THE AMERICAN LINE

THE AMERICAN LINE (1871–1902)

William Henry Flayhart III

W. W. Norton & Company
New York • London

Copyright © 2000 by William Henry Flayhart III

For information about permission to reproduce selections from this book, write to
Permissions, W.W. Norton & Company, Inc., 500 Fifth Avenue, New York, NY 10110.

The text of this book is composed in Janson
with the display set in Bank Gothic
Manufacturing by
Book design and composition by Germaine Clair

Library of Congress Cataloging-in-Publication Data
Flayhart, William H., 1944–
The American Line (1871–1902) / by William Henry Flayhart III.
    p.   cm.
Includes index.
ISBN 0-393-04710-5
1. American Steamship Company—History. 2. Steamboat lines—United States—History.
3. Shipping—United States—History.
I. Title.
HE945.A4F58 2000
387.5'0973'09034—dc21   98-38743
                                            CIP

Frontispiece: *The* St. Paul *(11,600 tons) and her sister,* St. Louis *(11,629 tons), were the largest passenger liners built in the United States during the nineteenth century. They were constructed by the William Cramp Shipyard, Philadelphia, Pa., for the American Line's New York–Southampton Service and delivered in 1895.*   Raphael Tuck & Sons' *Oilette.*

W.W. Norton & Company, Inc., 500 Fifth Avenue, New York, N.Y. 10110
www.wwnorton.com

W.W. Norton & Company, Ltd., 10 Coptic Street, London WC1A 1PU

1 2 3 4 5 6 7 8 9 0

To My Family and Friends

CONTENTS

FOREWORD

The story of the development of the American Merchant Marine remains one of the most glorious chapters in the early history of the United States. The foundation was laid in the Colonial Era when the vast virgin forests of eastern North America provided the materials for an almost unlimited number of sailing ships. These ships flew the flag of Great Britain as long as the "First Empire" endured. After independence, from 1776 to 1861, American sailing ships, both great and humble, carried the Stars and Stripes around the world with honor to the nation and profit to their owners.

The American Civil War (1861–65) proved to be a catastrophic watershed in the history of the American Merchant Marine. Confederate privateers swept Union shipping from the high seas both through successful cruises and by virtue of soaring insurance rates. The disastrous effects of the war on American shipping were compounded by the general changeover from sail to steam, and from wood to iron that occurred in the same period. After 1865 the American shipping industry never regained its prewar position, and, in fact, continued a sharp, steady decline as aging vessels were not replaced.

The condition of the American Merchant Marine deteriorated to the point that by 1870 there was not a single American-flag passenger liner on the North Atlantic, nor were there any under construction, nor were there any being planned. This was indeed a lamentable situation for a nation which so shortly before had boasted one of the finest merchant fleets in the world. The situation was a sad blow to national pride in the principal seaports of the United States.

Yet few concrete proposals for rectifying this state of affairs were forthcoming as the nation's eyes were turned Westward toward an immense continent that absorbed virtually all the available financial resources. A quarter of a century would pass before American citizens would be able to cross the Atlantic on a first-class American owned, operated, and manned steamer.

Small groups of shipping men after 1870 were interested in establishing American-flag steamship lines capable of assuming a major role in the movement of passengers and cargo across the North Atlantic, but the process of development and growth would be difficult indeed. The first mildly successful attempt—in that it even survived—was the American Steamship Company of Philadelphia (1873). Its lineal descendant would be the great American Line of 1893, which would restore American prestige by the middle of the 1890's. The story of the American Line is a window through which the problems and successes of the American Merchant Marine in the period 1870–1900 can be seen.

Correspondingly, the story of the founding and growth of the International Navigation Company (Red Star Line, 1873) illustrates the utilization of American capital to develop foreign-flag steamship enterprises. If the cost of building and operating a fleet under the American flag was too great, then the alternative of establishing a steamship line under a flag-of-convenience, such as Britain's, proved attractive to some American owners. The key figure in this instance was Clement Acton Griscom, a Philadelphia Quaker and one of the most influential men in America in the period 1870–1900. Griscom's creation and development of a number of shipping lines ultimately would lay the foundation for the International Mercantile Marine in 1902.

While the growth of the merchant marine provided the stimulus for this book, considerable effort was made to recover tales of the sea. Many of these stories briefly captured the newspaper headlines over a century ago and then were consigned to an undeserved obscurity. The American Merchant Marine on the North Atlantic possesses an exciting and dynamic story in the period 1870–1900 well worth telling.

ACKNOWLEDGMENTS

The researching and writing of *The American Line* occurred over a span of thirty-five years. It was not the only work occupying my mind, but it was never far from my thoughts. The quest for information brought me into beneficial contact with a wealth of friends, libraries, and organizations around the world. Under such circumstances it is virtually impossible to provide appropriate acknowledgment of every person and every organization who assisted me. Therefore, I begin by thanking everyone who ever helped me in any way, and by apologizing to anyone who I offend by unwittingly omitting them.

My greatest debt is owed to four individuals who set the course and left me to steam on. My maternal uncle, C. Albert Laux, a deltologist of the first magnitude, never ceased to encourage me to expand my imagination and collecting instincts. A postcard of the great North German Lloyd liner *Kaiser Wilhelm II* bought by him for me at the age of eight, was the first acquisition in a substantial collection of information. Some of the illustrations in this work were acquired by him for me before his passing in 1971.

Two professors, Loring Benson Priest and Robert H. Ewing at Lycoming College, Williamsport, Pennsylvania, my undergraduate alma mater, not only honed my rough skills as a historian but, far more importantly, inspired high professional standards that I hope I have honored by practicing during my career. Arguably the greatest single maritime historian of the twentieth century was Noel R. P. Bonsor of Jersey, the Channel Islands, whose five volume history, *North Atlantic Seaway*, is unlikely to be superseded. I will never cease to marvel at the events that brought an American student, bound for a year of study at the University of Edinburgh, to Noel Bonsor's attention in 1964, but it remains an honor to have been among the few disciples encouraged and influenced by him. Our friendship spanned twenty years during which we rarely were out of contact. His personal research standards were among the highest I have ever known in academia, even if he never was associated with a university.

I also owe an enormous debt to my parents, William Henry Flayhart and Naomi Laux Flayhart, who made many sacrifices to encourage me in my career. The fact that my father will have the pleasure of seeing this book published is a unique joy. My brother, Martin Albert Flayhart, with whom I shared many adventures and who often was my mentor, also has my deepest gratitude.

My literary agent in New York, Eleanor Wood, has seen me through a number of difficult times and never thrown me overboard even when she must have been sorely tempted. My editor at W. W. Norton & Company, James Mairs, has given me encouragement and time when I needed it. The entire team at W. W. Norton causes one to appreciate the fine art of crafting a book, in a house where it is still an art form. After three books published by W. W. Norton, I think I can say this with some authority.

Over the past 30 years Delaware State University, Dover, has given me a professional home and much encouragement. Today I owe a significant debt of gratitude to the present leadership of the university: President, Dr. William B. DeLauder; Provost, Dr. John Tolliver; Academic Dean, Dr. Tommy Frederick. Over the years promotion and tenure were granted with the support of the late President, Dr. Luna I. Mishoe. I also had the pleasure of working for a number of other academic deans, including Dr. M. Milford Caldwell, Dr. H. Ruth Williams, Dr. Henry Tisdale, and Dr. James Lyons. The various Faculty Development Committees of DSU have been of continuous and inestimable value in funding research, as well as the Office of Sponsored Research, and the Center for Excellence in College Teaching. I also was encouraged over the past 25 years in my research efforts by the Delaware Humanities Forum.

Among maritime organizations I wish to acknowledge the warm comradery and encouragement of the members of the North American Society for Oceanic History (NASOH), the Steamship Historical Society of America, the Canadian Nautical Research Association, the United States Naval Institute, the World Ship Society (UK), and last, but far from least, the International Maritime Economic History Association and its headquarters' staff, led by Dr. Lewis Fischer at the Maritime Studies Research Unit, Memorial University of Newfoundland, St. John's, which is one of Canada's greatest gifts to the preservation of history.

I wish to extend my grateful thanks to the staffs of the following American research centers: the Historical Society of Pennsylvania, Philadelphia; Alderman Library, the University of Virginia; Science Library, the University of Virginia; Photographs and Reproduction Services, the University of Virginia; William C. Jason Library-Learning Center, Delaware State University; University of Delaware Library; Hagley Museum and Library; the Philadelphia Free Public Library (particularly the History Reference people); Van Pelt Library, the University of Pennsylvania; Temple University Library (particularly the staff in the Urban Archives Collection); Mariners Museum Library; Lycoming College Library; New York Public Library; Baker Library, Harvard Business School, Harvard University; St. Louis University Library; Smithsonian Institute; Library of Congress; Library of Congress Prints and Photographs Division; National Archives; Dover Public Library; James V. Brown Public Library, Williamsport, Pennsylvania; Mystic Maritime Museum Library; Peabody Museum; Kendal Whaling Museum; United States Naval Academy Library; Bermuda Maritime Museum; Independence Maritime Museum, Philadelphia. Particular thanks go to the leadership and staff of the Naval History Division, Washington Navy Yard, who have been so helpful on so many occasions.

Overseas the following libraries and organizations have been of considerable value: Leiden University Library, Leiden, The Netherlands; Mitchell Maritime Library, Glasgow, Scotland; the Royal Library, Den Hague, The Netherlands; University of

Edinburgh Library; University of Liverpool Library; University of Southampton Library; University of Glasgow Library; Public Records Office, London; British Library, London; British Museum, London; City Heritage Services, Southampton, U.K.; Antwerp Maritime Museum, Antwerp, Belgium; the Netherlands Maritime Museum, Amsterdam, The Netherlands; the Prins Hendrik Maritime Museum, Rotterdam, The Netherlands; Musee de Marine, Paris, France.

Among individuals who must be thanked for their assistance over the years are the members of the Department of History, Political Science and Philosophy, Delaware State University, of which I have been a member since 1970 and chair since 1993. Special notice here needs to be made of the sustaining influence of two colleagues, who just happen to be secretaries, Mrs. Peggy Bingham and Mrs. Pam Trego. I also am deeply indebted to Mr. and Mrs. John H. Shaum, Jr., of Baltimore. Jack, my coauthor for *Majesty At Sea* (1981), always provides a willing ear and both he and Martha are valued advisers. Mr. and Mrs. John Nicholson of Leeds, England, are friends of many years standing, and John's paintings have enhanced a number of works. The same is true of Mr. Stephen Card of Bermuda, who generously gave permission to use his painting of the *Veendam* (I).

A research year in 1994–1995 permitted me to accept an invitation to become the Visiting Professor of Maritime History at the University of Leiden, The Netherlands. This invitation was extended by Professor Jaap Bruijn, the distinguished Dutch maritime historian, who was my mentor for the year. The writing of this work was finished during that time. I also had the pleasure of serving as "Distinguished Lecturer" at the Nederlands Scheepvaart Museum, Amsterdam, where the staff made researching and working very worthwhile. A deep personal acknowledgment must go to Drs. Joost Schokkenbroek and Josie Schokkenbroek-Smit, whose professional brilliance is outstanding and whose friendship continues to be deeply valued. This is also true of Mr. Joop Duindam, whose ability to alleviate problems and sustain friends is matchless. The leadership and staff of the British School in The Netherlands provided a remarkable educational opportunity for our daughter Jennifer.

Finally, the greatest sustaining influence over the past twenty years has been my wife, Debbie, and my children, Thomas, Catherine, and Jennifer, who often had to put up with quite a few distractions. All of these friends, family, and organizations combine to make life worth living. To you all goes my heartfelt thanks.

The professional debt acknowledged to many individuals and institutions in no way conveys any responsibility for the shortcomings of this work. They are mine, but I fervently hope that I will not have led too many readers astray.

William Henry Flayhart III
Delaware State University
Dover, Delaware
October 1999

THE AMERICAN LINE

Chapter 1

THE ORIGINS OF THE
AMERICAN LINE OF PHILADELPHIA

T he development of truly large industrial and transportation enterprises on the American economic scene occurred in the period immediately following the American Civil War (1861–65). This era brought a transformation in the character of the American merchant marine as sailing vessels increasingly gave way to steam. In technological terms, the rapid development of the American Industrial Revolution after 1865 made possible the construction in American yards of iron-hulled, oceangoing steamships. In financial terms, the expansion of the American railroad industry provided the financial resources for investment in complementary services of all natures, including steamships. The dynamic, transcontinental railroads pushed westward, while the even more powerful eastern railroads strove to expand their interests and consolidate their control over the transportation market by developing through-lines with services coordinated over vast distances. An integral part of this stage of American economic development involved transatlantic expansion as American companies began to develop substantial international ties.

The prosperous Pennsylvania Railroad Company (PRR) held the distinction of being the most powerful and influential business enterprise in the nation. One of the greatest rivals of the PRR was the New York Central Railroad, which was admirably positioned to greet the constant stream of immigrants crossing the Atlantic to New York, and to assist those passengers on their way to the hinterland of the United States. This was a challenge that could not go unanswered after the conclusion of the Civil War. As early as November 1865 the board of directors of the Pennsylvania Railroad passed a motion offering to invest $500,000 in the stock of any steamship company willing to establish a line between Philadelphia and Liverpool.[1] Whatever the Pennsylvania Railroad wanted, ultimately, it usually got.

The Pennsylvania Railroad Company definitely wanted to expand its operations to ensure a through service for immigrants and trade from Europe to the interior of the United States. Its leadership expected transatlantic trade to expand for the rest of the century. That expectation combined with the desire to offer customers a single freight bill or passenger ticket to any destination in the United States. In the eastern United States continental rivalry fostered transatlantic competition in an effort to develop global control of the transportation of passengers and freight from European points of origin, across the North Atlantic, and to destinations throughout North America. This prompted the PRR to encourage international trade either by establishing American-flag steamship lines or by acquiring foreign-flag concerns. The steamship schedules and

J. Edgar Thomson (left) and Thomas A. Scott, third (1852–1874) and fourth (1874–1880) presidents of the Pennsylvania Railroad Company, were two of the most important backers of the American Steamship Company and the International Navigation Company.

Free Public Library of Philadelphia

services could be dovetailed with those of the Pennsylvania Railroad to provide a universal transportation network. Within the United States, the expansion drive of the Pennsylvania Railroad during the period 1870–73 saw the company's profits increase by some 40 percent.[2]

Everything seemed perfect for new economic advances, but the challenges were manifold. Two key figures in these efforts would be J. Edgar Thomson, president of the Pennsylvania Railroad, and Thomas A. Scott, vice president of the Pennsylvania Railroad. Both men were respected transportation magnates. Of the two, Scott led the way in seeking to develop Philadelphia as a major North Atlantic terminus for trade and commerce. The first move was to secure a regular steamship service for Philadelphia, but this would be more difficult than expected. The initial idea involved the outright purchase of a reputable and established European-flag transatlantic steamship line. Instantaneously this would create the through-service from Europe to the Great American West by way of the Port of Philadelphia that the Pennsylvania Railroad desired.

Thomas Scott did not want to be bothered with the labor of creating an entirely new steamship line if it was possible to gain control of one of the existing European-flag concerns. The goal was to establish the steamship service as quickly as possible. A general survey of the smaller yet prosperous European lines led the Pennsylvania Railroad into negotiations with the owners of the Anchor Line of Glasgow, Scotland. The Anchor Line had been founded in 1856 by Nicol and Robert Handyside, two Scottish brothers, and a third partner, Captain Thomas Henderson. Earlier they had engaged in trading activities to Russia (1838), Australia (1852), and Portugal (1854). In 1854, the *Vasco da Gama* (1854, 170 tons) of the Glasgow and Lisbon Steam Packet Company was advertised as opening a service to Lisbon under the management of Handyside & Company, which thus entered the age of steam and began a century of steamship management. Subsequently they had one of their new iron sailing ships, *Tempest* (1855, 866 tons), converted into a screw steamship in 1856. When the *Tempest* sailed from Glasgow to New

York on October 8, 1856, she flew a house flag featuring a red anchor against a white background and carried the Anchor Line name into maritime history. The *Tempest* completed one successful round-trip and another crossing to New York in December 1856, but she went missing on her eastbound crossing of February 1857 and was never heard from again. The Indian Mutiny (1857) saw a number of Anchor Line vessels chartered by the British government to carry troops to southern Asia, and the North Atlantic service was suspended for the better part of two years.

On April 15, 1859, the Anchor Line instituted the first regular service between Britain and the St. Lawrence River using the *United Kingdom* (1857, 1,255 tons). The elimination of other competitors on the River Clyde made the Anchor Line the only regular steamship line between Glasgow and New York (1859). In the next five years the trade to Portugal, Gibraltar, and the Mediterranean picked up so much that the last of the line's sailing ships was converted to steam. A feeder service was established in 1869 from Christiania (now Oslo), Norway, and Gothenburg, Sweden, to Leith, Scotland, from whence Glasgow was only a short train ride. When the Suez Canal was opened with a grand flourish in November 1869, the *Dido* of the Anchor Line was the first commercial vessel in 2,500 years to sail from the Mediterranean to the Red Sea. That same year, a formal agreement was concluded between the Anchor Line and the Peninsular and Oriental Steam Navigation Company (P&O) and the British India Steam Navigation Company (British India) to carry cargo and passengers from Glasgow out to Alexandria. Once Anchor passengers arrived in Egypt, they then traveled overland to Suez and onward by the steamships of the other lines.[3] The upshot of all this activity was that Scott and the Pennsylvania Railroad were after no mean concern when they tried to catch the Anchor Line.

In 1870, negotiations with Captain Thomas Henderson, the surviving partner, reached agreement on the transfer of the American terminus of the Anchor Line from New York to Philadelphia. Unfortunately, they fell apart on the PRR's demand that the books and total direction of affairs also cross the Atlantic and be reestablished in Philadelphia. "This was too much to ask of an individualist like Thomas Henderson and the deal fell through."[4]

Scott was frustrated, but Henderson had not spent the better part of his life building up the firm of Handyside and Henderson (Anchor Line) just to leave Scotland at the behest of an American railroad, no matter how attractive the offer might be. The financial condition of the Anchor Line was strong enough that it needed to fear no competitor. The Scottish line landed more than 25,000 passengers in New York during 1870 alone. The Pennsylvania Railroad Company and Thomas A. Scott were after an attractive prize—and it got away.

The reversal suffered by Thomas Scott in his transatlantic expansion plans prompted him to take another course of action. Since the end of the Civil War, civic forces in Philadelphia centering on the Commercial Exchange had urged the establishment of an American-owned steamship link with Europe. In November 1870, the board of directors

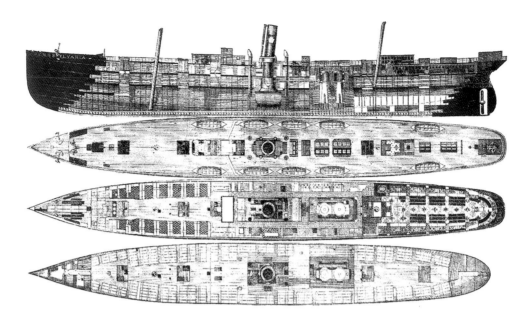

An "Arrangement Plan" of the Pennsylvania *(1873, 3,104 tons, 343 feet by 43 feet, 12 knots), inaugural vessel of the American Line constructed by the William Cramp Shipyard and delivered to the Line in 1873. Note the "keystone" symbol of the Commonwealth of Pennsylvania and the PRR on the funnel.*
Society of Marine Architects and Marine Engineers, *Historical Transactions 1893–1943* (New York, 1945), 66

of the Pennsylvania Railroad took the initiative and announced its willingness to provide substantial financial backing for an American-flag steamship line if interested Philadelphia citizens would undertake the establishment and operation of such a concern.[5] The commercial interests of Philadelphia responded enthusiastically to the railroad's overture, and the *Philadelphia Commercial List and Price Current*, a weekly journal of commerce for the Philadelphia community, lent heavy editorial support to the project. In December 1870, the American Steamship Company was formed and American Line financing established through a combination of $700,000 in stock and $1,500,000 in 6-percent bonds. The bond issue was guaranteed by the PRR.

The Commercial Exchange membership lent their money and prestige to the new steamship enterprise. What could go wrong with the mighty Pennsylvania Railroad guaranteeing the results? The *Annual Report* of the Commercial Exchange, published on February 4, 1871, provides details of the new steamship business. The American Line was to consist of no fewer than four steamers—the minimum deemed necessary for a weekly service—to ply between Philadelphia and Liverpool or any other suitable European port. The formal charter for the company was to be obtained from the next session of the Pennsylvania General Assembly. Minimum capital was set at $700,000, with provisions for its eventual rise to $5,000,000 when conditions warranted. The Pennsylvania Railroad Company subscribed $400,000 of the stock and guaranteed both the principal and the interest on the $1,500,000 bond issue. The commitment of the

Railroad to the American Line was very substantial indeed. The bonds were to run for twenty-five years, initially it was thought to offer them at 5 percent interest, but market conditions forced an increase to 6 percent. The title of the new enterprise was established as the "American Steamship Company of Philadelphia," but the concern would always be known as the American Line.[6]

To secure public support for the American Line, the Commercial Exchange established a committee composed of ten of its most distinguished members. The sale of the bonds in the new venture needed some pushing, since they received only a lukewarm reception from the general public. The committee must have done its work well, though, because it was announced two weeks later that $1,100,000 of the bond issue had been sold, with only $400,000 outstanding. Optimistically it was stated that "as soon as the $400,000 still unsold shall have been disposed of, the corporation will be at liberty to commence operations without further delay."[7]

Early in January it was announced that all the stock in the new company had been subscribed and the bonds were expected to sell quickly.[8] The Pennsylvania General Assembly passed legislation on February 7, 1871, permitting the Pennsylvania Railroad Company, or any other Pennsylvania chartered corporation, to purchase stock and securities in the new firm.[9] On March 16, 1871, the board of directors of the Pennsylvania Railroad was informed that all of the bond issue and $300,000 in stock had been sold to the public. Therefore, the PRR honored its agreement to purchase the remaining $400,000 in stock.[10]

The commissioners of the American Steamship Company of Philadelphia met in the Merchants' Exchange on March 28, 1871, and accepted the list of stock subscribers. John O. James was elected chairman of the committee on a motion of J. Edgar Thomson, president of the Pennsylvania Railroad, and the formal organization meeting was scheduled for April 4, 1871, at the Merchants' Exchange.

One of the first orders of business was the election of a president and the first board of directors. Many members of the Commercial Exchange Committee now became formal members of the board of directors of the steamship line. The vote resulted in the election of Herman J. Lombaert as president, with E. C. Knight, Washington Butcher, Josiah Bacon, John Rice, B. H. Bartol, J. Price Wetherill, Henry D. Welsh, and D. B. Cummins as directors. All were successful Philadelphia businessmen with numerous other commercial interests.[11]

The Commonwealth of Pennsylvania, through its General Assembly, granted a charter for the American Steamship Company on April 18, 1871. The charter was issued "for the purpose of establishing a line of first class steamships to run between Philadelphia and Liverpool; the steamers to be constructed in American ship building yards, and as entirely as possible of American Materials."[12] On the same day the board of directors of the American Steamship Company met for the first time to organize its affairs, including the creation of bylaws. Edmund Smith, secretary of the Pennsylvania Railroad Company, also was elected at this time to the joint position of secretary and

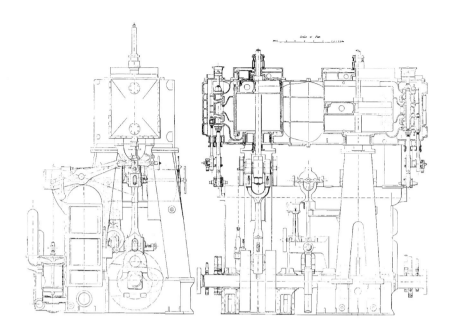

The initial American Line quartet were powered by some of the earliest compound engines constructed in the United States. These were built by the engine works at the William Cramp Shipyard, and drove the ships at 11.5 knots.
Library of Congress

treasurer of the American Steamship Company. Events moved very quickly as the board met again on April 22, 1871, to approve the new bylaws of the company and to create the two most pressing committees: "On Ships," with a membership of Bartol, Bodine, Butcher, Cummins, Welsh, and Wetherill; and "On Finance," with a membership of Bacon, Bodine, Butcher, Cummins, Welsh, and Wetherill. At the same meeting, Bartol, on behalf of the Committee on Ships, submitted to the board a formal prospectus soliciting bids from shipyards for construction of the inaugural fleet.[13] The ship prospectus was approved and distributed to the appropriate builders.

All bids were due by August 1, and the board of directors of the American Steamship Company met next on August 9, 1871, for the purpose of considering the various bids from the shipyards. Four builders had submitted bids—William Cramp and Sons, John Roach, Neafie and Levy, and Dialogue and Wood. William Cramp and Sons were serious about obtaining the contract for the American Line vessels—their bid was $520,000 per unit (on the basis of an order for four ships), which was $34,750 per unit under the next highest bid, $554,750 from John Roach. Neafie and Levy's bid of a flat $660,000 per ship and Dialogue and Wood's bid of $600,000 per ship were not even close and may have represented courtesy bids, rather than serious efforts.

The bid from Cramp was for vessels of approximately 3,016 tons, with a length of 336', a beam of 43', and a hold of 32'2". The board of directors of the American Steamship Company promptly awarded the contract to William Cramp and Sons, who began planning construction immediately.[14] Cramp may have had a few reservations about the final contract—the American Line board required the builders to provide a mortgage on the vessels, an assignment of all policies of insurance that might be taken

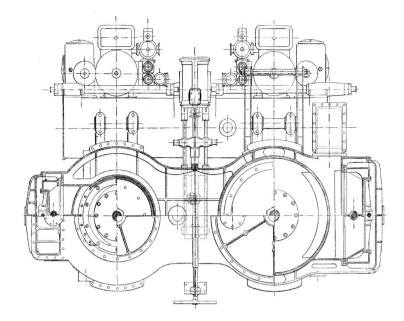

An overhead view of the compound engines built by Cramp with a small cylinder diameter of 57 inches and a large cylinder of 90 inches. The stroke was 48 inches. The engines received steam from three boilers heated by 18 furnaces. The ships could carry 720 tons of coal in their bunkers and burned approximately 40 tons a day.
Library of Congress

out on the vessels, and "personal security to the amount of $100,000 on each vessel; the parties to be satisfactory to the Steam Ship Co."[15] This requirement would prove onerous to the builder.

Philadelphia's civic pride in the new enterprise was vividly underlined on February 3, 1872, in the inaugural address of William Brice, president of the Commercial Exchange Association. On this occasion, Brice remarked:

> The merchants and capitalists of our city in connection with that great and
> enterprising corporation, the Pennsylvania Railroad, are now having built—and
> built, too, on our broad Delaware—a line of steamships to run between this city
> and Liverpool, not under a foreign flag, gentlemen, but under the glorious flag
> of our Union, our own Stars and Stripes. . . . It will be for us, and the entire
> mercantile interests of our city, to make that line so eminent a success that
> other lines will follow in such rapid succession that we will remain not the sec-
> ond city in the Union, but second to none.[16]

Despite such patriotic and civic enthusiasm, the financial future of the American Line was uncertain. At times in 1871, the company's bonds were offered on the Philadelphia Stock Board without finding a buyer, even with a discount of 5 percent. This, however, did not deter the directors of the new enterprise from their appointed duties.

The formal contract for the four American liners was signed with William Cramp and Sons on August 30, 1871. The Cramp Shipyard had been founded by William Cramp in 1830, and by 1870 was under the guidance of his son, Charles Henry Cramp.[17] Charles Cramp remains one of the most creative leaders of the American Industrial

A comparison of the principal Atlantic liners that were competitors of the American Line ships in 1873. The Pennsylvania (1873) at 343 feet ranked comfortably in the middle of the list.

Scientific American, June 7, 1873

Baltimore, N. G. Lloyd's line—Length 185 ft., beam 29 ft.; length to breadth, 6·38.

Peruvian, Allan line—L. 270 ft., b. 38 ft.; length to breadth, 7·11.

Moravian, Allan line—L. 290 ft., b. 39 ft.; length to breadth, 7·44.

Leipzig, N. G. Lloyds' line—L. 290 ft., b. 39 ft.; length to breadth, 7·44.

Minnesota, Williams & Guion line—L. 332 ft., b. 42 ft.; length to breadth, 7·90.

Rhein, N. G. Lloyds' line—L. 332 ft., b. 40 ft.; length to breadth, 8·30.

Westphalia, Hamburgh line—L. 340 ft., b. 40 ft.; length to breadth, 8·50.

Pennsylvania, American S.S. Co.—L. 343 ft., b. 43 ft.; length to breadth, 7·91.

Russia, Cunard line—L. 358 ft., b. 43 ft.; length to breadth, 8·33.

Queen, National line—L. 358 ft., b. 41 ft; length to breadth, 8·73.

Ville du Havre, French line—L. 423 ft., b. 49 ft.; length to breadth, 8·63.

City of Montreal, Inman line—L. 433 ft., b. 44 ft.; length to breadth, 9·84.

Atlantic, White Star line—L. 435 ft., b. 41 ft.; length to breadth, 10·61.

The Pennsylvania *(1873) is shown here packed with American troops bound for the Spanish-American War (1898). Her funnel is painted in the colors of the American Line, a black funnel with a white band, that the fleet bore after the Inman and International merger (1886) and the subsequent establishing of the new American Line (1893).*

Revolution and the single most outspoken promoter of the American merchant marine in the second half of the nineteenth century. The strain of financing the expansion of the Cramp Shipyard in order to build the American Line quartet was so substantial that the Cramp family petitioned the Pennsylvania legislature for a corporate charter in 1872. This was granted and the firm became the William Cramp and Sons Ship and Engine Building Company.[18] The Cramp contract stated that all four vessels were to be alike in model and machinery and, with regard to the terms of the charter, of American materials as far as possible. The contract stipulated that each vessel was to be "furnished with independent, compound, vertical, direct-acting, surface-condensing, propeller engines."[19] The compound engine was the state-of-the-art form of marine propulsion. The directors of the American Line wanted nothing but the very best for their ships.

Each of the liners was to be outfitted to carry 75 first-class and 854 steerage-class passengers. The names *Pennsylvania, Ohio, Indiana,* and *Illinois*—for the states along the PRR's main line from Philadelphia to Chicago—had been assigned to the four ships on September 18, 1871, before the keels were even laid. The total price for the four vessels was $2,080,000. The ships were designed by the marine architect Barnabus H. Bartol,

This excellent broadside shows the Pennsylvania *(1873) after 1886. She may have been in the Red Star Antwerp–New York (1887–91) or Antwerp–Philadelphia service (1892–97) when this picture was taken.*

one of the directors of the line, and Charles H. Cramp of the Cramp Shipyard. The completion dates proved optimistic. According to the contract the premier unit, the *Pennsylvania*, was to be ready by September 1, 1872; the *Ohio* by November 1, 1872; the *Indiana* by December 1, 1872; and the *Illinois* by January 1, 1873.

Within the American shipbuilding community, a battle raged between the advocates of the new compound engines and defenders of the more traditional marine engines. Among the more traditional-minded, the thought of all the modifications in boiler and engine construction was hard to bear. The new engines certainly contained unknown risks and augmented costliness in construction, but the potential savings in fuel consumption were enormous. Much ink was shed. In America, MacFarland Gray, a leading marine authority who wrote for the prestigious journal *Engineering*, led the fight, which vindicated the claims of the compound engine and contributed to its introduction.

In Britain, John Elder (1824–1869) was the driving force behind the widespread introduction of compound engines, although a number of individuals participated in the building and popularizing of the engine. Elder was one of the most distinguished of the great nineteenth-century marine engineers who contributed so much to the evolution of marine architecture and propulsion. Elder was born in Glasgow, Scotland, on March 8, 1824, and served an apprenticeship in the shipyard and engineworks of Robert Napier. Napier played a crucial role in the design and construction of the first Cunard liners in the 1840s, and David Elder, John's father, was a major figure in the yard. In time, John Elder rose to be assistant manager of the Napier yard under his father, but he wanted to strike out on his own. In 1852, he joined the millwright firm of Randolph, Elliott and Company, with his name replacing Elliott's in the firm's title. In 1854, Randolph, Elder and Company built the first compound engines for the steamer *Brandon*, which proved

The Pennsylvania *(1873) is shown with all sails set in this painting. Besides "Old Glory," she is flying the American Line house flag featuring the keystone with a Red Star (indicating International Navigation Company management), her name, and the United States Mail flag.*   The Elwin M. Eldredge Collection, courtesy the Mariners Museum, Newport News, Virginia

not only the feasibility of the new system of marine propulsion but also its enormous economy. The firm built a new boiler shop in 1854 and moved into shipbuilding in 1860. Elder leased a site in Govan until 1864, when he was able to acquire the old Fairfield farm nearby. Here the famous Fairfield Shipbuilding Company was created, and the extensive manufacturing of ships with compound engines was begun. The value of this marine engineering advance was its economical use of steam, which permitted it to expand successively in two cylinders. The compound engine could contribute to either a faster ship or one far less expensive to operate.[20]

As part of the preparations for building the American Line vessels, Bartol recommended that Charles Cramp, the dominant force in the Cramp Shipyard, go to Europe to make an exhaustive analysis of the compound-engine question. Cramp and J. Shields Wilson, Cramp's managing engineer, drew $10,000 from the treasury of the American Steamship Company and made arrangements to sail for Europe. Wilson had been selected by Cramp to head the new engine-building department, which was part of the expansion of the Cramp Shipyard. He already had designed successful compound engines for

The Ohio *(1873, 3,104 tons, 343 feet by 43 feet, 12 knots) was the second of the American Line quartet. Here she is shown after substantial enlargement and improvements to the deck house. Her original passenger accommodations for 76 cabin and 854 third (steerage) had been augmented by 75 intermediate. An iron bridge had replaced the original wooden structure after the* Pennsylvania *lost hers in 1874.*

the steamer *George W. Clyde*. Bartol stipulated "that he would oppose the construction of any steamers until he became convinced that they would be of the most advanced type in everything that pertains to most modern requirements."[21]

The two American marine specialists were particularly interested in the new Elder compound engine, so they sensibly booked passage on the National Line's *Italy* (1870, 4,169 tons), which Charles Cramp later described as "the first trans-Atlantic steamer with compound engines of John Elder's make and type, whose reported performance in economical coal consumption was considered at that time marvellous."[22] As soon as the *Italy* cleared the end of the pier in New York, they immediately set out to learn all they could about her propulsion system. "We soon made the acquaintance of the chief engineer of the ship, whose name also was Wilson [W. R. Wilson], and Mr. Wilson practically lived with him. He was permitted to 'take cards' [measure coal usage] under varying conditions, and secured an accurate account of coal consumption and of all other matters likely to be of interest."[23]

Steamship Docks on the Delaware by Frederick B. Schell shows the American Line Pennsylvania *arriving at Philadelphia and the Red Star Line* Vaderland *at her berth in an active river scene. The piers of the Pennsylvania Railroad, Red Star Line (Antwerp–Philadelphia), and American Steamship Company (Philadelphia–Liverpool) are identified. The view dates to the mid-1870s.* Library of Congress

Cramp and Wilson's enthusiasm for their subject knew almost no bounds. As soon as they reached Liverpool, they toured the Laird's Shipyard and then set out to visit every great marine engine and shipbuilding works along the Rivers Thames and Clyde. Cramp was under no illusions about the reputation of the Cramp Shipyard in Britain. It was unknown! As American shipbuilders, they were greeted with much kindness and consideration, but no little curiosity, wherever they went. They started with the Thames, "whose shipyards at that time stood higher in the *art* of ship-building and in the proficiency of marine-engine construction than the Clyde shipyards."[24]

From the beginning, Cramp and Wilson maintained a totally open policy of stating the reason for their interest in order to establish goodwill for the future and to remove completely any suspicion of industrial espionage or design theft. At the firms they visited, they signed themselves in as "shipbuilder" and "constructor." One of the first London firms they visited led to their introduction to a Mr. Zamuda, who, having been apprised of the fact that they were knowledgeable, invited them to lunch and provided them with letters of introduction to all the shipyards they wanted to visit so that none of their time would be wasted with underlings. In later years, Cramp commented with some humor that the superintendent initially delegated to show them around had thought in terms of a perfunctory visit—in one door and out the other. When the two

Americans began to pepper him with questions showing they knew their business, the whole relationship soon attained a different footing.

Many British shipbuilders they visited were astonished to learn what the Cramp Shipyard had accomplished, and that all of the ownership and most of the employees were native-born Americans. Industrial cross-fertilization and transatlantic communication in the 1870s were distinctly limited. Of course, in terms of industrial development, the United States was just at the beginning of its own Industrial Revolution, while Great Britain had experienced its own nearly a century earlier, in the 1780s.

Cramp and Wilson remained quite biased toward the new compound engines, regardless of what they heard from various naysayers along the Thames. Then they traveled north to view the great shipyards of the River Clyde and western Scotland. Whatever doubts they may have had were totally abandoned when they saw the fabulous engine erection shed at the Fairfield Works, Clydebank, Scotland. Cramp reported enthusiastically:

> We saw there *thirteen compound engines* in various states of completion, with their various parts ready for assembling, some about ready for installation in the ship, the whole exhibiting everything in the way of finish and arrangement both in their various parts and in the whole erection.[25]

Prior to this, the two Americans had seen engines of every kind and description—oscillating, trunk, plain vertical, and horizontal—assembled in every varying form of construction. In other words, the two men had seen nothing decidely different from what they were familiar with at home. Cramp rejoiced: "Now, without any preparation whatever for it, this vision of thirteen actualities of the new departure burst upon our view."[26]

Cramp and Wilson spent a day in the Fairfield Works, examining every detail of the construction process and the finished products. They found as much novelty in the boiler construction as in the engines. Never bashful, they also sought to show a couple of American techniques that they thought superior to methods being used in Britain. After viewing the work of John Elder at the Fairfield Works, Cramp and Wilson did not consider anything else worthy of delaying their departure for Philadelphia, and they booked passage home. Uppermost in Cramp's mind must have been the contract deadlines for the new American Line ships and the fact that little or nothing had been accomplished yet on them, even though six months had passed. Among the ameliorating factors was Bartol's refusal to approve the construction of any vessel that was not state-of-the-art—which placed considerable responsibility for any delay upon the American Steamship Company itself. The other factor was that the construction of the new ships necessitated the building of almost an entirely new shipyard in order to handle the workload and the advanced technology.

Cramp and Wilson's visits to the British yards certainly represent one of the earliest instances of transatlantic cross–fertilizations in the modern industrial era. It is somewhat extraordinary that it occurred while the ill will generated by the depredations of

Confederate commerce raiders still remained a sore point between the two governments, if not the two peoples. The settlement of outstanding American claims against Britain—known as the "Alabama Claims"—remained several years in the future (1877).

By late February 1872, construction of the new steamships for the American Line was well underway at the Cramp Shipyard, and an optimistic assertion was made that the fleet would be completed on schedule. "The ribs of two are already up and we learn that nearly a thousand men are busy at work making that point on our river one of special public interest at this time, and giving it a feature of unusual activity."[27] Workmen from all over Pennsylvania, New Jersey, and Delaware were lured to the Cramp Shipyard by the construction of the four liners. There also was the potential for steady work in the future owing to Charles H. Cramp's determined efforts to secure new contracts. All along the waterfront, support industries and facilities blossomed to assist the shipbuilding effort and to provide for the needs of the greatly augmented workforce. The dollars spent on the American Line ships recirculated several times through the Philadelphia business community. Furthermore, the early 1870s were a time of prosperity and economic growth in the United States—a heady period of business expansion apparently destined to go on forever.

Philadelphia's civic pride in the American Steamship Company and the enthusiasm of the board of directors of the Line were vividly stated in a newspaper article accompanying the *First Annual Report*.

> Silently, but steadily, this new enterprise, which the sages of New York and
> Boston have so confidently predicted would prove a fiasco, and which others
> pretended had no existence save on paper, is progressing towards a successful
> completion, and a few weeks hence we hope to be able to present to citizens
> and strangers, the novel spectacle, in American waters, of the launch of an

A Winter Arrival *by M.J. Burns underlines the fact that icebergs were not the only icy peril when one crossed the North Atlantic. The stability of even the most well-founded vessel could be jeopardized by an extra hundred tons of ice high on the superstructure. The small group of friends and relatives who have braved the freezing temperatures obviously are greatly relieved to see the liner nearing her pier.*

Harper's Weekly, January 23, 1886

American iron steamship, built of American materials, owned by American capital, and to be manned by American seamen.[29]

It was reported that 7,047 shares of stock at $100 each had been subscribed, and that the company's treasury had received the money for nearly all of these shares ($696,020, with a balance due of $8,680). The Cramp Shipyard was required to furnish a rather steep bond of $400,000 for the faithful performance of its contract—this represented nearly 20 percent of the value of the order. The sale of the American Steamship Company's bonds was continuing, although, as of April 1872, not all had been disposed of to the public. Nevertheless, $1,358,000 of the $1,500,000 to be raised in this manner had been secured and was in the company's hands. During the first annual meeting, Herman J. Lombaert was reelected president, and the board of directors was increased from ten to eleven members by the addition of Samuel T. Bodine.[30] Bodine was elected on the basis of a resolution that stipulated that the public shareholders should have a wider representation on the board of directors. In concluding their report, the board of directors of the American Line "deem it proper to express their high appreciation of the services of their esteemed colleague, B. H. Bartol, Esq., whose long experience as a mechanical engineer, and whose sound judgment have been of the greatest importance to the interests of the Company. In the selection of the model, the arrangements of the details of the plans and specifications, and in the preparation of the contract with the builders, his services have been especially valuable."[31]

A serious campaign was underway to secure a federal subsidy, or favorable mail contract, at the earliest possible opportunity. The president of the United States was Ulysses S. Grant, but there does not appear to have been any intention of approaching him directly, although he was invited to visit the Cramp Shipyard in January 1873 during a visit to Philadelphia. Instead, an American Line delegation traveled to Washington to solicit the assistance of the secretary of the Treasury, the postmaster general, and the secretary of the Navy. Subsequently, the secretary of the Treasury sent a message to Congress:

> After careful consideration of the whole subject, I am prepared to advise the passage of a law guaranteeing to persons who may employ in the foreign trade American-built first-class iron steamships of not less than two thousand tons burden each, an annual payment, for the period of five years, of the sum of thirteen dollars per ton. The subsidy should be proportionately less to vessels of lower classification.
>
> In making this recommendation, I do not assume that there is no other practicable method of restoring our commerce, but I present it as the method which appears to me to be the most efficient and economical.[32]

The postmaster general stated:

> In previous reports I have called attention to the importance of judicious legislation to encourage the establishment of American mail steamship lines....
>
> It is a very gratifying fact, in this connection, to state that, amid all the discouragements of the present situation, a new line of American iron steamships, to ply between Philadelphia and Liverpool, consisting of four first-class propellers of 3,000 tons each (old measurement), are now being built on the Delaware, for the American Steamship Company of Philadelphia, of materials exclusively of American manufacture. They will be completed and ready for service early in the fall of 1872, and will form a regular weekly line between the above-named ports. The proprietors of this pioneer line of American iron steamships are among the most enterprising merchants and capitalists of Philadelphia, and deserve such encouragement in their praiseworthy undertaking as can properly be extended by Congress. A reasonable compensation for conveying the mails, in excess of the postage receipts, is probably the only government aid needed to insure the permanent establishment of this or any other similar line of American ocean steamships plying between our own and foreign

ports; and, in my judgment, the granting of such incidental aid, in connection with proper legislation to encourage the construction by American builders of first-class iron steamships, is the most simple, economical, and practical method of establishing American lines of ocean steamers and advancing the general commercial prosperity of the country.[33]

Yet little movement was noticed in Congress. Therefore, on April 25, 1872, a special "Memorial of the American Steamship Company," formally requesting a subsidy for all American-built ships engaged in foreign trade, was drawn up by J. P. Wetherill, director, approved by the board, and sent to Congress.

J. Edgar Thomson, the president of the Pennsylvania Railroad, was traveling to Europe on business and was asked by the board of directors of the American Line to evaluate Liverpool as the European terminus of the service. Thomson wrote from England on July 29, 1872, that he had visited Cardiff, Wales, and wondered whether that port did not represent a better location than Liverpool for the ships to dock and refuel. In Thomson's view, some of the advantages of Cardiff over Liverpool were that Cardiff was a half day nearer Philadelphia; that the insurance on ships and cargo would be one-sixteenth percent less; that the cost of coaling the steamers would be $1.50 less per ton; that the dock dues would be one half those at Liverpool; that there would be no drayage at Cardiff as the cars of the Great Western, the Midland, and the London and North Western (railroads) could come alongside the ship; that Cardiff was nearer by rail than Liverpool to more than half the population of England and Wales; and that it had rail or steamer communication with all of England, Ireland, Le Havre, France, Spain, and Mexico. Thomson wrote, "Talk this over with our Steamer people and write me."[34] However, whatever doubts Thomson may have had about the European terminus were resolved shortly thereafter when he visited Liverpool. On August 24, 1872, Thomson wrote to his friend Edmund Smith, secretary of the Pennsylvania Railroad Company:

> I have been here five days looking after the Steamer matters. The result of my investigations is to induce me to abandon the Cardiff idea.
>
> I think that with the active opposition [competition] that exists among Steamship Companies, that Liverpool is the only point from and to which we could expect success.
>
> I have not yet arrived at a conclusion in relation to the Agency here, but at present my preferences incline towards Richardson, Spence & Co.
>
> Geo. Warren & Co., is the stronger firm but his interests and feelings though American are strongly towards Boston. I will remain here a few days longer. All Well.[35]

In a postscript, Thomson indicated that he had visited Laird's Works the day before and that they had quoted him £110,000 for a ship the dimensions of the American Line quartet. This was approximately equal to $528,000, which would compare very favorably with the Cramp bid of $520,000—eliminating the idea that

American construction costs were 30 percent higher than British prices for similar ships. While visiting Liverpool, Thomson discussed matters further with Mr. James Spence of Richardson, Spence and Company. On August 29, 1872, he wrote from Leeds, England, to inform the directors of the American Steamship Company that he had made arrangements with Richardson, Spence and Company on August 26 to take the agency of the American Line. The terms had been agreed to, and Thomson had instructed the English firm to make arrangements for the arrival of the first American Line ships. Thomson informed the American Line directors:

> Mr. Spence is a member of the Dock Board and will be able to secure the best berth attainable, which is a matter of importance in starting a new line.
>
> Room in the docks on the liverpool side is now difficult to secure, but I think that it is almost necessary that we should be on that side. I went over all of the Docks both on the Liverpool & Birkenhead side of the Mersey and fixed upon the Waterloo Dock as in all respects the most desirable for us, and Mr. Spence will endeavor to secure a berth on it.[36]

The spring and summer of 1872 wore on without the long-awaited launching ceremony at the Cramp Shipyard. Charles The building operation for hulls and engines was plagued by shortages of skilled craftsmen and materials. Getting the iron hull plates in sufficient quantity, for example, substantially taxed the production capacity of local industry. After all, this was occurring at the very beginning of the American Industrial Revolution, even if Philadelphia and Pennsylvania were the centers of such activity in the United States. The boom conditions of 1870–72 also meant that Cramp was not the only builder in need of iron products. Nevertheless, the great iron bow of the *Pennsylvania* soared into the air over the Delaware River waterfront, and her launching day arrived at last.

All Philadelphia, Camden (New Jersey), and the surrounding area declared a holiday on Thursday, August 15, 1872, when the *Pennsylvania* was launched. The crowd at the foot of Beach and Norris Streets, where the Cramp Shipyard was situated, and in every possible vantage point, was the largest that observers could remember. One reporter wrote: "Great interest was attached to the event by men of all classes in the community, and it was not surprising that the attendance was immense. The popular curiosity and excitement in the Richmond district ran very high, and in some industrial establishments a half holiday was allowed the operatives."[37] Given what is known of the nineteenth-century industrial mentality, virtually of the "Dickensian" school, this *must* have been a great civic event to warrant a half-day respite from remunerative labors.

The Commercial Exchange Building on Second Street was decorated with bunting and flags for the occasion and closed for the day, since the members had voted to attend the launching en masse. Many of them held both stock and bonds in the American Steamship Company and were actively engaged in assisting the construction of the vessels in any way they could. These businessmen definitely had a vested interest in viewing the success of their great undertaking.

The scene at the Cramp Shipyard immediately before the launching was exciting in the extreme. All the piers along the river were decorated with patriotic bunting. All available steamboats were pressed into service as excursion vessels, and all of them flew every decorative flag possible. In addition, an armada of lesser craft was so thick that the fleet almost made a bridge across the Delaware. All were crowded with human beings to such an extent that it was a wonder no disaster occurred to mar the festivities.

As the reporter for the *Philadelphia Commercial List and Price Current* wrote:

> All eyes were turned again to the quiescent mammoth on the stocks, decorated with hundreds of streamers, signal flags and other bunting. There lay the mighty monster of the deep awaiting the word that would baptize her in the element where she is hereafter to exist. She looked like an inanimate body, patiently pausing for that breath of life which would perfect, figuratively, the existence of the ship—the vessel destined to bear our flag aloft as the representative of peace and plenty to the lands across the seas.
>
> The launching of a vessel, especially one of the dimensions of the *Pennsylvania*, is a very complex and critical operation, and it was not without some difficulty and danger that her baptism by water was effected. At precisely twelve minutes past ten o'clock the elder Mr. Cramp gave the order to the axe-men to cut away the remaining pinions and shores, which was the work of a moment, and then the noble craft started toward her future home. She moved gracefully down the ways for the space of a minute, amidst the cheers of the vast throng, the blowing of a hundred steam whistles, and a salvo of artillery. In a few minutes the noble craft the *Pennsylvania* was afloat, and she indeed looked like a "thing of beauty and a joy forever" as her massive form floated on the waters of the Delaware.[38]

Rarely has any vessel received more glowing praise. She would serve the American merchant marine and fly the Stars and Stripes for forty-five years.

Contemporary observers commented that now that the great enterprise was underway, it was up to Philadelphia merchants to make it a success. The foreign commerce of Philadelphia was adequate to support such a steamship line *if* the mercantile community would just ship everything possible on their ships. The exports through the port during the previous fiscal year were up more than three million dollars over 1870, even if two-thirds consisted of petroleum. As one business reporter commented:

> Our import trade has heretofore been mainly transacted through New York, and notwithstanding the introduction of the new system of transporting goods in bond, hundreds of importers persist in following the old pathways of their forefathers, and New York continues to monopolize much of the profit and

credit accruing from the trade of the city [Philadelphia] and the State [Pennsylvania]. With the opening of this new line of trans-atlantic steamers, we should be able to date a new era of prosperity to the city, and no doubt this result will be achieved, if our merchants do their simple duty in co-operating with the zealous and well directed efforts of the Pennsylvania Railroad Company, to whom we are mainly indebted for this new element of progress. Let all good citizens take a practical interest in the success of the enterprise, and it will be assured from the outset.[39]

By 1871, the manufacturing capacity of Philadelphia exceeded a million dollars a day, not counting the steady growth in the petroleum trade and raw materials of the state of Pennsylvania. Even a portion of this should have been enough to sustain the American Line quartet.

The joy over the successful launching of the *Pennsylvania* must have been tempered in the minds of those intimately connected to the venture by the knowledge that she took to the Delaware barely two weeks before the completed liner was supposed to have been delivered (September 1, 1872), and she was far from being ready to sail. The schedule for the new transatlantic service obviously was impossible. The *Ohio* followed her sistership down the ways on October 30, with considerably less fanfare, and at that time it was announced that the maiden voyage of the *Pennsylvania* was planned for February 1873. February came and went, as did the remainder of the winter, without the liner sailing, although the third vessel, the *Indiana*, was launched on March 25, 1873.

The city of Philadelphia was so proud of the American Line that Mayor William S. Stokley wrote the directors on December 28, 1872, and, on behalf of the city council, presented four brass Dahlgren howitzers (twelve pounders) from the city arsenal to be used as signal guns on the four ships of the line. The board of directors was delighted to accept this testimonial of community support.

The second annual meeting of the American Steamship Company stockholders was held on April 7, 1873. E. C. Knight was reelected president of the company. The *Annual Report* dryly stated: "The execution of the contract with Messrs. William Cramp and Sons for the construction of four iron screw steamers for the company has been considerably delayed, so that as yet none of them have been delivered."[40] Note was taken of the fact that the first three ships had been successfully launched, and the iron plating on the hull of the *Illinois* was nearly completed, with hopes that she would be launched around May 15. Cramp's explanation for the delay was that there had been difficulties in getting the large castings for the engines. The *Pennsylvania*'s trial trip was planned for late April, and this was achieved for all practical purposes when the liner slipped out of the Cramp Shipyard and steamed down the Delaware for extended trials during the week of May 3, 1873. A satisfactory performance over a forty-eight-hour period in terms of speed and coal consumption having been achieved, she was turned

The American Line of European Steamers—
Sketches on the Indiana *drawn by C.S.
Reinhart. The "Bridge," "Ladies' Saloon,"
"Smoking Room," and "Dining Saloon" are
shown in this series of rare vignettes. The gold
"Keystone," symbol of the State of Pennsylvania
graced the American Line funnels from 1873–84.
The basic funnel color was a brilliant red with a
white band and a black top.*

Harper's Weekly, April 10, 1880

over to the American Line, which appointed Captain George Sumner as her first master, and preparations were made for the maiden sailing.

The *Annual Report* stated that a mail subsidy was being sought from the United States government. During the winter of 1872–73, a subsidy bill prepared by the board of directors of the American Steamship Company was placed before Congress by Representative Leonard Myers. The bill authorized the postmaster general to contract with the American Line for the establishment of an ocean mail steamship service between the United States and England. The American Line bill was read twice before the House, after which it was referred to the Committee on Commerce, where it languished without action prior to adjournment. The Line intended to pursue the matter aggressively in the halls of Congress during the coming year.

The final step in the organization of the American Steamship Company's transatlantic service was the establishment of the head offices of the firm in the United States and in Europe. In Philadelphia, Louis C. Madeira was appointed general superintendent of the company and opened the new offices of the line at 237–239 Dock Street. The staff consisted of Madeira, R. B. Hancock (freight agent), and ten clerks. Across the Atlantic in Liverpool, England, the old and well-established shipping firm of Messrs. Richardson, Spence and Company was retained to oversee the British and European affairs of the Line. This firm handled the business of a number of important steamship accounts, including the Inman Line, which would figure so prominently in the future of the American Line itself. In late May 1873, a wide-ranging European publicity campaign was begun to familiarize the public with the services of the American Line. Among the attractions of directing either passengers or freight to the new steamship line was the ease of access in obtaining through connections, or bills of lading, to the "interior" of the United States via the Pennsylvania Railroad Company.

The *Pennsylvania*, having satisfactorily passed her trials, was prepared for her maiden sailing. Philadelphia newspapers were unstinting in their praise of the liner. She "combines in a remarkable degree, all the qualities desirable in a vessel of her class, being swift, strong, and economical in consumption of coal." In her interior appointments, it was stressed that each room was supplied with a hair mattress and long, silk-striped terrycloth curtains of the finest quality. Each cabin on the ship was decorated with a different fabric, although uniform in style, thus "increasing the attractions of the eye of the visitor without destroying the harmony and symmetry of the whole."[41]

The majestic *Pennsylvania* backed out into the swirling Delaware River on May 22, 1873, for her maiden sailing. She carried fifty-six cabin-class passengers, with the passenger list headed by Major and Mrs. Thomas T. Firth. Firth was an important figure in the Pennsylvania Railroad Company and had shown considerable interest in the development of the American Line. He had reserved the first cabin to be sold for the crossing. The majority of the cargo shipped on the liner came from firms owned or controlled by members of the board of directors or stockholders in the American Steamship Company. The import-export house of E. C. Knight and Company enjoyed the privilege of placing the first cargo in the hold of an American Line ship—which was only appropriate, since Knight was the president of the steamship line.

With her single towering funnel and two graceful masts, the *Pennsylvania* was a beautiful sight underway. Her masts were outfitted to carry full-brig rigging, and the sails she carried were always kept ready for service. This proved fortunate even on her maiden voyage, when some of the blades were knocked off her propeller in mid-Atlantic, and she arrived under sail off the Mersey at Liverpool. The sails were set because of the need to conserve coal, owing to the slower crossing and the substantial vibration experienced when the propeller was employed. Upon her arrival in Liverpool, the propeller was repaired in drydock.

The machinery and boilers of the new American-built liner attracted considerable attention in Britain, according to Charles Cramp. "Two great changes in mechanical method and practice in certain details of engine building took place in Great Britain as a result of our visit and the arrival of the '*Pennsylvania*,' the first of the American Line; although we took no active measures in that direction."[42] Cramp went on to discuss the art of "flanging boiler plates," or heating and bending the plates in such a manner as to interlock them, which was common among American shipbuilders but unknown in Britain, where the boiler heads were secured by angle bars in the corners. Charles Cramp rarely restrained his ego or his pronouncements on subjects far and wide, maritime or not, and tact was never his strong suit:

> We called the attention of the British builders generally to this superiority in boiler construction, but little or no attention was paid to what we said at that time; but when the four ships of the new line arrived in Liverpool, draughtsmen from all quarters were sent to make sketches of the boiler work, and of many other devices new to them, besides the boiler constructions, one of which was the use of white metal in bearings and journals. This feature in engine construction the British had not taken up when we visited their works.
>
> We can claim to have introduced boiler flanging and the use of white metal in British ship construction on account of our recommendations, and the practical illustration of their utility on the arrival of the ships of the American Line.[43]

Sampson Fox was regarded by Cramp as one of the most creative of British shipbuilders by virtue of the early adoption of the flanging method at that yard. Conversely, Cramp acknowledged that he learned much about making corrugated furnaces from Sampson Fox. Subsequently, he applied the technique to new boilers he installed in the yacht *Corsair*, built for George Osgood, and the yacht *Stranger*, constructed for Charles Osbourne. The exchange of industrial information between American and British shipbuilders as a result of Charles Cramp's visit in 1871, and the subsequent construction of the *Pennsylvania* quartet, were not insignificant.

In Britain, the *Pennsylvania* definitely was newsworthy. The *Liverpool Journal of Commerce* reported on Monday, June 23, 1873, that the liner was ready to sail after her repairs, and that she had a full complement of passengers, as well as a fair cargo. The initial voyage of the *Pennsylvania* was followed by that of the *Ohio* in August, the *Indiana* in October, and the *Illinois* in January 1874. The initial American Line fleet was complete, but the economic storm warnings on the horizon were not at all auspicious for the firm. The commissioning of the fleet coincided with the beginning of the first post-Civil War economic depression. This resulted in a severe contraction in trade in 1873–74 and poor cargoes on the North Atlantic. Furthermore, when a depression was underway, prospective immigrants frequently were discouraged from crossing the Atlantic to seek a new life in America, and passenger revenues fell accordingly. This occurred at the worst possible time for the new steamship line—just as it was beginning operations.

Chapter 2

UNCERTAINTY AND DISCONTENT

The financial affairs of the American Steamship Company in the fall of 1873 were nowhere near as satisfactory as anticipated by the optimistic predictions of the founders and the Pennsylvania Railroad Company. The *Pennsylvania* and her sisterships were nine to 12 months late being delivered, and even though all four ships were to be in operation by January 1874, the delays experienced in putting the liners into service cost the company dearly in unsustained overhead.

During 1873, the vessels of the American Line completed 14 round-trip voyages between Philadelphia and Liverpool. The gross receipts from those trips amounted to $577,692.02, but the disbursements for running expenses were $524,372.27, leaving a gross profit from ship operations of only $53,319.75. From this figure had to be deducted the costs of the head office on Dock Street, which totaled $18,000 for office rent, salaries of personnel, insurance, furniture, fixtures, and all other office expenses. In Philadelphia, bills also had been incurred for a wharf—at $7,900. This expense could be regarded as nonrecurring, since the improvements were permanent additions to the pier, but they still contributed to the financial strain. Furthermore, there was little point in having a steamship line in either Liverpool or Philadelphia if no one knew of its existence. The costs of "placarding" and widespread advertising on both sides of the Atlantic accounted for an additional $22,000. Ads featuring the ships and sailing schedules of the four American Line vessels were placed in all the major newspapers of the British Isles, and far and wide in the United States, with emphasis on the route of the Pennsylvania Railroad Company to the west.[1]

The personnel cost for the officers and crews of each American Line ship ran $3,915 per month, $46,980 per year. The highest paid position was the captain with a salary of $3,600 a year, next was the chief engineer at $1,800, and then the chief steward at $1,200. The captain led a Sailing Department staff which—with their annual salaries—consisted of first ($1,500), second ($780), third ($660), and fourth officers ($540), a purser ($900), docker ($900), carpenter ($540), 4 quartermasters ($480@), 16 able seamen ($360@), 4 ordinary ($240@), a messroom steward ($300), and a sailors' mess boy ($180). Under the chief steward—who posted a bond of $5,000—was a second steward ($720), pantryman ($540), storekeeper ($540), barber (no salary), first stewardess ($300), second stewardess ($240), porter ($540), 8 waiters ($240) (number variable according to the number of cabin passengers booked), chief cook ($900), second cook ($660), third cook ($540), baker ($660), and butcher ($480). In the Engineering Department under the chief engineer was a first assistant engineer

($1,200), second assistant ($1,020), third assistant ($900), 3 oilers ($660@), storekeeper ($600), 12 firemen ($600@), 9 coal passers ($480@), and 1 firemens' mess boy ($180). The *Pennsylvania* and her sisters were manned by a crew of 85 divided into 34 in the sailing Department, 21 stewards, and 30 in engineering.[2]

The first 14 round-trip voyages of the American Line ships had demonstrated that the Port of Philadelphia commanded enough trade to permit full outward-bound cargoes at rates equal to those charged from any other Atlantic port—meaning New York. The inward-bound trade from Liverpool was beginning to build, and if it continued to do so, gave promise of providing full cargoes in each direction. Furthermore, the steamers had received good reviews with compliments on their speed and comfort, so it was hoped that the passenger trade would show a marked increase in the future.

In the final analysis for 1873, the net profit from the 14 round-trip voyages was $427.50—before any effort was made to pay those holding the securities of the company. The bond holders were owed a minimum of $90,000 interest (6 percent on the issue of $1,500,000), which the Pennsylvania Railroad Company, as the guarantor, had to loan the American Steamship Company. Thus the overall picture for the first full year of operations was a loss of $89,522.50, with nothing put aside for the insurance fund or replacement. The much-heralded American Steamship Company had come into existence, but it had not exactly proven to be a gold mine!

The directors of the Line noted: "The contract price for the construction of the four steamers, together with the cost of fitting them out, and other expenses of their construction not included in the contract, has exceeded the aggregate of capital stock and bonded debt. This deficiency is being met by a loan from the Pennsylvania Railroad Company."[3]

The plain facts of the matter were that the cost of building and putting into operations the initial quartet had totally exhausted the resources of the American Steamship Company. Were it not for the extension of a line of credit from the Pennsylvania Railroad Company, the steamship enterprise would have failed before the conclusion of the first calendar year of operations. Certain retrenchments were required immediately, and the board of directors took them in December 1873.

A "Committee on Reorganization" was created by the American Line board of directors, which reported to the full board on December 31, 1873.[4] A number of potential courses of action were considered, including declaring bankruptcy, but none held as much appeal as sharing expenses through a consolidation of management with the firm of Peter Wright & Sons, which also was the managing agent for another new Philadelphia-inspired maritime enterprise, the International Navigation Company (Red Star Line). Negotiations were undertaken to establish joint management for the two steamship lines, effective January 1874. Peter Wright & Sons agreed to assume responsibility for the American Line ships for a commission of 2 percent on freight and passage money, originating in America. Operations in Philadelphia and Liverpool for the two lines were combined to cut costs.

This might well be entitled A Cold Winter's Watch on the Bridge *and is by Henri Cassiers (1858–1944), the most celebrated Belgian artist and illustrator of his day. Over a period of fifty years he was commissioned to do numerous works for the International Navigation Company (Red Star Line) and the American Steamship Company.*

In fact, the International Navigation Company was intimately associated with the Pennsylvania Railroad Company from its inception in 1870. The PRR guaranteed the principal and interest on a $1,000,000 bond issue of the International Navigation Company and invested in a substantial block of the $1,500,000 in stock issued by the new concern.[5] It was chartered only a month after the American Line to run a fleet of steamships from Philadelphia to Liverpool, England, and Antwerp, Belgium. Whether the Red Star Line—as the company is more familiarly known—and the American Line were rivals at any time is doubtful. In 1873, however, the Red Star Line did run two British-flag steamships, the *Abbotsford* and the *Kenilworth*, in an active Liverpool–Philadelphia service along the same route as the American Line ships. The fact that the Red Star ships and the American Line vessels ran on complementary schedules appears to eliminate any possibility of their being competitors. The combining of the interests and steamers of the two lines permitted the establishing of a weekly service between Philadelphia and Liverpool, since six ships were available.

The original American Line advertisement, which ran in the Glasgow Herald *in 1873. Captain Sumner is listed for the* Pennsylvania *and Captain Morrison for the* Ohio, *but the other masters had not been chosen yet. The first Westbound sailing of the* Pennsylvania *was scheduled from Liverpool on June 18 with a call at Queenstown for additional passengers. Cabin-class fares were offered at 15–18 guineas with steerage rates "as low as any other line" indicating the competitive nature of that trade. Richardson, Spence & Co., an English Quaker firm, were listed as the agents.*

At the same time Peter Wright & Sons assumed responsibility for the operations of the American Line, a new contract was negotiated with the Liverpool firm of Richardson, Spence & Company that was much more favorable to the American Line. Prior to this, Richardson, Spence & Company already had been the agents for both steamship lines in Liverpool. Furthermore, the Philadelphia and Liverpool agents for the two lines had a multitude of interlocking business relationships, in addition to the two steamship lines, and had been closely associated for some years. Their ability to cooperate on all matters was well established, and their principal officers were well known to each other as business associates of long standing.

The recently opened head offices of the American Steamship Company on Dock Street in Philadelphia were closed, and, in the business terminology of the day, General Superintendent L.C. Madeira, Freight Agent R.B. Hancock, and the numerous clerks engaged there were "retired to private life."[6] Early in 1874, a significant boost to the morale of the American Steamship Company was the first public recognition of its existence from the United States Post Office, which finally granted the American Line ships the right to carry the mail from the United States to Britain. However, the reward even to an American-flag carrier amounted to a minuscule subsidy. The American-flag vessels of the line were to receive both the inland and the sea postage from any mails carried by them, but even this was better than nothing. The munificent sum earned in 1874 for 15 trips from Philadelphia to Queenstown, Ireland, was $701.17—in return for carrying 15,858 letters.[7]

Mother Nature proved to be unkind to any steamship braving the North Atlantic during the fierce winter of 1873–74. It was one of the worst seasons the transatlantic trade ever experienced. Even though the term *hurricane* was used in the 1870s to describe a broader variety of severe weather than now, contemporary newspaper accounts report hurricane after hurricane howling across the sea lanes with gale-force winds and mountainous seas. The American Line vessels did not escape unscathed, yet not one vessel was lost—in itself a major accomplishment. One crossing, in particular, deserves a place in the annals of American maritime lore.

The *Pennsylvania*, premier unit of the American Line, lay at Liverpool on February 21, 1874, preparing to sail. The liner had loaded all the freight available, which was worth the substantial sum of approximately $250,000. The Liverpool ticket agents sold passage on such vessels until the gangplank was pulled away, since money was money and in the winter every transaction helped make ends meet. One last passenger, an individual with a definite air of the sea about him, bought a ticket and boarded about an hour before departure. He gave his name to the Richardson, Spence & Company representative as "C.L. Brady." The anchor was raised about 2:30 P.M., and the *Pennsylvania* steamed down the Mersey bound for Delaware Bay under the command of the experienced and reliable Captain Lewis T. Bradburn. Bradburn, who had sailed the North Atlantic for 25 of his 42 years and had been with the ship since her commissioning, as first officer and then master, was on his last voyage. He had just been appointed port captain at Liverpool. While

"Steamer chairs" were available on American Line ships by the late 1880s at the nominal charge of fifty cents. Prior to this, passengers wanting deck chairs had to bring their own, at considerable inconvenience.

the American liner was carrying a substantial general cargo, she had only two saloon passengers and 12 steerage passengers for this dead-of-winter crossing.

The *Pennsylvania* passed down the Mersey without incident and crossed the Irish Sea in good time. The first two days were unexceptional, but as the liner rounded the coast of Ireland and headed into the open Atlantic, she encountered stormy westerly gales that continued for the next four days. On February 27, at 46°37' north latitude and 31°46' west longitude (barometer 27.90), the direction of the wind shifted slightly to the northwest and a violent hurricane began to slam the liner about. The crew was forced to exert the utmost effort to keep the vessel under control. The scene was horrifying, as mountainous waves and highly confused seas washed over the ship and carried away everything movable from the decks. The ship labored and strained very hard against the pounding from the heavy seas. During the night of February 27, the *Pennsylvania* shipped the first of several colossal waves, which broke over the bow with such force that it fractured and stove in the forward end of the "social hall" and sent seawater sweeping down the length of the ship through the saloon. When this happened, most of the passengers and some of the crew apparently felt that the ship was doomed, and that her end was near. The ship's carpenter, assisted by other crew members and desperate male passengers, proceeded to repair and reinforce the forward part of the deckhouse in an effort to prevent the seas from flooding the saloon even more.

Around midnight, when the ship appeared to have entered the eye of the storm, the *Pennsylvania* received a reprieve. However, even when the winds abated temporarily, very severe cross seas were running from southwest to northwest, and the liner still was laboring and straining hard to maintain any forward movement. The worst was yet to come.

While the crew was changing watches at midnight, the *Pennsylvania* encountered an extraordinarily huge wave, which loomed out of the darkness on the starboard bow and broke with a thunderous crash over the superstructure of the ship. The mountainous sea carried away a portion of the bridge, the wheelhouse, the mates' house, four of the lifeboats and all of the life rafts; unshipped the ventilators; ripped off the railings; broke the stanchions; and stove in all four of the forward hatches. The force of the wave was so great that it broke the foreboom and flooded both the steerage and saloon areas of the ship until they were about one-fourth full.[8]

The *Pennsylvania* appeared bound for a watery grave. The liner was completely disabled and in a very dangerous position. She lay in the trough of the seas, rolling heavily and losing all headway or direction. Those below decks were stunned by the concussion of the monster wave, cold and wet from the insurge of seawater, and dizzy from the wild rolls of the ship. As they wondered what had happened, additional information brought home the magnitude of the disaster.

The mammoth wave that struck the *Pennsylvania* and sent thousands of tons of water cascading across the decks had torn away the bridge and swept to their deaths Captain Lewis Bradburn, First Mate Henry Sweetman, Second Mate James Ross, and two seamen, Joseph Chapman and James Davis, who had been at the wheel. None of these five men were ever seen again. This was a tragedy of staggering proportions. Drownings at sea were common on the North Atlantic, but the loss of the three senior officers and two experienced seamen from one gigantic wave certainly was unsurpassed as a disaster.[9] The perilous position of the vessel was not helped when the third officer, Charles Rivers, upon whom the command of the liner devolved, took one look above deck at the rampaging seas and refused to take command! Rivers remained in the uncertain safety offered below decks and refused to accept responsibility for the stricken steamer. Under the circumstances, anyone might have cracked, but the fate of the ship and her passengers appeared bleak, with no one in command.

Cornelius L. Brady had been the last person to pay his six guineas ($31.50) to purchase a ticket for the February 21 sailing of the *Pennsylvania*, and he shared the saloon accommodations with only one other gentleman, Charles Walton of London. Brady had no intention of going to a watery grave. While technically a passenger, he held a master's certificate in steam and was determined to do everything conceivable to save the ship and the lives of those still on board. He already had worked alongside the ship's carpenter to shore up and reinforce the forward end of the deckhouse when it had been ruptured by waves earlier in the evening. Now the situation was infinitely more perilous for the ship and all concerned.

Brady had narrowly survived one shipwreck less than a year earlier, when he had been third officer on the ill-fated *Atlantic* (1870, 3,707 tons) of the White Star Line. Battling heavy gales late in March 1873, the *Atlantic* had run short of coal because of the violent weather, and her captain had decided to make for Halifax, Nova Scotia. During the night of April 1, in the midst of a raging storm, the White Star liner narrowly missed the entrance to Halifax Harbor and plowed onto the rocks. The *Atlantic* was torn in two by the accident. The stern of the liner soon broke away and sank, with a loss of 585 lives out of 1,038 passengers and crew. Only the courageous action of Brady, who fought his way through the surf to the Canadian shore with a rope tied around his waist,

The Indiana *(1873, 3,104 tons, 343 feet by 43 feet, 12 knots) is shown sailing from Philadelphia with a cargo of American grain destined for famine relief in Czarist Russia. The Cramp Shipyard reconditioned a number of vessels and built a small cruiser,* Zabiaca, *for the Imperial Russian Navy in the latter part of the nineteenth century. Hence, in Philadelphia and the Delaware Valley sympathies ran high for starving Russians.*

made it possible to save those who did survive. The *Atlantic* was the worst disaster in the period 1873–74, but 11 other liners were lost between January 1873 and November 1874 on the North Atlantic, and collision figured in only a single case.

Brady had no desire to repeat his narrow brush with death on the *Atlantic*. When the monster wave hit the *Pennsylvania*, he had been helping the carpenter repair the forward part of the deckhouse. The sounds made by much of the superstructure of the ship being ripped away hardly went unnoticed. As the men were struggling to make repairs inside the corkscrewing ship, Williams, the chief steerage steward, came aft and informed the men that heavy seas had stove in all the forward hatches and that the ship was filling with water. Brady ran forward to see the damage and found the majority of the crew and passengers standing around Third Officer Charles Rivers, who was leaning against a pump well with a lamp in his hand and saying nothing.

The lamp may have given some comfort but no salvation. The chief engineer, Mr. Eddons, said to Rivers, "Why don't you take your men on deck!" He replied, "I can't find a man to go on deck." The purser then said, "Go on deck yourself and set your men an example," but instead of so doing, "he continued walking up and down."[10] The third officer seemed paralyzed by the magnitude of their imminent peril and refused to take action.

Brady took one look at the scene and seized control of the situation below decks.

The Ohio *is shown at Dominica, February 20, 1896, during a Caribbean voyage. The substantial additions to the super-structure are evident, but less obvious are her triple-expansion engines, installed in 1887 by James Howden (Glasgow).*

Conditions could not have been worse. The *Pennsylvania*, with her hatches stove in, was lying in the trough of the sea in the midst of a hurricane. The most critical need at this point was to stop the flow of water into the ship. Brady issued orders for all those present to divide into three gangs in order to strip the lower decks of their hatches and pass them up to the upper decks, so that the stove-in hatches could be resecured and thus keep the ship from filling further. The chief steward, Mr. Peterson, the second steward, Mr. Brennan, and their two assistants, together with the quartermaster and the carpenter, set out to lift the lower hatches. C.H. Walton, the sole saloon passenger, gave them considerable credit for securing the hatches and saving the ship. Mr. Gamble, the fourth officer, was laid up with an injured foot.

Immediately after issuing those orders, Brady saw Captain Bradburn's steward, Edwin Coleman, a 12-year veteran of the North Atlantic, standing nearby. Brady sent Coleman on deck to tell Bradburn what had been done and to obtain the captain's sanction for the emergency measures. He then turned on Third Officer Rivers with amazement and demanded to know whether or not he was an officer of the ship. When Rivers said he was, Brady demanded to know "why he was not at his post on deck attending to his duty or trying to save the ship, to which the third officer responded, 'What can I do? What do you want me to do?' "[11] Brady then ordered Rivers to go forward and assist the crew in getting the hatches secured. The third officer immediately obeyed and Brady did not see him again for at least two hours.

Cassiers' Two Flemish Peasant Girls *watch a two-funnel Red Star liner steaming by. The vessel may be the* Westernland *(1883), but probably is the* Vaderland *(1900) or* Zeeland *(1901). Cassiers was an expert on the provincial dress of Dutch and Belgian peasants, which he captured in a number of scenes.*

In the meantime Coleman, the captain's servant, with great courage had gone on deck at Brady's request and in the turmoil of the storm had not been able to find his master. Coleman stumbled back to Brady with the horrifying news that the ship was steaming along with a quartermaster at the helm in the midships wheelhouse but minus all her officers who had been on deck! In the words of Brady, "This knowledge greatly increased the excitement, confusion and consternation among all on board."[12] Those passengers and crew members within hearing clearly were at the limits of their endurance. Brady did not hesitate. He felt the preservation of the lives on board and the cargo and the ship required that he assume command immediately. On his own authority and by his own judgment, he decided to do so. His decision would soon be reinforced. As Brady headed for the open deck, he was met by a delegation consisting of the ship's surgeon, the purser, the first assistant engineer, the quartermaster, the carpenter, and others who implored him to take command for the sake of saving the ship and the lives and property of all on board.

With this vote of confidence, or desperation, Brady struggled through the gale to the midships wheelhouse, where he found Michael Murphy, quartermaster, at the wheel. Murphy informed Brady that the captain had gone forward to the bridge some time before and had not been heard from since. Brady told Murphy that he was assuming command for the time being, and the quartermaster appeared greatly relieved. The first step was to slow the liner and heave-to so that she could regain some stability and sea-worthiness. This might make it possible for the deckhands to try to secure the hatches. Brady rang down to the engine room to reduce the *Pennsylvania*'s engines to dead-slow. Simultaneously, the helm was put hard aport and the ship's heading was brought from southwest to west-northwest. Hove-to in this manner, the bow was turned into the wind and just sufficient revolutions were maintained to keep the ship under control. Murphy later testified: "Without Captain Brady I believe we would never have reached port."[13] Brady left the quartermaster and with great effort made his way to a point where he could inspect the forward section of the ship. He saw the twisted and mangled portion of the bridge that remained. The bridgehouse itself had completely disappeared. No trace of it existed anywhere on the *Pennsylvania*. Brady clawed his way back to the mid-ships wheelhouse, where he told the quartermaster what he had (or had not) seen. The storm continued to rage around the stricken liner, while Brady remained in the wheel-house trying to save the ship. All able-bodied crew members not needed in the engine room worked frantically against the seas to resecure the hatches; after three hours, they managed to replace one. This information was brought to Brady by Rivers, who acknowledged Brady's command by reporting to him and taking orders from him.

During the remainder of the night, the exhausted crew managed to secure the remaining hatches, giving the liner a chance to survive. As the immediate crisis lessened somewhat, Brady could let his mind move ahead to thinking about navigating the ship. Brady soon discovered that the location of the *Pennsylvania* on the broad North Atlantic was virtually unknown, since the dead officers had been able to make only one observation after leaving Liverpool a week earlier. On the morning of February 28, the storm finally broke, after five days, and Brady mustered the crew on deck. He informed them that he had assumed command at the request of a majority of the officers and asked them if they were satisfied with his leadership. All were! The third officer acquiesced during the proceedings, standing behind Brady and accepting the temporary position of first officer under Brady. Rivers told Brady that this was his first trip on a steamship, having previously served all his time in sail, "and that he did not understand handling them."[14] Brady received reports of the fuel and provisions remaining on board, and, since they were adequate for proceeding to the United States, he gave orders for the *Pennsylvania* slowly to steam southward toward smoother seas.

Later on the same day, the *Pennsylvania* encountered the sailing ship *Charles A. Farwell*, which also had been through the storm, and which to Brady's surprise was commanded by a friend, Captain Streeter. The *Charles A. Farwell* and the *Pennsylvania* approached each other so closely that Brady could tell Streeter what had happened without the use of a trumpet. He asked his friend to report the news in Europe when he got there. Streeter encouraged Brady to transfer and cross with him, but Brady elected to remain with the American liner, since he did not feel anyone else on board was capable of navigating the *Pennsylvania* safely to port. As fate would have it, the *Pennsylvania* was not yet finished with foul weather; she encountered gales on March 3 and 4. Ultimately, on March 8 the *Pennsylvania*, under the

Cassiers' peasants watch the Red Star Line Finland *(1902, 12,760 tons, 560 feet by 60 feet, 15 knots) on the Scheldt River near Antwerp (Anvers), Belgium. The Belgian mail subsidy was vital to the survival of the Société Anonyme de Belge-Américaine, the Belgian associate of the International Navigation Company.*

command of Captain Cornelius L. Brady, passed the capes of Delaware Bay and picked up a pilot off Lewes, Delaware. The next day, March 9, the *Pennsylvania* was secured alongside an American Line wharf at Philadelphia, and the exhausted survivors staggered ashore. The liner was 17 days out from Liverpool on what was normally a 10-to-11-day voyage. The tributes of both passengers and crew to Brady's courage and seamanship were of the first magnitude. Brady was hailed as a hero, while Rivers was placed on the "retired list."

The log that Brady presented to Peter Wright & Sons, agents for the American Line, was the essence of simplicity:

> Steam-ship *Pennsylvania*, Brady, from Liverpool, Feb. 21, with merchandise to Peter Wright & Sons. Cabin passenger, Mr. Charles Walton, of London, and twelve in steerage.
>
> The *Pennsylvania* encountered a succession of heavy westerly gales, with high cross seas; Feb. 27, Latitude 46 degrees 37' North, Longitude 31 degrees, 46' West, encountered a violent hurricane from south-west to north-west, barometer standing 27.90 with high confused seas running.
>
> Feb. 27, midnight, shipped a tremendous sea sweeping forward deck of everything moveable, washing away forward house and a portion of the forward wheel, and carrying overboard Captain Bradburn, Mr. Sweetland [sic], first officer, Mr. Ross, second officer, and two seamen, all of whom are lost. Captain

C.L. Brady, an experienced officer in the North Atlantic trade, who has been in the employ of the Liverpool Agency of the line for eleven years, was on board, and, by request of the remaining officers, took command of the ship. From the Banks took a southerly course, and experienced strong south-west winds, with thick and unsettled weather. Used the after steering apparatus.

Feb. 28 (no latitude, etc.,), spoke ship *Charles A. Farwell*, bound east; March 6, latitude 40 degrees 25' North, Longitude 62 degrees 1' West, exchanged signals with ship *Cornelius Grinnel*, bound east. The *Pennsylvania* anchored off Brandywine Light at 10 P.M., 8th instant. The hull, engines and spars of the ship are all sound.[15]

Local journalists commented upon the fact that for all he had gone through, Captain Brady was a man of few words.

The nearly bankrupt American Line was faced with a big problem. What would be a suitable reward for an individual like Captain Brady, who had saved one of their four passenger liners, the lives of all on board, and a valuable cargo, under horrendous conditions? After some deliberation, the board of directors of the American Steamship Company passed a glowing resolution of thanks, which was presented to Captain Brady by the president of the Line, E.C. Knight.

Whereas after the loss of the Captain and the first and second officers, Captain C.L. Brady (a passenger) assumed the command and by his skill and seamanship prosecuted the remainder of the voyage in safety, therefore—

Resolved that the sincere thanks of this board are hereby tendered to Captain C.L. Brady for his noble conduct in taking the responsibility of commanding the ship under such trying circumstances and the President be and is hereby requested to address to Captain Brady a letter expressing our gratitude to him and requesting him to accept the sum of one thousand dollars as an earnest of the appreciation of the valuable services rendered this company.[16]

The board of directors of the American Steamship Company erred greatly on the side of conservativism when they voted Brady the munificent sum of $1,000 for saving a $600,000 vessel and cargo worth another $250,000—not to mention the passengers' lives. Brady indignantly returned the company's check, and Philadelphia sat back to watch one of the more interesting legal tussles of the 1874 season.

Brady filed a libel suit against the American Line for salvage in connection with services rendered. The documents submitted to the District Court of the United States requested that compensation be awarded to Brady on the basis of the value of the passenger liner *Pennsylvania*, the cargo she was carrying, and the cost and expenses that Brady was sustaining in pursuing the matter. A four-month court case was held before Judge John Cadwalader. During the trial, the testimony of those involved in the struggle to save the *Pennsylvania* weighed heavily in Brady's favor. Depositions taken from such individuals as Joseph Pullius, quartermaster and later second officer of the liner, substantiated all of Brady's version of the story. Pullius stated: "If Captain Brady had not taken command when he did, and stopped the speed of the ship, the next sea that boarded her would have filled her, and sunk her, as no vessel could stand taking so much water in board in the condition she was in."[17] In this a number of other American Steamship Company employees heartily concurred. The dead captain's steward, Edwin Coleman, testified "that only Captain Brady's prompt and efficient actions saved the ship and all lives on board."[18] Coleman also testified that Captain Brady, after he assumed command of the *Pennsylvania*, never left the deck day or night until he was sure the ship was safe. Peter McCarroll, another quartermaster who had been a seaman for 16 years, swore under oath: "My opinion is Captain Brady was the only man on board capable of bringing the ship safely into port. If there had been nobody on board who understood handling the ship as Captain Brady did, she could not have lived through the night."[19] Frank Reedstone, a seaman for nine years, stated: "What I give Captain Brady credit for is for doing what he did at the time, slowing the vessel and putting her head to the sea; without that I don't believe she would have lived through the night."[20] George Keabea, a sailor for 20 years and one of the most experienced hands on board, summed up the reaction of everyone who had been there: "I am satisfied the steamer would never have lived through the night if Captain Brady had not taken command when he did."[21]

Brady's attorney was able to cite a substantial number of admiralty cases as precedent where an individual, suddenly finding himself serving in an extraordinary capacity, was entitled to liberal compensation as salvage. In reply, the American Steamship Company lawyers pointed out that when a vessel was in danger of sinking, it was the responsibility of anyone on that ship capable of rendering assistance to do so, since their own neck and property were at stake along with everyone else's. They also pointed out that Brady made no effort to support or assist Third Officer Rivers, but simply usurped command of the ship from him. They also questioned how competent an officer Brady was if his previous experience had only carried him to the rank of third officer—the same rank as Rivers—on a White Star liner.

They sought to drive home the point that it was not a question of whether Rivers was the most competent navigator on board the *Pennsylvania*, but whether he had *sufficient* competence to bring the liner into port. The American Steamship Company attorneys certainly raised some questions, but the testimony of those on the scene and the action of the board of directors in congratulating Captain Brady undermined their position. In the end, Brady's attorney cited precedent that underlined the point that no passenger was required to stand by a vessel in time of danger (which Brady had done when he had declined to leave the *Pennsylvania* at the time of speaking the *Charles A. Farwell*), and that, by so doing, he had established a clear and justifiable claim for appropriate compensation. Brady's lawyer laid claim to a more substantial compensation based on the extraordinary character of the services that he had rendered and that were confirmed by numerous members of the crew of the *Pennsylvania*.

At the end of the four-month trial, Judge John Cadwalader reviewed the testimony and handed down a ruling that increased the award to Captain Brady by 420 percent but fell short of any judgment based upon pure salvage. Brady received the substantially increased sum of $4,000, plus $200 for expenses. This hardly represented clear profit, however, since he had to deduct legal fees of $1,650, ending up with $2,550 as his compensation for saving nearly $1,000,000 in private property from the North Atlantic. The buying power of $2,550 in 1874 represented a significant legacy, and Brady appears to have been content with the outcome, even if he had hoped for more.

During the annual meeting of the American Steamship Company on Monday, April 6, 1874, the horrendous weather conditions in February on the North Atlantic were mentioned with considerable relief expressed that all the units of the fleet had survived zand proven themselves thoroughly seaworthy. The loss of the commander, two officers, and two seamen from the *Pennsylvania* was acknowledged with deep regret.

It was also announced that E.C. Knight had declined to serve another year as president of the company, or as a director of the line. Knight was formally thanked in a resolution "that the stockholders regret the determination of E.C. Knight, Esq., to retire from the gratuitous position of executive officer of this company, believing that in thus recognizing his services during the inception and early progress of this enterprise, we fully acknowledge the loss the company has sustained, but trust that under all circumstances we may have the advantage of his interest and advice for the furtherance of our project to full success."[22] In the election that followed, Henry D. Welsh was chosen president, with a board of directors consisting of Josiah Bacon, John Rice, B.H. Bartol, John Price Wetherill, D.B. Cummins, M. Baird, N. Parker Shortridge, Strickland Kneass, Edmund Smith, and William D. Winsor.

During the early months of 1874, the American Line appears to have entered upon somewhat better times. The four members of the original quartet—*Pennsylvania, Ohio, Indiana, Illinois*—were all in service with the British-flag *Abbotsford* and *Kenilworth* of the International Navigation Company. Among them, the six liners could provide a weekly service when required. The *Indiana* sailed from Philadelphia for Liverpool on February 19 with 35 passengers, a large general cargo valued at $247,854.65, and nine well-filled mailbags. The Line was sufficiently encouraged to announce that the *Indiana* and the *Illinois* each would have an extra deck added in the near future. These plans appeared warranted by developments later in the year, when the *Indiana* returned to Philadelphia on June 8 with more than 400 steerage passengers—the largest number yet carried by an American Line vessel. At £6.6s a head, the steerage passengers contributed a substantial sum to the profitability of that crossing.

The agents were keeping a close watch on crossing times, with the idea that they might be able to compete with the Guion Line at some future date for the mail contract. Just before her disastrous voyage, the *Pennsylvania*, bound for Liverpool, made the best time between the two ports that she ever had made, with a crossing of 10 days and 4 hours from Cape Henlopen to the Mersey pilot. Upon arriving in Philadelphia, the *Pennsylvania* was unloaded and then surveyed in connection with the damage sustained in the storm. Subsequently, the liner was sent to her builders for repairs. Her new master was Captain Thomas R. Harris of Maine, who had left his last command when he reached San Francisco and returned as a passenger to Philadelphia in order to take charge of the *Pennsylvania*.

The *Ohio* also would have a rough time during a late-winter voyage. While outward-bound to Liverpool, she lost two lifeboats, and her after wheelhouse was destroyed. Coming home in mid-March, she battered her way through a gale that damaged her bow in the heavy seas.

On her April sailing from Philadelphia, the *Illinois* cleared the wharf and headed down the busy river without difficulty. Opposite the Philadelphia Navy Yard, she encountered four canal boats making their way upstream. In short order, the *Illinois* sank the four canal boats, but without loss of life and without sustaining any damage herself. Those iron hulls from Cramp were tough, and she continued on her voyage to Liverpool.

The *Ohio* made the headlines in May 1874 when some of her cargo caught fire in mid-Atlantic, and part of the deck burned before the flames were extinguished. Considerable cargo was destroyed, and the *Ohio* put into Queenstown on May 4 in order to secure the situation. Subsequently, the liner continued on her voyage to Liverpool, but when she arrived there on the afternoon of May 5, she was on fire again. The hatches were kept battened down to prevent draft, in hopes that such action would starve the fire of oxygen. Ultimately, steam pumps were employed to extinguish the blaze, and repairs were quickly made to the ship.

Thursday, June 18, 1874, was selected as a gala occasion for the American Steamship Company. The *Indiana* was in port and the president of the Line, Henry D. Welsh, and the board of directors paid a festive visit to the liner. Captain George Sumner, commodore of the Line, was on hand to greet them as the excursion steamer *George Birkbeck* brought the party from Pier 1 North River to the Erie Basin, where the *Indiana* was anchored. Sumner took his guests on a tour of the liner to show off the very latest in accommodations, featuring bathrooms, a smoking room, and a barbershop. The *Indiana* had berths for 75 in saloon and 700 in steerage. The main saloon was 115 feet by 43 feet, running the entire width of the liner. The paneling was English walnut and the room had a Waters piano at the upper end and a "finely covered bookcase" at the lower end. The tour was followed by dinner and toasts exchanged among the dignitaries, who returned to Philadelphia later that evening very pleased with their ship, the Line, and themselves.

The popularity of the American Line steamers was underlined during the summer of 1874 when the *Ohio* sailed for Liverpool with more than 400 passengers, including the members of the Athletic and Boston Baseball Clubs, who were crossing for some exhibition games. Unfortunately, the auspicious international economic forecasts were not to hold. Banking failures in Vienna and New York disturbed financial institutions on both sides of the Atlantic, with widespread reverberations. In September 1873, Jay Cooke and Company in New York became one of the largest financial institutions to collapse in the history of the world monetary system until that time. As a result, confidence in American

The discovery of gold in Alaska brought a rush of miners willing to pay any amount to get to the gold fields. American-flag ships were at a premium in 1898 and Griscom sold three of the original American Line quartet for service in the Pacific, where they never were more profitable than in the run from Seattle to Nome. Even as late as June 1906 the Ohio *is shown leaving Seattle packed with passengers. She was wrecked in Alaskan waters, August 26, 1909.*

banks plummeted, and extensive amounts of capital were withdrawn by European institutions. The American financial system also was influenced by the numerous financial scandals of the Grant administration, many of which, such as Credit Mobilier, received widespread public notice in 1873–74. Even the announcement in 1874 of the discovery of extensive deposits of silver in Nevada was not enough to improve the American and international financial climate. The recession deepened into the first post-Civil War depression, and transatlantic trade dried up for several years. This affected all steamship enterprises on the North Atlantic, but few were operating with resources as slim as those of the American Steamship Company. It would take the better part of a decade before boom conditions would occur again. The disastrous combination of too many ships chasing too little cargo and passengers would be the future of the American Line. A major stockholders' investigation of the Pennsylvania Railroad Company even forced the board of directors of that powerful institution to be very cautious.

One asset of Philadelphia as a major port was the presence of the Philadelphia Navy Yard, with its floating drydock. Vessels of the American Line needing repairs usually could be accommodated quickly and expeditiously. In February 1875, the *Pennsylvania* suffered damage to her propeller, which necessitated drydocking in order to change it. On Tuesday, February 10, the liner was standing by, preparing to enter the drydock, when the rods connecting the engines of the drydock with the pumps parted and the drydock sank to the bottom of the Delaware within minutes. The loss of the drydock was substantial, in that it was only nine years old and had cost $400,000 to build, but the inconvenience to the American Line would be monumental. Thereafter, a significant irritant to anyone operating large vessels on the Delaware was the absence of a major drydock in Philadelphia. This meant that ships periodically had to be sent to New York for drydocking, which was both expensive and time-consuming. In this instance, the *Pennsylvania* had to miss a sailing and steam in ballast to New York for the necessary change of her propeller. Happily, though, not all accidents and repairs required a trip to New York.

The annual meeting of the American Steamship Company on Monday April 6, 1874, was not a happy occasion. The treasurer reported that the revenues of the Line

The sea has inspired many composers. William Church composed a piece called "On the Sea," which was copyrighted by J.M. Stoddart & Co. (1877) and published by F.A. North & Co., Philadelphia, with a suitable cover vignette of an American Line vessel.

The Illinois *was sold in 1898 to the United States Navy and renamed* Supply. *As such she served from 1898 to 1921 through both the Spanish-American War and World War I. In 1921 the* Illinois *was sold again, and survived until 1928, when at the advanced age of 55 she finally was scrapped.*

U.S. Naval Historical Center photograph

during its first complete calendar year of operations had grown to $976,458.61, which was a substantial increase over the $577,692.02 reported for the partial year of 1873. Yet expenses had more than kept pace with revenue as a result of the economic downturn. Totals were $828,558.01 for operating expenses, $39,122.96 for advertising, $8,671.32 for wharf expenses, $60,555.25 for extraordinary expenses including salvage suits, and $88,465.33 for agency expenses. This gave the American Steamship Company a loss of $48,914.26 for the first full calendar year of operations (1874). The floating debt of the company had grown to the awe-inspiring sum of $351,656.17, accounted for in part by the fact that the original quartet had cost $153,106.02 more than the total capital raised by the sale of stocks and bonds in the company. The American Line had been left totally without working capital at its beginning and had begun operations only as a result of the loan from the Pennsylvania Railroad Company. Insofar as the board of directors of the American Steamship Company was concerned, it was felt that if the general depression in trade had not occurred during the previous year, the balance sheet would have shown a substantial profit. The total income of $976,458.61 included $288,932.97 from passenger fares and $683,502.13 from freight. Freight rates had been exceptionally low, and if they had been within the normal range, this would have contributed to the solvency of the line. It was noted that the major steamship lines serving New York had experienced an aggregate decline in receipts for 1874 in excess of $27,000,000, so in contrast with that figure, the American Line may be considered to have done remarkably well. The *Annual Report* ended on a cheery note: "The next year promises to be a highly prosperous one for our favorite line, and a dividend to the stockholders may be confidently predicted."[23] This was whistling in the dark.

There was sufficient demand for saloon accommodations on the American Line vessels that the decision was made to increase the number of cabins available. Apparently on some occasions, not all passengers who had wanted to cross had been able to find berths. The *Ohio* was the first vessel to be reconfigured, and in April 1875 she emerged from the builder's yard with accommodations for 100 instead of the original 75.

One of the chartered vessels of the American Line was the *Abbotsford* (1871, 2,554 tons), which originally had run between Liverpool and Philadelphia in the service of the International Navigation Company. The liner was launched on March 29, 1873, by Gourlay & Co., Dundee, Scotland, for Williamson, Milligan & Co. of Liverpool and intended for the South American trade. The opportunity for a profitable charter was not to be overlooked and the International Navigation Company was looking for ships. It was stated that: "The steamer is not intended for passenger traffic, but her cabins are fitted up in a costly manner, and will accommodate 20 persons."[24] After January 1874 when Peter Wright & Sons was managing both the INC and the American Line the brig-rigged vessel took sailings for either line as needed. On July 8, 1875, the *Abbotsford* sailed down the Delaware and began a normal summer crossing to the Mersey. Thirteen days later, near the end of the voyage, she was steaming in darkness with reduced visibility up the Irish Sea toward Liverpool. Suddenly land appeared out of nowhere, and the *Abbotsford* struck the shore in Cummoes Bay, Anglesey, Wales, on July 21. The liner hung on the rocks for about 48 hours and then settled into the sea on July 23, without loss of life. The British underwriters sold the wreck as she lay on October 26, 1875. This was the first and only loss of an American Line vessel, and it was fortunate that the vessel was chartered.[25] The American Steamship Company insured none of its property, for an estimated annual savings of $300,000, and while this was a legitimate business decision, they could not afford another cent of fixed expenses, no matter what the benefits.[26] Richardson, Spence & Company, Liverpool agents of the American Line, immediately chartered the *City of Limerick* (1855, 2,536 tons) to fill the gap, since she was available and ready. The *City of Limerick* took the sailing of the ill-fated *Abbotsford* on July 28, within a week of the accident, and remained part of the American Line service through May 1878 for 11 round-trip voyages.

The inventive genius of Peter Wright & Sons, managers of the American Line, was forever directed at finding new means to augment the freight and, therefore, the revenue of the company. As shipping rates continued to tumble, no venture was considered too great a risk. Out of this search for profitable new avenues for freight arose the

"Delaware peaches incident." A mild winter followed by a warm spring at the time when the vast orchards of Delaware peach trees were in blossom had resulted in a bumper crop of the luscious fruit. Balmy temperatures, gentle rains, and the long summer days had contributed to perfect conditions for one of the finest peach crops within memory. Enormous quantities of fruit were available. The farmers' markets of Pennsylvania, Delaware, and Maryland were flooded with what were described as "cherry ripe" fruit, and prices plummeted accordingly. Someone in the firm of Peter Wright & Sons conceived the idea that it would be wonderful if some of this delicious and overly abundant American fruit could reach the British market, where it could command a premium price. Refrigeration was in its infancy, but Quaker inventiveness was not. Accordingly, a formal announcement was made that on Thursday, August 26, the first shipment of peaches would leave for Liverpool on the liner *Ohio*, which would sail from the Washington Street wharf.

In support of this venture, the American Line stated:

> . . . to keep the fruit in merchantable order, it is proposed to operate by means of fans, forcing air over ice with such rapidity that the temperature is quickly reduced to 38 degrees. . . . No outside air is admitted, and the same air over and over again is passed quickly through and through the fruit with scarcely any moisture, and there being no currents of air of different temperatures there is not over one-third the consumption of ice that attends any other process. The gases emitted from the fruit are said to be drawn to the ice and the fruit is always dry and in the best possible state, although kept for weeks in this condition.[27]

Throughout Delaware, notices were posted that all persons proposing to ship peaches in the specially ventilated compartment on the *Ohio* should have their fruit in crates at stations along the Delaware Railroad by noon on Wednesday, August 25, so that a special train of eight freight cars, with a capacity for 350 crates each, could pick them up at the stations. The train was then to run directly to the siding alongside the liner, so that the fruit could be transferred to the iced compartment in preparation for her sailing the next day. The train met with an enormous response at every stop, and more than 4,500 baskets of fruit were delivered to the ship. The *Ohio* sailed on schedule, and it was noted that the Delaware peach shippers awaited news of the venture with no little anxiety.

August 1875 was a hot month, and the black iron hull of the *Ohio* efficiently absorbed the rays of the sun. Even the cold waters of the North Atlantic were not enough to counteract the effects of the sun, the compound engines, and the boiler fires. In mid-Atlantic, the ice gave out and the temperature in the hold began to rise precipitously. The luscious fruit soon passed the best condition for marketing, then became exceedingly soft, and finally decomposed into a slushy mess akin to peach butter. The cargo of peaches festered for several days in the hold of the *Ohio* before the liner reached the Mersey, and when the hatch was removed in Liverpool, a pillar of fruit flies rose heavenward. The newspaper

Supply (*ex-*Illinois) *in a magnificent stern shot taken by a U.S. Navy photographer in 1902 on the West Coast. The solid iron hull and beautiful lines of the original American Line quartet clearly are shown.*

U.S. Naval Historical Center photograph

article reporting the results of this noble pre-refrigeration experiment was headlined "A COMPLETE FAILURE," concluding with: "We presume that this failure will settle the question for the present at least."[28] The Delaware and Maryland peach growers were most unhappy at the news, and there were rumblings about damage suits. One can only guess at the consternation of the *Ohio*'s crew when the officers and sailors learned that they had more than 4,500 baskets of very rotten fruit to scrape out of the hot iron hold of their ship before she could take on cargo for the return voyage.

Once burned was not enough, however, for the agents of the American Line. The steamship *Illinois* sailed from Philadelphia for Liverpool in November 1875 with 30 head of dressed beef, 140 sheep, and a quantity of poultry and oysters that were placed in a "refrigerator" supplied with eight tons of ice and a high-pressure engine to maintain a flow of cold air. Hope was expressed that the experiment with a solider cargo than peaches might prove successful. This time, the ice held out and the perishable cargo reached Liverpool in "apple-pie order." The shippers were Messrs. Martin, Fuller, & Company, who were so delighted with the results that they immediately expanded their plans, and the *Illinois* sailed on December 25 with a hundred head of dressed beef in her cold-storage compartment.[29] These may well be the earliest successful attempts to deliver fresh meat from American farms to British tables. The potential for such a trade, given the teeming masses of Europe and the substantial supply of cheap protein produced by American farms and ranches, was enormous. Visionaries were willing to take the risks in the mid-1870s, although efficient, dependable refrigeration would require another 20 years of development and would have to involve something more sophisticated than rooms with fans rotating over blocks of ice.

Shipments of cotton began to figure large in the cargo manifests of American Line vessels. In February 1876, two of the steamers each carried about 1,600 bales from Philadelphia to Liverpool, representing one of the largest single movements of that commodity through the port.

The American Line received a temporary shock when the *Indiana*, inbound from Liverpool, went ashore on Bulkhead Bar on Tuesday, February 29, but the liner was freed the next morning without damage. The stout iron hulls of the Cramp Shipyard were proving to be solid pieces of work, and the reputation of the American Line vessels increased accordingly.

The fifth annual meeting of the stockholders of the American Steamship Company was held on Monday, April 3, 1876, at the firm's office, 230 South Third Street, in Philadelphia. There was a quite good attendance of city businessmen who had an interest in the line. Christian J. Hoffman chaired the meeting, and Robert W. Smith served as secretary and treasurer. Colonel H.D. Welsh, president of the company, presented the fifth *Annual Report* of the directors, covering the year 1875. The four steamships of the line had completed 34 round-trip voyages, with earnings of $791,138.59 for freight, $288,309.14 for passengers, and $1,872.29 for miscellaneous. Gross receipts from operations came to $1,081,320.02, breaking the million-dollar mark for the first time. Set against this was $886,258.89 for operating expenses, $87,289.87 for shore expenses, $29,050.04 for advertising, and $10,225.82 for wharf expenses at Liverpool and Philadelphia, which left a balance of $68,495.40. Unfortunately, from this also had to be deducted $38,033.40 in extraordinary repairs and expenses for the four steamers, but even with all this, the American Steamship Company still posted a profit for 1875 of $30,462 when many North Atlantic lines had suffered severely reduced incomes because of the depression. Colonel Welsh took considerable satisfaction in pointing out to his fellow businessmen that the actual turnaround since 1874, when the Line had lost nearly $50,000, was in the neighborhood of $80,000.

The $30,000 had been drawn from the agents, Peter Wright & Sons, and all the indebtedness of the American Steamship Company was paid off, with the single exception of the sum owed the Pennsylvania Railroad. In addition, supplies of dock furniture, spare propeller blades, shafts, boiler tubes, and numerous other marine equipment, valued at $17,827.52, had been acquired and stored at Philadelphia and Liverpool for emergency purposes. The ships had used supplies costing $5,892.75 during 1875, but these had mostly been replaced, so the value of the stores remained at $17,269.01 as of January 1, 1876.

Colonel Welsh took pains to underline the fact that trading conditions on the North Atlantic remained acutely depressed. Receipts from the steamers in 1875 actually show a decrease of more than $700 per voyage over those of 1874. The principal loss was in the area of passenger receipts, where the number of individuals carried was 1,206 fewer in 1875 than in 1874. Only the facts that rates being charged were considerably higher and that there had been stringent cost-cutting in operation of the vessels made it possible to convert the loss into a profit. The reduction in expenses per voyage totaled nearly $3,300 and was altogether remarkable. Colonel Welsh attributed it to efficient and fiscal management both in Philadelphia and in Liverpool, as well as on the part of the commanders of the steamers whose aid had been solicited in cost-cutting. Welsh stated:

> This reduction in expenses has been effected, it is believed, without in any way impairing the efficiency of the service, while the steamers have been kept in thorough repair. The commanders have positive instructions never to incur any risk to accomplish a rapid passage, and while many instances exist of exceptionally rapid trips by steamers of our competitors, yet we may well be satisfied with the regularity of the departures and arrivals during the past year. The average time, without allowance for stoppages, of outward passages of the four steamers having been 9 days, 20 hours, 5 minutes, and of inward passages, 10 days, 20 hours, 18 minutes.[30]

The crunch in 1875 had come halfway through the year, when it was realized that the ships had lost $46,305.25 for the first six months of operations in the fiscal year. Stringent provisions were put into effect, and in the second half of the year a gain on expenses of $76,767.25 was realized, which made possible the $30,462 profit for the year. That certainly represents one of the most spectacular turnarounds in business annals, given the depression atmosphere. The profitability of the American Steamship Company did not make it possible for the concern to meet the interest on its $1,500,000 bonded indebtedness and the Pennsylvania Railroad once again advanced enough money to the company so it could meet the sums due upon the bonds.

The report of the Treasurer, Mr. Robert W. Smith, was next presented and read as follows:

```
DEBIT
To Capital Stock                                          $ 701,400.00
To Mortgage Bonds                                         1,500,000.00
To Bills Payable                                           465,683.46
To Profit and Loss                                          96,407.75
                                                         $2,763,491.21


CREDIT
By coupon account interest on bonds                       $346,350.00
By advances for the operations of
   the steamers and purchase of supplies                  $ 66,545.19
By construction and outfit:
   Steamship Pennsylvania        $585,518.85
      "      Ohio                $589,367.54
      "      Indiana             $587,317.17
      "      Illinois            $586,802.46
                                                         $2,349,006.02
By cash on hand                                              1,590.00
                                                         $2,763,491.21

Robert W. Smith, Treasurer, January 1, 1876.[31]
```

In the election of officers that followed, Colonel Henry D. Welsh was reelected president of the company, with a board of directors composed of Josiah Bacon, B.H. Bartol, John Price Wetherill, D.B. Cummins, M. Baird, N. Parker Shortridge, Strickland Kneass, William D. Winsor, G.B. Roberts, and George Allen. The American Steamship Company appeared to be enjoying stable leadership and to have a promising future in 1876.

The depression of the mid-1870s would take a severe toll on manufacturing and immigration. In the immigrant trade, the figures plummeted 50 percent in 1875 over previous years. In imports, the value of goods moving through the Port of Philadelphia continued to slide. The high year after the Civil War was 1873, when the value of imports totaled $29,186,925 through the port, but by 1875 this figure had dropped to $24,011,014, a decline of one-sixth (17 percent) within two years. Had economic conditions continued to prosper as they had in the early 1870s, the earnings of the Line would have been very substantial indeed, but at least the American Line ships had made a profit. There might be light at the end of the tunnel.

Chapter 3

THE CENTENNIAL CELEBRATION AND A RUSSIAN OFFER

The Departure of General Grant for Europe—The Parting in Delaware Bay *by Frederick B. Schell was drawn for* Harper's Weekly *when ex-President and Mrs. Ulysses S. Grant began their celebrated tour around the world in 1877. The American Line's* Indiana *had the privilege of carrying the Grant party from Philadelphia to Liverpool. In the engraving the Delaware River sidewheeler* Twilight *has just delivered the Presidential group to the liner off Newcastle, Delaware. General and Mrs. Grant had elected to board downstream in order to avoid the crowds at the Philadelphia pier.*

The biggest event in Philadelphia during 1876 was the opening of the Centennial Exposition in honor of the *Declaration of Independence*, and the first century of America's existence. The Centennial Commission chose Fairmount Park as the site. A nationwide competition was held for architectural designs including one for the largest building in the world. Henry Pettit and Joseph M. Wilson submitted the winning plans, which ultimately covered 21½ acres and extended for a third of a mile through the park. Generous use of glass and iron, as in the Crystal Palace of the London Exposition, provided a light, airy atmosphere for the huge structure, whose principal hall was 120 feet wide and 1,832 feet long. In all, there would be more than 200 buildings within the exposition area, enclosed by a fence three miles long.

The Centennial Exposition was opened to widespread acclaim on May 10, 1876, by President Ulysses S. Grant and Emperor Dom Pedro of Brazil. The two statesmen actively participated in the opening ceremonies in a unique way by turning valves that supplied steam to the huge Corliss Engine in the Machinery Hall. This monster engine, with its twin 44-inch cylinders and 10-foot stroke, turned a 30-foot, 56-ton flywheel 36 times a minute, to produce 1400 horsepower. This supplied the power to turn some 800 other pieces of machinery at the fair. The Centennial Exposition as a whole was a magnificent tribute to American science and industry, and it symbolized the success of America's Industrial Revolution. One of the star attractions of the exposition was the arm and torch of the new statue soon to be erected in New York Harbor—the Statue of Liberty.

The first day's attendance totaled 186,272 and was confined largely to natives of Philadelphia, but newspaper and magazine accounts of the Centennial Exposition carried the news across the United States. During the summer and fall of 1876, this created the first great wave of tourism in the history of the nation. The Pennsylvania Railroad established "Centennial excursion fares," which encouraged many people for the first time in their lives to plan a vacation away from their homes. Before this occasion, travel for pleasure had been the exclusive domain of the affluent. By the close of the Centennial Exposition, admissions to the fair totaled 10,164,489, of whom 8,047,601 had paid 50 cents a head.[1]

During the centennial year, the American Line and Red Star Line vessels were superbly positioned to benefit from this movement of goods and people across the Atlantic. Early in 1876, bookings for space on the ships were proceeding so well that it was announced that all of the inbound steamers of both lines from March through May were expected to be carrying exhibits for the Centennial Exposition.[2]

Early in 1876 the board of directors of the American Steamship Company evaluated the existing fleet and decided that two new ships capable of carrying 4,000 tons of cargo were needed if profitability was to be possible during the next economic upswing. The basis for their reasoning was that a ship capable of carrying 4,000 tons eastbound and securing 4,000 tons westbound would net a profit of $23,707.31 per voyage; if carrying 4,000 tons out and only 2,000 tons home, $17,196.06; if carrying 4,000 tons out and nothing home, $10,685.50. The Cramp Shipyard had been consulted and made a bid of $645,000 to build each of the new ships and to deliver them in 12 and 14 months.

When the American Steamship Company approached the PRR board in January 1876 for additional funds to build the two additional ships of at least 4,000 tons, the management of the railroad balked. They might recognize the need for the ships, but could not agree to extend any more credit, or offer any more guarantees to the steamship line.[3] Chartered tonnage would have to serve, and arrangements were made in the

A rare early photograph of the Westernland *(ca.1883) shown at the Antwerp Pier of the Red Star Line. Workmen are unloading barrels of goods from the hull of the liner.*

United Kingdom to fill the need. In addition to their other financial committments to the American Line during 1875 the PRR board found itself also being forced to guarantee short term bank loans, which, even if the steamship line was making payments on these, still represented yet another liability.

The American Line board apparently did not feel the rebuff from the Pennsylvania Railroad was unreversible. Henry Welsh continued to push the PRR to underwrite the cost of the two new ships. In March 1876 he informed them that he was sure the steamship line could raise $750,000 toward construction costs by issuing bonds, if the railroad would agree to furnish in cash the additional $600,000 needed.[4]

The Pennsylvania Railroad board was determined to go no further, and instead established a committee to review the financial relationship between the railroad and the steamship line. By January 1877 the steamship line owed the railroad $501,302 without hope of payment. The solution to the accounting problem posed by the indebtedness of the American Steamship Company to the Pennsylvania Railroad was arrived at amicably. A joint committee of the two concerns decided that the American Steamship Company would issue the PRR 5,000 shares of stock at its par value of $100.00, and pay the

A beautiful Cassiers view of the four Red Star steamers, Vaderland *(II),* Kroonland, Zeeland *(II), and* Finland, *which were ordered after 1898 to enhance the service. The* Vaderland *(1900) and* Zeeland *(1901) were built by John Brown on the Clyde, while the* Kroonland *(1902) and* Finland *(1902) were constructed at William Cramp on the Delaware. The hope was to transfer the first two to American Registry, but the necessary legislation never passed Congress.*

Red Star Line
ANTWERPEN-NEW YORK

STEAMERS:
Vaderland
Kroonland
Zeeland
Finland

railroad $1,502.00 in cash. Everyone knew that the stock was virtually worthless, but now the railroad could tidy up its books.[5]

Why would the Pennsylvania Railroad continue this relationship? The answer is simple. The American Steamship Company constantly produced income for the railroad from freight and passengers with every ship that docked or sailed. In 1875 the Pennsylvania Railroad earned from the American Steamship Company operations $206,154.40 in freight and passenger revenue. When set against annual charges of $90,000 for the interest on the bonds, the railroad still benefited greatly and was willing to provide a subsidy when the government would not. 1875 was not a good year for the American Line, and it is assumed that these earnings were among the lowest that the railroad received from the steamship line. No figures for any other year have been found.

In the meantime, Welsh continued his plans for new tonnage. Announcement was made in May 1876 of plans to order two new American Line vessels, to be named *Missouri* and *Kansas*. It was thought that the order would go to the William Cramp Shipyard in Philadelphia. Subsequently, in March 1877, it was announced that the American Steamship Company "closed a contract with Messrs. Wm. Cramp & Sons for the construction of two additional steamships. They are to be modeled after the British steamship *Lord Clive*, now in the service of the company, and the keels will be laid soon."[6] There is no evidence that the keels of these ships ever were laid down because of the continuing economic recession, and the fact that the Pennsylvania Railroad refused to finance construction.

At the same time during 1877 the Pennsylvania Railroad could not deny the rapid expansion of the fresh-meat trade between Philadelphia and Liverpool. Fresh meat, carried in "cold compartments" was becoming the most profitable single cargo that the American Line was transporting. The debate over hiring British steamers continued. In the end the decision still went with chartering foreign tonnage.

More consideration went into long-term charters, often of newly built tonnage. In December 1875, when the American Line released the *Kenilworth* to Red Star, they chartered the larger *Lord Clive* (1872, 3,386 tons), which had proven herself on the North Atlantic. The *Lord Clive* originally was ordered for G.M. Papayanni of Liverpool and had been trading between Liverpool and Boston. Thus began a long association between Papayanni, as shipowner, and Peter Wright & Sons, as charterer, with the ships taking American Line sailings. The plans for the *Missouri* and the *Kansas* were scrapped because of the uncertainty of trading conditions, in favor of chartering additional tonnage from Papayanni and other friendly British associates. In 1879, Papayanni ordered an improved *Lord Clive* for charter to the American Steamship Company. She was launched as the *Lord Gough* (1879, 3,655 tons) and became the largest ship in the American Line fleet. Both the *Lord Clive* and the *Lord Gough* ultimately would be purchased by the American Line, but not until 1888, when completely different owners were directing affairs.

William Cramp and Sons greatly enhanced its value to the Line by building a major new drydock, which was commissioned on May 22, 1876. The new Cramp drydock was capable of accommodating the largest class of oceangoing steamers and was 100 feet longer than those vessels operated by the American Line. On the wharves adjoining the new dock were machine shops, blacksmith shops, and a marine railway capable of taking out vessels of 1,000 tons. The first vessel to christen the drydock was the Red Star Line's *Nederland*, which went in on Thursday, May 25, 1876, for repairs to her bottom. Having a first-class drydock nearby meant enormous savings to the American Line and other Philadelphia maritime concerns. No longer did their ships have to make the long trip to New York in ballast just to use a drydock. This had been their lot since the Philadelphia Navy Yard floating drydock had sunk three years earlier.

In spite of the fact that the American Steamship Company never earned the interest on its bonds during the period 1873–84, the concern worked closely with another Liverpool concern, the British Shipowners Company, to obtain new tonnage. Short-term and spot chartering meant uneven and undependable service, hence undesirable over the long run. It is difficult to believe that the British Shipowners Company did not represent American capital in some way, since British-flag tonnage was so much cheaper to build and operate than American counterparts.

In 1878, the newly built *British Empire* (1878, 3,361 tons) was delivered by Harland and Wolff, Belfast, and immediately took her first sailing for the American Line on

The British Princess *(1882, 3,864 tons, 420 feet by 42 feet, 12 knots) was built by Harland and Wolff, Belfast, for the British Shipowners Company—a holding company—and chartered by Peter Wright & Sons for the Liverpool–Philadelphia service of the American Steamship Company. She was from the next generation of ships, which were built abroad because of prohibitive cost in the United States. Altogether six ships were acquired in this manner:* British Empire *(1878),* British Crown *(1880), British Queen *(1881),* British King *(1881), and* British Prince *(1882). Between 1884 and 1892 American Line ships had a red star in the center of the yellow Keystone, symbolic of International Navigation Co. ownership.*

September 25. She was followed by the *British Crown* (1879, 3,563 tons) on October 15, 1879; the *British Queen* (1881, 3,558 tons) on January 31, 1881; the *British King* (1881, 3,559 tons) on April 9, 1881; the *British Prince* (1882, 3,871 tons) on April 12, 1882; and the *British Princess* (1882, 3,864 tons) on April 28, 1883. There can be little question that these vessels represented the next generation of American Line ships, which for economic reasons and because of the failure of an American postal subsidy could not be built and operated under the American flag. In fact, these ships were built for charter to Griscom and, while they took American Line sailings, there is no evidence that the earnings ever became part of the American Line cash-flow. Owing to trading conditions, not all these vessels were maintained in the American Line service at all times. With the addition of these ships, the British-flag side of the American Line far exceeded the American-flag tonnage in the 1880s.

Many of the American Line captains were famous figures of their time, earning reputations that far surpassed even their immediate shipboard responsibilities.

Captain Lecky, the famous author of *Wrinkles in Practical Navigation*, a book probably found in every blue water ship afloat, ran between Philadelphia and Liverpool in command of the *British Crown* in the American Line. Captain

John Reilly, who commanded the *British King*, in the same Line, was a good seaman and a Shakespearian scholar to boot. Once he appeared on the stage of the old Walnut Street Theatre in the place of the leading man with Robert Mantell in *King Lear*. The equally famous Captain Shackford was in command of another ship in the same service.[7]

The amenities and food on the American Line vessels made them quite popular, particularly with immigrants. Every effort was made to provide new travelers with through tickets to their ultimate destinations in the United States, in order to minimize the disorder, if not terror, of arriving in a new country.

Passenger bookings in 1876 slumped to 11,535 from 13,890 in 1875, which increased the pressure on trimming expenses. Cost-cutting had become a fine art in the American Steamship Company, and eventually it extended even to salaries of seagoing officers of the Line. In 1873, the commanders of the original quartet had received $3,000 a year as their salary; this had been maintained until March 1877, when, as a result of the economic downturn, the captains received an undisclosed cut in pay. It was emphasized, however, that when the captains of American Line vessels were off duty or awaiting a ship, they were boarded at first-class hotels.

The Lord Gough *(3,655 tons, 383 feet by 40 feet, 12 knots) was built by Laird on the Mersey and went directly into the service of the American Line (1879). After ten years she was bought outright and continued in the Liverpool–Philadelphia service until 1896, when she was sold to the Aberdeen Atlantic Line and finally scrapped around 1899.*

The Indiana *dressed out with all flags, probably on the occasion of General Grant sailing for Europe, May 17, 1877. The crossing was described by Grant as being very rough, but he said that he and his wife had been very good sailors.*

Sometimes individuals tried to smuggle goods off American Line vessels to avoid United States Customs. One of the more unusual instances was that of a young lady discovered disembarking from an American Line ship with a violin "peeping out from under her pull-back skirt. She was pulled back, and enough violins brought forth to start a small parlor orchestra."[8]

The high point of the 1877 sailing season occurred when ex-President Ulysses S. Grant sailed from Philadelphia for Liverpool aboard the *Indiana.* Grant's round-the-world tour was to take nearly two and a half years. At Philadelphia on the sailing day, May 17, 1877, the Civil War hero and politician enjoyed a champagne breakfast in his honor attended by Governor John F. Hartranft of Pennsylvania, General William T. Sherman, Hamilton Fish, George W. Childs, and Senator J. Donald Cameron, among many notables. The departure festivities, in fact, would continue through the day. The *Indiana* was fully decorated with all her flags when she backed out into the Delaware, but the ex-president and his party were not on board. The decision had been made to let the liner get away from her Philadelphia pier and to have the Grant party join the ship downstream, away from the crowds. "The most extensive arrangements had been made for the departure. The ex-president, in charge of a Committee of Councils, embarked on the steamer *Twilight,* and was transferred to the *Indiana* near New Castle, Delaware. Mrs. Grant followed him in the revenue cutter *Hamilton* and boarded the outgoing steamer near the same place. The scene upon the river was one of the most exciting ever seen here. All the shipping in the harbor were decorated, the yacht clubs were out in full force, while tug boats made themselves hoarse from whistle blowing."[9]

One hitch in the proceedings occurred when Grant entered his stateroom on the *Indiana* and found his former valet, Bill Barnes, unpacking his clothes. Barnes had attached himself to General Grant during the siege of Vicksburg and had served him well, as the story goes, when sober. Grant had dismissed Barnes from his service and taken him back innumerable times, but Mrs. Grant finally had demanded and received the general's promise not to reemploy the valet. Upon finding Barnes unpacking his shirts, Grant sought out the captain of the *Indiana* and indicated in no uncertain terms that either he or Barnes would leave the liner immediately. "If Bill Barnes is to sail on this boat I shall leave with the pilot. It depends on you, Captain; either you arrange for the departure of Bill Barnes, or I go, but Mrs. Grant must not know until Bill is safely ashore."[10] Barnes left the *Indiana* as expeditiously as possible, and presumably without Mrs. Grant discovering his presence.

Grant wrote from London to a Philadelphia friend, George W. Childs: "After an unusually stormy passage for any season of the year and continuous seasickness generally among the passengers, after the second day out, we reached Liverpool Monday afternoon, the 28th of May. Jessie and I proved to be among the few good sailors. Neither of us felt a moment's uneasiness during the voyage."[11] President and Mrs. Grant had intended to leave Liverpool immediately for London because Judge Pierrepont, U.S. minister to the Court of St. James, had accepted invitations on their behalf and scheduled receptions, but the ex-president was surprised to find nearly all the shipping in the harbor decorated with flags, including the Stars and Stripes, flying from their mainmasts in honor of his arrival. "The docks were lined with as many of the population as could find standing room, and the streets to the hotel where it was understood my party would stop were packed. The demonstration was, to all appearances, as hearty and as enthusiastic as in Philadelphia on our departure."[12] As a result of this generous reception on the part of what was considered pro-slavery Liverpool, Grant and his party remained in the city for an additional day before traveling to Manchester and Leicester en route to London. In Britain, Grant received a reception usually accorded royalty on state visits. He remained in London for most of June and experienced a continuous round of entertainment and receptions, culminating with dinner as a guest of the Prince of Wales and a concert at Buckingham Palace as a guest of Queen Victoria. Ultimately, the ex-president would complete a circumnavigation of the world and return to San Francisco from Yokohama on September 20, 1879, aboard the *City of Tokio*. The crossing of the Pacific was much calmer than the trip across the Atlantic 28 months earlier.

In 1878, after five years of false expectations, the Pennsylvania Railroad Company was anxious to rid itself of the liability of the American Steamship Company. The deteriorating diplomatic climate in Europe seemed to make war inevitable, particularly where Russia was concerned. Russia's feelings recently had been badly burned by her erstwhile friend, Prince Otto von Bismarck, at the Congress of Berlin (1878). This diplomatic gathering had been called by Bismarck, chancellor of the German Empire, to settle out-standing differences among the major powers. Alexander II (1855-1881), czar of Russia, had expected significant help from Bismarck with the Russian goal of expanding south-ward into the lands of the Ottoman Empire in order to secure a warm-weather port on the Mediterranean. The rest of the European states, including Great Britain, France, and Austria-Hungary, were not willing to permit Russian aggrandizement at the expense of the Turks, and Bismarck had cooperated in frustrating the czar.

Relations between Britain and Russia were so strained that the czar's government was unwilling to have any naval ships built in British yards. At that time, a substantial percentage of the world's naval tonnage was built in Britain. It was not unusual to find vessels destined for many different foreign navies lying side by side in British fitting-out basins. With the deterioration of relations in the 1870s and 1880s between Russia and Britain over affairs that ranged from the Khyber Pass to the Dardanelles, it was impossi-ble for St. Petersburg to patronize British yards.

Accordingly, in the early part of 1878, a Russian naval delegation was sent to the United States—the only major industralized power that had not attended the Congress of Berlin—for the purpose of surveying American shipyards. The goal was to have some fast units built for the Imperial Russian Navy in the United States, where they would be superbly positioned to ravage the North Atlantic sea-lanes as commerce destroyers if war should break out. The success of the Confederate raiders built by British shipyards against Union shipping during the Civil War had not gone unnoticed. The Russians were willing to wager some money that they could beat the British at their own game with the assistance of American shipbuilders.

During the American Civil War ships had been built by British shipyards for the Confederate Navy and this violated the laws of neutrality. The Union had protested vehemently, particularly with regard to the most famous Confederate raider, CSS *Alabama*. When the North won the Civil War claims were made for damages and losses to American shipping. These claims were assigned by Britain and the United States to an international arbitration commission meeting in neutral Switzerland. The whole issue of the "*Alabama* claims" only was settled in 1877 as a result of Swiss arbitration between the United States and Great Britain. The memory of the Confederate raiders and the rancor against Britain still remained vivid in the minds of many Americans. The fact that Britain had paid the very substantial claims of the American claimants seemed to have been forgotten.

The chartered HAPAG steamer *Cimbria* (1867, 3,037 tons) brought about 60 Russian officers and some 800 Russian sailors to Bar Harbor, Maine, early in 1878. The Russian officers were royally entertained by the Americans, but the enlisted men found New England singularly inhospitable as they went along the streets of prohibitionist Maine "searching for vodkha in vain."[13]

The American agent for the Russian government was the Philadelphia banking con-cern of Barker Brothers. Wharton Barker soon paid a call on Charles Cramp with some very welcome news. "Mr. Barker informed Cramp that he was delegated to arrange for the conversion and fitting out of a number of auxiliary cruisers for the Russian navy and that he had selected the Cramp Company as the professional and mechanical instrumentality for the purpose."[14]

Captain Semetzschkin, chief of staff of the Grand Duke Constantine, who was General-Admiral of the Russian Navy, had traveled to the United States separately from the *Cimbria* group. Captain Semetzschkin was the leader of a Russian naval committee to oversee the acquisition and conversion of suitable tonnage. He and Wharton Barker discussed a number of alternatives before selecting the Cramp Shipyard. Since war between Britain and Russia was expected at any moment, speed was of the essence. "The purpose of the Russians was to fit out a small fleet of auxiliary cruisers or commerce destroyers to cruise in the North Atlantic in the route of the great British traffic between the United States and England. Their idea was that the fitting out of such a

The International Navigation Company (Red Star Line) also operated a small fleet of tugs to assist its liners. This rare view shows the tug Newcastle *in the Delaware Bay off Newcastle, Delaware, on the occasion of* General Grant *sailing on the* Indiana *for Liverpool (1877).*

fleet with its threatening attitude toward their North Atlantic commerce might or would deter the British from armed intervention in behalf of the Turks."[15]

An atmosphere of the utmost secrecy surrounded everything about the project. Russian officers were spirited in and out of the Cramp Shipyard while plans were completed and agreements struck. The quickest means of filling the Russian order was to buy three or four up-to-date merchant ships and transform them into cruisers. Naturally, Cramp wanted to work on ships with which he was familiar, and he also was well aware of the attitude of Thomas A. Scott, the new president of the Pennsylvania Railroad, who wanted to rid the railroad of any connection with the American Line. The Russians appeared to have a happy solution to everyone's needs. They wanted ships as fast as possible; Cramp wanted ships he knew; the Pennsylvania Railroad wanted to get rid of a financial albatross. All that was needed was the swift agreement of the American Line management to unload its fleet on the Russians at a handsome profit.

Accordingly, Cramp made an offer to the American Line management to purchase three of the Line's four ships. To the amazement of Cramp and Scott, the American Line board of directors refused the offer, perhaps hoping for even more money from the desperate Russians, and the deal fell through. The result was a parting of the ways between the management of the Pennsylvania Railroad and that of the American Steamship Company. Scott was furious that the American Line board of directors had not been prepared to act as quickly as the occasion required. He let them know in explicit language that they need not look to the PRR for any additional assistance. Subsequently, Cramp was able to purchase three other vessels (at very substantial prices), which were converted for the Russians. The success of this effort then brought Cramp an additional order from the Imperial Russian Navy for a small cruiser, the *Zabiaca*.

If the mighty Pennsylvania Railroad was irritated by the intransigence of the American Line, this in no way affected the common sense of the PRR board of directors, nor its ability to smell profits. The potential of Philadelphia as a major North Atlantic port had been proven by the business activities of the American Line and the Red Star Line. In spite of the worst depression up to that time in American history, the Pennsylvania Railroad decided to make a major investment in docks and transshipping facilities within the Port of Philadelphia. The PRR purchased the old Navy Yard property—involving 23 acres of land and five more under water, with deepwater wharves—for $1,000,000, and tracks were laid to connect the wharves with the Delaware Extension. Three new piers and a freight shed were added in 1879. These soon proved inadequate, and in 1881 a major construction project was begun for the railroad along the waterfront. With the completion of this improvement, "the Pennsylvania railroad Company will be in possession of nine piers, six of them 500 feet long and 100 feet and upwards wide, extending from the southside of Christian Street to the north side of Reed Street, a distance of five squares."[16] The new wharves were christened by the *Illinois* of the American Line and the *Montreal*, a chartered vessel of the Red Star Line, on April 6, 1882, with considerable fanfare.

The American Line agents, Peter Wright & Sons, under the guidance of Clement Acton Griscom, always sought to obtain the maximum free publicity from newspapers. Periodic news releases garnered favor with the press and publicity for the American Line. On February 18, 1882, it was announced that the very popular Captain Lecky and Purser Large of the *British King* were to be promoted to the fine new steamer *British Prince*, which was similar in size to the *British Crown* and due to arrive in Philadelphia on her maiden voyage about April 1. It was noted that the *British Prince* would make the tenth ship in the service of the American Line. Subsequently, in March 1882, an article described the fleet of the American Line as consisting of:

Pennsylvania	3,104 tons	*British Prince*	3,859 tons
Ohio	3,104 tons	*British King*	3,559 tons
Indiana	3,104 tons	*British Queen*	3,559 tons
Illinois	3,104 tons	*British Crown*	3,487 tons
Lord Gough	3,665 tons	*Lord Clive*	3,386 tons

The article announced: "The addition of the *British Prince* steamer gives the line two departures per week from Liverpool, and you will thus see that, even should the large number of passengers carried by us during 1881 (32,378) be exceeded, there will be no difficulty in providing for them comfortably."[17]

The *British Prince*, with Captain S.T.S. Lecky in command, was soon proving a valuable addition to the fleet. On May 17, she sailed from Liverpool on her second voyage and crossed in nine days, 19 hours, 49 minutes, bringing 1,208 passengers. No indication of distance or knots was provided, but the voyage certainly was a good one, or it would not have been noted in the press. The outlook for trade in the 1882 summer season appeared so good that the steamship *British Empire*, which had run for the American Line and then been chartered to the Alexander Line (running between New York, Havana, and Veracruz), would again fly the house flag of the American Steamship Company. Unfortunately, the liner *Pennsylvania* had experienced some trouble and was going to be receiving visitors at the Cramp Shipyard for some time.

The stockholders of the American Steamship Company held their annual meeting on Tuesday, April 4, 1882. Once again, while there were 10 ships in the fleet and six of those vessels chartered, the report dealt exclusively with the performance of the four original units. The directors' report for 1881 showed that the 35 round-trip voyages made by the four vessels produced freight receipts of $453,763.76; passenger receipts of $410,269.64; and miscellaneous income of $3,785.94, for a gross income of $867,819.34. Disbursements for operations consumed $707,804.53, leaving a balance of $160,014.81. From this had to be deducted shore-based and extraordinary expenses of $67,753.59 (agencies), $19,495.81 (advertising), $14,957.02 (wharf), $6,023.93 (general office), $67,649.12 (extraordinary), $90,690 (interest on bonds), for a loss of $106,554.66.[18]

In the seven and a half years during which the American Steamship Company had been in operation, it had lost something over half a million dollars, representing 19 percent of the original capitalization of the business. The almost continuous stream of deficits was not encouraging and appeared unending. Passenger revenues had almost doubled over the years, but income from freight had steadily declined as a proportion of the overall income.

Whether any accounting was ever made of the income and outgo from the chartered tonnage remains a mystery. The *Annual Reports* of the American Steamship Company cover nothing but the original American-flag quartet—which, admittedly, were more expensive to operate than foreign-flag vessels. That being the case, it stands to reason that there should have been some profit somewhere from the cheaper chartered tonnage, which represented over 60 percent of the gross tonnage of the fleet. One possible explanation is that the vessels, while technically assigned to the American Line, actually were wholly owned or chartered by other parties, or the firm of Peter Wright & Sons. If so, one is left wondering why so many additional vessels were chartered when the cargo and passenger earnings were so badly needed by the original quartet. Any income siphoned off to any other pocket would contribute to the miserable financial performance of the American Steamship Company and drive that concern deeper into the red. At the same time, there do not appear to have been any irate stockholders at the annual meetings, and no charges of mismanagement brought against anyone.[19]

Even when the American Steamship Company chose to complain about something, it was always in terms of the four original vessels and what was happening to them. In April 1882, a bald comment appeared: "The four steamships belonging to the American Steamship Company which sail between this port and Liverpool have, since the Line was started, paid about $100,000 to the English lighthouse monopoly in fees for the maintenance of the lighthouses on the English Coast."[20] Since the United States Coast Guard had the responsibility for this service in the United States, the inference was that the English charges were unwarranted.

Early in 1882, another recession struck the American economic scene, and the brief period of prosperity between 1879 and 1881 became but a fond memory. At the same time, the organization of labor on even a limited scale was evident for the first time when the stevedores of the American Line and the Red Star Line indicated late in March 1882 that they would demand a 50 percent increase in their wages for the often-dangerous night work. Managements' responses are not noted, but since no further labor unrest was evident, apparently some accommodation was reached between the lines and the stevedores working the Philadelphia piers. Evidence of the prosperity of Philadelphia as a center of commerce and trade was the reversal of the normal flow of agricultural products. In March 1882, the American Steamship Company brought in large quantities of potatoes, cabbage, and sauerkraut. The farmlands of Pennsylvania, Delaware, and New Jersey apparently were not equal to the demand, or such products never would have been arriving from overseas. The American Industrial Revolution was coming of age in the eastern United States.

The recession of 1882 produced devastating results quite quickly in the fortunes of the American Line. In June, the newest pride of the fleet, the *British Prince*, was chartered to the Red Star Line to run between New York or Philadelphia and Antwerp as required. In July, at what should have been the height of the summer season, a solemn announcement appeared:

> The American Steamship Line, owing to the diminution of freighting in the trans-atlantic trade at present, will reduce its fleet in active service. The steamer *British King* has been taken off and chartered at Liverpool for a voyage to the East Indies, the *Lord Clive* and another of the British chartered fleet will be taken off at the end of their next eastward voyage, and the *Ohio* and the *Pennsylvania*, when they again come this way, will be docked here for repairs. In the course of a month the line will be reduced to five steamers, with weekly sailings, but will be again expanded as soon as freighting warrants."[21]

The fleet that had boasted 10 ships in March was cut in half by July—90 days that turned the fortunes of the American Steamship Company upside down. Such were the vagaries of competing on the North Atlantic.

An additional unkind blow was dealt by the U.S. District Court, when judgment was finally rendered in June 1882 in the case of *Schooner H.B. Hume vs. American Line*. The *Pennsylvania* had run down and sunk the sailing ship in 1878, resulting in a lawsuit for damages. Ultimately, in 1882, the owners of the *H.B. Hume* were allowed 50 percent of their damages (indicating that the *Pennsylvania* was not wholly at fault) and their court costs. Nevertheless, in a time of short money, any additional drain was unwelcome. At almost the same time, it was noted that the American Line employed men with lifebuoys on its vessels' sailing days to rescue persons who might accidentally fall overboard. It sounds incredible, yet there must have been sufficient concern to warrant the expenditure. As an additional safety precaution, the wooden pilothouse on the front of each ship was replaced with an iron one. The *Pennsylvania* missed one round-trip voyage in the summer of 1882 so that this alteration could be accomplished.

The recession of 1882 deepened into a full-scale depression, which significantly reduced trade and commerce for the better part of five years. This time, the strain was more than the board of directors of the American Steamship Company could accept. There did not appear to be any light at the end of the proverbial tunnel. In 1883–84 a crisis loomed that required immediate action. The 10-year-old quartet of American Line ships was surveyed, and it was discovered that they required immediate major maintenance totaling over $25,000 per ship. The repairs involved strengthening the hulls, after ten years of hard service, and could not be delayed. In fact, the surveyors indicated that unless the ships' keels were strengthened they should not be permitted to sail again. The expenses were completely beyond the ability of the American Line to meet, and the board of directors informed the Pennsylvania Railroad Company that they had no realistic alternative except winding up the affairs of the concern.

The only buyer on the scene was the International Navigation Company (INC) whose management had handled the day-to-day operations of the American Line ships through the firm of Peter Wright & Sons since 1874. However, the INC was not prepared to invest a great deal of its own money in the acquisition of the American Line. The Pennsylvania Railroad Company was a major investor in the International Navigation Company and was not above applying a little pressure if that would solve the problem. Accordingly, the PRR's solution to the INC lack of funds was to have that steamship line issue an additional 14,500 shares of stock at par, which the railroad then bought for $725,000. The board of directors of the Pennsylvania Railroad Company approved the purchase of the INC stock on October 8, 1884, and the deal was consummated on November 25, 1884. There was no particular urgency since the money never was destined to leave the treasurer's office of the PRR. The railroad money was deposited in the account of the INC who then used it to purchase the American Line quartet of ships. The sale price for the ships was $725,000, plus the current debt of the vessels equal to another $25,000. The purchase of the American Steamship Company ships for this sum was approved by the steamship board on October 14, 1884, and confirmed by the stockholders on November 6, 1884. On November 25, 1884, the American Steamship Company then used the money transferred to its account with the railroad to repay its short-term loans from the Pennsylvania Railroad Company. The indebtedness of the American Steamship Company to the Pennsylvania Railroad Company came to $690,000, to which was added interest of $88,851.65 for a total of $778,851.65. Since the amount received for the four ships was only $725,000, the American Steamship Company gave the railroad a due bill for the remaining $53,851.65 in order to close the books. The Pennsylvania Railroad Company lost $900,000 on the American Steamship Company stock it owned, assumed responsibility for all the 6 percent $1,500,000 bond issue of the steamship company, and was left holding a worthless due bill for an additional $53,851.65. The bond issue matured on October 1, 1896, and the bonds were burned with appropriate ceremony. The American Line continued to sail as a wholly owned subsidiary of the International Navigation Company, whose largest corporate stockholder was the Pennsylvania Railroad Company. A period of more frequent interchanging of vessels did occur, with American and Red Star ships taking each other's sailings whenever vacancies appeared, but this was only natural when one line had a ship available and the other possessed an open sailing date. The existing interlocking corporation between the INC and the PRR became even closer than it had been before, and the foundation was laid for a major international expansion of American owned shipping on the North Atlantic.

Chapter 4

THE INTERNATIONAL NAVIGATION COMPANY—RED STAR LINE

The progressive economic trends of the early 1870s in the United States created a climate conducive to the establishment of new business ventures, of which the American Steamship Company was only one manifestation. On May 5, 1871, the General Assembly of the Commonwealth of Pennsylvania also authorized a charter for the International Navigation Company. This occurred less than a month after the approval of the charter for the American Steamship Company.

The International Navigation Company was representative of those American shipping interests who wanted to establish a transatlantic steamship line but who did not feel that such a business could be run successfully under the American flag. These financial interests, even though headquartered in the United States, built their fleets in foreign yards, operated the vessels under foreign flags, and manned their ships with foreign crews. Such was the case with the International Navigation Company (always known as the Red Star Line for the Red Star on its white house flag), whose foreign-flag operations were exactly the opposite of the American Steamship Company's American-flag organization.

The chief American organizer and general agent for the International Navigation Company was the shipbroking firm of Peter Wright & Sons,[1] one of the oldest, most respected, and most financially prosperous of the Philadelphia import-export houses. The principal financial backer of the new shipping line was the Pennsylvania Railroad Company,

Clement Acton Griscom (1841–1912), a Philadelphia Quaker, was the principal force behind the creation of the International Navigation Company (Red Star Line). He was made a partner in the Philadelphia import-export house of Peter Wright & Sons at the age of 22. In 1902 he was the founder of the International Mercantile Marine and remained Chairman of the Board of the shipping trust until his death in November 1912.

which provided a crucial guarantor for the $1,000,000 bond issue with which to build the initial fleet; purchased a substantial block of stock in its own right; and provided free wharfage and facilities at Philadelphia. The importance of the Pennsylvania Railroad Company to the founding of the International Navigation Company was of the first magnitude. The initial issue of $1,500,000 in International Navigation Company stock was purchased by a small group of investors including the Peter Wright & Sons partners and the upper management of the Pennsylvania Railroad Company—and their friends.

On its part Peter Wright & Sons provided invaluable expertise. The firm controlled a large fleet of sailing ships, many of which were engaged in carrying petroleum, in both barrels and cases, to the European market from the relatively new oilfields of western Pennsylvania. Oil was first discovered at Titusville in western Pennsylvania in 1857, and the boom that occurred heralded all those petroleum extravaganzas of the future.

The problems associated with the movement and storage of a liquid product presented quite a challenge in the middle of the nineteenth century. Whaling vessels met the problem by storing large quantities of the rendered-out oil in barrels, but the dimensions of the challenge were altered dramatically with the enormous quantities of Pennsylvania petroleum to be moved to European markets. Peter Wright & Sons initially tackled the shipment of oil in 1861 by chartering the 224-ton brig *Elizabeth Watts*. They loaded her with a full cargo of Pennsylvania oil contained in the traditional barrels for delivery to London. As the management of Peter Wright & Sons soon realized, this was an expensive and time-consuming method. Some better system had to be developed for moving large quantities of petroleum overseas. The Philadelphia firm's next step was in 1863, when the sailing ship *Romney* was fitted out with a few tanks in her hold so she could carry some bulk oil in addition to the traditional barrels, which still were stowed between decks. By 1864, the amount of oil exported from the United States—largely through the Port of Philadelphia to Le Havre and Antwerp—reached 31,745,687 gallons. This was in spite of the demands placed upon American production by the Civil War!

The next innovation in the movement of petroleum products overseas was exemplified by the 794-ton sailing vessel *Charles*, which was outfitted in 1869 with 59 iron tanks built into her holds. These were filled to the top, allowing only minor air spaces between and around the tanks. A small fleet of sailing vessels was outfitted similarly to the *Charles*, but these early "sailing tankers" were not regarded as a success. The iron tanks were too heavy, and the problems in maintaining their structural integrity were too great when the sailing ships were pounded by heavy North Atlantic seas. A ruptured tank (or tanks) during a violent gale at sea must have been one of the worst disasters imaginable in the age of sail, particularly with the omnipresent threat of fire. The *Charles* operated as a "sailing tanker" for only three years, until 1872.[2] By 1871, the total export of petrochemical products from the Port of Philadelphia had grown to 54,000,000 gallons, valued at $13,255,805. Peter Wright & Sons was the largest exporter of oil in the Commonwealth of Pennsylvania and the second largest in the nation.[3]

The shipping affairs of Peter Wright & Sons were largely in the energetic and capable hands of one vigorous young man—Clement Acton Griscom, who was born in 1841

In this Henri Cassiers monochrome two elderly Belgians watch one of the Red Star liners of the Antwerp–New York, Boston, or Philadelphia service being assisted by tugs in the Scheldt River. The tall spire of Antwerp's famous Our Lady of Sorrows Cathedral (1352–1584) is in the left background.

The Southwark (1893) or Kensington (1894) is shown by Cassiers sailing down the Scheldt from Antwerp. These ships were ordered from British yards for the American Line but transferred to the Red Star Line in 1895 for the Antwerp–New York service. Two Belgian watermen work their boat past the bow of a sailing ship.

into a well-established pre-Revolutionary Quaker family. His father, Dr. John D. Griscom, was a prominent physician and his mother, Margaret Griscom (née Acton), was from an old New Jersey Quaker clan. In his family background, Griscom could trace descent from the earliest Quaker settlers of Pennsylvania and New Jersey. Andrew Griscom, an early ancestor, arrived in "Penn's Woods" in 1680, two years before William Penn himself first saw the Delaware. A maternal ancestor, Thomas Lloyd, had served as the proprietor's deputy during Penn's long absences from the colony. The family thus ranked among the oldest European settlers in the colony and had maintained its Quaker heritage.

When Elias Hicks of Long Island advocated a more liberal interpretation of life and split the Society of Friends into two rival camps early in the nineteenth century, Griscom's father joined the "Hicksite" (liberal) group of American Quakers. The ill will

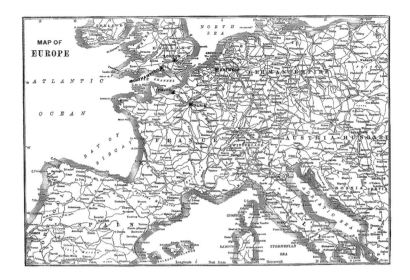

This Map of Europe was included in the International Navigation Company's Facts for Travellers *(1897) produced for passengers on American Line and Red Star Line ships. The most significant European ports noted were Antwerp, Southampton, and Havre with London and Paris also highlighted. Tradition has it that in 1871 Griscom strode across his office toward the map of Europe with a pointer aimed at the industrial center and hit Antwerp as his future European terminus.*

between "orthodox" and "Hicksite" Quakers continued unabated in the Philadelphia region well into the post-Civil War period.

Griscom's parents may have been "liberal" Quakers, but they did not patronize the theater, allow cards or alcohol or even a piano in the house. Attendance at Philadelphia society parties was deemed unacceptable to Griscom's parents. Apparently he disagreed with these restrictions, however, because his own children were permitted much greater freedom and became the first generation of the family to play an active role in Philadelphia society. Clement Griscom never forgot his Quaker heritage, but his adventuresome mind encompassed a much broader world.

Griscom was given the best education available for a young Philadelphia Quaker at the Friends Academy. In 1857 at the age of 16, he left school and began his business experience as a clerk with the firm of Peter Wright & Sons. Griscom's working career spanned five and a half decades—from 1857 until his death in 1912. He ranks among the most important American industrial leaders of the period. In time Griscom, besides having maritime interests, would become a close associate of J.P. Morgan and John D. Rockefeller; a director of the Pennsylvania Railroad Company, the Insurance Company of North America, and numerous banks; and one of the organizers of the National Transit Company, then the largest oil pipeline in the world. Griscom's career coincided with the formative age of the American Industrial Revolution, and he played no small part in the proceedings.

At Peter Wright & Sons, the intelligent, discerning, and aggressive young clerk soon made his mark and caught the attention of the senior partners in the firm. In particular, James A. Wright, one of the principal owners, encouraged the affable but serious young man. Griscom's rise in the firm can only be described as "meteoric," since between 1857 and 1862 he rose from clerk to partner by the age of 22. Peter Wright & Sons was an established import-export house specializing in china and luxury goods.

Griscom was disturbed by the high cost of freight rates for these items and broadened the firm's interests by purchasing sailing ships just as the Civil War was beginning. He filled the ships' holds with general cargo from other firms, westbound, and petroleum products, eastbound. His company prospered accordingly, and profits were aided by the wartime charter market, which Griscom worked to the advantage of the firm.

Clement Acton Griscom was also a close business associate and friend of J. Edgar Thomson, third president of the Pennsylvania Railroad and the man most often credited with creating the single most powerful corporation in the nation. The Pennsylvania Railroad Company was chartered in 1846, but Thomson's presidency (1852–74) stretched across the formative period when the line achieved greatness, as well as encompassing the unique challenges of the Civil War. Under Thomson's iron-willed leadership, the PRR created a unified transportation system stretching from New York City and Philadelphia in the east to St. Louis and Chicago in the west, and from Lake Ontario in the north to Baltimore and Washington, DC, in the south. The Pennsylvania Railroad served the heartland of the American Industrial Revolution and would prosper accordingly when the United States came of age as an industrialized economy.

Griscom also would be a lifelong business associate and friend of Thomas A. Scott, vice president, and later the fourth president (1874–80) of the Pennsylvania Railroad. Scott was well known as an affable diplomat among the great industrialists of his day and he was unique for his ability to handle public-relations issues and crisis situations. Thomson regarded Scott as his right-hand man, the person to whom he most often turned in a difficult situation. Scott was the one who had been assigned to cool the civic temperature in Pittsburgh in the mid-1850s after the PRR had blocked the Baltimore & Ohio Railroad from gaining entrance to that wealthy market. The PRR wanted no competition from any other major railroad in the fiefdom of Pennsylvania. Scott said it was the greatest challenge of his career to get the citizens of Pittsburgh to accept the Pennsylvania Railroad's plans for the area.

Thomas A. Scott was the vice president of the Pennsylvania Railroad most intimately associated with the creation of the Red Star Line and the American Line. The strain of managing the Pennsylvania Railroad and all its subsidiaries clearly took a toll on men. Thomas A. Scott rose to be the fourth president of the PRR but only served from 1874 to 1880 before retiring.

The Friesland *(1889, 7,116 tons, 437 feet by 51 feet, 15 knots) was one of the most beautiful of all the ships in the Red Star fleet. She had four masts and a distinctive clipper bow. The* Friesland *had accommodations for 226 in first, 102 in second, and 600 in third (steerage).*

After the conclusion of the Civil War, when the PRR was anxious to develop the international trade of the Port of Philadelphia, there was no more likely combination than Griscom and Scott, operating with the benevolent approval of J. Edgar Thomson. Philadelphia had large quantities of grain, pig iron, and oil for export, but no regular steam transportation system to serve the trade. Griscom, with the support of the Pennsylvania Railroad and the Standard Oil Company, encouraged the establishment by local Philadelphia commercial interests of the American Steamship Company, while remaining in the background himself. The Pennsylvania Railroad Company was represented on the board of the American Steamship Company by Herman Lombaert, vice president and former comptroller of the railroad; Thomas A. Scott, senior vice president of the railroad, sat on the board of the Red Star Line.

According to Ambassador Lloyd C. Griscom, Clement Acton Griscom's son, in 1872 his father and Thomson of the PRR had a conference during which it was decided to start a foreign-flag steamship line from Philadelphia to continental Europe. This would complement the service of the American Line between Philadelphia and Liverpool. Griscom raced back to his offices and called for the largest map of Europe the firm owned and ordered it hung on the wall. "With a red pencil he dotted the principal manufacturing towns of England, Belgium, France and Germany. From the far side of the room he aimed a pointer at the center of the red spots and strode forward. The tip struck exactly on the ancient city of Antwerp, formerly a busy port, but then so isolated by the silting of the Scheldt that no steamer of any size could reach it."[4] By so casual a method, according to family lore, was the European terminus of the future steamship line determined. Griscom was a man of action. Upon arriving home that evening, he informed his young wife, Frances Canby Griscom, that he had to leave for Europe immediately and that she was to accompany him. She informed him that she would not go without their baby son, so the next day all three, plus servants, set out for Europe. Arriving in Antwerp, Griscom found the burgomaster and the council willing to undertake major improvements to the harbor facilities, but only if they had the backing of King Leopold. If there was any thought this would put off the American businessman, they were mistaken.

Griscom took the train to Brussels, where he collared the American minister, John Sanford, and received every assistance. According to the family story, King Leopold responded to Sanford's request for an audience immediately, and the American minister introduced Griscom to the king with the statement: "Your Majesty, here's a young American with a scheme which should boom Belgium's foreign trade."[5]

Historically, King Leopold is known as a shrewd businessman and an individual with an acute desire for wealth. In the 1870s, Belgium had only been in existence for 40 years, and the monarch was capable of energetically championing the expansion of his kingdom. Griscom explained his ideas and King Leopold was impressed. Griscom's son recalled what he had been told about the interesting exchange that occurred:

> "Your plan seems sound, Mr. Griscom. However, since it's so late I'd like you to dine with the Queen and me. Afterwards we can discuss it further."
>
> Father, who was unused to royal etiquette, replied bluntly, "Sorry, Your Majesty, it's impossible."
>
> Sanford's expression registered consternation, but the King, somewhat amused, inquired: "It's seldom we have our invitations refused. Won't you tell me your reason."
>
> "Well, Sir, my wife and young baby are back at the hotel in Antwerp. Before I left this morning she made me promise to return for dinner."
>
> The King shook Father's hand. "You could not have a better reason. Another time you must bring Mrs. Griscom. And don't worry about a charter or a postal subsidy. I'll see that Parliament grants you everything you need."[6]

Whether or not everything went quite as smoothly that, the bond between Griscom's Red Star and Antwerp would endure.

Certainly the foundation for the Belgian connection had been laid long before with the Antwerp business ties of the firm of Peter Wright & Sons. Two Belgian business associates and friends were John Bernard vender Becke and William Edouard Marsily, prominent Belgian shipowners who controlled prosperous firms that had dealt with Peter Wright & Sons for years. As early as 1854, J.B. vender Becke was a well-known Antwerp shipowner with a fleet of five sailing vessels. During the 1860s, the vender Becke firm became an important importer of petroleum products to the Continent, the oil coming from the newly discovered fields of western Pennsylvania. Since one of the most active U.S. exporters of such products was Peter Wright & Sons, there were numerous business ties between the Philadelphia and Antwerp concerns.

When vender Becke entered the oil import business in the 1860s and thereby established trading interests with Griscom of Peter Wright & Sons, the cases of oil were shipped from Philadelphia to Antwerp in American and Belgian sailing ships.

The negotiations were fruitful under the benevolent patronage of King Leopold, and the necessary statutes establishing the Belgian-based concern under the name "Société Anonyme de Navigation Belge-Américaine" (Red Star Line) were published in the *Moniteur Belge*, the Belgian government gazette, on September 27, 1872. The founding officials of the company were listed as John B. vender Becke, president, and William E. Marsily, administrator. Peter Wright & Sons had the right to nominate three members of the board of directors; they chose H.H. Houston, Clement A. Griscom, and Thomas A. Scott.

The commitment of the Pennsylvania Railroad Company to the Société Anonyme de Navigation Belge-Américaine could not be underlined any more explicitly than by the presence of the senior vice president of the railroad on the board of directors of the new steamship line. Of course, this was the same railroad that was underwriting the bonds of the American Steamship Company and of the International Navigation Company. The simple fact of the matter was that the PRR did not regard the two steamship lines as competitors, whatever any member of the public might think.

Nevertheless, the idea has been put forth that the International Navigation Company and the American Steamship Company were competitors. This arose, in part, from the fact that some contemporary newspapers described the two lines as competitors in their columns. Furthermore, the Red Star Line ran two chartered steamers, the *Kenilworth* (1872, 2,595 tons) and the *Abbotsford* (1873, 2,554 tons) on the same Liverpool-Philadelphia run as the American Line from May to December 1873. A composite chart listing the sailing dates of the Red Star Line and the American Line ships for 1873 strongly indicates that the schedules were coordinated to provide a weekly service, and that there was no competition between the two concerns (see Table 1). When this information is considered along with the mutual interest of Thomas A. Scott and the enormous financial investment of the Pennsylvania Railroad in both lines, it appears likely that the two were never competitors. The perfect integration of the sailing schedules of the Red Star Line and the American Line in 1873, and the fact that both lines would be under the American management of Peter Wright & Sons after January 1874, further indicates close connections and assured cooperation from their inception.

The importance of petroleum products in the import-export affairs of both the American and Belgian backers of the Red Star Line provides a ready explanation for the peculiar construction of the first Red Star liner, the *Vaderland* (1873, 2,748 tons). The *Vaderland* was designed from the keel up to carry the unusual and (to today's sensitivities) uninviting combination of passengers, general cargo, and petroleum products. The famous British nautical journal *Mitchell's Maritime Register* on August 30, 1872, announced that "on the 21st instant there was launched from the iron shipbuilding establishment of Messrs Palmer & Company, Jarrow, an iron screw steamer named the *Vaterland* [sic].

Table 1[1] — Sailing Schedules

Weekly Sailing Date, Liverpool Departure	American Steamship Company (American Line) Vessel	International Navigation Company (Red Star Line) Vessel
1873 May 10		*Abbotsford*
(June 18)[2]	(*Pennsylvania*)	
June 23	*Pennsylvania* (M/V)	
June 26		*Abbotsford*
July 11		*Kenilworth*
July 30	*Pennsylvania*	
(August 7)[3]		*Abbotsford*
(August 13)[4]	(*Ohio*)	
August 20		*Kenilworth*
August 27	*Ohio* (M/V)	
September 10	*Pennsylvania*	
September 17		*Abbotsford*
October 1		*Kenilworth*
October 8	*Ohio*	
October 22	*Pennsylvania*	
October 29		*Abbotsford*
November 5[5]	*Indiana* (M/V)	
November 12		*Kenilworth*
November 19	*Ohio*	
December 3	*Pennsylvania*	
December 10		*Abbotsford*
December 17	*Indiana*	
December 24		*Kenilworth*
December 31	*Ohio*	
1874 January 14	*Pennsylvania*	
(Peter Wright & Sons assumes management of both lines)		
January 21		*Abbotsford*
January 28[6]	(*Illinois*) *Indiana*	
February 4		*Kenilworth*
February 14	*Illinois* (M/V)	
February 21	*Pennsylvania*	
February 28	*Ohio*	
(March 4)[7]	(*Abbotsford*)	
March 11	*Abbotsford* (F/V)	
March 18	*Illinois*	
March 25[8]	*Kenilworth* (F/V)	

1. Taken from the complete record of all American and Red Star Line sailings compiled by N.R.P. Bonsor.
2. *Pennsylvania* was delayed by repairs and did not sail until June 23.
3. Liverpool sailing not verified, but the *Abbotsford* left Philadelphia on its return trip August 28.
4. *Ohio* was unable to sail, skipped a week, and took the next American Line alternate sailing date.
5. Originally scheduled for November 19, but sailing advanced.
6. *Illinois* sailing taken by the *Indiana*.
7. First American Line sailing of the *Abbotsford*: initial sailing was delayed by one week.
8. First American Line sailing of the the *Kenilworth*.

The steamer is 319 feet in length, 38 feet in breadth, 2,333 tons register [sic], and is built upon the double bottom principle, and is divided into several compartments, perfectly air, water and gas tight."[7] The last statement, referring to five compartments designed to carry petroleum products, was intended to meet any objections from the public that there would be noxious fumes from the cargo throughout the liner. The general belief was that the simple movement of air currents over the vessel while at sea would be inadequate to remove the fumes of such a cargo.

A number of historical points of interest emerge from the article in *Mitchell's Maritime Register*, which has a justifiable reputation for contemporary accuracy. The reporter went on to comment that the liner was owned by the Philadelphia Steam Navigation Company Red Star Line, and that the vessel was intended for the Antwerp-New York trade. With due acknowledgment to the fact that the affairs of the company were still in a formative stage, the name "Philadelphia Steam Navigation Company" would never be heard again. That apparently was a brief title of convenience to Griscom. Second, the name "Red Star Line" is used without reference to any Belgian interest. Third, the launching of the *Vaderland* occurred nearly three weeks before the Société Anonyme de Navigation Belge-Américaine (Red Star Line) officially came into existence.

Clement A. Griscom's trip to Europe to negotiate with the Belgian interests also permitted him to be present at the Jarrow yard for the August 1872 launching of his first steamer. With considerable pride, he cabled the news: "*VADERLAND* LAUNCHED TODAY" to the *Philadelphia Commercial List and Price Current*. It was immediately included in the next issue of the newspaper, three days after the event.[8]

The Pennsylvania Railroad, as part of the stimulus for its founding, entered into a traffic agreement with the International Navigation Company (Red Star Line). "The railroad company agreed to provide free dockage or wharfage at its own piers or elsewhere and to protect the Philadelphia differential in its rate making. The Pennsylvania constructed a new terminal at Girard Point for the use of this line, with warehouses and elevators capable, it was thought, of handling fifteen million bushels of grain in a year. The company also made large additions to its other terminal properties, such as additional coal docks at Greenwich Point, facilities for handling petroleum from shore to ship, and a large new freight house on Delaware Avenue at Dock Street."[9] The guarantee of free dockage and other services was a powerful incentive from the Pennsylvania Railroad to the Red Star Line, yet for good reason the Pennsylvania Railroad did not wish to be too closely identified with the Red Star Line and the International Navigation Company. Contemporary accounts made little or no mention of the railroad's interest in the foreign-flag steamship line. Even a lengthy newspaper account of the inspection of the terminal site by officials of the port and a committee representing the Red Star Line records nothing more than the fact that satisfactory arrangements had been made with the Pennsylvania Railroad for the rapid conveyance of freight to the wharves.[10] The Pennsylvania Railroad was keeping as quiet as possible about any connection with the Red Star Line in order that nothing might stand in the way of its other endeavor, the American-flag American Line, receiving a federal mail subsidy.

A public-relations article on the Red Star Line was released to the press by Peter Wright & Sons and published in the *Philadelphia North American United States Gazette* on January 13, 1873, just prior to the maiden voyage of the *Vaderland*. The newspaper reported:

> We publish this morning the announcement by the general agents, Messrs.
> Peter Wright & Sons of the Red Star Line, of regular steamship service

between Philadelphia and Antwerp, via Southampton, appointed to carry the Belgian Mails. Although sailing under the Belgian flag in consequence of having been built abroad, these steamers are chiefly owned in Philadelphia.

They are of iron built in the English style, of the highest class. Their bottoms are double and everything is in accordance with the strictest regulation of English Lloyd's. For passengers the most elegant and comfortable arrangements have been made, the saloon and first class staterooms being upon the main deck amidships, where the least amount of motion is felt, and where the best ventilation is assured.

These steamers will be run regularly. The first of the Line, the *Vaderland*, Captain Van der Hayden, 2,800 tons, is now ready and will sail from Antwerp January 18th, and from Philadelphia February 15th. The other two, *Nederland* and *Switzerland*, each 3,000 tons, are building and nearly completed and as soon as they are finished the line will be made fortnightly. Especial attention will be given to the comfort of steerage passengers, as it is the purpose of the general agents to enter vigorously into the competition for the immigrant business. Tickets will be sold here good from Antwerp to all interior points in the United States via the Pennsylvania Railroad and at its lowest prices. This is the arrangement to which we have often referred while advocating the establishment of lines of European steamers to be run in connection with the Pennsylvania Railroad (Company), passengers being ticketed through from any point in the United States to any point in Europe and vice versa. The rates of passage will be found quite reasonable. The eminent firm of J.B. Von der Beeke [sic], of Antwerp is the general European agent of the line.

The same arrangement holds good with reference to freight with this line, which will be received at all points in the west and south at the railroad offices, and through bills of lading issued for Antwerp, London, Hull, Leith, Bremen, Hamburg, Rotterdam, Amsterdam and all prominent points in the interior of Europe. It will, of course, take time to have people of two continents appreciate thoroughly the advantages of this wide spread system. But it will work its way as fast as it is felt understood. The people of the interior, south and west, will soon perceive that by this arrangement the steamships sailing to and from Philadelphia are for the benefit of the whole country. Antwerp and Southampton are the most favorable points that could be selected for the trade of London and the south of England on the one hand, and of the Netherlands, Germany, eastern France and Switzerland on the other hand.

The Liverpool connection already established and soon to be greatly extended would of itself not suffice to enable our foreign commerce to recuperate. It needed a connection like this which has been established by a few prominent citizens under the management of one of the most experienced and enterprising mercantile firms in Philadelphia, and has been arranged in the most careful and comprehensive manner.[11]

The commentator wrote with unbridled civic pride of the fact that prior to this, the goods imported by Philadelphia from Belgium, Holland, and Germany had entered the United States via the Customs House of New York, and now they could come directly. It was mentioned that while the American Steamship Company was chartered first, the great energy of Clement A. Griscom and the other founders of the Red Star Line had enabled them to "open the ball."

A Summer Holiday Abroad—No 1: "Experiences During a First Voyage in an Ocean Palace" *by G.A. Davis. The "First Morning Out" and the rolling of the liner has brought distress and second thoughts to the minds of the young ladies as their cabin turns topsy-turvy. The appearance of the steward with a cup of tea and the observation "A little fresh this morning" does not help. Later in the voyage "The British Female Taking a Constitutional" with dog in tow was observed, while "The American Female Takes Her Ease." "The Purser" has seen it all many times before.*

Frank Leslie's Illustrated Newspaper, June 16, 1883

A SUMMER HOLIDAY ABROAD.—No 1: EXPERIENCES DURING A FIRST VOYAGE IN AN "OCEAN PALACE."
FROM SKETCHES BY MISS G. A. DAVIS.—SEE PAGE 374.

Chapter 5

THE RED STAR AT SEA

The remarkable Vaderland *(I) (1873, 2,748 tons, 320 feet by 38 feet, 13 knots) was the first passenger liner of the International Navigation Company. She was constructed by the Palmers Yard in Britain and was one of the earliest vessels built to carry oil in bulk. Governmental authorities balked at carrying oil and passengers on the same vessel, and the* Vaderland *never carried petroleum, replacing that bulk cargo with grain.*

The maiden voyage of the *Vaderland* began in Antwerp on January 20, 1873. Captain Van der Hayden's seamanship was tested, as the crossing was not without incident. Apparently trouble occurred shortly after leaving Antwerp, because the *Vaderland* is next described as leaving the Port of Falmouth on January 30! While Falmouth is a gateway to the Atlantic from the west of England, there is no explanation for what she was doing there, nor for the hiatus of 10 days. Shortly after leaving Falmouth, the *Vaderland* ran into a series of North Atlantic gales that gave the new liner a royal baptism. So much coal was consumed by the furnaces that Captain Van der Hayden had to take his ship into Halifax for refueling. The premier unit of the Red Star fleet left Halifax on Valentine's Day, February 14, 1873, and finally arrived at Philadelphia three days later, with 105 passengers and a good cargo. The maiden voyage took 17 days for what normally would have been a 10-day crossing. Nevertheless, the *Vaderland* received a warm reception in Philadelphia, where Griscom had been beside himself about the whereabouts of the first Red Star steamer.

Lloyd Griscom later commented about his father at home:

> It was not easy for the head of a great shipping business to remain even-tempered under the weight of never-ending responsibility for the lives and

The Belgenland *(1879, 3,692 tons, 403 feet by 40 feet, 14 knots) was nearly a thousand tons larger than previous Red Star liners. She proved a very popular ship for Red Star, was transferred to the American Line in 1895, and was sold in 1904.*

The Belgenland *(1879) is shown turning in the Scheldt River at Antwerp with Our Lady of Sorrows Cathedral in the background. She was built by the Barrow Shipyard in Britain and flew the Belgian flag for the Société Anonyme de Belge-Américaine.*

The Rhynland *(1879, 3,689 tons, 403 feet by 40 feet, 14 knots) was a sistership of the* Belgenland *and maintained the Antwerp–New York service for fifteen years before being transferred in 1895 to the American Line for the Philadelphia–Liverpool run. She was sold for further service in 1906.*

A rare shipping document of the Red Star Line with the Belgian Société Anonyme de Belge-Américaine and the American International Navigation Company framing a bold "Red Star Line" and star. The general European agent is Von der Becke & Marsily, Antwerp, and the general agent is Peter Wright & Sons, Philadelphia and Bowling Green, New York.

property of others. Our household peace was always being disrupted by the arrival of messages and telegrams—engines broken, boilers burst, rudders or propellers off, fires in cotton cargoes, ammonia leaks in cold-storage plants, ships aground. The most disturbing news was that a vessel was overdue and unreported. Father would pace up and down with a worried face; if a wire came that all was well, he would brighten up immediately; but the loss of a ship meant weeks of gloom.[1]

The basic construction of the *Vaderland* heralded that of all future oil tankers. Her funnel and engines were placed aft between the mainmast and the mizzen, leaving a long, unencumbered tank area running the length of the vessel toward the bow. Her lines would raise considerable interest at the time and would not be repeated in the fleet. She had accommodations for more than 800 passengers—30 in first class, 800 in steerage. The oil pipelines were not finished, and the *Vaderland* carried grain on her first eastbound crossing. Clearly, the American authorities had expressed their displeasure with the concept of petroleum products and passengers on the same ship. Furthermore, the character of the trade for which the ships were intended may have changed with the possibility of a mail subsidy from the Belgian government. Whatever the case, the *Vaderland* was described as carrying both passengers and "liquid freight" when she sailed from Philadelphia for Antwerp on February 25.[2] If the *Vaderland*, as a passenger liner, did carry oil or petroleum products in crossing, it was probably the only time in her career that she did. Publicly, her cargo on this crossing was described as bark, hides, lard, tallow, tobacco, and a substantial shipment of bacon. Thereafter, ordinary merchandise and grain appear to have been substituted for the potentially volatile "liquid freight." The *Vaderland* was the only Red Star liner in the Philadelphia–Antwerp trade from January until September 1873 when she was joined by the chartered vessel *Rydal Hall* (nd, 2,100 tons), and soon thereafter by her consort, *Nederland*, whose maiden voyage began on December 6, 1873. The third consort, *Switzerland*, did not have her maiden sailing until May 15, 1874. Both the *Nederland* and the *Switzerland* had engines amidships in the traditional model. Hence, they were consorts of the *Vaderland*, but not sisterships, since the *Vaderland*'s lines were unique.

Chartered tonnage always would play a major role in the operations of the International Navigation Company. Griscom was a professional when it came to moving in and out of the charter markets to meet the immediate or long-term needs of his fleets. The economic collapse and depression of 1873 occurred simultaneously with the first sailings of the International Navigation Company (Red Star Line). Like the American Steamship Company, Red Star would have a very difficult time surviving the unexpected economic downturn, but the cost of operating the foreign-flag tonnage was less. When retrenchment was mandatory at the end of 1873, the general management of the American Line was assigned to Peter Wright & Sons and Griscom took over the operation of both fleets. As of March 1874, the same general advertisement would be run in all newspapers, with the American Line maintaining the Philadelphia–Liverpool service and the Red Star Line the Philadelphia–Antwerp connection. Thereafter, the Red Star Line ships technically would not sail for the International Navigation Company when in the Liverpool service.

Expansion plans for the International Navigation Company included the concept of a New York–Antwerp service. The Belgian government, with the encouragement of King Leopold, offered a subsidy for the creation of an Antwerp–New York line, and Griscom was more than willing to accept. The decision had far-reaching repercussions for the International Navigation Company. The government of Belgium offered a mail contract stipulating an annual payment of $100,000 for 10 years, with free port and wharfage privileges at Antwerp worth another $30,000. The successful contractor was to provide a fleet of 14-day steamers. All of the terms were specifically tailored to meet the aspirations of the Société Anonyme de Navigation Belge-Américaine (Red Star Line). The first sailing from New York occurred on March 11, 1874, with the *Cybele*, chartered from the Donaldson Line. The Philadelphia service of the Red Star Line was maintained by the *Vaderland* and the *Nederland* until well into the 1880s. Almost immediately, the primary concentration of the International Navigation Company would be the New York market.

During its early years, the Red Star Line was plagued with teething troubles both on land and at sea. Lloyd Griscom remembered one occasion:

> We were startled to see our living room invaded by a committee of elders of the Race Street Meeting; although Father had become "worldly" he had continued a member in good standing. The leader gravely addressed him:

A Cassiers portrait of one of the two-funnel quartet (Vaderland, Zeeland, Kroonland, Finland) of 1900–2 in the Scheldt River near Antwerp, Belgium. A sailing barge, which often would be instrumental in redistributing the Red Star cargoes within the European market, is shown on the right.

"We have been reliably informed thee is operating sixteen saloons where
  alcoholic beverages are sold."

"What's that? What's that?" Father indignantly protested his ignorance.

"Has thee not sixteen ships?" the spokesman persisted.

"Quite true; what has that to do with it?"

"Does not each ship carry a bar?"

"Oh, that's it, is it? Well, sit down." And Father began explaining to his practical-minded visitors that the sale of liquor was essential to his business. However, he was not satisfied with convincing them by argument. An hour later, hearing a clink, I peered around the door. The elders had drawn up to the table, each with a glass in his hand, judiciously sniffing and tasting. No further objections were ever raised by the Meeting.[3]

The *Nederland,* the second unit of the Red Star Line fleet, was referred to on at least one occasion by the *Philadelphia Commercial List and Price Current* as an "ill-fated steamer."[4] Since this newspaper was a solid backer of new commercial efforts in Philadelphia, and a substantial supporter of the Red Star Line, such publicity upset Griscom a great deal. The label *ill-fated steamer* was hardly a welcome one to be bestowed on a new passenger liner of a new steamship company. The unfavorable publicity was an outgrowth of the second voyage of the *Nederland* from Antwerp to Philadelphia, which had taken two months!

The *Nederland* left Antwerp on her normal sailing date and suffered unspecified damage several days out, necessitating a detour to Liverpool for repairs. When these were completed, the *Nederland* sailed again for Philadelphia, only to go ashore on the Brigantine Shoals near Atlantic City on April 16, 1874, less than a day's steaming from Philadelphia. The liner attracted considerable publicity, and for a while it was feared that she would be a total loss. However, she was refloated within a week, with what the newspapers described as "superficial" damage, and proceeded to port. The damage was extensive enough to require nearly three months to repair, and the *Nederland* did not take a sailing again for the Red Star Line until August 29. She was to have made the third of Red Star's New York–Antwerp sailings in the new service, but this proved impossible. The near-disaster prompted the labeling of the *Nederland* as an "unfortunate ship" and disrupted the 1874 summer sailing schedule of the International Navigation Company. Hasty early assessments are not always justified, however. The *Nederland* was to serve the Red Star Line well for 30 years (1873–1906) and never sailed under another flag.

The construction in Philadelphia of new piers for the International Navigation Company fulfilled the commitment of the Pennsylvania Railroad Company to the shipping concern. The grain elevators and wharf facilities at Girard Point, near the confluence of the Delaware and Schuylkill Rivers, were designed to make a major corporate statement. The main granary building was 200 feet by 100 feet, with a height of 115 feet. "It contained 36 bins with a capacity of 15,000 bushels each, and 23 bins with a capacity of 10,000 bushels of grain each. Twelve elevating machines were capable of lifting 4000 bushels of grain per hour and 24 railroad cars could be unloaded at once."[5] This represented one of the most significant integrated transportation systems of its day. The surrounding wharves could accommodate up to six oceangoing steamers of 3,000 tons each, or 12 sailing vessels of 1,000 tons each. The first vessel to use the new terminal was the *Vaderland*, when she loaded a cargo of 20,000 bushels of red winter wheat in October 1874 for delivery in Antwerp.

The early history of the International Navigation Company saw two major ship losses. One of these involved the *Abbotsford*, in July 1875, shortly after the transfer of that vessel to the American Line's Philadelphia–Liverpool service. Her sistership, the *Kenilworth*, was to meet an equally untimely end. The liner had proven so satisfactory as a partner for the *Switzerland* in the New York–Antwerp service that negotiations were undertaken to buy her early in 1877. Just before the start of her eighth voyage for the International Navigation Company, the name of this ship was changed to *Rusland* (Flemish for "Russia"), indicative of her new ownership. The *Rusland* sailed from Antwerp on March 5 and 12 days later went hard ashore at Long Branch, New Jersey. Telegrams were sent, cargo was unloaded, and pictures of the liner were taken for publication. Expectations were raised that the *Rusland* would come off at the next spring high tide. Unfortunately, the hopes for the vessel were unfounded, and she became a total loss. The Red Star Line was left with only a single vessel on the New York run once again, and this situation had to be rectified. The Belgian mail contract was at stake.

Griscom was forced to take drastic action. The Philadelphia–Antwerp service of the International Navigation Company was suspended for approximately a year (March 1877 to February 1878). This permitted the *Vaderland* and the *Nederland* to partner the *Switzerland* in the New York–Antwerp service.

The *Java* (1865, 2,866 tons) was obtained from the Cunard Line in April 1878. After satisfactory service for three voyages, she was renamed the *Zeeland* to bring her

The Rhynland *(1879) was one of the most elegant and popular vessels of the Red Star Line. Here she is shown with the old Inman funnel colors, which probably indicates she is in the Philadelphia–Liverpool service of the American Line after 1895.*

into line with the rest of the fleet. This gave the Red Star Line a dependable vessel with a proven track record on the North Atlantic at a reasonable price and an acceptable delivery date. The *Zeeland* would sail under the Red Star for 11 years until sold for further trading in 1889.

Operation of the combined International Navigation Company and American Steamship Company fleets, plus the extensive sailing-ship interests of Peter Wright & Sons and allied firms, provided enough business for Griscom to create a small fleet of tugs. The *Juno* and the *Hercules* were new construction from the Wood and Dialogue's Works, Camden, N.J., in 1876, while the *Newcastle* was described as being only two years old. The *Newcastle*, named for a town in Delaware, had the honor of escorting President Grant to the steamship *Indiana* when he began his round-the-world trip in 1877. The three tugs were managed by Peter Wright & Sons, and with the number of vessels handled by the firm, plus the activity of the port, it may be assumed that they rarely lacked employment.

The International Navigation Company weathered the depression of 1873 quite well. The strength of the Red Star Line is shown by the fact that in the midst of the shipping depression of the late 1870s, Griscom was able to order two ships far larger than any previously owned by the company. In 1879, the 403-foot, 3,692-ton *Belgenland* was delivered by the Barrow Shipbuilding Company, Barrow-in-Furness, Scotland, to the Red Star Line and began her maiden voyage on March 30, 1879, from Antwerp to Philadelphia. She had accommodations for 150 in first class and 1,000 in steerage. The first voyage to Philadelphia showed her off to the owners before she became a regular on

The Belgenland *(1879) is shown here in a rare advertising print under full sail shortly after her commissioning. The print probably was created for travel agencies or agencies of the Red Star Line. As a single-screw vessel, sails could be fundamental to survival. Many a steamship arrived under sail after losing her only propeller.*

the New York–Antwerp service. The *Belgenland* would be a popular vessel for the Red Star Line and serve the International Navigation Company well for 25 years (1879–1904).

Lloyd Griscom provides a highly interesting reminiscence of a crossing on the *Belgenland* when he was eight years old:

> The *Belgenland*'s gangplank slid aboard with a rattle and bump, hawsers were flung free, bells clanged, the whistle boomed.
>
> "Come on, Roddy," I shouted above the clamor, "I'll race thee to the bridge."
>
> Simultaneously we dived for the ladder but Rodman, who was ten, two years older than I, pushed ahead and was first aloft, waving and calling good-by to Father across the widening sliver of water between us and the Philadelphia pier.

The Griscom boys were crossing to Europe for the purpose of attending an elite preparatory institution, the Haccius School, near Geneva, Switzerland. They were in the care of their mother, Frances Griscom, and their grandfather, Dr. John Griscom. Also in the Griscom party was a baby sister, Pansy, who was two, so Frances Griscom more than had her hands full. Lloyd Griscom continued:

> We were looking forward to the voyage as a great adventure. Mother would be busy taking care of our two-year-old sister Pansy, we knew we could take care of our grandfather, Dr. John Denn Griscom, and, being sons of the President of the line, we would have the run of the ship. For dinner we ordered all the dishes on the menu, and at bedtime retired to our own cabin, well pleased with our independence.
>
> Towards dawn we awoke to find the three-thousand-ton *Belgenland* dancing about like a cork. With every lurch our baggage skidded over the floor, stopped with a thud, and skidded back. We braced ourselves in our bunks and waited for morning, then gazed sadly at each other and decided we preferred to stay where we were. The steward appeared with breakfast but we were not interested. As the hours dragged along, nobody else came near us; Mother was always seasick and Grandfather apparently did not miss us.
>
> That day passed, and another and another, and still the gray-green waves banged on the porthole. When darkness closed down, our only light was a dim glow from a candle behind a piece of ground glass in the wall. The atmosphere in our tiny cabin grew thick and foul. Rod groaned, "I wish I were at Dolobran [the family mansion near Philadelphia]," and I agreed with him heartily. A half-hour at our new home in Haverford now seemed to us worth ten Atlantic crossings as they were in the winter of 1881.
>
> It was seven days before the sea began to subside and we were recovered enough to stagger on deck. A few breaths of fresh air made us feel ourselves again, and, delighted to discover the ship coated with sleet, we patted some of it into balls with which we stormed the bridge. Bushy-bearded Captain Randle put up only a slight resistance. We pursued him all the way to his cabin, messed his papers, fingered excitedly the revolver which he told us he kept to quell mutinies.
>
> After we had once investigated the ship from stem to stern, we were impatient for the end of the voyage. Our ice was soon exhausted, and sour milk, rancid butter, strong meat, added to the choking fumes of kerosene from the swinging lamps in the dining room, almost made us ill. Worse still our coal supply was low. One day during the gale we had slipped backward thirty knots while steaming full speed forward. Even though we used our sails, it was nip and tuck whether the fuel would last. When we finally docked at Flushing at the mouth of the Scheldt, we had no more than a few tons left in the bunkers. We had to take the train to Antwerp because the river was frozen for the first time in years.[6]

A sistership of the *Belgenland*, the *Rhynland* (1879, 3,689 tons), was another popular liner. The *Rhynland* was three tons smaller and one inch shorter than the *Belgenland*, but

The Rusland *(1877), originally the* Kenilworth *(1873, 2,595 tons, 345 feet x 37 feet, 10 knots), was purchased by the Red Star Line after she had run for them in the Liverpool–Philadelphia service for over a year. Renamed the* Rusland, *she sailed from Antwerp on her first voyage and ran aground at Long Branch, New Jersey, in dense fog on March 17, 1877, while seeking the entrance to New York Harbor. Hopes to refloat her were lost when it was found that her hull was sitting on another sunken wreck, which broke her back.*

"otherwise" identical, with a straight stem, single funnel, and four nicely spaced masts—all of which were rigged with sails when needed. The *Rhynland* was constructed by the Barrow Shipbuilding Company and launched on March 10, 1879. Fitting-out proceeded swiftly, and the new liner was ready for her maiden voyage from Antwerp to New York on June 10, 1879. She also had a long career under International Navigation Company ownership, not being sold until 1906, just prior to scrapping in Italy.

The *Belgenland* and the *Rhynland* made it possible for the Red Star Line to maintain a strong Antwerp–New York service in the early 1880s. Furthermore, the Cunard liner *Russia* (1867, 2,960 tons) was bought by Griscom and sent to the builders for extensive alterations. The reconditioned liner was renamed *Waesland* (1880), and her tonnage was radically increased to 4,752 tons by lengthening the hull 77 feet (358 to 435 feet). Her magnificent lines were at least partially preserved by the addition of a fourth mast. *Waesland*, the largest liner flying the Red Star, had accommodations for 120 in first class and 1,500 in steerage. The replacement of her machinery in 1880 with compound engines greatly enhanced her performance, and she proved so satisfactory that she was reengined again in 1889 with triple-expansion machinery. The *Waesland* served the various units of the International Navigation Company for 22 years until sunk after a collision with the *Harmonides* off Anglesey, Wales, March 5, 1902, with the loss of two lives. Another Cunarder bought by Griscom in 1882 was the *Algeria* (1870, 3,428 tons). Improvements to this vessel, renamed *Pennland* (1882), simply involved the addition of compound engines by J. Jack & Company, Liverpool. The reengining proved particularly gratifying when the *Pennland* became one of the fastest units in the fleet. In January 1886, she crossed from the Scilly Isles to Sandy Hook in nine days, 16 hours. Two years later, a new spar deck was added, increasing the liner's tonnage from 3,428 to 3,760 tons. The vessel proved highly successful as a money-earner for the International Navigation Company and remained in the fleet until sold in 1903 for scrapping in Italy. The addition of the *Belgenland, Rhynland, Waesland,* and *Pennland* between 1879 and 1882 permitted a weekly service between Antwerp and New York and ultimately forced the White Cross Line and the Engels Line out of the trade to the Scheldt. Between 1878 and 1882, the Philadelphia service was left in the hands of the original *Vaderland* and *Nederland,* although other units occasionally took Antwerp–Philadelphia sailings as needed. Griscom very much wanted to enhance the service to Philadelphia if trade and circumstances warranted.

A major move on the part of the International Navigation Company was the ordering in 1883 of the largest unit ever built for the fleet. An order was placed with Lairds of Birkenhead for a ship of well over 5,500 tons to be the flagship of the Red Star Line. This highly important vessel was named *Westernland* (1883, 5,736 tons), and was unique in a number of ways. She was the first Red Star liner constructed of steel, marking the beginning of that transformation in the fleet, and she also was the first unit in the fleet to have two funnels. Her method of construction was unusual in that Lairds was short of building berths and therefore built the liner in its drydock and "launched" her by floating her out on August 4, 1883. The *Westernland* took her maiden sailing from Antwerp to New York on November 3, 1883, and was the first Red Star Line vessel to carry three classes of passengers, since she had accommodations for 80 first-class, 60 second-class, and 1,200 steerage. With remarkable fidelity, the *Westernland* was a stalwart of the Antwerp–New York service for nearly 20 years (1883–1901) before being shifted around the fleet, and she served until sold for scrapping in 1912.

Another magnificent addition to the fleet of the International Navigation Company was the *Noordland* (1884, 5,212 tons) built for the company by Lairds of Birkenhead

The title page for a Red Star Line information booklet intended for transatlantic passengers in the 1880s.

A brilliantly designed postcard featuring two Cassiers pictures of the Vaderland *(1900) and Christopher Columbus'* Santa Maria *(1492). The card emphasizes the Red Star Line's "Antwerpen–New York" and "Antwerpen–Boston" services.*

immediately following the *Westernland*. The *Noordland*, the second steel unit in the fleet, was launched on November 1, 1883, two days before the *Westernland*'s first sailing. At 400 feet, she was almost 40 feet shorter than the *Westernland*, although virtually the same breadth (47 feet), and she was graced by a single funnel. Some early publicity for the *Noordland* described her as having two funnels like the *Westernland*, but she was not fitted out in that manner. She was equipped with compound engines capable of 13 knots and had accommodations for 63 first-class, 56 second-class, and 500 steerage passengers. Her maiden voyage was from Antwerp to New York, March 29, 1884, and she also was a workhorse of the Antwerp–New York trade for 17 years (1884–1901). Her last voyage occurred in 1908 for the American Line in the Liverpool–Philadelphia trade, after which she was scrapped.

The decade 1873–1883 brought great changes for the International Navigation Company (Red Star Line). The sizes of the largest ships operated by the line doubled. In 1874, the first four steamers of the Red Star Line totaled 10,736 tons. In 1884, each new ship was twice as large as the original vessels, and they totaled 10,948 tons. Passenger totals increased more than 10 times for the Antwerp–Philadelphia trade alone. In 1874, the ships of the International Navigation Company carried 3,174 passengers, and in 1875, 7,093. In 1880, the total for Philadelphia was more than 30,000 and for 1881 more than 40,000. The combined transatlantic and transcontinental services offered by the Red Star Line and the Pennsylvania Railroad proved very popular among European immigrants, since one ticket took the wary individual from Central Europe to Chicago.

Griscom was not bashful about trumpeting the virtues of the ships and services of the International Navigation Company. As far as he was concerned, the Red Star Line was an outgrowth of the public demand "to reach the Continent of Europe at some central point, so as to avoid the English fogs, a long, tedious, and uninteresting railroad journey through England, as well as the ever-dreaded crossing of the British Channel in small and poorly appointed boats."[7]

The American traveling public by the early 1880s represented a discerning and critical force that the Red Star Line was out to capture. First, however, it was necessary to convince Americans that European travel was available, affordable, and safe on a Red Star Line vessel.

These improved facilities have materially tended to promote travel between America and the Continent of Europe, as the yearly increase in the number of American searchers after pleasure, health, or science in Europe, is ample proof that a sojourn in the Old World is becoming not alone "the proper thing to do" but a general movement. Americans are keen observers, and a few weeks sojourn in the cradle of civilization suffices for them to become familiar with the people and customs of the lands of their forefathers. In former years the "proper thing" was to visit Newport, Long Branch, Lake George, or some other home watering-place where expensive toilets, exorbitant hotel charges, very little comfort, and a poor *cuisine* were the only returns for a large outlay. The rich could only enjoy this privilege, and persons in more moderate circumstances had to content themselves to pass the summer months in the sweltering cities. It is, however, not so at present. The natural restlessness of the American people, their spirit for investigation and enterprise and thirst after knowledge have done much to break through these old society rules, and since it has become a fact that a three months' trip to all the points of interest in Europe can be accomplished for *less* than it would cost the sojourner at a home watering resort for a month's stay, Americans of every station in life from the banker to the mechanic can now be found admiring the beauties of the birth place of the arts, science and literature.[8]

Red Star Line
Antwerpen—New York
Boston Philadelphia.

Another Cassiers print features one of the Vaderland *quartet of 1900 steaming up the Scheldt River, Belgium, past some traditional sailing barges.*

The Westernland *(1883, 5,736 tons, 440 feet by 47 feet, 14 knots) was nearly two thousand tons larger than her predecessors. She is shown at the Liverpool Landing Stage in the American Line Philadelphia–Liverpool service after 1901.*

The blandishments were difficult to ignore. The Red Star Line brochure quoted a Mr. T Buckler Ghequier, whose letter describing his travels in Europe was published in the American *Architect* (February 25, 1882). Mr. Ghequier wrote that in 1881 he had spent $110 for his transatlantic steamship ticket, and that he had kept a detailed register of all the expenses of his trip, which totaled $156, or $3.33 per day while in Europe, including hotel rooms, meals, steward's fees, all entrance fees to buildings, etc., and fees to porters. "These being absolute facts, will show with what economy such a journey can be made, and how absurd it is to talk about the great expense."[9]

What better way could the American public travel than on the ships of the Red Star Line? The brochure states:

> The *Westernland* and the *Noordland*, the latest additions to the fleet, are magnif-
> icent specimens of naval architecture, built entirely of *steel*. They are literally
> floating palaces, and are intended to eclipse in *size, speed, elegance, and comfort*,
> every previous effort of the line, and will not be excelled by any steamer afloat.

The brochure continues:

> Their passenger accommodations are of a very superior and extended nature.
> The first and second cabins, saloons, social halls, smoke and bath rooms are, as
> in the other steamers of the Red Star Line, amidships between the upper and
> main decks, an arrangement which has met with universal approbation. The

The elaborate figurehead of a young girl on the bow of the Friesland *(1889) is well defined in this unusual dockside picture of the ship. The liner has coaling barges alongside.*

staterooms are mostly outside rooms; large, light and thoroughly ventilated, the latter being perfected by a new method which renews the atmosphere every few minutes (even in the roughest weather, when all portholes and usual modes of ventilation are battened down) without creating a draught.

Considerable attention had been paid to the appointments in the staterooms:

The first cabin staterooms are supplied with two berths and a sofa which can be converted into a berth. In the larger rooms these sofas can be converted into an upper and lower berth. There are also a number of very large rooms (family rooms) which contain a lower double berth, an upper berth and a very wide sofa, capable of being converted into a berth. The woodwork is of polished mahogany and other hard woods, and the upholstering is in the finest quality of Utrecht velvet.

Staterooms are furnished with a new patent toilet and drawers or lockers, and placed in communication with the steward's department by electric pneumatic bells. The ships are lighted throughout with electric lights.[10]

The interest of the Red Star Line in the immigrant trade saw Griscom paying particular attention to the facilities offered this profitable portion of the passenger traffic. On the *Westernland* and *Noordland*, single men were housed in the front of the ship and families toward the stern. Whereas many immigrant ships had unlighted, open dormitories devoid of privacy, accommodations were handled with more concern on the Red Star Line vessels. The family area, in particular, was divided into cabins or staterooms, each with a folding door that provided a rare degree of privacy. Tables and benches had been fitted in the steerage areas so that meals could be served properly and immigrants could partake of their meals with some degree of comfort and satisfaction.

At the same time, class distinctions were clearly maintained. First- and second-class passengers did not ever have to associate with steerage passengers. The promenade for

RED STAR LINE
NEW YORK — ANTWERP.

S.S. FRIESLAND | APPROACHING FLUSHING ON THE WAY TO ANTWERP.

The Friesland *(1889) is shown approaching Flushing (Vlissingen), The Netherlands, up the Scheldt River en route to Antwerp, Belgium. Flushing guards the entrance of the Scheldt; upon occasion the river was completely frozen and passengers had to disembark there and travel by train to Antwerp.*

the cabin passengers was on the spar deck, above the upper deck—entirely removed from the steerage passengers on the deck below. The ladies' public rooms and library were carefully situated in the deckhouse, well away from the kitchen and thereby avoiding any unsavory odors.

It was stated in connection with the *Westernland* and the *Noordland:*

> The woodwork is of the finest-selected and highly-polished hardwoods and lincrusta [inlay], thereby combining elegance with durability. The upholstering is in leather, Utrecht velvet, and French silk brocade. In one word, no money nor pains have been spared to make the cabin accommodations of the *Westernland* and *Noordland* the *non plus ultra* [sic] of elegance without sacrificing comfort, in fact, to place them at the head of the list of floating palaces.[11]

In regard to safety, Griscom was very concerned about the image of ships, particularly in view of the dismal record of the White Cross Line of Belgium running in competition with Red Star. The ships of the International Navigation Company were fitted with watertight compartments meeting the highest standards of the British Lloyd's and French Bureau Veritas, under whose inspection the new ships were constructed.

The fame and good fortune of the Red Star fleet became well known to the knowledgeable traveling public. Griscom was an expert at public relations, and whenever favorable notices about his ships reached the head offices, or appeared in the press, he

One of the Vaderland *(1900)*
*quartet passes Flemish fishermen in
the Scheldt estuary.*

sought a much wider readership. Sometimes special news releases were made available to the press; on other occasions, these letters were included in an annual *Notice to Travellers* created by Peter Wright & Sons to be an early pocket guide to Europe as well as a sales stimulus for the line.

Griscom's formal schooling may have ended when he left the Friends Academy in Philadelphia, but his mind was highly inquisitive about the design and working of the vessels he so ably managed for Peter Wright & Sons and then owned as founder of the International Navigation Company. His thirst for knowledge about the technical aspects of the ships he operated caused him to go far beyond mere interest in their potential earnings. Informally at first, but with considerable expertise gained over the years, Griscom ultimately commanded the respect of the professional marine architects and engineers of his day as few businessmen ever have. The depth and extent of his experience and training in marine architecture and design were testified to by the fact that in 1893 he was elected the first president of the United States Society of Naval Architects and Marine Engineers (SNAME) and one of three honorary associate members of the prestigious British Society of Naval Architects. He also served as one of the American delegates to the International Maritime Conference for Revising the Rules of the Road at Sea, which met in Washington during the winter of 1889–90 with representatives from 28 nations. At the time, this international meeting was considered one of the most distinguished gatherings of experts on a subject ever to meet for any purpose. As a result of his keen interest in the subject, no vessel constructed for Griscom was ever built without considerable input from the owner. He knew what he wanted from a ship in terms of appointments, comfort, size, and speed, and he was knowledgeable enough about marine science to create specifications that challenged a builder to excellence. Only Albert Ballin of the Hamburg-American Line, among the great merchant-marine figures, shared the same level of thoroughness and genius that Griscom exhibited.[12] Ballin

The Pennland *(1882) originally was built as the Cunard* Algeria *(1870, 3,760 tons, 361 feet by 41 feet, 13 knots). In 1888 Red Star enhanced her accommodations with a new spar deck as shown. She was transferred to the American Line Philadelphia–Liverpool service in 1895 and scrapped in Italy in 1903.*

The Waesland *(1881), originally was built as the Cunard* Russia *(1867, 2,960 tons, 358 feet by 43 feet, 13 knots). In 1880 she was lengthened (4,752 tons, 435 feet) and given compound engines. Her passenger capacity of 100 first and 1,000 third made her an attractive addition to the Red Star fleet. In 1889 she was given triple-expansion engines and in 1895 was transferred to the American Line for the Liverpool–Philadelphia service. She was lost in collision with* Harmonides *off Anglesey on March 7, 1902.*

The Westernland *(1883, 5,736 tons, 440 feet by 47 feet, 14 knots) was built by Laird Bros., Birkenhead, England, in drydock and floated out. Her maiden voyage was November 3, 1883, from Antwerp to New York, where she became a fixture of the trade for eighteen years. Her original accommodations were for 80 first, 60 second, and 1,200 third. She is shown here with her Red Star Line funnel colors.*

ultimately would create and manage a far larger fleet, but Griscom's interests in shipping, railroads, oil transportation, banking, and insurance would be far broader. Only a thorough "workaholic" could have attempted all that he did.

At the same time, Griscom obviously enjoyed and relished the perquisites that came with great wealth and economic power. He definitely was one of the leading industrial lords of his day, living in a society where membership in the aristocracy was defined by an individual's bank balance.

Lloyd Griscom provides a rare insight into what this meant:

> The era of great fortunes which permitted individuals to own whatever they
> desired was also the era of unparalleled privilege. Because I was my father's son,
> I could walk into any telegraph office, compose as long a message as I wished,
> sign his name to it, and walk out; I could express anything I wanted anywhere
> free of all charge; I could step on any steamship and be transported to any point
> in the Seven Seas; I could board any train and ride from Portland, Maine, to
> Portland, Oregon, without paying a cent. I can still remember my humiliation
> when, obeying an Interstate Commerce Commission ruling, for the first time I
> had to stand at the window and buy a ticket like everybody else.[13]

Lloyd Griscom also wrote of his father's relationship to the Pennsylvania Railroad:

> As a director of the Pennsylvania Railroad, Father wore a little gold medal on
> his watch chain. If he were suddenly called to Chicago, he did not have to go
> into Philadelphia; the station agent at Haverford flagged The Limited for him.
> Once I was accompanying Mr. Frank Thomson along a platform of the Broad
> Street Station. On both sides a train was waiting; we turned into one and sat
> down. The conductor bustled up: "Mr. Thomson, this is an express which
> doesn't stop at Merion."
>
> "Well, stop it," commanded Mr. Thomson.
> It stopped.[14]

On one occasion, Grand Duke Alexander Mikhailovitch of Russia was a houseguest at Dolobran, the Griscom mansion in Haverford, Pennsylvania. Frank Thomson, president of the Pennsylvania Railroad Company, was giving a dinner in honor of the grand duke and to help his friend extend American hospitality to visiting royalty. Griscom was justifiably proud of his stable, which was managed by an Irish man, Augustus Archfield, who was devoted to him even if he quaked in his boots every time he had to present the stable accounts for audit. Archfield apparently had heard stories of how well disciplined Russian servants were, so he worked out a scheme to impress the grand duke. Lloyd Griscom recalled:

> Augustus, resplendent in breeches and claret jacket with primrose facings and
> pipings, yellow and black striped waistcoat, shiny leather boots, and curved top

The Westernland *was transferred to the American Line in 1901 and ran in the Liverpool–Philadelphia service, as shown. In this trade she carried a revised total of 170 second and 1,200 third. After May 1906 she briefly resumed the Red Star Antwerp–New York service until 1907 and then did a few more voyages for the American Line before her retirement in 1908. She was scrapped in 1912.*

The Noordland *(1884, 5,212 tons, 400 feet by 47 feet, 13 knots) was one of the most popular of all the Red Star Line ships. She was a good sea boat. Outfitted with passenger accommodations for 63 first, 56 second and 500 third, she carried less than half the total of comparable ships, but far more cargo.*

hat, brought our fastest team of trotters so that Father might put on a show. Father took the reins, the Grand Duke mounted beside him, the rest of us filled the sleigh and, leaving Augustus standing at attention, we skimmed out of the yard. A crack of the whip and we darted down Gray's Lane so swiftly that the Grand Duke was breathless. In less than half an hour we shot through the Thomson entrance, steam rising from the horses' backs. There on the steps, standing at attention exactly as we had left him at Dolobran, was Augustus.

The Grand Duke blinked. "Why, isn't that your coachman? How could he be here?"

"Oh," replied Father, who himself had no idea, "I told him to meet us and I expect my servants to follow my instructions."[15]

The Noordland *(1884) was transferred to the American Line in 1901 (as shown) for the Philadelphia–Liverpool service. Accommodations were revised to 160 second and 500 third, reflecting the age of the ship. Between 1906 and 1908 she filled in when needed and was scrapped in 1908. Another fine ship who spent her entire career under the Red Star and American Line flags.*

Lloyd Griscom held back from the group as it entered the Thomson mansion in order to satisfy his curiosity about how the coachman had managed to get there ahead of them. Archfield told the younger Griscom that as soon as their sleigh had left, he had jumped into another that was waiting and raced to the Haverford Railroad Station. At Haverford, he had leaped on a train that was just about to depart, and then got off at Merion. There he had lumbered as fast as his size and bunions would permit to the entranceway of the Thomson mansion, reaching his position seconds ahead of Griscom's arrival. Griscom was surprised at finding his coachman there, but not so stunned that he could not pretend that it was simply his due as an American industrialist and a member in good standing of the "American aristocracy." The Griscom family fondly remembered and laughed about the incident for years. Lloyd Griscom would retell the story as an example of the devotion his father could inspire in men. Griscom could and did lose his temper at people, but he also had a gift for compromise. Because of both his strictness and his fairness, there would be little labor unrest in the history of the International Navigation Company.

In 1884, Griscom was set for expansion. At the age of 43, he had been involved in the shipping business for nearly 25 years. He knew from his friends and associates that the Pennsylvania Railroad Company was very enthusiastic about disposing of the steamers of the American Line and winding up the business of the American Steamship Company. Financial success and a significant federal subsidy had eluded the grasp of the American concern, whose ships were more expensive to build and crews more expensive to maintain than foreign-flag tonnage. The efforts of Charles Cramp of the Cramp Shipyard, and Thomas A. Scott of the Pennsylvania Railroad to sell the original American Line quartet to the Imperial Russian government in 1878 fell through when the officers of the American Steamship Company were not prepared to act as quickly as was required. Thereafter, the Pennsylvania Railroad Company would welcome any excuse to unload the shipping line, which could neither earn the interest on its bonds nor repay the railroad its loans.

In 1884, when the financial situation of the American Steamship Company became desparate, the Pennsylvania Railroad management insisted that Griscom take over responsibility for the American Line. Griscom does not appear to have been thrilled at the prospect, but when the railroad agreed to put up virtually all the money, he hardly could refuse. The PRR was by a long measure the strongest single corporate backer of the International Navigation Company upon which the fortunes of that steamship company also depended. Hence, the offer of the PRR to purchase 14,500 shares of INC stock in order to provide the $725,000 in financing for Griscom to buy the four ships of the American Line could not be refused. Besides, Griscom was familiar with the ships, after managing them for ten years, and definitely felt that with some solid hull repairs and new engines and boilers, they probably had many more useful years in them. On the part of the board of directors of the American Steamship Company, the offer from Griscom and the International Navigation Company to purchase their ships could not be ignored since they had no other alternative and the PRR was insistent. The original investors in the American Steamship Company lost heavily, as did the Pennsylvania Railroad Company, when the business was sold. Griscom, for his part, acquired the name and goodwill of the American Line as well as four fine steamers, all of which were solid performers on the North Atlantic. Few grounds exist for the much lamented demise of the American Line, since the name, services and ships of the line remained virtually unchanged under Griscom's continuing management. What occurred in 1884 was nothing more than the reorganization of a diversified shipping enterprise for the purpose of eliminating a reluctant backer, the Pennsylvania Railroad Company. The American Line continued to exist and to operate a Philadelphia–Liverpool service just as it had since its inception. The only novelty was a greater flexibility of tonnage, which found American Line steamers sailing for the Red Star Line and vice versa. The International Navigation Company of Philadelphia assumed the role of the American holding company for both the American Steamship Company (American Line), and the Société Anonyme de Navigation Belge-Américaine (Red Star Line). The development and expansion of Clement Acton Griscom's shipping interests did not stop with the adjustments of 1884. The owner of the International Navigation Company was laying the groundwork for an even more important acquisition—the Inman Line, one of the oldest and most respected British-flag operations on the North Atlantic.

Chapter 6

Inman Steamship Company Limited— Inman and International Navigation Company

"NEW YORK."

Under the guidance of Clement Acton Griscom, the International Navigation Company bought control of the Inman Line in 1886 and set out to restore its fortunes on the North Atlantic. The New York *(1893), originally the* City of New York *(1888, 10,499 tons, 528 feet by 63 feet, 20 knots), was the largest liner in the world. Her 20,000 horsepower engines drove her twin screws at over 19 knots, making her a Blue Riband liner. She was given American Registry in 1893.*

*I*n the 1860s and 1870s, the Liverpool, New York & Philadelphia Steam Ship Company—universally known by its nickname, the Inman Line—was one of the premier maritime enterprises on the North Atlantic. It remains one of the most famous and celebrated of all the great nineteenth-century steamship lines carrying on the trade between Europe and America. While the primary route served was from Liverpool to Philadelphia and New York, feeder services from the Continent, such as the Port of Antwerp, resulted in a wider casting of the net for cargo and passengers.

The origin of the Inman Line lies with William Inman of Leicester, England (1825–1881).[1] Early in his career, he joined one of the leading Liverpool shipbroking firms, Richardson Brothers & Company. Richardson Brothers (Liverpool) were joint owners, with Richardson, Watson & Company of Philadelphia and New York, of a regular line of sailing packets trading between Philadelphia and Liverpool. In time, the firm would own steamers and be the earliest concern to carry steerage passengers on its ships.[2] William Inman was one of the earliest ship managers to have a keen appreciation of the immigrant trade in steamships and the profits to be derived from it.

The Inman Line of Royal Mail Steamers was founded in 1850 by William Inman as the Liverpool & Philadelphia Steam Ship Company. In 1857 "New York" was added to the title, and in 1875 the name was revised to "Inman Steamship Company Limited." The line was sold to Griscom and his associates in 1886. The liner shown here is the City of Richmond *(1873).*

Inman Line of Royal Mail Steamers.

In 1850, Thomas Richardson and William Inman created the Liverpool & Philadelphia Steam Ship Company. The new line bought the iron-hulled, screw steamship *City of Glasgow* and announced that a sistership, the *City of Philadelphia*, was building. The *City of Glasgow* left Liverpool on her first voyage for her new owners on December 11, 1850.[3] The Liverpool & Philadelphia Steam Ship Company elected to maintain the *City of* — designation of the builders, Tod & McGregor. Afterward, virtually all the ships operated by the line would be named for various cities. The name of the new sistership was altered before launching, however, and she went down the ways as the *City of Manchester* (1851, 2,109 tons). Maiden westward passages appear to have been agonizingly slow for Inman vessels. The *City of Manchester* took 40 days getting to Philadelphia in July 1851, but she romped across in March 1852 in well under two weeks, delivering her mails to America on the same day as the Cunarder *Niagra*, which sailed only 12 hours after her for Boston.

The bold decision was made between 1850 and 1852 to enter the immigrant trade with steamships—a trade that heretofore had been the market of sailing vessels. Class prejudice stated that truly first-class passengers would never be willing to book passage on a vessel, no matter how luxurious, if smelly, vermin-ridden immigrants were stuffed below decks. It also was thought that the income to be derived from immigrants would not equal the cost and problems of handling them on the fastest vessels. William Inman felt differently and offered steerage tickets at six guineas, while merging all cabin accommodations into a single class and charging according to the type of cabin booked (13 to 20 guineas). The response more than justified his expectations. Soon Inman liners were crossing with hundreds of steerage passengers on a regular basis, which made a substantial contribution to the balance sheet for each voyage.

The outbreak of the Crimean War in the spring of 1854 saw the British and French governments seeking to charter every vessel they could lay their hands on to transport troops and supplies to the Black Sea. Tempting offers were made by the French government for the *City of Manchester*, but William Inman's two partners, the Richardson brothers, were Quaker and would not consent to the military use. In the end, the

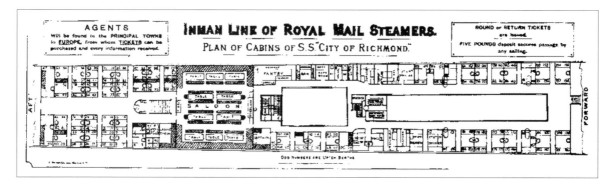

The interior accommodations of the City of Richmond *(1873, 4,607 tons, 441 feet by 43 feet, 14 knots) are presented in an original passenger information sheet. She had accommodations for 132 cabin class and 1,310 third.*

problem was solved by buying out the brothers and creating a new firm, Richardson, Spence & Company.

James Spence, one of the founding partners, was born in the north of Ireland in 1829 but emigrated to Philadelphia, where he went to live with an uncle, a Mr. Clarke, one of the partners in the Quaker shipping firm of Richardson, Watson & Company. The Philadelphia firm owned a line of packets that sailed between the Delaware and the Mersey. In Liverpool, the British agent of the packet line was Richardson Brothers (managed by another Richardson brother), with which William Inman would be associated. James Spence and William Inman knew each other well as business associates and friends, even if their principal cities of commerce were on opposite sides of the North Atlantic. James Spence returned to England from the United States in 1854 and became one of the founding partners in Richardson, Spence & Company, which would remain closely associated with Thomas Richardson and Company of Philadelphia and New York. The new firm would succeed quite well and exercise a major influence on the trade and commerce of Liverpool.[4] In the early 1870s, Richardson, Spence & Company would become the Liverpool agents of the American Steamship Company and the International Navigation Company when those concerns began operations.

The Inman Line, as it usually was known, was one of the big three British-flag lines, sharing the Royal Mail Contract with Cunard and White Star. Mail ships sailed on Tuesday, Thursday, and Saturday and the Inman Line was responsible for the Thursday departures of the Royal Mails.

The removal of the Richardson brothers from the ownership of the Liverpool & Philadelphia Steam Ship Company permitted William Inman to accept the French charter offer.[5] At the conclusion of the Crimean War, Inman had a first-class fleet available for the North Atlantic. The Philadelphia trade no longer was sufficient, and a new service from Liverpool to New York began on December 31, 1856. The simple economic and historical facts of the matter were that with the great success of the Erie Canal and subsequent canal projects, plus the growth of railroads, New York had outstripped Philadelphia as the largest city and most important commercial center in the United States. The Liverpool & Philadelphia Steam Ship Company joined the growing number of lines serving the New York market and in March 1857 added "New York" to its title to become the Liverpool, New York & Philadelphia Steam Ship Company. Also in 1857, a number of Inman ships were chartered by the British government in connection with the Sepoy Mutiny in India.

William Inman, always open to new opportunities, created a feeder service from Antwerp to Liverpool that ran from 1857 to 1873, when the International Navigation Company commenced its direct line from Belgium to the United States and abruptly garnered all the trade. When William Inman began having his ships call at Queenstown, Ireland, in 1859, he began a tradition that would last for more than half a century for mailboats sailing from Liverpool, and, on many occasions, those from Southampton as well.[6] So sensible was the decision to call at Queenstown that Cunard followed suit in November 1859, and a steady stream of cabin passengers, mail, and immigrants soon left Ireland by this route. The American Civil War saw the withdrawal of virtually all American-flag tonnage from the North Atlantic and an enormous boom in cargoes and passengers for those in a position to take advantage of the situation. The conclusion of the war in 1865 brought a decline in freight bound for America as the wartime demand slackened. In the immediate postwar period of 1866–68, a recession checked the expansion of the American economy and forced severe retrenchment on the North Atlantic steamship lines. William Inman and other Liverpool shipping magnates recognized that the Liverpool–New York trade could not possibly support the 40 or 50 passenger liners operating on the route owned by the "Big Four" (Inman, Cunard, National, and Guion), let alone lesser firms. Inman reduced sailings from weekly to biweekly.

In 1867, negotiations with the British postmaster-general also brought Inman a share of the Royal Mail to be carried from Liverpool to New York. The Inman Line won the right to carry the mail on the Wednesday sailing to New York, to fly the Royal Mail ensign, and to advertise themselves as "Royal Mail Ships." A revised contract starting July 1869 called for a service from Liverpool to New York via Queenstown upon payment of a subsidy of £35,000 a year. The Inman Line, because of the speed of the new vessels and the desire of the post office for three sailings a week, agreed to shift its midweek departure from Wednesday to Thursday. While Inman handled the Thursday sailing, Cunard would supply ships for the Tuesday and Saturday departures. The penalty for failing to make a scheduled mail sailing was £300.[7]

To the delight of William Inman, the third of the new ships, the *City of Brussels* (1869, 3,081 tons), proved to be the "record breaker" he was after. This liner was the first iron-hulled, propeller-driven record breaker never beaten by a paddlewheeler.

The renewal of economic prosperity after 1870 saw the Inman Line in an excellent position to benefit from the increase in passengers and freight. The fleet totaled an impressive 38,811 tons, with most of the 16 larger vessels being of fairly recent construction. The results showed in the figures for passenger movement from Liverpool and Queenstown to New York. The American records show the Inman Line with 68 crossings (only two fewer than Cunard), and if Inman ships carried only 3,635 cabin-class passengers to Cunard's 7,638, they transported the enormous number of 40,465 steerage passengers to Cunard's 16,871. The Inman Line's grand total for 1870 was 44,100 passengers—a number that made the Liverpool, New York & Philadelphia Steam Ship Company the largest maritime operation on the North Atlantic.

William Inman had three great challenges in his immediate future. The sea provided one when the *City of Boston* sailed from New York with 177 passengers and crew on January 25, 1870, and, while reported off Halifax three days later, was never heard from again. The second challenge was the invention and perfection of the compound engine in 1869. Almost overnight, the compound engine reduced fuel consumption by 50 percent and made it necessary to reengine almost the entire fleet. The third challenge was the creation of the White Star Line by Thomas Henry Ismay in 1871. Of the three challenges, White Star would be the most severe and within five years would force the Liverpool, New York & Philadelphia Steam Ship Company into a major reorganization. Within 15 years, it would threaten the very survival of the Inman Line.

William Inman already had a most impressive liner on order, *City of Montreal* (1872, 4,451 tons), nearly 50 percent larger than any previous unit in the fleet. The *City of Montreal* would be a worthy addition to the Inman fleet when she began her maiden sailing on February 8, 1872, but she never would be the equal of the White Star liners for speed, and her accommodations simply were far surpassed by the new competition. Desperate to upgrade his fleet wherever possible, Inman took the two-year-old *City of Brussels* out of service temporarily. Her upper deck area, including the wooden deckhouse and high bulwarks, were ripped out in order to fit an iron deck in an arrangement similar to that of the new White Star liners. This increased her tonnage from 3,081 to 3,747 but did little for her earning power except for making her more competitive as a first-class unit. These measures were not considered enough, in and of themselves, so William Inman ordered two large new liners.

Just as the *City of Chester* and the *City of Richmond* were ready in 1873, a major shipping depression set in. To make matters even more critical, the establishment of the Red Star Line's Antwerp–New York service robbed the Inman Line of yet another source of revenue. In 1871, the Canadian mail contract was lost to the Allan Line, which had strong Canadian and Scottish ties. The financial stress of building a major new vessel every year for four years, and the promise of future challenges, forced William Inman to

The City of Montreal *(1872 4,451 tons, 419 feet by 44 feet, 13 knots) was a celebrated unit of the fleet. In 1876 the Inman Line replaced her machinery with compound engines. She burned at sea on August 10, 1887; all her passengers and crew were rescued by the Furness liner* York City.

The City of Richmond *(1873) was a sleek two-funneled, three-masted, clipper-bowed unit of the Inman fleet. On one occasion she had a cargo of cotton bales catch fire through spontaneous combustion and barely made it into Queenstown, with her decks and bulkheads extremely hot.*

form a public company in 1875, with himself at its head, in an effort to provide the extra capital that was so badly needed.[8] The competition to have the fastest ship in service on the North Atlantic was financially murderous. By the spring of 1876, the shipping depression had become so severe that the Inman and White Star Lines, in spite of their bitter rivalry, were forced to come to a working agreement on their sailings before they bankrupted each other.[9] This agreement markedly reduced the sailings of the two lines. By 1883, Inman owned seven aging liners, though much of the older and more-expensive-to-operate tonnage had been disposed of in one way or another. The *Buenos Ayrean* (1880, 4,005 tons), commissioned for the Allan Line, provided an excellent working example of the advantages of steel over iron in ship construction. Hence, Inman decided to take the plunge and ordered a steel liner of some 8,000 tons from the Barrow Shipbuilding Company. With the relatively new metal in short supply, Inman grudgingly agreed to the construction of an iron steamship. The work proceeded rapidly, and on

The City of Chester (*1873, 4,566 tons, 445 feet by 44 feet, 14 knots) was built by Caird. She had accommodations for 132 cabin and 1,310 third. In 1893 she became the* Chester *of the American Line and in 1898 was sold to the U.S. government and became the* USS Sedgwick. *She was sold again in 1905 and scrapped in 1907.*

The City of Rome (*1881, 8,415 tons, 560 feet by 52 feet, 16 knots) was three thousand tons larger than any other unit in the Inman fleet. She was ordered from the Barrow Yard and designed to be a steel-hulled record breaker. A shortage of steel made it necessary to build the hull of iron, and the result was a slower vessel with less cargo capacity. The* City of Rome *was one of the most beautiful vessels ever built for the North Atlantic and a total financial disaster. The Inman Line threw the vessel back on her builders after six voyages. She had a varied career thereafter. Here she is shown in the colors of the Anchor Line.*

The City of New York *(1888, 10,499 tons, 528 feet by 63 feet, 20 knots) was ordered to rejuvenate the fortunes of the Inman and International Line. She was designed to be the largest and fastest ship in the world. This is an early impression of the vessel showing her with a full set of sails. She was a twin-screw ship and the sails were dispensed with shortly after her commissioning. It is doubtful that she ever used them.*

June 14, 1881, the new liner was launched as the *City of Rome*. In appearance, the new liner was the most stately and well-proportioned steamship ever built.[10] Certainly the *City of Rome* underway must have been a glory to behold. The clipper-bowed liner possessed the lines of a thoroughbred racer, and her superstructure was crowned with three slender, stately funnels and four evenly spaced pole masts. When commissioned with a tonnage of 8,415, a length of 560 feet, and a breadth of 52 feet, the *City of Rome* was the largest liner in the world in active service. Unfortunately, however, beauty was not enough for the new vessel. On her maiden voyage, October 13–22, 1881, she plowed from Queenstown to New York, taking more than two days longer than the *Arizona*, which she had been built to beat! This was a disastrous performance for a liner upon which the Inman Steamship Company had staked everything. When the *City of Rome* then took a day longer than the *Arizona* to steam home, the disaster became a catastrophe. The new liner promptly underwent a major six-month overhaul and then took four more voyages for the Inman Line. In mid-August 1882, the beautiful *City of Rome* was thrown back in disgust on her builders by the Inman Line.[11]

On July 3, 1881, the management of the Inman Steamship Company was weakened by the premature death of its founder, William Inman, who was only 56 at the time. Inman died just a few days after the launching of the *City of Rome*; therefore, the great shipping man never lived to know of the vessel's shortcomings. The rejection of the *City of Rome* after five voyages may be considered a somewhat hasty reaction by the new Inman Line management. Greater consideration might well have been given the liner if William Inman had been alive. The *City of Rome* probably would have been an asset to

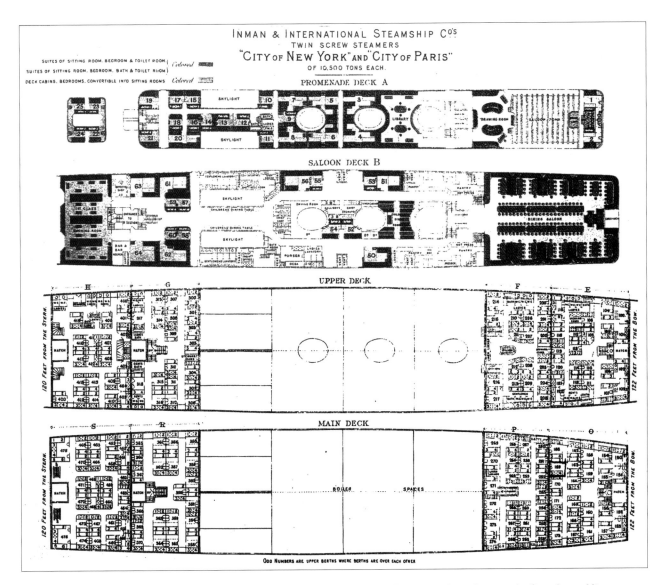

The deck plans showing the interior layout of the City of New York *and* City of Paris, *with emphasis on the first-class public rooms on Promenade and Saloon Deck and the staterooms on Upper Deck and Main Deck. The liners had accommodations for 540 first, 200 second, and 1,000 third.*

the aging Inman fleet, even if she was not a record breaker, but the liner would never be given the chance.[12] The Inman Line bought a new 6,000-ton liner on the stocks and named her *City of Chicago,* but this was not enough.

With its back to the wall financially, the Inman Steamship Company faced the hour of decision. A stockholders' meeting was called in Liverpool on October 18, 1886, to discuss the courses of action open to the company. Debts and obligations exceeded the value of the fleet by nearly £100,000 and were mounting steadily.[13]

Frames of the *City of New York*, looking forward—July 19, 1887, *is the title of this engraving, which shows the steel plates of the double bottom being installed, approximately eight months before her launch.*

The critical financial straits of the Inman Steamship Company were common knowledge and became of particular interest to Clement A. Griscom and the International Navigation Company through Richardson, Spence & Company, their Liverpool business associates. The Griscom shipping interests, including Peter Wright & Sons of Philadelphia and backed by the Pennsylvania Railroad, had purchased some of the debts of the Inman Line and therefore were primary creditors. Since the Inman Line fitted nicely into the expanding operations of the International Navigation Company, Griscom received encouragement from the Pennsylvania Railroad to enter into negotiations for the purchase of the line. The major British stockholders of the Inman Steamship Company knew of the American move when the stockholders' meeting was called. On October 18, 1886, it was decided that the company should go into voluntary liquidation and thus pave the way for the American purchase.

A Stern View, Showing Twin Screws *is an engraving that shows the mounting framework for the propellers. Twin screws were still rare and drew attention because only a very large vessel could have a hull large enough to justify them. In this case the design was faulty, because the* Cities *would suffer numerous propeller and/or shaft failures through metal fatigue.*

The City of New York *(1888) took her maiden voyage from Liverpool to New York on August 1, 1888. She was the largest and fastest ship in the world and drew the cream of the trade. The Hon. James G. Blaine, a prominent Republican politician, crossed on the maiden voyage and the welcome he and the ship received upon her arrival at New York was about equal. The Battery fired a salute as the* City of New York *came up the bay dressed out in all her flags. A fleet of smaller vessels greeted the new queen of the North Atlantic and escorted her to the new American Line pier.*

Harper's Weekly, August 18, 1888

Within two weeks a new name, the Inman and International Steamship Company Limited, replaced the Inman Steamship Company Ltd and the transatlantic passenger lines were confronted with a rejuvenated giant where an imminent demise had been expected. An active role in the management of the new concern was assumed by Richardson, Spence & Company, Liverpool. The Inman owners received a sum of £205,000 for their five liners and the use of the company name. From this amount was deducted the large debt already owed the American purchasers. Discussions appear to have taken place over whether the new company name should be the "International, Inman and American Line," but the final choice was Inman and International.[14] This was wise, for the longer name was much too bulky for advertisement purposes. Furthermore, since the Inman Line was a subsidized British mail line, there was no need to offend or upset the British government by emphasizing that American investors had just purchased one of the premier British-flag North Atlantic lines. The situation vis-à-vis the British government and the new Inman owners was to deteriorate soon enough anyway.

The first order of business for the new owners was the rebuilding of the fleet in a grand manner. Clement A. Griscom had planned and prepared some 20 years for the day when he would have a free hand to establish a truly first-class transatlantic line. He

Few vessels ever have had more beautiful and graceful lines than the City of New York *and* City of Paris. *The latter took her maiden sailing from Liverpool to New York on April 3, 1889.* "Steamer Day" *in New York, drawn by J.O. Davidson, shows the* City of Paris *outward bound passing the Inman and International piers with a White Star liner astern. This is one of the most majestic pictures of these liners ever published.*

possessed a strong foundation for doing so in the two divisions of the International Navigation Company that he already controlled. The Société Anonyme de Navigation Belge-Américaine (Red Star Line) was maintaining a prosperous Antwerp–New York trade, and the American Steamship Company (American Line) operated a growing Liverpool–Philadelphia service. Neither of these concerns was ever in a position to obtain the respect of the great British North Atlantic lines. Both Cunard and White Star had long looked down on Griscom's efforts as unworthy of attention while he built up the smaller lines. With the acquisition of the tottering Inman Line—over which Cunard and White Star had been ready to say the last rites—Griscom suddenly emerged as one of the world's largest owners of steamships. The reaction of the competing British lines was first stunned silence, and then a flurry of activity. Griscom, they were convinced, was the very essence of the fox among the chickens, and he had waited years to play the part.

Upon acquiring the Inman Steamship Company, Clement A. Griscom caught the next steamer for Liverpool to discuss the future plans of the Inman Line with his British associates, James Spence and Edmund Taylor of Richardson, Spence & Company. He carried with him the committment of the Pennsylvania Railroad Company to provide $2,000,000 toward the building of a new ship—second to none in the world.

The City of New York, *shown under construction at the J. & G. Thomson Shipyard on the River Clyde, Scotland. This is a general view of the frames of the liner on June 25, 1887, nine months prior to her launch. She was newsworthy as the largest ship under construction in the world. The artist was C. Butler.*

The advance in construction of the City of New York *is evident in this view done on July 19, 1887, at the Thomson Yard. Much more of the steel framing is evident that would make this ship and her sister,* City of Paris, *two of the strongest ships ever built for the North Atlantic.*

This magnificent view of the City of New York *ready for launching captures the majesty of the vessel. No less a figure than Lady Randolph Churchill, the American-born mother of Sir Winston Churchill, traveled north to Glasgow, Scotland, to christen the liner on March 15, 1888, in a cold, torrential rain.*

The Cities *combined beauty and majesty from almost any angle. This starboard view of one of the sisters inward bound to New York is exceptional. She slices through the sea with all flags flying.*

Scientific American, *ca. 1889*

Immediately upon landing he discussed his plans with his old friend and agent, James Spence, and then set out for Scotland. There was a deep recession along the Clyde and the shipyards were hungry for work. Before Griscom returned negotiations were completed with James R. Thomson of J. & G. Thomson Shipbuilding Yard, Clydebank, Scotland, for the building of the two largest, fastest, and finest commercial vessels in the world, calculated to far surpass any existing competitors.[15] Griscom notified James Wright in Philadelphia of what he had done in ordering two vessels, and Wright wrote an urgent letter to the president of the Pennsylvania Railroad explaining their position. The opportunity was tremendous, but the cost was nearly double at $1,850,000 per ship. Griscom's arguments about the age of the Inman fleet, the need to revive its fortunes, and the savings to be realized on an order for two crack liners, apparently won the day. The Pennsylvania Railroad Company agreed to underwrite the acquisition of sufficient funds to pay Thomson for, not one, but two liners larger than anything else in service.

The delivery of the new vessels was two years away and additional tonnage was needed immediately. The *Ohio* was fresh from a major overhaul during which triple-expansion engines were installed—producing spectacular crossings at more than 14 knots by the 14-year-old liner. The four original American Line vessels were all doing well in these years, and they were considered to be in good enough condition to be overhauled and rejuvenated.

Griscom was determined to make the greatest possible impression upon the steamer trade with his new liners. The keel of the *City of New York* was laid in June 1887 and that of the *City of Paris* soon thereafter. The two new vessels were to be as nearly unsinkable as possible—each liner was constructed with 15 transverse bulkheads that ran from the keel all the way up to the saloon deck, with no breaks in the partitions below this level. The two liners were the most perfectly subdivided transatlantic vessels ever built.

The first of this famous pair was ready for launching by March 1888. A contemporary observer described the scene:

> The *City of New York* stands on the ways ready to be launched, while the other steamer, the *City of Paris*, is in an advanced state. The former, as she now stands in the yard, presents a fine appearance. Her great length of 560 ft., her beam 63 ft., and her height, 44 feet, might well attract the attention of passengers on the river steamers. With the buildings on deck, she measures close to 10,500 tons, making her the largest passenger steamer in the world.[16]

Of particular note was the figurehead that graced the clipper bow of the new liner. The female figure, greatly admired, had been carved by the sculptor James Allan of Glasgow. Traditionalists were particularly pleased that the new owners of the Inman Line had elected to retain the clipper bow and figurehead, which had so long been associated with Inman ships.

Each vessel was outfitted with two completely separate engine rooms. The engines were of the three-crank triple-expansion type, having piston valves throughout, and each engine was capable of driving the ship at four-fifths the maximum speed in the event that either set of engines should have to be stopped for any reason. Each liner was constructed with a double hull so that if the ship should strike anything that might open her interior to the sea, the second skin would be there to keep the vessel safe.

On March 15, 1883, no less a figure than Lady Randolph Churchill came north to Scotland to name the new Inman and International liner *City of New York*. Her sistership was christened the *City of Paris* and launched on October 23, 1888, a little more than two months later than planned. Since the liners were constructed in a depression period along the Clyde, they were warmly regarded by the local populace. Their passenger accommodations surpassed anything in existence and set new standards of luxury. Of particular note were the magnificent vaulted dining rooms, complete with stained-glass windows and grand organs. The vaulted ceiling of the saloon area was meant to give first-class passengers the impression that they were in an elegant hotel or mansion instead of on a ship at sea, and this effect was fully achieved. The two liners had accommodations for 540 first, 200 second, and 1,000 steerage passengers.[17]

Unexpected disaster struck Griscom, however, before the commissioning of the new ships. In 1887, the British government reviewed the arrangements for carrying the mail across the North Atlantic and decided that two sailings a week, one by Cunard and the other by White Star would be adequate.[18] Both lines not only were British built and manned but also were British owned. Behind the scenes, revenge was taken for Griscom's audacity in buying Inman. The third mail each week, heretofore carried by Inman, was discontinued, and the subsidy paid to the line was canceled. Unofficially, Griscom was informed that the British government saw no reason to subsidize the new

The Friesland *(1889, 7,116 tons, 437 feet by 51 feet, 15 knots) was ordered by the Red Star Line from the J. & G. Thomson Shipyard, Glasgow, Scotland, which also was building the* Cities *for Inman and International. At 7,116 tons she was nearly 2,000 tons larger than any other Red Star liner, but still some 3,000 tons smaller than the speed queens for the first-class service.*

American owners of Inman and International even if it remained a British-flag steamship line. This action severely affected the solvency of Griscom's maritime empire. It was questionable whether the two new liners could be operated profitably without some form of guaranteed income through a contract to carry the mail.

The *City of New York* took her maiden voyage on August 1, 1888, and was the largest passenger liner in commission at the time. The *City of Paris* followed with her maiden sailing on April 3, 1889, and the two ocean greyhounds were hailed as the outstanding marine marvels of their day, with their gross tonnage of 10,500, length of 560 feet, and beam of 63 feet. The Inman and International *Cities* also were (and are) regarded as among the most beautiful passenger ships ever constructed. The *City of New York* and *City of Paris* possessed the unique Inman clipper bow and long, sleek black hulls. Each was graced with three majestic, evenly spaced funnels and three towering masts. Oddly enough, the builders deemed it necessary to outfit the liners with sails; the foremast was square-rigged, with the other two masts being fore-and-aft rigged. It is doubtful that the sails were ever used by these twin-screw, 20-knot passenger liners, and it appears that the crossbars and sails were soon removed. Both liners carried 22 lifeboats as a prominent portion of their exterior equipment, and it was firmly stated that "these will be capable of carrying all on board when the vessels are full."[19]

Majestic in their external appearance and most beautiful within, but could they capture the "Blue Riband" for speed? The award was traditionally given to the North Atlantic liner making the fastest crossing. The poor performance of the *City of Rome* must have haunted Griscom, Spence, and Taylor as their two great liners prepared for their maiden voyages. Their fears were probably accentuated when the *City of New York* took longer than expected to work out the kinks and, while turning in a creditable performance during her first six months in service, produced no new record crossings. The *City of Paris* made a comfortable maiden voyage (April 3, 1889), which was eagerly watched but which also established no new record. The *Paris* left Liverpool on her second voyage May 1, 1889, and after the usual stop at Queenstown (Cobh), rapidly pulled away from the Irish coast with 2,855 miles of the broad North Atlantic before her. Five days, 23 hours, and seven minutes later, the *City of Paris* arrived off Sandy Hook and steamed up the North River with the legendary Blue Riband of the Atlantic tacked to her foremast. The *City of Paris* had steamed at an average speed of 19.95 knots, which was .39 knot and two hours and 48 minutes faster than the Cunarder *Etruria* (1885, 7,718 tons) over a similar distance in May of the previous year (six days, one hour, 55 minutes, 2,855 miles, 19.56 knots). The Inman and International Steamship Company was the proud owner of the "Fastest Passenger Liner in the World." Clement A. Griscom, James Spence, and Edmund Taylor in one stroke had transformed the Inman Line from a loser into a blue-blooded winner—and in the process sending all their competitors scurrying to their builders. The *City of Paris* also was the first passenger liner to make an Eastbound crossing of the North Atlantic in under six days. "Later in the same month the *City of Paris* arrived at Queenstown after a voyage of 5 days, 22 hrs. 10 min. and thereby completed the 'double.' "[20] Now Inman and International could confidently proclaim to all the world that they had the "fastest liner on the Atlantic."

A year later, the *City of Paris* experienced one of the narrowest escapes from disaster in the history of the North Atlantic. At 5:30 P.M. on Tuesday, March 25, 1890, the liner was about 216 miles from the coast of Ireland, running at full speed.[21] The ship's triple-expansion engines, capable of approximately 18,000 horsepower, were at full ahead when the manganese collar of the starboard shaft wore away. The shaft wrenched loose and a chain of events destroyed the starboard engine room, while flying metal also punctured the bulkhead to the port engine room and simultaneously buried the seacocks, permitting seawater to enter. All method of propulsion was lost and the liner drifted to a stop. After two anxious days, early in the morning of March 28, the lights of an approaching steamer were seen. Rockets were fired by First Officer F.M. Passow and his men in a lifeboat, attracting the attention of Captain Roberts and others on the bridge of the White Star liner *Adriatic*, and course was altered toward the distress signal. Passow told Roberts that Captain Watkins wanted the *City of Paris* towed 200 miles to the Irish port of Queenstown. Roberts said he would go to the aid of the individuals on the *City of Paris*, but that he would not undertake a tow. Shortly thereafter, a small steamer bound eastward was sighted. It proved to be the *Aldersgate* of London, heading from Galveston, Texas, to Liverpool. Captain Cheshire of the *Aldersgate* was informed by Captain Roberts that it was not the *Adriatic* that needed assistance but the *City of Paris*, and he asked if the *Aldersgate* would undertake the tow. The captain of the little freighter promptly said yes.

Captain Roberts said he would stand by and accompany the *Aldersgate* to the *City of Paris* in the event any assistance was needed. As soon as they could proceed in safety, the two rescue vessels made for the *City of Paris*. The early dawn revealed the liner a derelict, wallowing in the slight westerly swell very far down by the stern. A throng of passengers could be seen crowding the deck forward as the *Adriatic* and the *Aldersgate*

The triple-expansion engines of the City of New York *and* City of Paris *each produced over 9,000 horsepower and were among the largest power plants in the world on land or sea. Their engine rooms can be described as "cathedrals of the industrial revolution," as they soared upward over 70 feet from the keel in the center of the ship.* Scientific American, September 15, 1888

The City of Paris *was steaming at full speed some 200 miles off the coast of Ireland on March 25, 1890, when the manganese collar supporting the starboard shaft wore away, the shaft wrenched loose, and the engine room self-destructed as huge chunks of metal flew in all directions. The wreckage in the engine room was photographed in Liverpool after the liner reached port.*

steamed up, and a great cheer greeted the arrival of the White Star liner. By that time, the *City of Paris* had been drifting dead in the water for 60 hours.

As the tow began, the passengers held a religious service on board the *City of Paris* to give thanks for their deliverance. Subsequently, the American Line's *Ohio* encountered the *Aldersgate* towing the *City of Paris* and turned around to escort the tow into safe harbor. The *City of Paris*'s anxious passengers finally would reach port at 4:50 A.M. on March 29, when their liner slowly entered Cork Harbor. By this time, the ship was drawing an incredible 35 feet astern, and her bow was high out of the water.

Plans were undertaken immediately to repair the ship and return her to service. Comments were made in newspaper accounts about the remarkable construction of the liner, which had permitted her to survive so devastating an explosion and to bring her passengers and cargo safely to port. Her watertight subdivisions had held and she had remained afloat with two of her largest and most vital compartments completely flooded.

It had been thought that a four-ship fleet would be adequate to maintain a weekly sailing schedule, with the addition of the two new liners. However, the accident to the *City of Paris* brought the aging *City of Chester* back into service for another year, with the occasional extra sailings being taken by the *City of Richmond*, which was finally sold in 1891. During its 43-year history (1850–93), the Inman Line suffered a number of marine disasters. The ninth and final loss of an Inman ship took place on July 1, 1892, when the *City of Chicago* went ashore in dense fog near the Old Head of Kinsale and became a total

This imposing stern shot of the City of Paris *(1889) in drydock underlines the vulnerability of her twin propellers. Since the hull lines curved inward toward the stern the propellers had to be supported by external struts projecting from the hull. This contributed to excessive vibration and vulnerability to external damage from debris.*
The Engineer, July 25, 1890

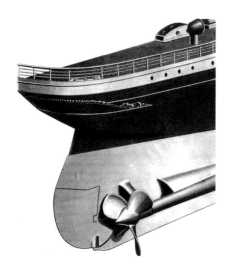

A cutaway drawing shows the rudder of the City of Paris *and the exposed position of the starboard propeller. When the liner was rebuilt in 1899 external improvements included extending the hull lines to completely enclose the propeller shafts and strengthen their supports. Internally, the liner was provided with quadruple-expansion engines and a new lease on life.* Scientific American, May 24, 1890

The City of New York *races through the night with the White Star* Teutonic *(1889) in hot pursuit. F. Adams did this sketch for* Frank Leslie's Illustrated Newspaper *(August 31, 1889). The view is an extraordinary night scene with the search lights of the* City of New York *playing forward and the great dome over the first-class dining room illuminated forward of the bridge.*

loss. There were no casualties, but once again the old *City of Chester* took a place in the sailing schedule, as she was the reserve ship—in a very active reserve capacity.

Inman was Griscom's flagship line in the late 1880s, but the Société Anonyme de Navigation Belge-Américaine (Red Star Line) was also most active. Between 1883 and 1889, the Red Star Line's New York–Antwerp service steadily expanded. An average of

The luck of the sailing schedule pitted express liners against each other on certain Atlantic crossings. In August 1889 the Inman and International City of New York *and the White Star* Teutonic *raced over 3,000 miles from Liverpool to New York. The two great rivals were in sight of each other most of the time. In this dramatic view from the stern of the* City of New York *her passengers are waving at those on the* Teutonic *as the two ships keep pace with each other. In the end the* City of New York *won and entered New York harbor first.*

25,000 steerage passengers per year were landed in New York, and there was a slow but relatively steady increase in the better classes—specifically, from 1,500 to 4,000 passengers per year. The Philadelphia figures greatly exceeded these, with a total of more than 40,000 passengers in 1882 alone. In 1888, the Red Star Line was able to order a much bigger vessel than ever before. The *Friesland*, built by Thomson's on the Clyde shortly after the Inman *Cities*, was the only Red Star liner constructed with a clipper bow. The new liner entered service late in 1889 with passenger accommodations for 226 first-class, 102 second-class, and 600 steerage-class passengers. Rumors of the sale of the *Vaderland* and the *Zeeland* had been making the rounds for at least seven years before the construction of the *Friesland* finally made this possible in 1889. The Red Star passenger totals continued to rise and during 1891 reached over 41,000 for the Port of New York. Hence, the Société Anonyme de Navigation Belge-Américaine was clearly prospering and carrying its weight in Griscom's International Navigation Company.

The *City of Paris* reentered the Inman Line service in May of 1891, just in time to help the *City of New York* meet the challenge of the White Star Line's *Teutonic* (1889, 9,984 tons) and *Majestic* (1890, 9,965 tons). These four liners were the most evenly matched pair of record breakers ever to compete for the transatlantic Blue Riband. Average crossing times were nearly the same, and record passages were lowered by only minutes as the four liners sought to obtain the coveted title for their owners. The competition was strenuous, and the White Star Line was a subsidized concern that could better stand the grueling pace in the long run.

Clement A. Griscom was fully aware of this fact and therefore redoubled his efforts to obtain American recognition for his line of first-class steamers. Congress was pressured to change the government policy on federal subsidies and to alter the rigidity of the American ship-registration laws. The reviving American interest in navies and maritime affairs aided this campaign, although it was slow to pick up speed and gain momentum. Nevertheless, Griscom and his associates (including the Pennsylvania Railroad Company) pushed the issue as forcefully and judiciously as possible. Griscom, in particular, must have felt that the entire survival of his multifaceted maritime empire hung upon the need for the United States government to recognize the importance of the American merchant marine and support the lines.[22]

Clement A. Griscom took the case of his American-owned line to the U.S. Congress. In testimony before the Senate Commerce Committee, the president of the Inman and International Navigation Company explained the situation of the Line, owing to the mistreatment it had received from the British government. The plight of the Inman Line, with two costly new express steamers and no subsidy to defray their operating expenses, was quite obvious. The prize that Griscom was after was American registry for his liners, which would permit him to apply for an American subsidy under the terms of the Postal Aid Act of 1891, the key to the puzzle.

Two distinct shipping subsidy measures had been placed before Congress in 1890; one concerned ocean mail steamers and the other freighters and sailing ships. Both bills had been drawn up by Senator William P. Frye of Maine, the Senate's leading proponent of government aid to the American merchant marine. Senator Frye had undertaken a detailed study of the state of the American shipping industry and of the fundamental costs of marine operations. He therefore was well versed in the condition and economics of the merchant marine.

The various amounts stated in the bill for subsidies to the shipping industry were accepted by the Senate. Unfortunately, the House of Representatives was of a different mind, as well as in a frantic haste to adjourn, when the measure came up for consideration. When an amendment was brought forward to slash the proposed subsidy for first-class liners by one-third, it was speedily passed—much to the displeasure of the bill's backers. The amended bill was immediately passed. In this manner was enacted the first significant piece of legislation to aid the American merchant marine in 32 years.

By the Act of Congress, the postmaster general was authorized to make contracts with American citizens for carrying the transatlantic mail for a period of five to ten years:

> Proposals must be invited by public advertisement three months before the letting of the contract. Vessels must be American built, owned and officered. The crew of a mail steamer must be at least one-fourth American for the first two years, one-third for the next three years, and one-half, thereafter.[23]

Since it was not reasonable to lay down the same set of requirements and subsidies for all vessels, four classes of mail steamers based on tonnage and speed were established. First-class steamers had to be at least 8,000 tons and be capable of maintaining a speed of around 20 knots. Second-class liners had to be at least 5,000 tons and be capable of maintaining a speed of 16 knots; third-class steamers had to be at least 2,500 tons, with a cruising speed of at least 14 knots; and fourth-class vessels had to be at least 1,500 tons, with a cruising speed of 12 knots. All ships in the first three categories had to be constructed of either iron or steel, while the fourth-class steamers could be of iron, steel, or wood.

SECTIONAL VIEW OF THE "CITY OF NEW YORK"
OCEAN STEAM-SHIPS, FROM THE "SAVANNAH" TO THE "CITY OF NEW YORK."

The City of New York, *as the largest and fastest ship in the world, was honored by* Harper's Weekly *with a detailed sectional that showed the magnificence of her internal subdivisions. The bulkheads reached to the Main Deck and made her one of the safest vessels ever built.*

THE STEAM SHIP "CITY OF NEW YORK."

The entry of the City of New York *into service was celebrated with a number of illustrations and a general panorama of the evolution of the transatlantic steamer. A dramatic broadside of the* City of New York *was featured.* Supplement to Harper's Weekly, *March 30, 1889*

It was intended that the major liners would serve as armed merchant cruisers (or troopships) in the event of war, and all steamers in the first three classes were required to be built under the general supervision of the Navy Department. The reward forthcoming to the owners of vessels qualifying for the different classes was fixed at a maximum of four dollars per mile for the first-class liners, two dollars per mile for the second-class vessels, and one dollar per mile for the third-class steamers. All those in the fourth class were to be compensated at a rate of 66⅔ cents per mile—an accountant's nightmare! All subsidies were to be paid only on the outward crossings of each voyage and not for the homeward passages, with a further restriction of not more than $12,000 per voyage for those liners serving between the United States and the United Kingdom.[24]

The Postal Aid Act did not result in a flood of offers to begin a first-class line of mail steamers on the North Atlantic. In fact, not a single offer was forthcoming, since a subsidy of only $12,000 per voyage was far from sufficient inducement to invest millions in a fleet of expensive ocean greyhounds. The offer could look attractive only to an established line in need of a subsidy, but there was no such commercial endeavor under the American flag.

There was, however, the American-owned and -operated Inman and International Navigation Company, which had been denied the British subsidy and was ready, willing, and able to undertake a transatlantic service under the American mail-contract terms. This was the moment when Clement A. Griscom ushered his two new express liners, the *City of New York* and *City of Paris*, both Blue Riband liners, before the Senate Commerce Committee. Griscom petitioned Congress to allow his two Atlantic champions American registry. In return, he offered to build two larger vessels in American yards to complete the quartet of superliners necessary for a regular weekly transatlantic service at a speed of 20 knots.

The dining room of the City of Paris *was one of the most elegant public rooms on any transatlantic liner. It soared two decks to a huge reinforced dome-skylight that was situated forward of the bridge on the liner. The chairs swung in to the long tables and entertainment was provided by a pipe organ.*

For several reasons, Congress did not have to hesitate over the Inman offer. It did not appear as though a transatlantic service would ever be taken up by an American concern. The Inman and International Line nearly filled this qualification, since the majority of its shares were owned by American citizens. Furthermore, the establishment of such a proud line of ships under the American flag would bolster American pride and interest in the American merchant marine. At the same time, the action was a slap at the British government, which apparently had tried to ruin the American investors. Finally, the offer to build two consorts for the brand-new and already famous *City of New York* and *City of Paris* in American shipyards promised to provide a great stimulus for the American shipbuilding industry, which sorely needed two such prestigious orders.

On May 10, 1892, Congress approved a measure giving American registry to the *City of New York* and the *City of Paris*, thereby paving the way for the return of the American flag to the North Atlantic in a most spectacular manner. The Inman and International Line changed its name to the American Line.

The Acts of Congress that created the Postal Aid Act of 1891 and gave American registry to the passenger liners *New York* and *Paris* were the first steps in the formulation of a merchant-marine policy by the United States government in the years before World War I. These acts represented the first major pieces of benevolent legislation toward the American shipping industry after a period of 30 years in the wilderness of statutory neglect.

Chapter 7

THE AMERICAN LINE OF 1893

The creation of the great American Line in 1892 brought a desire for a new pier and terminal for New York. This was constructed in lower Manhattan and became Pier 14 and Pier 15 of the American and Red Star Lines, North River. The pier was at the foot of Fulton Street, adjoining the Cortland Street Ferry of the Pennsylvania Railroad.

T he passage by Congress of the Postal Aid Act in 1891 heralded a new age in American maritime history. The new legislation created a general system of postal compensation based upon the tonnage and speed of ships with routes to be determined by the postmaster general. The rate of compensation in no way was regarded as liberal, however, since even first-class vessels would only receive $4 a mile, but at least it represented a start. Primary goals of the new legislation were stated as:

First.   To secure regular and quicker service to countries now reached;

Second. To make new and direct commercial exchanges with countries not now reached;

The Cities *moved south from Liverpool to Southampton and the principal American Line service was switched to Southampton–New York. This broadside shows one of the* Cities *approaching her new terminal at Southampton.*

Third.	To develop new and enlarge old markets in the interest of producers and consumers under the reciprocity treaties completed and in progress;
Fourth.	To assist the promotion of a powerful naval reserve; and
Fifth.	To establish a training school for American seamen.[1]

With the passage of the bill permitting American Registry for the *City of New York* and the *City of Paris,* Clement A. Griscom at last possessed what he had been striving for years to achieve—the ability to create and sustain a first-class American-flag passenger line on the North Atlantic.

In Britain, the new American Line management undertook a major alteration in the Line's European terminus. After 20 years, the American Line prepared to move its head-quarters south from Liverpool to Southampton. The move from the Mersey to the English Channel placed the American Line in direct competition with Hamburg-American and Norddeutscher Lloyd but reduced the direct threat to the Cunard and White Star Lines. Negotiations between Thomas Ismay, John Burns (Lord Inverclyde), and Clement Griscom saw Griscom agreeing to place emphasis on Antwerp as the European port of call for the International Navigation Company (Red Star Line) and to transfer the Inman North Atlantic operations, to be known as the American Line, to Southampton. In return for these "concessions," White Star was to pay Griscom

$20,000 a year for five years and Cunard was to pay Griscom $10,000 a year for the same period.[2] Subsequent negotiations modified these terms slightly. Griscom thereby obtained almost unbelievable help from his strongest competitors to cover the costs of the move south. There is reason to believe that Griscom was prepared to take the American Line to Southampton anyway!

Antwerp had been the principal European terminal for the Red Star Line since 1873, and one is left wondering what concession Griscom made here. None is apparent. With regard to the transfer of the first-class Inman and International ships to Southampton, this also appears to be what Griscom was prepared to do. The concessions (subsidies?) he obtained from Cunard, White Star, and the London and Southwestern Railway were very substantial indeed. New docks, and new special trains, while all the miscellaneous moving expenses were paid for by his erstwhile competitors. No wonder that Griscom was regarded as a hard-dealing shipping magnate. The American Line was the first of the British-based North Atlantic passenger services to make the move to Southampton, whose advantages were substantial in terms of proximity to London, tides (two a day), and deepwater channels.

The London and Southwestern Railway Company took possession of the Southampton docks on November 1, 1892, for a payment of £1,350,000. The quay wall, excluding the new docks planned for the American Line, was 1,800 feet long and included facilities for berthing the largest vessels afloat. Furthermore, the railway company committed itself to expend an additional £250,000 in the construction of a graving dock at Southampton capable of receiving the largest liners then planned. The Town Council of Southampton agreed to a nominal tax-abatement program and ceded to the railway 20 acres of land for the enlargement of the dock area. For the first time, it was mentioned that if all the pieces of the puzzle fell into place, the Inman Line vessels would begin running to Southampton in March 1893.

In America, a formal bid was submitted to the United States postmaster general for the North Atlantic mail routes. The fate of Griscom's efforts to secure the future of his maritime concerns through American mail contracts was followed closely on both sides of the Atlantic. It was reported in London that the International Navigation Company had "just submitted to the American Government their proposal for conveyance of mails from New York to Southampton," and that the results were eagerly awaited by the inhabitants of Southampton.[3] No one would have to wait long.

The news that the postmaster general accepted the tender of the International Navigation Company for the American Line's New York–Southampton service, and also for the Red Star Line's New York–Southampton–Cherbourg–Antwerp service, was greeted with great jubilation. When the formal contracts were signed by Postmaster General John Wanamaker on October 13, 1892, the future of Southampton looked as bright as that of the International Navigation Company. Optimistic individuals thought that the two mail contracts would require the construction of at least five new first-class vessels. The services were to commence in March 1893, under the terms of the new

American Postal Aid Act. This development from a nation that had neglected its merchant marine for 30 years produced considerable unrest in transatlantic shipping circles. The response in Britain was best expressed in the journal *Fairplay:*

> Dismal forebodings cannot be repressed. We remember the days when the
> Yankees had a practical monopoly of the Atlantic trade and the Stars and
> Stripes were found flying from the peaks of the smartest vessels afloat and in
> every European port. In the days of wooden ships the Americans gave us points
> in marine architecture. Nobody who knows anything of yachting but is power-
> fully impressed by the Americans' natural skill in construction and seamanship,
> wherein they cannot be ranked second even to ourselves. The demand for free
> ships in America is steadily growing into an articulate cry.... When Jonathan
> returns to reason in shipbuilding and shipowning we shall not have our troubles
> to seek. Meanwhile, the efforts made in America to meet the case of the
> American shareholders of the Inman Line and the ambitions of Philadelphia
> shipbuilders to add thereto are signs of the times which cannot be ignored.[4]

Improvements in New York included plans for the acquisition by the International Navigation Company, through its agents, Peter Wright & Sons, of a handsome new pier for the American Line. For several years, the company had wanted to secure a new pier, and this had become particularly urgent with the commissioning of the *City of New York* and the *City of Paris*, both of which were longer than the existing piers. For its part, New York City had since 1871 been pursuing a plan to encircle the island of Manhattan with bulkheads and, where appropriate, piers. As part of this "new plan" for the North River, West Street was to be widened from 70 to 250 feet. It was intended that Pier 14, as the next structure to be built was known on the plans, would lie between Vesey and Fulton Streets. The site became available late in 1891, and the International Navigation Company made its move. There were a number of applicants for the pier, including the Baltimore and Ohio Railroad, so the campaign to acquire the lease had to be handled subtly. On January 28, 1892, Wright appeared before the dock commissioners with an offer of $40,000 rent per year for the pier. He was told that he could have it for $42,500 and was given 10 days to make up his mind. The International Navigation Company readily accepted the lease at the figure the dock commissioners asked. Later, controversy ensued about how the lease was handled. The president of the Dock Board, J. Sergeant Cram, explained that if all the leases were given openly, the railroads would drive all the shipping lines out of Manhattan by driving the prices too high. Therefore, the New York dock commissioners, who were strongly pro-shipping, did not bother to list the important new dock as being available and simply undertook the awarding of the lease under the category of "new business" so that the railroads would not have time to act. By this means, the International Navigation Company acquired the lease on a highly satisfactory pier site.

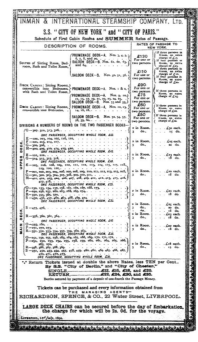

The Inman and International Steamship Company Limited possessed the two largest and fastest ships in the world by 1889. A weekly service was mandatory and this pamphlet shows the first-class sailings for July 20–November 30, 1892. Rates also are shown.

When the blasting and dredging was accomplished, the pier site was turned over to the American Line in April 1893, and construction of the above-water terminal began immediately. The dock commissioners renamed Pier 14 "Washington Pier," but it always would be more well known by its number. The architects for the American Line designed an imposing two-story structure of iron, with appropriately ornate embellishments. The first floor was to be used for cargo and provisioning, while passengers, for the first time, would be able to walk directly on board their liner from the second floor, which was reserved exclusively for them. This was considered a great advance in comfort and convenience, separating passengers from the dust and dirt that accompanied the loading of cargo and provisions.

The site was occupied on May 1, 1893. Pier 14 was the first one built by the city of New York for a steamship company under the new master plan for the harbor. The new pier was 720 feet long and 125 feet wide, making it the largest maritime terminal in New York—120 feet longer and 55 feet wider than any other steamship pier in the harbor. The completed structure was opened on Saturday, December 28, 1893, with the arrival of the *City of New York*. Passengers marveled that they were able to stroll off the ship and onto the second floor of the pier. The spacious second floor was devoted almost exclusively to passengers, with only a few offices for the Line at the eastern end. Ample facilities for baggage were created as part of the pier design, as well as convenient access to cabs and carriages. On the north bulkhead, the wing for storage of merchandise was 180 feet long; on the south bulkhead, it was 75 feet long.

Captain Frederick Watkins was the popular master of the City of Paris. *When the American Line obtained Congressional authorization in 1892 to give the ship American registry, Captain Watkins applied for American citizenship in order to retain his command, but this proved impossible to resolve. He was able to continue as master of the British-flag tonnage.*

The total cost of the structure and its fixtures was over $300,000. A major new asset of the International Navigation Company, Pier 14 made it possible for the Line to consolidate its business from two other locations, one in Jersey City and the other at the foot of Christopher Street.

Preparations for the transfer of the Inman vessels to the American flag included an effort to speed up the naturalization process for those senior officers of the Inman Line who were not American citizens and who wished to retain their positions with the new American Line. Griscom had no desire to lose the services of all the senior officers of the Inman Line, many of whom had spent decades in the employ of the concern and knew its vessels from stem to stern. The U.S. Treasury Department in Washington, D.C., was petitioned to speed up the paperwork so that the captains could remain in command of their ships when they were transferred to the American flag. The Act of Congress had stipulated that the officers of the ships must be American citizens, and there was no desire on anyone's part to try to modify that clause. The officers promptly took out their papers, but the probationary period of five years threatened to make them ineligible to retain their commands. The simple declaration of intent to obtain citizenship was not considered sufficient basis for fulfilling the requirements of the congressional act. As a test case, the Inman and International Steamship Company petitioned the Treasury Department to retain Captain Frederick Watkins as master of the *City of Paris* during his probationary period for naturalization. The commissioner of navigation already had handed down a ruling that any individual must fulfill all aspects of the naturalization procedure before he could legally be considered an American citizen and qualified to command an American-flag vessel. Secretary of the Treasury Charles Foster and

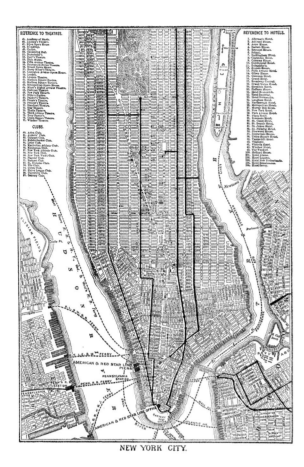

REFERENCE TO THEATRES.

REFERENCE TO HOTELS.

NEW YORK CITY.

A map of lower Manhattan with the American Line Piers and offices highlighted was provided to passengers. Passengers disembarked on the second floor of the new American Line terminal, which kept them away from baggage and cargo.

Commissioner O'Brien of the Navigation Bureau both were willing to make an exception if it could be done within the law, and if the attorney general would concur—in other words, if it could be done without too much protest. Some felt that only additional legislation could permit the exceptions to be tolerated within the law.

When questioned about the matter by reporters, Philadelphia shipbuilder Charles Cramp called the whole discussion just a trumped-up attempt to embarrass the new American Line. He made a point that there were two new vessels building in Britain that the British officers could command, and that there already were American officers in the employ of the Inman Line to whom the commands of the *City of New York* and the *City of Paris* could, and would, be given. Thus, the intent of Congress that the two ships be totally manned by American citizens after their transfer to American registry would be upheld without any manipulation of the immigration and naturalization laws.[5]

It seems apparent that Griscom was willing to go quite far to retain the services of popular and well-known masters of the *City of New York* and the *City of Paris*, and that the American owners of the Inman Line were prepared to bring pressure on the American government for a solution to their problem. However, they were not prepared

NAME.	Vessel's Dimension.			Engines.	Engine Cylinders.		Boilers.		
	Length.	Breadth.	Moulded Draught.	Indicated Horse Power.	Diameters.	Stroke.	Heating Surface.	Area Fire grate.	Working Pressure.
	ft. in.	ft. in.	ft. in.			ft. in.	in sq. ft.	in sq. ft.	lb.
SS. City of Rome..............	542 6	52 0	21 5½	11,890	$\frac{3}{46 \text{ in.}}$ $\frac{3}{86 \text{ in.}}$	6 0	29,286	1,398	90
" Normandie.......	459 4	49 11	19 9½	6,959	$\frac{3}{35\frac{7}{16} \text{ in.}}$ $\frac{3}{74\frac{7}{8} \text{ in.}}$	5 7	21,404	756	85
" Arizona.......	450 0	45 1½	18 9	6,300	$\frac{1}{62 \text{ in.}}$ $\frac{2}{90 \text{ in.}}$	5 6	..	..	90
" Orient	445 0	46 0	21 4½	5,433	$\frac{1}{60 \text{ in.}}$ $\frac{2}{85 \text{ in.}}$	5 0	..	..	75
" Stirling Castle................	420 0	50 0	22 3	8,396	$\frac{1}{62 \text{ in.}}$ $\frac{2}{90 \text{ in.}}$	5 6	21,161	787	100
" Elbe	420 0	44 9	20 0	5,665	$\frac{1}{60 \text{ in.}}$ $\frac{2}{85 \text{ in.}}$	5 0			
" Umbria and Etruria	500 0	57 0	22 6	14,321	$\frac{1}{71 \text{ in.}}$ $\frac{2}{105 \text{ in.}}$	6 0	38,817	1,606	110
" Aurania.	470 0	57 0	20 0	8,500	$\frac{1}{68 \text{ in.}}$ $\frac{2}{91 \text{ in.}}$	6 0	23,284	1,001	90
" America................... ...	432 0	51 0	26 0	7,354	$\frac{1}{63 \text{ in.}}$ $\frac{2}{91 \text{ in.}}$	5 6	22,750	882	95
" Servia........................	515 0	52 0	23 3½	10,300	$\frac{1}{72 \text{ in.}}$ $\frac{2}{100 \text{ in.}}$	6 6	27,483	1,014	90
" Alaska	500 0	50 0	21 0	10,500	$\frac{1}{68 \text{ in.}}$ $\frac{2}{100 \text{ in.}}$	6 0	..	..	100
" Ems.......	430 0	46 10	20 7½	7,251	$\frac{1}{62 \text{ in.}}$ $\frac{2}{86 \text{ in.}}$	5 0	19,700	780	100
" Aller.........................	438 0	48 0	21 0	7,974	$\frac{1}{44 \text{ in.}}$ $\frac{1}{70 \text{ in.}}$ $\frac{1}{100 \text{ in.}}$	6 0	22,630	799	150
" Ormuz.....	465 6	52 1½	..	9,000	$\frac{1}{46 \text{ in.}}$ $\frac{1}{73 \text{ in.}}$ $\frac{1}{112 \text{ in.}}$	6 0	26,000	850	150
" Lahn.........................	448 5	49 0	..	9,500	$\frac{2}{32\frac{1}{2} \text{ in.}}$ $\frac{1}{68 \text{ in.}}$ $\frac{2}{85 \text{ in.}}$	6 0	.	..	150
" City of New York	560 0	63 3	25 0	20,000	$\frac{2}{45 \text{ in.}}$ $\frac{2}{71 \text{ in.}}$ $\frac{2}{113 \text{ in.}}$	5 0	50,265	1,293	150

The "Hulls and Engines of Atlantic Steamers" ranging from the City of Rome *(1881) to the* City of New York *(1889) were provided for comparison by* Scientific American *(September 15, 1888).*

to fight a damaging public relations battle over the issue of citizenship for a few officers. When the entire problem became too complex and was being aired too thoroughly in the newspapers, the Inman and International management dropped the issue and let Charles Cramp defuse the situation.

The issue of deck officers was one matter, that of engineers another. Secretary of the Treasury Foster bluntly informed George Uhler, president of the Mechanical Engineers' Brotherhood Association (MEBA), "that he doubted the competency of American engineers to run the engines of the *New York* and the *Paris*, and that he interpreted Section 4.131, Revised Statutes of the United States, which states that "Officers of American vessels shall be American citizens," as meaning that a declaration of intention to become American citizens was all that was necessary to be done by aliens before having licenses granted to them."[6] Uhler informed a meeting of the MEBA No. 4 in Chicago, Illinois, that an appeal against Secretary Foster's ruling had been filed in the U.S. Circuit Court, New York, and that protest meetings were being held throughout the lake ports to drum up public awareness and unite the engineers against the ruling. Nearly 300 engineers

The City of Chicago *(1883, 5,202 tons, 431 feet by 45 feet, 14 knots) was ordered for the Dominion Line but bought on the stocks and launched for Inman. A valuable addition to the fleet after the refusal of the* City of Rome *(1881), she was unusual in the Inman fleet in that she had a straight stem. The* City of Chicago *had accommodations for 140 first, 100 second, and 850 third. She ran aground in dense fog at the Old Head of Kinsale, Ireland, July 1, 1892.*

and pilots were present at the Chicago meeting and entered their protest against the action of the International Navigation Company and ex-Secretary of the Treasury Foster, who had just left office.

The first American master of the *City of New York* was Captain John C. Jamison who had been in the employ of the International Navigation Company for many years. Previously, Captain Jamison had commanded the *Switzerland, Belgenland,* and *Westernland* of the Red Star Line and made a considerable reputation for himself as a skillful sailor, a tireless worker, and a genial conversationalist. Captain Jamison was quite a small man physically, but the trust of the directors of the Line was shown when they gave him the command of the flagship. It was also intended that Jamison's appointment would blunt some of the criticism about alien officers on the American-flag vessels of the International Navigation Company.

Inman and International suffered one additional ship loss on July 1, 1892, when the *City of Chicago* hit the Old Head of Kinsale, a rocky promontory along the southern coast of Ireland, and became a total loss. No lives were lost, but new tonnage was going to be needed. As a result of the passage of the American legislation, the contract for several new steamers went to William Cramp and Sons, Philadelphia, who had built the original American Line quartet. The announcement of the signing of the contract between Griscom and Cramp was leaked to the press in August 1892. The contract was regarded as an opportunity for an American builder to show the British shipyards what could be done with a first-class ship.

The summer and fall of 1892 dealt kindly with both the *City of New York* and the *City of Paris.* Between August 18 and 23, the *City of New York* crossed from New York to Queenstown in five days, 19 hours, 57 minutes at 20.12 knots over a 2,814-mile track. Daily runs were impressive at 394, 467, 460, 475, 468, and 76 miles, resulting in the Inman liner beating the record of the White Star *Teutonic* by one hour, six minutes, when the latter's average speed had been 19.78 knots. The *City of New York* at last appeared to be coming into her own on the North Atlantic. Between October 14 and 19, the *City of Paris* streaked across from Queenstown to Sandy Hook in five days, 14 hours, 24 minutes, with an average speed of 20.70 knots over a 2,782-mile track. Daily runs totaled 448, 508, 503, 505, 530, and 288 miles. The 530-mile run on one day broke all previous daily records as well. The *City of Paris* beat her previous best by one hour and 34 minutes, which to contemporaries seemed altogether remarkable for its margin. She was the indisputable Queen of the Atlantic.

A table shows how the North Atlantic record had been reduced over the previous two years:

VESSEL	TIME OF PASSAGE			AVERAGE HOURLY SPEED
City of Paris	5 days	19 hrs.	18 min.	20.01
Majestic	5	18	08	20.10
Teutonic	5	16	31	20.35
City of Paris	5	15	58	20.48
City of Paris	5	14	24	20.70[7]

Captain Watkins and his officers and crew were confident that the Blue Riband passage of the *City of Paris* would not be surpassed until the new Cunarder *Campania*, still under construction in Britain, entered the lists. Even then, they had high hopes for the new ships being built at the Cramp Shipyard in Philadelphia. It was announced that the *City of Paris* would have the honor of taking the first sailing from Southampton on March 3, 1893.

The Westernland *is shown on the Delaware River approaching Pier 53 of the American Line at the foot of Washington Avenue, Philadelphia.*

THE BIRTH OF THE
GREAT AMERICAN LINE

The Frontispiece of the International Navigation Company's Facts for Travellers booklet (1897).

The formal transfer of the *City of New York* to American registry, and the official date of the establishment of the American Line, was planned for February 22, 1893. The occasion was one of great public interest. Advance notice was given to the American press, which responded with stories about the festivities on Washington's Birthday. The date was described as a "Red Letter Day" for the American Line, as Old Glory would be hoisted over the renamed *New York* and she would become the largest ship in the American merchant marine. President Benjamin Harrison, members of his cabinet, and hundreds of other dignitaries from Maine to Virginia were to be present. A special presidential train was to leave Washington for Jersey City. There the official guests would transfer to a steamboat, which would convey them to the liner, anchored off The Battery, for her rechristening. Simultaneously, the steamer *Howard Carroll* was to leave Pier 43, North River, with the New York contingent, and the two

Saluting another passing vessel, the City of New York *is outward bound for Southampton.*

On February 22, 1893, the American flag was raised by President Benjamin Harrison over the new American liner New York, *symbolizing the rebirth of the American merchant marine. The artist's depiction fails to note that the event took place in one of the worst blizzards of the century.*

steamers were to come alongside the *New York* at about noon. The American flag that the president was to hoist was made of silk, and for the first time it was announced that the house flag of the new American Line would be a blue eagle on a white field. The rechristening was to occur immediately upon President Harrison's arrival, and the event was to be heralded with a 21-gun salute from the USS *Chicago* and The Battery. Following the ceremony, the *New York* was to steam out as far as Sandy Hook with her load of dignitaries while they enjoyed a feast of Olympian proportions. She was to return to the pier at sunset. No human effort was spared to make the day one of the most memorable in American maritime history—but nature intervened.

As an observer drolly commented:

> Weather more bleak than that which attended this ceremony could hardly have been dreaded. But the gale that filled the air with frozen rain and snow and whipped the harbor into its angriest mood had no deterrent effect upon the enthusiasm of the occasion. It was a hurrah event from start to finish, and it tried the lungs and stirred the blood of a company on board the ship such as

has been seldom brought together, and of uncounted spectators in a surrounding fleet that swarmed on the bobbing waters on all sides of the big ship and on shore lining the Battery walls and near-by shores of Jersey.[1]

Everything that could go wrong did. A fierce winter low-pressure system blanketed the East Coast from New England to Virginia. In Virginia and Maryland, icy rain and scattered snow squalls lashed the countryside. The farther north one went, the rain turned to sleet and then to heavy snow. The Pennsylvania Railroad had mustered every available man and piece of snow-removal equipment to keep the track clear. President Harrison boarded the Presidential Express accompanied by a large group of cabinet officials, naval officers, congressmen, and senators, and the train left the nation's capital on schedule.

So many dignitaries had accepted the invitation of the American Line directors to the flag-raising ceremony that the official party was divided between two trains, and additional Pullman cars were added to the Southern Express of the PRR, which departed Washington ahead of the Presidential Express. The powerful engines and heavy Pullman cars made excellent headway as far as Philadelphia, when disaster struck. The Southern Express stopped at Broad Street Station for more guests and departed at 10:25 A.M., beginning to pick up speed as it curved around West Philadelphia. The track conditions were very icy and treacherous. Engineer Thomas "Jockey" Jones of the Express did not see a danger signal on the control tower ordering the train to stop. As the Southern Express slammed by the tower, Jones caught sight of the danger signal out of the corner of his eye, but it was too late. Suddenly, to his horror, he saw a local train slowly crossing the main line just ahead of the Express. The local was pulling into South Street Station. Jones made frantic efforts to apply the brakes, but the massive momentum of the Southern Express was not to be stopped, and the steel cowcatcher of the express engine slammed into the middle of the last car of the Morton commuter train, throwing the lightweight car 50 feet from the track. Jones leaped from the cab seconds before the impact, although his fireman remained at his station. There was no damage to the heavy engine of the Southern Express, and no one was injured on board. On the other hand, the last car of the Morton commuter train was a mangled wreck, with four persons killed instantly, 15 injured seriously enough to require hospitalization, and a number of others who accepted treatment for wounds before being released.

The Southern Express slid to a stop, and the air was filled with the cries of individuals trapped in the wreckage. A crowd of excited people soon gathered, as the victims were rushed to University Hospital. Some of the dignitaries, including Congressmen Dingley and Belknap, ex-Postmaster General Frank Hatton, and Senator Washburn left the Southern Express to render assistance to the wounded until the ambulances arrived. Congressman Belknap was particularly praised for his courage and resourcefulness in assisting the injured. It was Belknap who found the severed head of one woman and tenderly placed it with her body, which was some distance away. Mr. and Mrs. Edward L. Minzer had died instantly in the crash, which had decapitated both of them. Their 10-year-old son survived with a vivid memory of the express train's engine suddenly

The stern of the New York *is surrounded by tugboats as President Benjamin Harrison raises Old Glory. The speeches and reception were cut short by the blizzard.*

coming through the side of the commuter car. He was taken to the hospital without knowing the fate of his parents. Thomas Jones, one of the most experienced engineers on the railroad, was devastated by the disaster, and, after doing all he could to help the victims, was sent to his home in Philadelphia. Some of the dignitaries on the train had had enough excitement for the day and left the train to return to Washington.

Within half an hour, the wreckage of the commuter train was sufficiently cleared for the Southern Express to continue to New York. At first word was flashed ahead that the Presidential Express had been in the wreck, but this was false, and the train with the president on board simply was held a little behind the Southern Express until the track was cleared. The accident meant President Harrison was about an hour late arriving in Jersey City.

Throughout the morning, the snow continued to fall, and freight trains in northern Pennsylvania and central New York were moving only with the assistance of four and five engines. The blizzard was being compared with the Great Blizzard of March 1888, which had shattered all known records. Snowfalls in some instances reached three feet, with extensive drifting. The scene in New York was torturous, with a 25-to-35-mile-an-hour gale whipping across the harbor and sending snow and spray everywhere. The sailors on the *New York* were forced to sweep the decks constantly in order to keep ahead of the drifts on the ship.

The *New York*, under the command of an American, Captain John C. Jamison, had been polished as never before. Jamison backed his big charge out into the North River at midmorning during a temporary break in the snow squalls and brought the liner down to the tip of Manhattan. There the *New York* was anchored between Bedloe's Island and The Battery, with her bow headed somewhat north of the new Statue of Liberty (1886) and her stern toward Castle William. Around her, a large flotilla of

President Harrison Raising the Flag on the Steamer *New York, as drawn by T. de Thulstrup. Everyone was dressed as warmly as possible for the event as gale-force winds whipped snow across New York Harbor.*
Harper's Weekly, March 4, 1893

pleasure craft gathered to view the raising of the flag. The snow squalls whipped across the harbor with such vengeance that the smaller boats bobbed and dipped constantly, while periodically neither the flotilla nor the shore was visible because of the blizzard.

The *Howard Carroll* brought the New York contingent from Pier 43 around noon, and she was packed with dignitaries. Governor Roswell Pettibone Flower begged off with a plea of pressing business at the last moment, but Mayor Thomas F. Gilroy was present. The excursion steamer was held for a half hour because some of the public figures had been attending a funeral across town and had to fight their way to the pier through the snow. Massed on the two decks of the *Howard Carroll* were some of the cream of American industry and commerce. Andrew Carnegie of Carnegie Steel, J.V.S. Oddie of the New York Yacht Club, George Wilson of the Chamber of Commerce, Aaron Vanderbilt, Samuel Wanamaker, Charles Cramp of the Cramp Shipyard, and George Hall of the Harland and Hollingsworth Shipyard were only a few. Among the representatives from the steamship companies were F.W.J. Hurst of the National Line, R.J. Curtis of White Star, William Coverly of the Anchor Line, Emil L. Boss of HAPAG, O.A. Taylor of Fall River, and Oswald and Harold Sanderson of the Wilson Line. Most of the major railroads were represented, led by a large delegation from the Pennsylvania Railroad, which had played so large a role in the creation of the first American Line 20 years earlier. The Pennsylvania Railroad delegation included President George B. Roberts, Vice President Frank Thomson, and General Manager C.E. Pugh, with many others. It could be argued that there were several men on the *New York* that frigid February day who were far more powerful than the president of the United States.

Clement A. Griscom, as president of the American Line, led a party of directors consisting of H.H. Houston, Joseph D. Potts, William H. Barnes, and William G.

Warden, all of whom greeted President Harrison when he finally reached Pennsylvania Station. The presidential party, including five cabinet members, quickly moved to the steamer *San Sloan*, which took them to the *New York*. Even if this patriotic occasion was almost the last official act of Harrison's administration, it remains amazing that Secretary of State John W. Foster, Secretary of Agriculture Jeremiah M. Rusk, Secretary of the Navy B.F. Tracy, Secretary of War Stephen B. Elkins, and Postmaster General John Wanamaker all should have been there. With a blare of bugles and a rendering of "Hail, Columbia," the president and his party filed on board the liner.

Owing to the weather and the hour, no time was wasted, and the dignitaries made their way immediately to the stern of the *New York*. A roped-off area marked the space reserved for Harrison and the most distinguished guests, while about 400 or 500 others crowded around. As one observer noted, no one minded the crush, because it was so terribly cold out in the blizzard-swept harbor. The wind was getting in its best licks, and no one could stand it for long. An observer commented that the company assembled on the open stern area of the liner was "made up of the class of men for whom pneumonia goes gunning," owing to their age and portly nature.

> As the President took his place in front of the halyards, he looked wan and pale, but apparently he was less mindful of the weather than those who surrounded him. The collar of his fur-lined coat lay folded in place, and his hat needed no extra pulling to keep it where it belonged. [Congressman W. Bourke] Cockran presented a contrasting picture. He bunched his shoulders up to his ears until his upturned overcoat collar and pulled-down hat met. He presented at the moment a fair type of the other spectators as he stepped forward to perform the office assigned him.[2]

To Cockran went the honor of representing the steamship line because he had introduced the bill into the House of Representatives permitting American registry for the *New York* and the *Paris*. He was well prepared for the occasion, even if he was almost frozen stiff.

> Mr. President: I have been asked by the officers of the company whose hospitality we enjoy to open the ceremony of the day. That ceremony consists of replacing a foreign flag by the flag of our country at the masthead of this triumph of the shipbuilder's art.
>
> It is a magnificent occasion. It marks a peaceful conquest—a conquest of civilization which we celebrate—when we annex this splendid specimen of marine architecture to the American merchant marine. Conquests such as these are alone compatible with the civilization of this age. Believing, as we do, that this celebration inaugurates a splendid revival of American shipbuilding, voicing, as I believe, the sentiments of the people obedient to the wishes of the company. I turn, Sir, to you, who stand before the world today a high type of citizenry, a

heroic defender of its integrity, an ornament to its magistracy and commit to your hands the patriotic task of unfurling from the masthead the flag which typifies American statesmanship, national liberty, and enlightened progress.

The conclusion of Congressman Cockran's remarks was greeted with loud applause. Captain Jamison then removed the silk American flag from its special case and began to secure its fastenings as the president stepped forward. President Harrison's remarks on the occasion were difficult to hear because of the full gale blowing across the harbor, but he is reported to have said:

> Mr. Cockran and Gentlemen: It gives me pleasure to consummate here to-day, by the act of lifting this flag, legislation to which I gave my hearty support. [Applause] I have felt as a citizen and as President the mortification which every American must feel who examines into the standing of the United States in the merchant marine of the world. I believed that we had reached an epoch in our development when the great work of internal developments was so far consummated that we might successfully take up the work of recovering our fair share in the carrying trade of the world. [Applause]
>
> We lift the flag today over one ship—a magnificent specimen of naval architecture—one of the best afloat on any sea. That event is interesting in itself, but its interest to me is in the fact that the ship is the type and precursor of many others that are to float the flag. [Applause]
>
> I deem it an entirely appropriate function that the President of the United States should lift the American flag.[3]

President Harrison's remarks were greeted with loud cheering from the throng on the stern of the *New York*, and he quickly raised the American flag to the top of the sternpost, where the wind whipped it straight out. Simultaneously, the new house flag of the American Line was broken out from the mainmast, and the blue eagle against a white background first saw the light of day.

The patriotic citizens by the thousands who lined The Battery and braved a freezing nor'easter in order to see the president raise the flag on the *New York* only knew that this had been accomplished by what followed. The Naval Reserve presented arms and cannons thundered from the decks of the cruiser *Chicago* and from the batteries of Castle William. The weather cooperated slightly with a temporary break in the clouds, which brought a weak ray of sunshine on the flag before it vanished in another snow squall. For the dignitaries on the *New York*, the bar was open, and a generous buffet was available in the main dining saloon.

President Harrison and the most important individuals present took their refreshment in the ladies' cabin. The foul weather and the delay because of the train wreck resulted in the cancellation of the cruise to Sandy Hook. The Presidential Express was made ready early, and Harrison left the ship at 3:20, after a stay of less than two and a

Sailing Schedule

1893 — NEW YORK TO SOUTHAMPTON

PARIS	Saturday,	May 6th,	9.00 a. m.
Berlin	Saturday,	May 13th,	4.00 p. m.
NEW YORK	Saturday,	May 20th,	9.00 a. m.
Chester	Saturday,	May 27th,	4.00 p. m.
PARIS	Saturday,	June 3d,	8.00 a. m.
Berlin	Saturday,	June 10th,	2.30 p. m.
NEW YORK	Saturday,	June 17th,	8.00 a. m.
Chester	Saturday,	June 24th,	2.30 p. m.
PARIS	Saturday,	July 1st,	7.00 a. m.
Berlin	Saturday,	July 8th,	1.00 p. m.
NEW YORK	Saturday,	July 15th,	7.00 a. m.
Chester	Saturday,	July 22d,	1.00 p. m.
PARIS	Wednesday,	July 26th,	3.30 p. m.
Berlin	Saturday,	Aug. 5th,	11.30 a. m.
NEW YORK	Wednesday,	Aug. 9th,	3.30 p. m.
PARIS	Wednesday,	Aug. 16th,	9.00 a. m.
Chester	Saturday,	Aug. 26th,	4.00 p. m.
NEW YORK	Wednesday,	Aug. 30th,	7.30 a. m.
PARIS	Wednesday,	Sept. 6th,	2.00 p. m.
Berlin	Saturday,	Sept. 16th,	10.00 a. m.
NEW YORK	Wednesday,	Sept. 20th,	1.00 p. m.
PARIS	Wednesday,	Sept. 27th,	7.00 a. m.
Chester	Saturday,	Oct. 7th,	3.30 p. m.
NEW YORK	Wednesday,	Oct. 11th,	7.00 a. m.
PARIS	Wednesday,	Oct. 18th,	11.30 a. m.
Berlin	Saturday,	Oct. 28th,	8.00 a. m.
NEW YORK	Wednesday,	Nov. 1st,	11.30 a. m.
PARIS	Wednesday,	Nov. 8th,	6.00 a. m.
Chester	Saturday,	Nov. 18th,	1.00 p. m.
NEW YORK	Wednesday,	Nov. 22d,	3.30 p. m.
PARIS	Wednesday,	Nov. 29th,	10.00 a. m.
Berlin	Saturday,	Dec. 9th,	6.00 a. m.
NEW YORK	Wednesday,	Dec. 13th,	8.30 a. m.

14

Sailing Schedule

1893 — SOUTHAMPTON TO NEW YORK

PARIS	Saturday,	May 20th,	12.00 noon
Berlin	Saturday,	May 27th,	12.00 noon
NEW YORK	Saturday,	June 3d,	12.00 noon
Chester	Saturday,	June 10th,	12.00 noon
PARIS	Saturday,	June 17th,	12.00 noon
Berlin	Saturday,	June 24th,	12.00 noon
NEW YORK	Saturday,	July 1st,	12.00 noon
Chester	Saturday,	July 8th,	12.00 noon
PARIS	Saturday,	July 15th,	12.00 noon
Berlin	Saturday,	July 22d,	12.00 noon
NEW YORK	Saturday,	July 29th,	12.00 noon
PARIS	Saturday,	Aug. 5th,	12.00 noon
Chester	Saturday,	Aug. 12th,	12.00 noon
NEW YORK	Saturday,	Aug. 19th,	12.00 noon
PARIS	Saturday,	Aug. 26th,	12.00 noon
Berlin	Saturday,	Sept. 2d,	12.00 noon
NEW YORK	Saturday,	Sept. 9th,	12.00 noon
PARIS	Saturday,	Sept. 16th,	12.00 noon
Chester	Saturday,	Sept. 23d,	12.00 noon
NEW YORK	Saturday,	Sept. 30th,	12.00 noon
PARIS	Saturday,	Oct. 7th,	12.00 noon
Berlin	Saturday,	Oct. 14th,	12.00 noon
NEW YORK	Saturday,	Oct. 21st,	12.00 noon
PARIS	Saturday,	Oct. 28th,	12.00 noon
Chester	Saturday,	Nov. 4th,	12.00 noon
NEW YORK	Saturday,	Nov. 11th,	12.00 noon
PARIS	Saturday,	Nov. 18th,	12.00 noon
Berlin	Saturday,	Nov. 25th,	12.00 noon
NEW YORK	Saturday,	Dec. 2d,	12.00 noon
PARIS	Saturday,	Dec. 9th,	12.00 noon
Chester	Saturday,	Dec. 16th,	12.00 noon
Berlin	Saturday,	Dec. 23d,	12.00 noon
NEW YORK	Saturday,	Dec. 30th,	12.00 noon

15

half hours, to begin the return to Washington. The main New York contingent also was anxious to reach home and left the ship around 4:30 to plow through the icy harbor and the drifting snow after reaching Pier 43.

The events of February 22, 1893, were regarded as a step forward toward the freeing of the American merchant marine from the unfair restrictions under which it had labored for 30 years, but many authorities felt that the true revival of American shipping would occur only if American owners were able to build and buy vessels wherever they wanted and still register them in the United States. In a blistering editorial, the *New York Times* stated:

> The way to encourage American shipping is to give it freedom and a fair
> chance. The letting down of restrictions, even in the case of two steamships,
> paltry as the beginning may be, is a hopeful sign, like the reciprocity conces-
> sions of the McKinley tariff. It is an abandonment of the "principle" of restric-
> tion in a limited way and an admission that there is advantage in liberty. That
> admission is much and is destined to undermine the whole policy of encourag-
> ing trade by loading it with burdens and putting obstacles in its way.[4]

The people of Southampton gave the *New York* a warm welcome on her first arrival, March 4, 1893. As soon as the liner was signaled off The Needles, the American flag was run up over the Bargate and flown from all the municipal buildings, while church bells rang and a salute was fired from The Battery. As the *New York* passed Hurst Castle, the

Sailing Schedule 1893 — NEW YORK TO ANTWERP

Westernland	Wednesday, June 7th,	11.00 a. m.
Noordland	Wednesday, June 14th,	5.00 p. m.
Waesland	Wednesday, June 21st,	11.30 a. m.
Belgenland	Saturday, June 24th,	2.30 p. m.
Friesland	Wednesday, June 28th,	5.00 p. m.
Rhynland	Wednesday, July 5th,	10.00 a. m.
Pennland	Saturday, July 8th,	1.00 p. m.
Westernland	Wednesday, July 12th,	4.00 p. m.
Noordland	Wednesday, July 19th,	10.00 a. m.
Waesland	Wednesday, July 26th,	4.00 p. m.
Friesland	Wednesday, Aug. 2d,	8.30 a. m.
Belgenland	Wednesday, Aug. 4th,	3.00 p. m.
Rhynland	Wednesday, Aug. 16th,	9.00 a. m.
Pennland	Saturday, Aug. 19th,	11.30 a. m.
Westernland	Wednesday, Aug. 23d,	2.00 p. m.
Noordland	Wednesday, Aug. 30th,	7.30 a. m.
Waesland	Wednesday, Sept. 6th,	2.00 p. m.
Friesland	Wednesday, Sept. 13th,	7.30 a. m.
Belgenland	Saturday, Sept. 16th,	9.30 a. m.
Rhynland	Wednesday, Sept. 20th,	1.00 p. m.
Westernland	Wednesday, Sept. 27th,	6.30 a. m.
Pennland	Saturday, Sept. 30th,	9.00 a. m.
Noordland	Wednesday, Oct. 4th,	12.30 p. m.
Waesland	Wednesday, Oct. 11th,	6.30 a. m.
Friesland	Wednesday, Oct. 18th,	11.30 a. m.
Rhynland	Wednesday, Oct. 25th,	4.30 p. m.
Belgenland	Saturday, Oct. 28th,	8.00 a. m.
Westernland	Wednesday, Nov. 1st,	11.00 a. m.
Noordland	Wednesday, Nov. 8th,	5.30 a. m.
Pennland	Saturday, Nov. 11th,	7.00 a. m.
Waesland	Wednesday, Nov. 15th,	9.30 a. m.
Friesland	Wednesday, Nov. 22d,	3.30 p. m.
Rhynland	Wednesday, Nov. 29th,	10.00 a. m.

30

Sailing Schedule 1893 — ANTWERP TO NEW YORK

Waesland	Saturday, June 3d,	3.30 p. m.
Belgenland	Wednesday, June 7th,	7.00 a. m.
Friesland	Saturday, June 10th,	9.00 a. m.
Rhynland	Saturday, June 17th,	3.30 p. m.
Pennland	Wednesday, June 21st,	7.00 a. m.
Westernland	Saturday, June 24th,	9.00 a. m.
Noordland	Saturday, July 1st,	2.30 p. m.
Waesland	Saturday, July 8th,	7.30 a. m.
Friesland	Saturday, July 15th,	2.30 p. m.
Belgenland	Saturday, July 22d,	7.30 a. m.
Rhynland	Saturday, July 29th,	2.00 p. m.
Pennland	Wednesday, Aug. 2d,	3.30 p. m.
Westernland	Saturday, Aug. 5th,	7.00 a. m.
Noordland	Saturday, Aug. 12th,	1.30 p. m.
Waesland	Saturday, Aug. 19th,	6.30 a. m.
Friesland	Saturday, Aug. 26th,	1.00 p. m.
Belgenland	Wednesday, Aug. 30th,	2.30 p. m.
Rhynland	Saturday, Sept. 2d,	6.00 a. m.
Westernland	Saturday, Sept. 9th,	1.00 p. m.
Pennland	Wednesday, Sept. 13th,	2.30 p. m.
Noordland	Saturday, Sept. 16th,	6.00 a. m.
Waesland	Saturday, Sept. 23d,	12.00 noon
Friesland	Saturday, Sept. 30th,	3.30 p. m.
Rhynland	Saturday, Oct. 7th,	12.00 noon
Belgenland	Wednesday, Oct. 11th,	1.30 p. m.
Westernland	Saturday, Oct. 14th,	3.00 p. m.
Noordland	Saturday, Oct. 21st,	10.00 a. m.
Pennland	Wednesday, Oct. 25th,	1.00 p. m.
Waesland	Saturday, Oct. 28th,	2.30 p. m.
Friesland	Saturday, Nov. 4th,	10.00 a. m.
Rhynland	Saturday, Nov. 11th,	2.30 p. m.
Westernland	Saturday, Nov. 18th,	8.30 a. m.
Belgenland	Wednesday, Nov. 22d,	12.00 noon

31

The 1893 sailing schedule for the Red Star Line in the first-class service from New York to Antwerp.

mayor and corporation of Southampton, accompanied by the Harbor Board and its officials, the directors of the Chamber of Commerce, the borough magistrates, the consuls and vice consuls of the port, press, and others led by the artillery and volunteer bands proceeded to the docks in full civic dress and boarded a ferry that took them downstream to the liner. Captain Jamison welcomed his British guests on board the *New York* and brought them back to the Empress Dock, where the American liner was assisted into her berth for the first time at about 8 o'clock. The ship was loudly cheered by a large crowd of spectators, while rockets shot up in the evening air and fireworks illuminated the darkness as the liner made fast to the dock.

The offices of the Harbor Board at the Empress Dock had been placed at the disposal of the American Line until its own headquarters could be completed. The mayor and corporation of Southampton planned a banquet for Captain Jamison and his officers, directors of the line, and visiting American dignitaries. For its part, the American Line announced that the *New York* would be thrown open to the public at a shilling a head for the duration of her stay, and that the proceeds would be donated to Southampton charities.

The advantages of Southampton over Liverpool for passengers bound to London or the Continent were substantial. The terminal facilities at Southampton were being completely rebuilt by the London and Southwestern Railway to accommodate the American Line vessels. The L&SW also had agreed to provide a special train from London to Southampton for the American Line ships. The terminal facilities at Southampton were infinitely easier to reach than the landing stage at Liverpool, which could be approached

The Empress Dock, Southampton, England, with the American Line's New York *in the background on the left (ca. 1903). The Empress Dock was opened by Queen Victoria in July 1890 and covered an area of 18.5 acres with 1,900 feet of quayage reserved for the American Line.*

only on certain high tides, and then only after navigating the twisting, often treacherous, and busy Mersey. The loss of the *City of Brussels* in July 1883, when that liner had been anchored at the Mersey Bar awaiting a favorable tide, had underlined the problem for Inman. The proximity of Southampton to London and to France meant that passengers landing at the Hampshire port reached the British capital with far less hassle than those landing at Liverpool, and those bound for the Continent had a variety of means of getting there. Passengers westward bound from the Continent to America would not have to spend the better part of three days traveling across France, the English Channel, and England before reaching an English-language transatlantic liner terminal. In the end it should be realized that the attachment of the new American Line to Liverpool was far less than that of the old Inman management, and if a move was to occur, 1893 was the time. New port facilities, new special trains, and the new ships soon to come combined to underline the importance of the move. From the historical perspective, the ultimate justification was that over the next 15 years, the White Star and Cunard Lines would follow.

The American correspondents who traveled from London to Southampton for the official welcome of the liner *New York* to the British port found the entire situation too remarkable to be believed. Here were British dignitaries traveling to greet the flagship of a new steamship line that did not fly the Union Jack and that had been transferred from British to foreign registry. The *New York Times* correspondent compared the junket to a group of American legislators attending the funeral of a colleague:

> The English, it is known, take all their pleasures sadly. They had more than the familiar temperamental excuse this time for the lugubrious aspect which, from first to last, yesterday's function presented. It was, I should think, the first time in history in which a large party of Englishmen had been got together to devote a day to festivities in honor of a national bereavement. They did their part with much decorum, cheering at the right places in the speeches, and eating, drinking, and smoking with a very tolerable assumption of enjoyment. But it was too

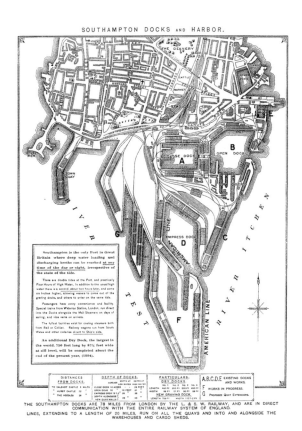

SOUTHAMPTON DOCKS and HARBOR.

The Southampton Docks between the River Test and River Itchen showing the existing docks of the American Line and the significant expansion work that was underway. The great advantage of the Empress Dock, Southampton, was that it was the only one in Britain permitting access to deep-water loading and discharging berths at any time.

much to ask of even British human nature to pretend that they were really happy about the change.

Probably no other country in the world would have made even the attempt at such a pretense. England's shipping list is such a gigantic, all-embracing affair that the loss from it of three or four big steamers makes no visible gap and attracts no special attention. But it is a far cry from the attitude of dated indifference, to the active stimulation of delight over the loss. One does not easily imagine the press of Berlin travelling to Wilhelmshaven to a luncheon celebrating the sale of the North German Lloyds to a Russian syndicate. One wonders, too, what kind of festivities San Francisco would get up to greet the passing of the Pacific Mail boats to the ownership of a British corporation.[5]

The only possible explanation was that the English after half a century of free trade all around the globe had achieved a higher level of sophistication than anyone else. They were capable of viewing the problems of international trade and contact from a broader and more impersonal standpoint than the rest of the peoples of the world.

The London and Southwestern Railway train that carried the entourage to meet the *New York* was brand new and had just been delivered to the railroad for the purpose of serving the American Line ships. The 80-mile run was made in 90 minutes without a

The New York *and a Union Castle liner preparing to leave the Empress Dock, Southampton, England, after April 1903. The* New York *had her triple-expansion engines replaced by William Cramp and Sons, Philadelphia, Pennsylvania, and her funnels reduced to two.*

stop. The train was described as a "vestibule" train because some of the cars were arranged with seats on each side and a large central aisle that constituted the vestibule. This differed from the normal English practice of smaller seating compartments on one side of the car and the aisle connecting all of them on the other side. The new L&SW train was very American in its design.

The representatives of proud and happy Southampton and the directors of the London and Southwestern Railway did most of the cheering during the sumptuous dinner in the main saloon of the *New York*. They were very pleased with the promise of prosperity for the port and additional earnings for the railroad. The principal American official present was the American minister to the Court of St. James, Robert T. Lincoln, son of Abraham Lincoln. (The senior American diplomatic representative in Britain held the rank of minister rather than the more exalted title of ambassador.) Minister Lincoln commented: "If I were an Englishman, I would be proud of the commercial supremacy of my country, but as an American, I congratulate America on the immense success it has reached within hardly more than a century. The sight of one's flag in a foreign port is thrilling. It is grand to see the flag borne abroad by the queen of the seas."[6] Ex-Secretary of the Treasury Foster got a little carried away with himself when he commented upon British energy and enterprise: "The finest things in America were of English origin, and the British race were splendidly represented there." Given the fact that Foster was traveling to Paris in order to negotiate a dispute with Great Britain that nearly had brought the two countries to blows, this was hardly an impartial statement and marked Foster as a bit of an Anglophile.

Yet there were problems about what to say at such an occasion.

> The British orators were painfully conscious, once they got on their feet, of the numerous things which, under the circumstances, it would be better not to mention. The American speakers, notably Minister Lincoln and ex-Secretary of State [sic] Foster, were even more obviously handicapped by these considerations of international reticence, and had the additional embarrassment of celebrating a final breach in the Chinese wall of anti-shipping laws which their own party had invented and so long maintained. When Mr. Lincoln deplored the decay and collapse of American shipping, the grins on scores of faces about him asked so pointedly "Whose fault is that?" that he seemed almost to have heard the question and hurried awkwardly on to another branch of his remarks.[7]

Success of Southampton as a major passenger terminal was felt to lie with the speed at which passengers and mails could be delivered to London. The ability to travel on one steamer from wharf to wharf without regard to tide, and then to be delivered in the British capital two hours later, was regarded as a significant advance.

The *City of Paris* sailed from Liverpool for the last time at the end of February, 1893 and made a fast crossing to New York under the command of Captain William G. Randle (2,862 miles; six days, two hours, 39 minutes). In so doing, she overtook and beat the *Teutonic*, which had departed 35 minutes ahead of her, by three hours. Upon her arrival at New York, the American flag was hoisted over her by Griscom's 13-year-old daughter, Frances C. Griscom, and the liner was rechristened *Paris*. The ceremony on the *Paris* occurred on March 7 and once again was held in the midst of a blinding snowstorm. An observer commented that if the grandeur of the proceedings on the *New York* two weeks earlier were lacking, the touching family scene as Clement Griscom and his daughter raised the American flag over the *Paris* had a charm all its own. Miss Griscom—whom everyone persisted in calling by her nickname, "Pansy," in spite of the dignity of the occasion—was dressed in a red frock and blue jacket, a combination that was soon made even more patriotic by large patches of white snow. The dashing Captain Randle was her escort, and several dozen guests were present this time instead of hundreds. The *Paris* was all decked out in bunting and flags for the occasion, which was held at her pier near the foot of Christopher Street. The new house flag of the American Line, featuring a large blue eagle on a white field, was also raised to the mainmast, and the new mail flag was hoisted to the mizzenmast. Waterfront wags had dubbed the mail flag "the Wanamaker flag" because of the prominent role that ex-Postmaster General John Wanamaker had played in having the Postal Aid Act passed by Congress.

The libraries on the New York and Paris were the finest products of the Thomson Shipyard on the Clyde in 1889.

Another view of the libraries on the Cities, with a spectacular skylight.

Victorian interior decorating left nothing unembellished. The drawing rooms on the New York and the Paris were the height of fashion.

The first-class dining room on the Paris was crowned by a magnificent domed skylight, which made it one of the most elegant rooms on any transatlantic liner.

The names of all the ships in the old Inman fleet were shortened to bring the nomenclature into line with the new policy. Sailings from New York would occur every Saturday. The *Paris* was registered through the collector of the Port of Philadelphia, making that city legally her port of registry. Both the *New York* and the *Paris* heralded the new service by establishing record passages on the route from New York to Southampton. The *New York* crossed from New York to Southampton, July 15–22, in six days, nine hours, 36 minutes, and the *Paris* bettered this with a run of six days, seven hours, 14 minutes, September 9–16, 1893. These crossings made it possible to deliver passengers to London far more quickly than via Liverpool. The American Line was able to commence operations with the image of a winner. This was fortunate, since the introduction of two new Cunarders, *Campania* (1893, 12,950 tons) and *Lucania* (1893, 12,952 tons), on the Liverpool–New York service would soon see those vessels capturing the Blue Riband for speed (May–October 1893). As the Cunard Line responses to the *Cities*, they were slightly larger and slightly more powerful. Few rivals existed for the moment on the Southampton route to challenge the *New York* and the *Paris*, which were advertised as the fastest liners to the Channel. They were able to hold on to that distinction for another four years. The *Fürst Bismarck* of North German Lloyd held the record for the fastest crossing from Southampton to New York, with a run of six days, 11 hours, 44 minutes over a 3,103-mile course (19.92 knots). In July 1893, the *Paris* steamed from The Needles to Sandy Hook in six days, nine hours, 37 minutes, which was heralded as a new record, but the distance was 51 miles shorter (3,052), and while the passage time was lowered by two hours and seven minutes, the *Paris* actually only crossed at 19.87 knots—.05 knot slower than her rival.

The debate over this was endless and heated. What was celebrated as remarkable in American newspapers was the fact that for the first time travelers had been able to breakfast in London on Saturday and dine in New York the following Friday. The privileged position of the American Line vessels in New York was underlined when Health Officer Jenkins steamed down the bay to meet the incoming liner so that she could be given her clearance papers immediately. This made it possible for the American-flag liner to bypass the quarantine station and proceed immediately to her pier for the speedy disembarkation of her grateful passengers. It is assumed they would not forget such preferential treatment the next time they booked an Atlantic crossing. Of course, it did not hurt that Lieutenant Governor Sheehan of New York and Senator Jacob A. Cantor also were arriving on the American liner.

The importance of the *New York* and the *Paris* to the United States as armed merchant cruisers in time of war was not ignored, and the Navy Department began work on the design of a powerful battery for each liner. The plans were completed and announced just before the recommissioning of the vessels under the American flag. In time of war, the American Line ships were to carry 12 six-inch breech-loading rifles— one on each bow and stern quarter and four on each broadside. In addition, there was a secondary battery of 20 six-pounder rapid-fire guns placed on the main and hurricane decks, and eight one-pounder rapid-fire guns mounted in the tops. Each of the two

The Friesland *was the largest ship in the Red Star fleet in 1889 and one of the most handsome ships on the North Atlantic.*

masts of the ships was to be given double tops at the next opportunity and each top would then contain two one-pounder guns in time of war. No mention was made of the effect on the masts of firing these guns.

On the extremities of the main bridge, commanding a fore-and-aft sweep, were to be fixed two Gatling guns, and plans were also announced to fit the liners with submarine guns in the bows. These would be placed so as to permit the firing of projectiles 10 feet below the waterline. A couple of turntable torpedo tubes were to be placed amidships and on each broadside. Each turntable would support two torpedo tubes and would be operated from the lower main deck at a height of 15 feet above the waterline. The battery was considered sufficiently powerful for the armed merchant cruiser to be able to defend herself against virtually any single warship afloat. Against a naval vessel, her primary defense would be speed of escape, but it was stated that she should be able to ram and sink any enemy ironclad because of the strength of her construction. Also, it was indicated that her secondary guns would be able to create carnage on the deck of any attacker. Where the battery was to be kept in peacetime remained unresolved and thus presented a problem for the incoming secretary of the navy in Grover Cleveland's administration. Suggestions were made that the guns might be stored permanently in the hold of the liner, or at the American Line's pier. The other alternative was to store the battery at the Brooklyn Navy Yard—the choice that was finally made.

In wartime, it was thought that the vessels would be able to raid the North Atlantic steamer lanes at will because of their speed and the amount of coal they could carry if normal bunkers, freight space, and lower decks were used for fuel storage. The utilization of all those areas would increase the normal capacity of 2,000 tons of coal to 4,500 tons. The *New York* and the *Paris* each was to have a complement of 800 officers and men. Since the liners were envisioned as commerce destroyers, sufficient manpower might be needed to be able to detach prize crews for up to 25 vessels. Fifteen officers and sailors were considered sufficient to man and bring a tramp steamer safely to port; 400 officers and crew would be the permanent complement of the armed merchant cruiser, leaving 400 free for prize-crew work. The only potential enemy mentioned was Great Britain![18]

The general reorganization of the three shipping companies in the conglomerate did not affect the Red Star Line's ships or schedules at first, but an immediate change was that all the vessels of all the lines adopted the old Inman Line funnel colors—a solid black stack with a white band. In 1893, the *Pennsylvania* and the *Illinois*, which had been fitted with new triple-expansion engines in 1891, were transferred from the Red Star Line's premier Antwerp–New York service, where they had been since 1887, to the Antwerp–Philadelphia run, where they would remain until 1898.

The disappearance of the strikingly colored funnels of the American Steamship Company—red stack, black top, gold band with a gold keystone in the center (surmounted by a red star after 1884)—and of the Société Anonyme de Navigation Belge-Américaine (Red Star Line)—beige stack, black top, and a red star—may be regretted. The result, however, was the creation of a much more uniform image for the fleet. The funnels of the ships in the Red Star fleet began to change in November 1894. The *Friesland*'s stack was repainted in Antwerp prior to sailing for New York, and the *Noordland*, which was at New York, had her funnels repainted there. The rest of the Red Star fleet followed suit as they reached port.

One result after 1893 was the diminution of the Belgian interest in the Red Star Line as the Belgian stockholders were gradually bought out. This may be regarded as a logical outgrowth of both the expansion of capital and the consolidation of operations within what had grown to be an international shipping conglomerate based in three nations.

The American Line's *Ohio* and *Indiana*, now averaging the ripe old age of 20 years, maintained the Philadelphia–Queenstown–Liverpool service in the company of the *Lord Gough* (1879, 3,655 tons), *Lord Clive* (1872, 3,386 tons), *British Prince* (1882, 3,871 tons), and *British Princess* (1882, 3,864 tons). An interesting development in 1888 was that the *Lord Gough* and the *Lord Clive*—which had been built for G.M. Papayanni of Liverpool but had never run for any other concern than the American Line—were purchased by Griscom and registered in companies bearing the names of the ships (LORD GOUGH S.S. Co., Ltd., LORD CLIVE S.S. Co., Ltd.). The owner of these two companies was the American Steamship Company. The close relationship of G.M. Papayanni and of another concern, British Shipowners Company, leads one to think that they represented British fronts for American money. This gave the American Steamship Company the tonnage it needed to expand services without the cost and expense of American building and operation.

Contracts were signed in Britain in September 1892 for two new liners supposedly to replace the aging *City of Chester* (1873) and *City of Berlin* (1875). In reality, the vessels were intended to rejuvenate the American Steamship Company's original Philadelphia–Liverpool service. When the twin-screw, steel-hulled *Southwark* (1893, 8,607 tons) and *Kensington* (1894, 8,669 tons) took their maiden voyages on December 27, 1893, and June 27, 1894, respectively, they were far superior in size and quality to anything the American Steamship Company had operated in the Philadelphia–Liverpool trade. They entered service with accommodations for 100 in second cabin, as well as 929 in steerage. Hence, the American Line introduced the "cabin-class" liner to the North Atlantic and further upset the competition. The *Southwark* and the *Kensington* were the first new ships to be described as catering only to second-cabin and steerage passengers.

The Kensington *(1894, 8,669 tons, 480 feet by 57 feet, 14 knots) was built by Thomson for the American Line but transferred in 1895 to the Red Star Line for the New York–Antwerp service. In 1903, under the International Mercantile Marine, the* Kensington *was reassigned to the Dominion Line.*

Since they were built in British yards, they could not fly the American flag, and Griscom may have felt that it was better not to have any first-class accommodations in order to sidetrack the argument that they should have been built in American yards.

There is no question that the *Southwark* and the *Kensington* greatly improved the Liverpool–Philadelphia service. They were nearly three times larger than the old American Line quartet, and their accommodations were far superior, as befitted vessels 20 years younger. In comparison with the old American Line quartet, whose accommodations had been downgraded for some time, the new tonnage was a spectacular improvement, and the increase in bookings underlined this fact. The *Ohio* was the only unit still carrying first-class, second-cabin, and steerage passengers. The *Pennsylvania* and the *Illinois* were described as carrying second-cabin and steerage passengers, but the *Indiana* handled steerage only. Any pretense of maintaining a first-class service to Philadelphia had long since gone by the boards. The introduction of the *Kensington* and the *Southwark* made it possible to release the *British Prince* and the *British Princess*, which briefly ran for the Dominion Line to Canada and then were sold to French buyers, becoming *Les Andes* and *Les Alpes* (1895).

In the fall of 1892, the International Navigation Company was very irritated with the health authorities in Philadelphia for holding up the disembarkation of passengers until they were fully satisfied about the absence of disease. Delays had begun with the outbreak of cholera in the German ports during the fall of 1891, and sporadic instances of the dread disease had occurred in western European immigrant ports throughout 1892. This had made many health inspectors and the American public jittery about the "importation" of disease via immigrants. The *Indiana* sailed from Liverpool for New York on September 10, 1892, with a full load of 753 steerage passengers. Those departing on the *Indiana* had to agree to a process of disinfecting their clothing and bedding before embarkation by exposure of not less than six hours to sulfurous acid gas. They also had to agree to undergo whatever quarantine might be imposed by the authorities in New York. The gas treatment was considered the only effective means of dealing with human parasites, such as lice, which transmitted the disease. The New York authorities developed a new fumigation vessel to meet the cholera threat, and all immigrants were required to take rigorous showers with strong soap, as well as to submit to especially thorough physical examinations.

The Philadelphia authorities appear to have been either more concerned or more zealous than their New York counterparts, and ships of the Red Star Line were delayed by lengthy quarantines. Tempers flared, since delays were costly. Accordingly, a "high official" of the International Navigation Company took the opportunity to let the press know that unless the situation in Philadelphia improved, the Red Star Line would transfer all sailings to New York and cease to serve Philadelphia. He was very pointed in his comments:

> It is all very well for the officials of a port like that of Philadelphia to exercise precautions for the preservation of the health of the people, and to be zealous in the discharge of their duties. But when it comes to taking advantage of the roundabout methods of "red tape" for the purpose of eking out the salaries of health officials, which the municipality is not able to pay otherwise, then the time has arrived when the steamship companies are justified in calling a halt. The proposed transfer of the business of the International Navigation Company to New York, so far as the Red Star Line is concerned, is simply in the interest of self-preservation.[9]

Nothing transpired of any note, since the cholera situation in Europe remained threatening throughout the fall of 1892 and the rigorous health inspections continued, although the Philadelphia "red tape" appears to have been brought in line with that of New York.

The problem of too many ships chasing too few steerage passengers on the North Atlantic forced the major steamship lines in 1894 to make a significant attempt to control sailings and ticket prices. Referred to as "the transatlantic steamship pool," it involved Cunard, American, White Star, North German Lloyd, and Hamburg-American,

A beautiful color view of the Vaderland *and* Zeeland *in the Scheldt at Antwerp with sailing barges and the spire of St. Peter's Cathedral in the background. The card was issued around 1902.*

as well as a number of smaller lines. The original attempt at some type of rate-fixing organization had occurred in 1885–86, but it had not survived for long. The new negotiations were followed in the American newspapers with some interest. Such a group of cutthroat robber barons was not to be domesticated easily, and the talks blew apart in April after nearly three months of bickering. The German lines were furious with the British lines for attempting to seduce a larger proportion of the continental immigrant trade, and the British lines regarded the German lines as being outrageously unfair in their control of the rich Central European traffic.

In October 1893, the British lines reduced the steerage fares to and from Scandinavian ports. Hamburg-American, under the redoubtable shipping genius Albert Ballin, responded with a new German line (Scandia Line) and began a direct service from Scandinavia to New York at rates lower than those charged by the British feeder lines. Furthermore, the ships of the Scandia Line were larger and better equipped than the competition, and the British lines began to lose passengers. A genuine trade war erupted.

The Thingvalla Line, a Danish concern, had operated a minor North Atlantic service from Copenhagen to New York since 1880. In 1894, the British lines encouraged Thingvalla, with certain guarantees about profitability, to lower its steerage rates below those of the German Scandia Line. Hamburg-American and North German Lloyd united temporarily against the British threat by lowering steerage fares for the whole of the North Atlantic to $18. This trade war, which broke out on April 19, 1894, would rumble on for nearly two years. The reduction in steerage fares was enormous, since the normal fare charged by all before the conflict began was around $28. If the new rate was $18, and the agents' commission was $2, the German lines were prepared to accept as little as $16 for carrying a passenger across the North Atlantic. These reduced rates were publicized in Britain, and the British lines promptly had a fit, but they immediately matched the German quotations. As long as this insanity existed, no one was going to make any money carrying steerage passengers on the Atlantic. Since the battle lines were drawn with Cunard and White Star on one side and Hamburg-American and North German Lloyd on the other, the American Line, the Anchor Line, and the Compagnie Générale Transatlantique were left chuckling on the sidelines until the reduced fares began to cut into their trade. Red Star nominally was part of the continental pool with the German lines and Holland-America, so this represented an entanglement for the International Navigation Company. A.E. Johnson, New York agent of Thingvalla, noted there was little hope for any rational settlement of the trade war among the "big four" until rates were reduced to such an extent that every voyage lost money and the hemorrhage of red ink threatened to drown everyone. Most observers tended to agree. By April 23, it looked as though the owners had come to their senses and no further disruptions of the trade would be allowed. The New York agents of the conflicting lines were informed of a tentative settlement, but it collapsed when General Manager J. Boumphrey of Cunard in London refused to accede to the division of spoils. Hamburg-American and North German Lloyd responded by lowering steerage rates another $2. Some German observers were not surprised at the failure of the agreement, since they doubted that Cunard was prepared to make the concessions required to share British traffic.

The American Line sought to protect itself and its market by matching whatever reductions the warring parties made in their steerage rates. The Liverpool and Southampton steerage rates of the American Line were adjusted downward, threatening to imperil the financial stability of the new line, which had so many big ships building. In May 1894, Mr. Lederer, general manager of the International Navigation Company, announced:

> We will protect our own interests at all hazards, and have met the German lines, but not gone below them. If the German lines go lower, so will we, and I cannot tell you what may be done in an hour from now. It all depends on the other people, but you may depend upon it that we will meet them in every move. At the same time, I don't know that we need to have reduced rates, for I believe people would rather patronize the American Line even if they paid a little more.[10]

This was whistling in the dark, since immigrants chose the cheapest fare available whenever possible.

The rate war during the summer of 1894 would bring the cheapest steerage fares seen for decades. The *New York Times* on July 15 carried a headline, "Ocean Travel Next to Free," and they were quite correct! Almost anyone could go to Europe if they could get the time off and comfort was not a factor. The American Line found itself in the thick of the fray by midsummer and announced steerage rates from Liverpool, Southampton, or Queenstown to any American port for 36 shillings ($8.64)! Furthermore, the American Line quoted round-trip fares in steerage at $18.64. Only the British ports were involved at this time, but Cunard and White Star were livid. If the beauties of a steerage passage across the Atlantic were not many, these nevertheless were astonishing rates. An observer in the United States commented:

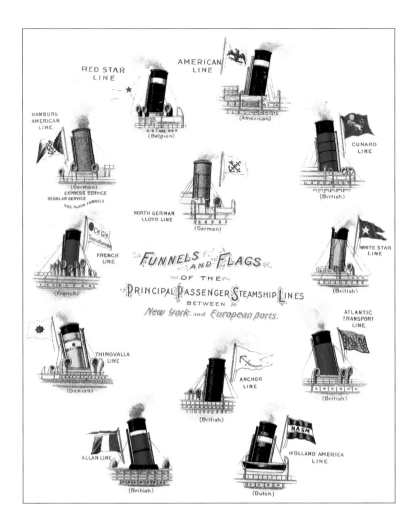

This further reduction makes an excursion to Europe seem as commonplace
and tawdry as a trip to the fishing banks. One who takes it cannot, of course,
look forward to superior accommodations. But what more in that line could be
expected for $18.64, when there are 6000 miles of blue water to be traversed,
and, at the lowest estimate, thirteen days of subsistence to be provided.[11]

It was marveled at that steamship lines could afford to transport passengers at that
rate. In fact, they could not, but the rate war—combined with a major depression in the
United States, the threat of cholera in European ports, and the corresponding greatly
reduced immigrant loads—meant that sweet sanity was totally absent from the proceedings. Some immigrants who had crossed the North Atlantic to find a better life for
themselves in the United States even were encouraged by the low fares to return home
in order to live out the economic depression in a place where survival was cheaper. In
1894, the eastbound steerage traffic was running heavier than the westbound.

Furthermore, the incredibly low rates prompted some young men, notably college students, to rethink their vacation plans and to decide on a trip to Europe at these rock-bottom prices. As long as the rate war persisted, every ship that sailed fitted the old adage of "a hole in the water into which one pours money." Griscom had authorized the lowest rates on the North Atlantic only two months after quoting a premium for the American Line ships. White Star immediately quoted $10 eastward and $15 westward. Cunard lowered its rates to $12 eastward and $15 westward, but neither matched the incredibly low American Line rates.

The pyrrhic struggle continued into the next year, when the lines were so exhausted and financially battered that some respite was imperative. The result was a conference at which the 1895 Declaration of Intent was hammered out. This pooling agreement required that the German lines withdraw from the Scandinavian trade in return for the British lines leaving the Mediterranean (except for the long-established Anchor Line). The German lines agreed to leave the British immigrant traffic both outward and home-ward, and the British lines were limited to 6 percent of the continental traffic. The agreement on steerage passengers so laboriously hammered out between 1892 and 1895 would last for three years. Efforts would be made to establish minimum cabin-class fares in 1896, and to define what was meant by "summer season (May 1 to October 31)," but the conference system began to disintegrate in 1898 concurrent with another major trade fluctuation, and another rate war was inevitable.[12]

A major reorganization of the American holding company occurred on June 6, 1893. The International Navigation Company of Philadelphia, which had been chartered by the Commonwealth of Pennsylvania in 1871, closed its books and ceased to exist. In its place, a new International Navigation Company—registered in New Jersey, which had easier corporation laws—was born with a capitalization of $15,000,000. The International Navigation Company, Inc., of New Jersey was given title to all the American-flag tonnage of the combined lines, and a British subsidiary, the International Navigation Company Limited, was established in Liverpool (July 13, 1893) to hold title to the *Berlin* and the *Chester*, which continued to be British-flagged. Clement Acton Griscom, as the foremost American shipping magnate of the day, was elected president of the new concern.

Griscom was going to need large sums of money to maintain his shipping conglomerate and to finish the new tonnage that the U.S. mail contract required that he order. The entire cash-flow situation was complicated by the steerage rate war, which lowered income even below the break-even point for 1894–95. Griscom's solution was to meet with his bankers. A large mortgage ($6,000,000) was negotiated with the Fidelity Trust and Safe Deposit Company, and this was ratified by the board of directors of the International Navigation Company at its annual meeting on May 8, 1894. The financial agreement was similar in every respect to a railroad mortgage, with bonds issued to the holders of the indebtedness. No financial undertaking of this dimension had ever before been undertaken by an American steamship line.

When Griscom placed the order for the Saints *with the Cramp Shipyard, he ordered the two largest ships to be built in the United States in the nineteenth century. Here the 11,600-ton* St. Louis *is shown in a dramatic sketch by F. Cresson-Schell.*

The $6,000,000 was to be used for improvements to the working fleet, most notably for the building of two new American greyhounds to partner the *New York* and the *Paris*, and to pay for the *Southwark* and the *Kensington*, which were approaching delivery from the Scottish shipyards. The collateral offered largely consisted of the ships of the fleet—namely, the *New York, Paris, Chester, Berlin* of the American Line; the *Friesland, Westernland, Noordland, Waesland, Pennland, Rhynland, Belgenland,* and *Switzerland* of the Red Star Line, and the *Illinois, Indiana, Ohio,* and *Pennsylvania* of what was described as the "Philadelphia–Antwerp line." The International Navigation Company also included as collateral its new pier and the favorable lease in New York. In other words, Griscom had to put up virtually every asset of his shipping companies in order to raise the necessary funds to take delivery of, or complete, the four ships under construction.

Within the financial community, the word on the street was that the bond issue had sold almost completely. It was mentioned that the success of the offering was ensured by the close alliance between the mighty Pennsylvania Railroad Company, on whose board of directors Griscom continued to sit, and the new American Line. An observer commented, "With the money thus obtained the company will be splendidly equipped for ocean service without waiting to earn money with which to pay for what its management thinks it should have."[13] At the annual meeting of the International Navigation Company, Griscom made the statement that the improvements underway ought to be convincing evidence that the company's financial condition and business were satisfactory. Griscom's high spirits and confidence may have been warranted, but there also were great financial risks at stake, and neither the prosperity of the American economy nor the international shipping market looked good.

Chapter 9

AND THE "SAINTS" CAME MARCHING IN

The St. Louis (1895) was delivered to the American Line in May and began her maiden voyage on June 5, 1895. At 11,629 tons she was the largest ship flying the American flag. Her dimensions were 554 feet by 63 feet and her engines gave her a service speed of over 19 knots. We can tell this is an early photograph because the slender funnels with cowls were replaced after the first season.

U.S. Naval Historical Center photograph

A key factor in the legislation permitting American registry for the *New York* and the *Paris* was the immediate ordering and construction of two similar units in an American shipyard. When congressional and presidential approval of the transfer of the American-owned Inman and International liners to the United States occurred on May 10, 1892, Clement A. Griscom took immediate action to convert this promise into reality. Contracts for the construction of two ocean greyhounds were signed with William Cramp and Sons Ship and Engine Building Company of Philadelphia. Griscom was a director of the Cramp Shipyard, but little issues like that did not matter in 1892. William Cramp & Sons had a long and honorable history of solid, dependable ship construction. At the time of the order, the shipyard was under the management of Charles H. Cramp, one of the most eloquent and forceful maritime spokesmen of the day. Rarely did Cramp pass up an opportunity to exhort his fellow Americans to think about the condition of the American merchant marine. In the early 1890s, the Cramp Shipyard was turning out a substantial number of warships for the United States Navy and was admirably suited to undertake the ambitious project of producing the first American transatlantic greyhounds.

During the summer of 1893 the Cramp Shipyard in Philadelphia was providing employment for more than 4,000 workers. Orders from the United States Navy were worth $20,522,000, covering seven new cruisers and battleships. The list included the battleships *Iowa*, *Indiana*, and *Massachusetts*; the armored cruisers *New York* and *Brooklyn*;

One of the official American Line postcards of the St. Louis *underway around 1900.*

and the triple-screw cruisers *Columbia* and *Minneapolis*, which were being heralded for their speed. The naval orders involved 64,142 tons (displacement) of warships, with engines capable of a total of 103,000 horsepower. The American Line order for five ships involved another 60,200 tons of shipping, with the two new express liners for the New York–Southampton service representing the greatest challenge. Challenges were nothing new to Charles Cramp, since he had agreed to naval contracts that specified both bonuses and penalties. The bonuses ran $25,000 to $30,000 for each quarter of a knot by which the warships exceeded their specified speeds. In virtually every instance, he was to win the wager and collect the incentive reward.

It was a source of no little pride to Cramp that the liners would be constructed "from the trunk to the keelson" of American material. He set out to ignore completely the tariff revisions permitting shipbuilders to import necessary construction materials without paying duty.[1] The two new liners were to be as competely American as Cramp

"Steamship St. Louis *now building for the International Navigation Company (American Line), by the Wm. Cramp and Sons Ship and Engine Building Company, Philadelphia, Pa."*
U.S. Naval Historical Center photograph

View of the large derrick (ca. 1893) used at the Cramp Shipyard in the construction of the St. Louis *and* St. Paul. U.S. Naval Historical Center photograph

could make them. Every order went to American rolling mills, foundries, and forges. The ¼-inch steel plates for the ships came from the Wellman Iron and Steel Company, while additional steel was to be supplied by Carnegie, Phipps & Company of Pittsburgh. As soon as the battleship *Massachusetts* was launched, the keel for the second of the express liners was laid on that building berth.

In the act permitting American registry for the *New York* and the *Paris*, it was stipulated that the new vessels must equal the earlier vessels in size and tonnage. In order to ensure compliance, the State Department requested the Navy Department to have Naval Constructor Hanscom, who was assigned to the Cramp Shipyard, examine the plans for the new steamers and report on their tonnage. Hanscom was presented with a bit of a problem, because the builder's plans for any given vessel will never reveal the exact tonnage of the finished ship. Variables always exist, but Hanscom at least could

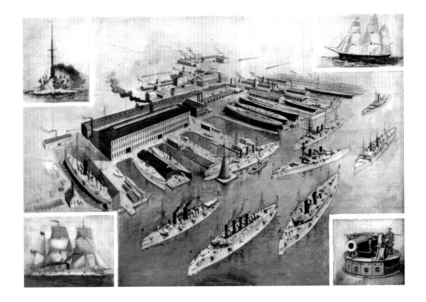

A view of the Cramp Shipyard, Philadelphia, Pa., at the time the two big American liners were under construction. Library of Congress

certify that the vessels would be equal in tonnage to the *New York* and the *Paris*. In fact, the Delaware ships, when commissioned, would come in at a thousand tons larger than the Clyde pair.

The two new American Line ships had the following dimensions:

Length overall . . . . 554 feet
Length on load waterline . . . . 536 feet
Extreme beam . . . . 63 feet
Depth of hold . . . . 42 feet
Gross registered tons . . . . 11,000 tons

In appearance, they differed significantly from the *New York* and the *Paris*, inasmuch as they had straight stems instead of clipper bows, two funnels instead of three, and two masts instead of three. The masts, being more ornamental than functional, were ordinary pole masts with a fore-and-aft schooner rig. Signor Marconi's success with wireless communication between ship and shore remained a couple of years in the future.

The newspapers had a field day with the hugeness of the American Line ships. They were described as more than a tenth of a mile long, or equal to the length of two New York city blocks. Twelve six-foot men standing on each other's shoulders would not reach from the ground to the main deck, while the stairways erected alongside the ships to reach the main deck contained 140 steps. A reporter standing on the forecastle was higher than a six-story building, and looking over the side of the ship provided the dizzying sensation of looking down a precipice.

In terms of construction, Cramp employed a different method than was common in Scotland. The hulls of the new liners were built out in a horizontal web to a steel frame having both bosses cast in one piece weighing about 68,000 pounds. The after deadwood

The boilers of the St. Louis *are shown in this view of the Cramp Shipyard.*

was cut away, and the keel sloped so that the shoe met the boss frame at the after end. This form of construction gave a decidedly fishlike appearance to the after ends of the two vessels. In 1888–89, when the *New York* and the *Paris* were among the first transatlantic liners to be built with twin screws, it was thought that struts projecting from the side of the hull would be sufficient to support the shafts and the propellers. This had not been the case, as was proven in the 1890 accident to the *City of Paris*. Both vessels had required immediate redesigning and reinforcing of the supports for the propeller shafts. This involved incorporating the shafts within bulges on the sides of the hull. Therefore, in the American vessels the hull was built out to incorporate the shaft bearings and to secure greater strength and stability. This hull modification was first noted in the *Campania* (1893, 12,950 tons) and the *Lucania* (1893, 12,952 tons) of Cunard when they were commissioned.

Each of the American liners was built with a double bottom for safety, with the two steel platings being 54 inches apart. The double bottom was capable of holding water ballast, but Charles Cramp was adamant that no additional ballast would be needed to keep any ship of his upright. Cramp was scathing in his comments about "foreign" builders who created ocean greyhounds that could only stay upright because of their ballasting. Cramp contended that every single transatlantic liner of British construction depended on water ballast for her stability. As far as Cramp was concerned, this meant that such a ship was liable to capsize if anything interfered with the working of the mechanism for supplying the water ballast. Furthermore, the provision made for water-ballast space materially reduced the cargo-earning capacity of the ship. Cramp barked:

> I dismiss the commercial aspect of water ballast or permanent deadweight with
> the remark any steamship owner who will accept a design that compels him to

lug around 1,000 tons or so of non-paying freight in her bottom for the life of his ship deserves what he gets and is not entitled to sympathy.[2]

Cramp was vociferously opposed to any ballasting system that made the safety of a ship dependent upon human judgment:

> In connection with the conventional English plan of indispensable water bal-
> lasting, it has been suggested as an ultimate refinement a system of ingress and
> expulsion of water to and from numerous compartments by means of valves and
> pump gear under electrical control from a central station. Let us suppose such a
> system perfectly developed so that an operator can sit at an electric keyboard
> with a button for each valve and for each pump, they then operate them like
> Paderewski plays the piano. This may be very pretty and very scientific, but
> after all, it involves the human factor, with its liability to err, in a manner that
> places the lives of a thousand passengers at the finger ends of the operator. I
> have during forty years of observation and experience in my profession, seen so
> much of the human factor under such circumstances that the elimination of it
> in every possible direction has almost become a passion with me. It is a first
> principle with me to provide as many absolute and unchangeable qualities of
> performance and safety as possible, and to place them beyond manipulation.
> The first and most important of such qualities is that of initial stability. With it
> the ship will stand up and float despite errors or misfortunes of management or
> condition. Without it she and all on board may at any time be at the mercy of a
> tipsy tank trimmer or a jammed valve.[3]

As they stood upon the stocks in the Cramp Shipyard, the new ships appeared almost flat-bottomed, though as a matter of fact there was considerable rise even amidships. Forward of amidships, they were unsually fine, while aft they were characterized by extremely easy lines. The sheerline forward was much sharper than the hulls of the *New York* and the *Paris*, and greater than that of the *Campania*.

The method of construction in the Cramp Shipyard followed a standard and familiar pattern. The keel was laid on blocks arranged at intervals of about three feet on an incline of about five-eighths inch per foot so as to give the requisite pitch for the launching. After the keel was laid, the two frames in the center of the boat were put up. Others forward and aft followed, until the sternpost and stem were fitted into place. The steel plates on the sides were then riveted into place until the hull was finished. As the launching day neared in the fall of 1894, two broad ways were built against the bottom of the vessel, and the keel blocks on which it had been resting were knocked away. Each launching ways consisted of upper and lower planking between which were spread thousands of pounds of the best tallow. At the bow of the boat, the upper and lower planks were clamped together, and when all was ready, they were sawed apart and the launching started. The upper part of the ways slid into the water with the vessel, and the lower part with the smoking tallow remained stationary on the shore.

Early stages in the building of the St. Louis *and* St. Paul *at the Cramp Shipyard.*

A launching at the Cramp Shipyard in the 1890s was normally a smooth occurrence, rarely lasting more than 12 seconds from start to finish, hence it was easy for the public to overlook the potential difficulties. Three things were absolutely necessary: The launch had to be on time, when the tidal water in the Delaware was highest; it had to be of sufficient speed so as not to stick on the downward trip to the water; it had to be accomplished without straining. So complex was a launching that the careful engineer in charge had to be able to calculate the strain on every part of the hull for every position it occupied on its way down the incline. There was one supreme moment of truth—when the vessel was two-thirds of the way into the water. The buoyancy of the water raised the hull and threw the weight onto that portion of the hull still on the ways and heading for the water. This was the point when the greatest danger of straining occurred. Should the ways break down, the hull might split and the vessel could be ruined. The potential loss on a liner such as the *St. Louis* or *St. Paul* would run more than $3,000,000.

The American liners were to have six decks and the most modern and powerful engines available. The engines were quadruple-expansion, designed to provide not less than 10,000 horsepower each—20,000 when working together—which compared with 18,000 on the *New York* and the *Paris*. Each engine had four cylinders of 36, 50, 71, and 100 inches in diameter. The piston stroke was 60 inches. Steam was provided by six steel double-ended boilers, each 20 feet long and 15 feet 7½ inches in diameter, which were designed to furnish steam at about 200 pounds of pressure. The fire room would have a battery of 48 Purves furnaces, 39 inches in diameter, fitted with Serve's Ribbed Steel boiler tubes. The total grate surface was 830 square feet, and the heating surface around 30,000 square feet. Crankshafts, eccentric straps, and connecting rods were of forged steel, and the piston rods were of ingot steel. The valve gear was the link type, controlled by a steam cylinder and also by auxiliary hand gears. Since this was the first time that quadruple-expansion engines of more than 4,000 horsepower were being used in a ship, Cramp was required to show during prolonged trials that the ship could maintain a speed of 20 knots.

A factor that had to be corrected as the launching days neared was the expected speed of the new liners. The *Campania* and *Lucania* had represented somewhat unknown quantities when the American liners were ordered. Early in 1893, some loose tongues spoke of Cramp building a pair of record breakers. By late 1894, it was realized that the new Cunarders were nearly 2,000 tons larger, with engines that produced 10,000 horsepower more than those planned for the Cramp ships. The American vessels never would be competitors for the Blue Riband, even if they would be the second and third largest liners in the world. Cramp obviously regretted that time and money had made it impossible for him to design and build vessels capable of wresting the speed records from the Cunarders. In a "sour grapes" retort, he said he did not feel a vessel over 600 feet was a good idea, and that structural failure was to be expected if anyone tried to create such a ship.

As a result of the different school of marine architecture and the different method of construction, the new Cramp vessels would be able to carry a great deal more cargo than the *New York* and the *Paris* and, while considerably smaller in dimensions than the *Campania* and *Lucania*, nearly as much cargo as the Cunarders. This would significantly enhance their earning capacity. Accommodations would be available for 1,540 passengers: 350 first cabin, 290 second cabin, and 900 steerage. In all classes, the refinement and luxury of the cabins and public rooms would surpass anything afloat.

The great day for the launching of the first of the twin steamships came on November 12, 1894. The weather was unseasonably cold and blustery along the Delaware, as President and Mrs. Grover Cleveland traveled from Washington, DC, for the purpose of launching the largest ship ever constructed in the United States. Cleveland had won the presidential election of 1892 and replaced Benjamin Harrison in the White House. A Presidential Special left Washington for Philadelphia at 8:15 A.M. on the Pennsylvania Railroad. It brought President and Mrs. Cleveland, Secretary of the Treasury and Mrs. John G. Carlisle, Secretary of the Navy Hilary A. Herbert and his son and daughter, and Attorney General Richard Olney, as well as a large number of military, naval, and congressional figures. Clement A. Griscom and Charles H. Cramp boarded the Presidential Special before it arrived at the shipyard in order to greet the president and welcome him to Philadelphia. Cleveland was in a very expansive and cheerful mood as the Presidential Special rolled to a stop at the front entrance to the Cramp Shipyard at 12:10. Griscom and Cramp were first off the train. Henry W. Cramp, secretary of the Shipyard, and a group of officials from the shipyard and the International Navigation Company stepped forward to greet President and Mrs. Cleveland as they alighted. Flowers were presented to Mrs. Cleveland and the other ladies in the official party, while introductions were made all around. The president then walked toward the launching site with Charles Cramp, while Mrs. Cleveland took Griscom's arm. Inside the Cramp Shipyard, the launching party walked up a slight incline to a small railed platform that had been erected right under the keel. On this

A bow view of the St. Louis *on the stocks.*

A stern view of the St. Louis *dressed out in flags for her launch on November 12, 1894.*

platform were Mrs. Cleveland, the president, Griscom, and Cramp. Owing to the small size of the platform and the large sizes of the participants, it was a tight fit.

All the buildings in and about the shipyard were gay with flags and buntings, and the national colors floated from the bow of the vessel. The flags of many nations were flown from a line that stretched from stem to stern of the ship. As soon as everyone was in position, the gates of the shipyard were opened to the public, and a large throng swarmed in and packed around the hull. More than 25,000 individuals jammed the shoreline and the river on chartered vessels to see the launching of this masterpiece of American naval architecture. When Henry Cramp received the official word that all was ready for the launch, he handed Mrs. Cleveland a gaily decorated bottle of champagne and instructed her on the best way to break the bottle. Mrs. Cleveland took the bottle, nodded and smiled in reply to Cramp's advice and stood waiting for the ship to begin to move. As the vessel slowly began to edge down the ways, Mrs. Cleveland swung the bottle of champagne by its multicolored ribbons and smashed the glass against the side, at the same time calling out in a clear voice: "I christen thee *St. Louis*!"

The liner slid down the ways and sped some distance out into the river from the launching site before waiting tugs caught her, and an anchor was let go to hold the steamship. As the new flagship of the American merchant marine took her maiden bow in the Delaware, there was no question that she was "the greatest single vessel ever constructed on this Continent."[4] Mrs. Cleveland was congratulated for her adeptness in swinging the bottle of champagne to christen the ship. The launching party then retired to the shipyard offices for a luncheon in their honor. Griscom served as master of ceremonies and, after the lunch, offered a toast to the Cramp shipbuilding firm and then to the health of the president of the United States. This was drunk with a round of applause. The president then spoke:

> I would not be entirely frank if I did not acknowledge the extreme personal satisfaction afforded me by the references just made to the part which fell to me as a high duty and privilege in the great work of creating an American navy, and at the same time stimulating American shipbuilding.
>
> I cannot, however, keep out of mind the feeling that the gratification appropriately growing out of this occasion is such as must be shared by every patriotic American, and that the important event which has just now taken place is of such national interest that it is fittingly witnessed by the highest officials of the government.
>
> We shall fail to realize the full significance of what we have seen today if we overlook the fact that the causes of our congratulation reach beyond actual accomplishment, and are not limited to the things already done, and within our sight. While we may well be proud because we have launched the largest and most powerful steamship ever built in the Western Hemisphere, and with two exceptions, the largest and most powerful in the world, and while we may find reason for additional pride in the fact that, notwithstanding general economic conditions not encouraging to such achievements, this great vessel has been built on American plans, by American mechanics, and of American materials. We must not forget that our greatest cause of congratulations is found in the hope and promise these incidents furnish of the revival and development of American commerce and the renewed appearance of the American-flag in foreign ports.[5]

Another substantial group of attendees came from St. Louis, the city in whose honor the liner was named. The official party from St. Louis was led by Mayor Cyrus

Mrs. Grover Cleveland, wife of the President of the United States, stands on the far right of the launching platform at the Cramp Shipyard. It was a blustery November day and she had traveled by train to Philadelphia in order to sponsor the St. Louis *at her launch.*

President Grover Cleveland acknowledges the cheers of the crowd as everyone awaits the right moment of high tide for the launch.

Packard Walbridge and brought a pledge to outfit the two libraries on the liner as a civic gift to the ship.

The second liner was to be christened the *St. Paul* and launched with only a little less fanfare 5 months later. The International Navigation Company attempted to make every American aware of the tremendous achievement that the two liners represented. Press releases and public-relations materials were churned out by the Line so that every potential traveler would know about the new American-flag ships.

In New York, new piers were constructed well up the North River for the new liners in order to provide a proper terminal for the American Line. In a day and age when the search for speed on the Atlantic could occasionally mean sacrificing safety, no effort was

A dramatic drawing by the artist Smith captures the instant the hull of the St. Louis *first parts the waters of the Delaware River. The hull is dressed out in flags, including that of the Cramp Shipyard and the "Blue Eagle" of the American Line.*

An official American Line photograph celebrates the launch of the St. Louis *with a bow shot just as the liner clears the ways and takes her baptismal splash in the Delaware.*

spared to make the *Saints* as safe as the *Cities*. The guiding principle was to make the vessels as safe and dependable as possible. If a record passage could be achieved, clearly the American Line would be very pleased, but safety would be paramount. Cramp told one audience that it was rumored that more than one record breaker carried substantial quantities of cement deep in the hold or against the keel in order to correct tenderness and to ensure that the vessel would remain upright. He would have none of that in any ship he was responsible for building. Cramp expressed horror at the idea and indicated that the *Saints* were designed so that they would remain on an even keel at all times without excessive and costly ballasting.

The launching of the *St. Paul* was scheduled for March 25, 1895, at the Cramp Shipyard. Festivities only a little less grand than those for the *St. Louis* were planned. A large party of dignitaries from St. Paul, Minnesota, had come east on the Pennsylvania Railroad via Chicago to stay at the Hotel Stratford as the guests of the International Navigation Company.[6] All the members of the Pennsylvania General Assembly were invited to view the launching from the Port of Philadelphia iceboat, which served as a civic yacht. Numerous other federal government officials were the guests of Charles Cramp. For the purpose of having complete nationwide coverage of the launching, Griscom and Cramp also had invited one of the largest gatherings of journalists ever seen in Philadelphia.

Cramp expected a very large crowd and was rewarded with some 25,000 spectators who lined the shore and packed numerous vessels in the river. Some 500 Philadelphia policemen participated in crowd control, and a double line of blue uniforms stretched from the Ball Street entrance of the shipyard to the stairway leading to the launching platform on the port side of the *St. Paul.* The entrance to the shipyard was profusely decorated with the national colors and Cumberland Street was roped off. All through the morning, a small army of workmen armed with cans of paint and paintbrushes touched up the sides of the hull as the shoring was removed preparatory for the launching. The sounds of the carpenters' hammers and wedges were accompanied by the noise of falling timber. Several hundred workmen took several hours to remove the shoring timbers wedged under the ship's bottom. Battering rams were used to drive the wedges under the shores, since the hull was so heavy. Each of the battering rams was manned by a squad of men distributed along the keel in a double column on each side of the ship. The pounding noise was deafening.

When the shores were removed, the ship rested in her launching cradle, which in turn rested on the ways. The driving of the wedges lifted the hull off the keel blocks and permitted removal of the blocks. A week earlier, the ways had been greased with a tallow and oil mixture in order to ensure success. Original plans had been to launch the liner six weeks earlier, but the bitter cold weather had delayed construction, and a new date was chosen.

At noon, a vast assemblage had collected in the shipyard and on the Delaware River. The two steamboats bearing the invited guests and the Pennsylvania legislators steamed up to the wharf, the delegation from St. Paul disembarked, and the members of the Gridiron Club of Washington and the legislators remained on board to view the proceedings from the river.

The guests invited to be on the launching platform took their positions by 12:30. Frances C. Griscom, daughter of Clement Acton Griscom, who was to launch the ship, was joined for the ceremony by Governor Daniel Hartman Hastings, Henry W. Cramp, and a few young friends from Miss Galbraith's School in Haverford. The thundering blows of the battering rams beneath the ship finally ceased, and everyone waited for the gigantic hull to begin to slide into the water. Minutes passed and nothing happened. The crowd waited to applaud and cheer. Miss Griscom continued to hold the bottle of

The bow of the St. Louis *is caught just as it leaves the ways at the Cramp Shipyard, November 12, 1894.*

The largest ship built in America in the nineteenth century has been successfully launched and everyone in the employ of the Cramp Shipyard can heave a huge sigh of relief.

wine with which to christen the ship once it began to move, but it did not. Strained silence followed. The *St. Paul* did not move.

Frantic consultations occurred. Charles Cramp was having a fit, and Clement Griscom was not pleased. In the meantime, a swarm of busy workmen began to labor under the bow of the liner with hydraulic jacks, trying to raise the hull enough to begin the launch. Nothing happened. Steam lines were run out from the engine room of the shipyard and superheated steam was blasted against the sticky, stiff tallow. Still nothing happened. Every effort on land having proven unavailing, a line was cast from the *St. Paul*'s stern to four tugs and a powerful city iceboat, and they tugged frantically to launch the ship. All effort was fruitless and, after two hours, Henry Cramp announced

A beautiful broadside of the St. Louis *underway.*

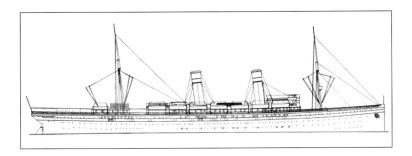

Scientific American *closely followed the construction of the American Line ships and published this line drawing of the* Saints *from the Cramp Shipyard plans, August 11, 1894, three months before the launch.*

the cancellation of the launch for that day because the tide had changed. Putting the best face possible on matters, the hosts served the formal luncheon to the guests, but the congratulatory speeches were omitted. This was the first failure to launch a ship at the Cramp Shipyard since the *Pennsylvania* stuck in 1873, and the experience was both embarrassing and humiliating.[7]

Analysis of the situation placed the problem on two causes. The weather had been so cold that the tallow had chilled and become more like glue than grease, holding the hull on the ways. Furthermore, the delay in the launch for more than six weeks because of the cold weather had resulted in the installation of more than 1,000 tons of additional machinery and fittings, which increased the weight to be moved down the launching ways. The *St. Paul*, festooned with bunting and flags, remained firmly positioned on her building berth at the end of the day. An enormous amount of work would be necessary to prepare the hull for launching a second time. The ship had to be shored up again, the launching cradle removed, the old tallow scraped away, new oil and tallow applied, the launching cradle reassembled, and the shoring removed once more. This would take approximately two weeks, since great care had to be exercised not to topple the huge hull as it was lifted.

Great emphasis had been placed on having the state legislators present, since it was felt that Philadelphia had been slighted when money was appropriated for such things as

The St. Louis *moving down the Delaware River on her trials.*

harbor improvements. Contemporary boosters of the port felt that the expenditure of only a relatively nominal sum for improvement of the Delaware River channel would produce great benefits in increased commerce and trade for the whole state. Unfortunately, the failure of the launch was complicated by a pushing and shoving fiasco on the iceboat assigned to the legislators, and they returned to Harrisburg ready to censure someone. A "Resolution of Indignation" was introduced into the Pennsylvania House of Representatives by Mr. Phillips of Chester, who sharply criticized the handling of the official parties in connection with the launching ceremony. It seems as though a large number of uninvited guests had pushed their way onto the boat reserved for the legislators, severely overcrowding the accommodations. Unanimous consent for the consideration of the resolution was asked, but Mr. Smith of Philadelphia rose in objection, feathers were smoothed, and the resolution was withdrawn, although the Cramp Shipyard and the International Navigation Company received an additional dose of bad publicity.

Two weeks of frantic activity ensued around the stranded hull of the *St. Paul.* Everyone was invited back for the second try on April 10, and many members of the official party from the city of St. Paul had enjoyed an extra two weeks in Philadelphia as the guests of the steamship line. The Cramps were confident of success, but Charles Cramp and his son Edwin took personal charge of the launching and spent the morning running around supervising workmen. Cramp was so sure that the problem with the unsuccessful launch lay with the gummy tallow, rather than additional weight, that construction on the liner continued. The two extra weeks had seen the addition of the iron framework for the bridge as well as considerable interior finishing. This time, the tallow was checked and checked again to ensure its runny consistency. Finally, the shores were removed and the hull rested on its cradle again. The only thing left to be done was the sawing away of the driving ways. Charles and Edwin Cramp stood among the workmen anxiously awaiting the creaking of the timber, which would signify the starting of the

ship. As the saws began to move and the work of cutting through the driving ways began, some yelled, "Get ready."

Frances Griscom, the young sponsor of the liner, was advised by Henry Cramp to stand nearer the hull. She took a step forward and placed one hand on the stem of the ship while she held the bottle of wine in the other. Throughout the yard, men took out their watches to time the launch. Charles Cramp stood on the top step of the landing from the gangway to the launching stand and anxiously waited as the seconds ticked by. Then, with a creaking and a thunderous crash of falling timbers, the giant hull began to move. If Frances Griscom ever said anything, the speech is lost to history, but she heaved the bottle of wine with precision and it shattered against the steel stem as the *St. Paul* finally slid gracefully toward the Delaware.

"She's off" was shouted from many throats, and the air was filled with the din of blowing whistles from river craft, factories, and train locomotives. The *St. Paul* began to move down the ways at 1:05, and exactly 60 seconds later the starboard anchor was let loose, quickly followed by the port anchor. The liner swung around in the river, bow down, and was soon secured by waiting tugs, which towed her to the wharf. When the anchors were dropped in the river and the guests on the stand were thoroughly satisfied with the launch, Charles H. Cramp triumphantly led the way across a special bridge to the old mould loft in the building facing on Beach Street, where a celebratory luncheon was ready.

Cramp and Griscom were accompanied by Governor Daniel Hartman Hastings; Deputy Attorney General Wilbur F. Reeder; ex-Minister to England Robert Lincoln; Henry D. Welsh, former president of the American Steamship Company and a director of the Pennsylvania Railroad; Mayor Charles F. Warwick; District Attorney Graham; the St. Paul visitors; and other invited guests. At the luncheon, a number of speeches were made by the governor, the mayor, Griscom, and Henry Cramp, although one of the

The St. Paul *is shown ready for her launch at the Cramp Shipyard, March 25, 1895. Unfortunately, the liner stuck on the ways and Cramp could not get her into the water until April 10.*

most famous guests of honor, who had been invited to the initial launch date, had left on a European tour. No less a literary lion than Samuel Langhorne Clemens had been invited to speak at the launch of the *St. Paul*. He had traveled to Philadelphia to be present in March when the hull refused to budge, but he could not wait two weeks for the second attempt. In spite of the fact that European engagements made it impossible for him to be present on April 10, "Mark Twain" left his written comments to be read:

> Day after tomorrow [March 27] I sail for Europe in a ship of this line, the *Paris*. It will be my fourteenth crossing in three years and a half; therefore my presence here, as you see, is quite natural, quite commercial. I am interested in ships. They interest me more than hotels do. When a new ship is launched I feel a desire to go and see if she will be good quarters for me to go to live in, particularly if she belongs to this line, for it is by this line that I have done most of my journeying. People wonder why I go so much. Well, partly for my health and partly to familiarize myself with the road. I have gone over the same road so many times now that I know all the whales that belong along the route and, latterly, it is an embarrassment to me to meet them, for they do not look glad to see me, but annoyed, and they seem to say, "Here is this old derelict again!"
>
> Earlier in life this would have pained me and made me ashamed; but I am older now, and when I am behaving myself and doing right, I do not care for a whale's opinion about me. When we are young we generally estimate an opinion by the size of the person that holds it; but later we find that that is an uncertain rule, for we realize that there are times when a hornet's opinion disturbs us more than an emperor's. I do not mean that I do not care nothing at all for a whale's

opinion, for that would be going to too great a length. Of course it is better to have the good opinion of a whale than his disapproval. But my position is that if you cannot have a whale's good opinion except at some sacrifice of principle or personal dignity, it is better to try to live without it. That is my idea about whales. Yes, I have gone over that same route so often that I know my way without the compass—just by the waves. I know all the large waves and a good many of the small ones, and also the sunsets. I know every sunset and where it belongs just by the color. Necessarily, then I do not make the passage now for scenery. That is all gone by. What I prize now is safety first, and in the second place, swift transit and handiness. These are best furnished by the American Line, and I am told by naval folks that this line's ships are the only ones in existence where water-tight compartments have no passage through them, no doors to be left open and consequently, no way for water to get from one of them to another in time of collision. If you nullify the peril which collision threatens you with, you nullify the only serious peril which attends voyaging on the great liners of our day and makes voyaging safer than by staying at home.

When the *Paris* was torn half to pieces some years ago enough of the Atlantic ebbed and flowed through one end of her during her long agony to sink the fleets of the world, if distributed among them, but she floated in perfect safety, and no lives were lost. This seems to me to be the only great line in the world, that takes a passenger from metropolis to metropolis without the intervention of tugs and barges or bridges—takes him through without breaking boat, so to speak. Upon the English side he lands upon a dock, on the dock a special train is waiting and in one hour or three-quarters he is in London. Nothing could be handier. If your journey were from a sandpit on one side to a lighthouse on the other you could make it quicker by other lines, but that is not the case. The journey is from the city of New York to the city of London and no other line can do that journey quicker than this one, nor anywhere even as conveniently and handily, and when the passenger lands on our side, he lands on the *American* side of the river, not in the provinces. As a very learned man said last voyage—he is the head quartermaster of the *New York* and starboard streak [sic] of the middle watch—when we land a passenger on the American side there is nothing betwixt him and his hotel but hell and the hackman. The American Line pays no difference to tides and loses no time by them on either side of the ocean. It sails at 11 from New York and at noon from Southampton, and lets the tide serve when it gets ready. I am glad with you and the nation to welcome the new ship. She is another pride, another constellation for a great country whose mighty fleets have all vanished and which has almost forgotten what it is to fly its flag at sea. I am not sure as to which St. Paul she is named for. Some think it is the one that is on the Upper Mississippi; but the head quartermaster told me that it was the one that killed Goliah [sic]. But it is not important. No matter which it is, let us give her hearty welcome and godspeed.[8]

Griscom responded to the toast that Clemens had written for the launch of the *St. Paul:*

> I thank you for the friendly manner in which you have received the toast to the International Navigation Company, and I wish, on behalf of our company, to express our warm appreciation of the presence here of the distinguished and influential delegation from the beautiful city of St. Paul—ladies and gentlemen who have left their homes and businesses and undertaken to travel at this unreliable season of the year 2,000 miles to manifest their interest in the launch of this steamship, and in our company's efforts to secure a share of the traffic of this country to our native flag.
>
> This, certainly, is a remarkable evidence of great sympathy, and it is most highly appreciated.
>
> It is this sort of public spirit, manifested in a thousand ways, that has made St. Paul the great city it is, and has developed, with unparalleled rapidity, the wonderful Northwest.

Griscom expressed admiration for Cramp's skill in building great ships, and complimented them on the successful launching of the *St. Paul*. He also chose to expound upon the decision of the board of directors of the International Navigation Company to name one of its new liners *St. Paul*. Griscom said that a request to name the ship for the capital of Minnesota had been received from citizens of that state, presumably with numerous other suggestions from many other areas. When the directors of the International Navigation Company had been discussing potential names, they found themselves bound to recognize the fact that the success of the Inman Line, which they had only recently renamed the American Line, was largely indebted to the enormous numbers of Scandinavian, German, and Swiss immigrants whom it had carried across the Atlantic to populate the Northwest.

> It is these brave yeomen and their descendants who have done so much to make your country what it is, to whom we must look not only for our future passenger service but also for much of the produce that must fill our cargo holds.
>
> The Inman Line was the first transatlantic line that made the comfort of the emigrant on the ocean its chief aim (previously they had been crowded into sailing vessels); but the Inman Line put the first fleet of steamships afloat devoted to improving the comfort of the emigrant.
>
> The American Line has lived up to the tradition, and we carry the emigrant today more comfortably and more speedily than the cabin passengers of a generation ago.[9]

Griscom was justifiably proud of the International Navigation Company's achievements over the previous ten years. Insofar as he was concerned, his was the first line to place twin-screw passenger vessels into service, the first to establish the fact that 20 knots from shore to shore was as feasible as 15 knots, and the first to give cabin

A starboard view of the St. Louis *with a bone in her teeth inward bound to Southampton.*

passengers such luxurious accommodations at sea as were previously considered impossible. "We can safely claim that to us belongs the credit of a great advancement in the comfort and safety and speed of transatlantic passenger service, and we are proud to point to the *New York* and the *Paris* and now to their sisters, the *St. Louis* and the *St. Paul*, as the work of our company."[10] Griscom was very concerned about the many comments that had been made about the "record-breaking" possibilities of the *Saints* and wanted to make clear the position of the company:

> Much has been written on the assumption that they were to be record-breakers. This is correct, so far as comfort is concerned; but not in the sense that they are expected to beat the speed record. They are to be running mates of their sisters, the *New York* and the *Paris*, and with them they are to make an even and regular performance, so that our patrons shall know not only that they are to sail at a fixed hour but that they are to arrive at a fixed hour as nearly as practicable, and they, therefore, can be indifferent to which of these steamers they take.
>
> It avails nothing to beat another steamer an hour or so. It is money wasted to try to gain this small advantage, and this waste of money for this small advantage we have tried to avoid.
>
> We intend to be commercially successful to the utmost degree, and it is only by making a fair return to those who have ventured their money that we can properly serve the public.
>
> We have studied this carefully—we shall give the speed the law requires of us—make a uniform and regular running, for the experienced travelling public have already shown their indifference to record-breaking, and very wisely so.
>
> I am very grateful for the good wishes which so complement your toast, and we shall strive to merit your patronage.[11]

The St. Paul *rests after her successful trials. The crisp fall breeze in 1895 blows the smoke from her funnels forward over the bow.*

The goals and ideals of the rejuvenated American Line were eloquently expressed by Griscom at the launching of the *St. Paul.* Griscom's remarks can be summarized quite simply: "The aim of the American Line is not to cut down the ocean record by one hour, but rather to produce steamers that should be trustworthy and comfortable in all winds and weathers, departing and arriving on schedule."[12]

Special care was taken with the members of the Pennsylvania General Assembly this time. The formal invitations to the lawmakers assured them that there would be no crowding or pushing because the International Navigation Company had chartered one of the largest Delaware River steamers, the *Columbia,* for their comfort. With these assurances and a little arm twisting by the mighty Pennsylvania Railroad, President G. Wesley Thomas of the Senate and Speaker Henry F. Walton of the House were persuaded to break off their deliberations once again for a daylong excursion to Philadelphia as the guests of the railroad, the builder, and the steamship line. A special train left Harrisburg at 7 A.M. and was taken around the city to the Washington Avenue wharf of the International Navigation Company, which was reached around 10:30. The *Columbia* awaited them there, but it was a little while before she departed, since every guest was required to present a special ticket in order to board the chartered steamer. This time, there was to be no overcrowding or unseemly shoving. Remarkably, 284 of the legislators and their friends traveled to Philadelphia with Governor Hastings and Lieutenant Governor Walter Lyon in order to avail themselves of the hospitality of the International Navigation Company. No expense was spared to wine and dine the members of the General Assembly on the pleasure steamer. The *Columbia* arrived off the Cramp Shipyard shortly after 11 A.M. in plenty of time for lunch on board and a good view of the launching ceremony. After the *St. Paul* successfully took to the water, the *Columbia* took the legislators for a run down the Delaware to show them the shoals blocking navigation in the lower stretches of the river. It was hoped that this would encourage them to vote in favor of a $500,000 appropriation for the improvement of the Delaware River channel. The *Columbia* returned to the wharf later in the afternoon, and

The elaborate first-class dining rooms of the St. Paul *(1895) and* St. Louis *(1895) were designed to impress any traveler. The American ships were built by the Cramp Shipyard to partner the* New York *and* Paris.

The Cramp Shipyard sought to make the first-class dining room of the St. Louis *the most magnificent afloat. Soaring more than two decks through the center of the ship, it represented the American version of Victorian interior decorating.*

the well-contented legislators boarded their special train for the return trip to Harrisburg. This time around, everyone agreed that the occasion was enjoyable.

The *St. Louis* slipped down Delaware Bay on May 25. She was under the command of the Cramp shipmaster, Captain R.W. Sergeant, as she backed out into the Delaware and turned parallel to the Cramp Shipyard. In midstream, she was turned over to the International Navigation Company, and Captain William G. Randle took command for the first time.[13] The *St. Louis* left her birthplace with the American flag flying from both the sternpost and the masthead, indicating that she was an American ship bound for an American port. As the liner got underway at 11:45 A.M., she was given a deafening ovation by an informal crowd that had gathered all along the river. On board were a few representatives of the shipyard and the line, and no one else. With justifiable pride, Clement Griscom permitted himself the pleasure of one of the suites for the trials. He was accompanied by Edwin Cramp and Professor J.H. Giles of Edinburgh University, consulting architect to the American Line. Members of the press were prohibited from boarding the ship, which was outward bound for three days of trials. The explanation for the secrecy was that the builders and owners preferred that information about the ship's speed and seaworthiness not become public before she actually entered service. Unofficially, there was some concern about the performance of the huge new quadruple-expansion engines and of the new hull design, which only the trials would answer.

Cramp stated again to the press that he wanted the ship to work up her machinery gradually and not to make any attempt to sustain 20 knots for four hours in order to fulfill the requirement for the United States mail contract. Since the mail contract did not go into effect until October, there was plenty of time for speed trials later in the summer. Furthermore, if the *St. Louis* maintained 20 knots for an entire Atlantic crossing, no additional trials would be required by the government.

At Philadelphia, immigrants landed from the ship and proceeded immediately to the second floor of Pier 53 to meet the Immigration officials. Note the railroad baggage cars loading trunks from the ship.

Chapter 10

THE BEST-BALANCED
NORTH ATLANTIC SERVICE

FLEET:

	Tonnage.	Length, Feet.	Breadth, Feet.		Tonnage.	Length, Feet.	Breadth, Feet.
ST LOUIS (twin screw)	11,629	554	63	ST PAUL (twin screw)	11,600	554	63
NEW YORK, "	10,803	560	63¼	PARIS, "	10,795	560	63¼
KENSINGTON, "	8,669	494	57	SOUTHWARK, "	8,607	494	57
FRIESLAND, . .	7,116	455	51	WESTERNLAND,	5,736	455	47
BERLIN, ...	5,526	510	44	NOORDLAND, . .	5,212	419	47
CHESTER, . . .	4,770	461	44	WAESLAND, . .	4,752	443	43
PENNLAND, . . .	3,760	374	42	BELGENLAND, .	3,692	423	40
RHYNLAND, . . .	3,689	423	40	OHIO, ...	3,392	355	43
PENNSYLVANIA, .	3,166	355	43	ILLINOIS, . . .	3,163	355	43
INDIANA, . . .	3,158	355	43	NEDERLAND, . .	2,839	338	39
SWITZERLAND, .	2,819	338	39	CONEMAUGH, .	2,328	310	37

The fleet of the International Navigation Company in 1896 shows 22 vessels of which the first-class service was composed of the St. Louis, St. Paul, New York, *and* Paris, *which represented the best-balanced first-class service on the North Atlantic.*

Fog obscured Delaware Bay as the *St. Louis,* the largest American-flag ship, slowly steamed down the bay. In fact, the fog was so thick that the liner did not drop the pilot and clear the Capes at the mouth of Delaware Bay until 6:15 A.M. on May 27, one day behind schedule. Finally she was able to bite her bow into the Atlantic swell and receive her formal baptism.

The *St. Louis* arrived at New York after her sea trials on May 29, 1895, and was spotted by the "observer" at Fire Island who reported ship sightings. She cleared The Narrows, slipped by quarantine, and made her first passage up the bay to the American Line pier at the foot of Fulton Street. All the way, the beautiful queen of the American merchant marine was greeted by the whistles of hundreds of tugs, ferryboats, and steam craft of every description. At 4 P.M., Captain William G. Randle maneuvered his new charge into her home berth, where she promptly became the center of attention in the city.

The International Navigation Company was besieged by the press and well-wishers who wanted to tour the *St. Louis.* They promptly announced that she would be open to journalists on Saturday and the general public on Monday, at a charge of 25 cents per person—the proceeds to be divided between the maritime charities of New York and the Pilots Benevolent Association.

When Clement Acton Griscom, president of the International Navigation Company, was questioned by reporters about the trip, he responded, "The trip was made for two reasons. The builders wanted to test the ship, and the owners wanted to be sure the machinery was in perfect order. The Chief Engineer informs me that he kept up a nominal pressure of 200 pounds to the square inch, and that the machinery worked beautifully. The builder's certificate will be delivered to the Government today, and the ship will be registered tomorrow."[1] Among the 150 passengers on the liner were many of the department heads from the Cramp Shipyard, who got a chance to admire their work while being available for consultation. One of the passengers who broke the cordon of secrecy said that the *St. Louis* at one time had achieved more than 22½ knots. A thrilling experience had occurred when the outward-bound *Paris* passed them off Sandy Hook and treated them to a thunderous salute on her horns, while her passengers cheered. The *Paris* ran up the house flag and dipped the colors to the newest addition to the fleet.

The signal flags of the *St. Louis* spelled out her call letters, HSPT, and were chosen by the First Lady, Mrs. Grover Cleveland, who had been her sponsor. Mrs. Cleveland selected signal flags composed entirely of the colors red, white, and blue. The first flag consisted of one red and one white perpendicular stripe, the second of a white background with a blue square in the center, the third of a blue background with a white square in the center, and the fourth of red, white, and blue perpendicular strips. Fortunately, the combination was easily visible and unlikely to be confused with any distress signals. The Bureau of Navigation was pleased to comply with the First Lady's selection and provide the *St. Louis* with the call letters HSPT. Her official American registry number was 116,669.

The official statistics of the *St. Louis*, upon final measurement, were:

Gross tonnage	11,629 tons
Net tonnage	5,895 tons
Length between perpendiculars	535.51 feet
Overall length	554 feet
Breadth	63 feet
Number of decks	6
Moulded depth	42 feet
Watertight bulkheads	17
Draught	26 feet
Collision bulkhead abaft stem	33 feet
Quadruple-expansion engines	20,000 hp

In recognition of the honor bestowed by the American Line in naming the new ship for the city of St. Louis, the citizens of that metropolis, led by Mayor Walbridge, made a gift to the ship of two libraries for the first-class and second-class passengers. The city of

The first-class staircase of the St. Paul *and the* St. Louis *sweeps down through the ship. The Act of Congress permitting American registry for the* New York *and the* Paris, *required the building of two larger ships in the Cramp Shipyard.*

St. Louis also gave 10 ornamental glass windows for the the first-cabin library, as well as a full set of flags, including the American ensign and the house flag in silk, and a large burgee bearing the name "St. Louis."[2]

Nothing ever appeared to go absolutely smoothly for the International Navigation Company. A morning newspaper in New York carried an article in which crew members of the *St. Louis* who had signed on in Philadelphia for the trial trip to New York accused the Line of having acted in bad faith toward them. According to some of the crew members, they should have been paid the normal wages of laborers, $1.50 a day, but instead had received only the $1.25 a day of sailors for the trial trip. James Wright, Jr., the American Line agent in New York, stated that those who had signed on in Philadelphia had been hired as sailors at wages stipulated by the company to bring the ship to New York. The *St. Louis* carried neither fare-paying passengers nor cargo on the trip north. It was understood that those who signed on in Philadelphia would have the opportunity to stay with the ship at sailors' wages if they wished. Only a few individuals were involved, and nothing further came of the incident.

Another concern voiced by the sailors was that the American Line intended to import cheap help from overseas to man the new liners and not to employ American crews, as required by the new Postal Aid Act. Wright assured all concerned that the entire crew of the *St. Louis* would be secured in New York, although he could not testify

The First Cabin Saloon (dining room), looking forward, on the steamships St. Louis *and* St. Paul. *The elaborate bank of organ pipes probably could make the domed skylight vibrate. The long boarding-house tables would be part of every Atlantic liner for another ten years.*

as to what percentage would hold American citizenship at the time of sailing. All the officers of the ships would hold American citizenship.[3]

When the liner was opened to the public, she was described as a floating palace of unparalleled beauty. A straight stem, elliptical stern, two pole masts, and two lofty smokestacks with cowls gave the *St. Louis* distinctive lines. The five passenger decks were designated orlop, main, upper, saloon, and promenade, with the last three plated from stem to stern. All decks were covered with wood planking for beauty and comfort. The promenade deck remained unbroken for the length of the liner, providing a broad, open expanse of deck space that would prove very popular. The *St. Louis* was fitted out to carry 350 first-class, 200 second-class, and 900 steerage passengers. Some cabins were intended to be interchangeable between first and second, according to bookings. In her first-class accommodations, she had more suites than any other vessel in service and the luxuriousness of their fittings, since many had private bathrooms, was unprecedented. The main saloon, or dining room, on the upper deck stretched 110 feet by 50 feet and was large enough to hold all the first-class passengers at one sitting. While the *St. Louis* may not have been first, this has remained a standard of excellence ever since. The

dining room was situated in the middle of the ship, where it was felt there would be a comparative absence of motion. Slender pillars supported a large dome that soared over the center of the main saloon and gave the room an airy atmosphere. At the same time, nearly all the available space in the room not occupied by woodwork was covered with paneling. On the aft end, the dome contained a heroic seated figure of Neptune, Roman god of the sea, with two large allegorical panels. At the base of the dome on each of the two sides was a series of panels featuring figures of harp and viol players. At the forward end of the dining room was a colossal electric pipe organ with 14 stops. It was elevated above the diners and occupied the arched space soaring to the dome. The base of the organ rested on the shoulders of a heroic mermaid figure, while the brass pipes totally filled the area. The console of the organ was played from a location on the saloon deck some 30 feet away. An electric battery supplied the power for operating the organ, with both the key mechanism and the blower being electrical. It was considered remarkable that a single two-volt battery was sufficient to supply the power to the organ, built by Jardine & Company of New York. A permanent organist was one of the musical positions on the liner's staff.

The walls of the dining room were divided into alcoves paneled with carvings of fish and fowl. The predominant wood was Mexican mahogany, and the seats were upholstered in a bluish-green plush. The dome of the dining saloon was, in fact, an immense

The St. Louis *and* St. Paul *are shown passing The Needles near Southampton, England. The Needles are a rocky promontory off the Isle of Wight that marks the beginning of the transatlantic run to New York. The card was by the American Litho Company of New York, which produced the new American Line advertising cards after 1893.*

skylight that emitted light to the room through stained-glass windows. Additional windows, not portholes, along the sides also lightened one of the most magnificent rooms in any ship afloat or any hotel on land. The second-class dining room, on the same deck as the main saloon but situated toward the stern, was fitted out in a manner equal to first-class facilities on other vessels.

The first-class smoking room for gentlemen was on the promenade deck aft, and it had every comfort a passenger could desire. Rich dark-mahogany paneling covered the walls, as in the very best men's clubs ashore, and the furniture was covered in dark leather. The carvings enhancing the smoking room dealt with the Bacchic origin of wine and the Indian origin of tobacco. The drawing room, or social hall, for ladies and non-smokers was executed with an emphasis on lightness and comfort. The drawing room was graced with silk tapestries and silk-paneled walls; the predominant tone was yellow with an abundance of floral patterns. The large first-class library soon proved to be the most popular room on the liner. The prevailing color was sepia, which contrasted nicely with the glass-doored oak bookcases lining the walls. The citizens of St. Louis had given the ship what was regarded with justification as the finest library afloat. One interesting feature of the library was the arrangement of more than one overstuffed chair around the pillars necessary for deck support, thereby utilizing to advantage what otherwise might have been an unsightly problem. Many writing tables were also supplied. The firm of Furness and Evans, architects, undertook the general scheme of interior decoration, which was executed by the builders and the American Line under the immediate supervision of Mr. Furness.[4] Their achievement was applauded for being in the lighter style favored by Americans in the year 1895 rather than the heavier Victorian and Wilhelmine styles of Europe.

A new type of mattress for the staterooms on the *St. Louis*, supplied by the Mechanical Manufacturing Company of Boston, Massachusetts, received considerable publicity. The mattress consisted of a sack of airtight rubber cloth with the back and front secured together. The outer covering was a strong cotton duck heavily coated with rubber and vulcanized. A foot bellows was used to inflate it. The cabin steward attached a long rubber hose to the valve of the mattress and inflated the mattress with a few pushes on the bellows. The tube was removed, the valve secured, and the bed was ready for making. One inflation would last as long as a year. The mattress could be pumped up hard, a passenger could lie down on it, and air could be let out until the individual felt as comfortable as on his or her own bed at home. No mention was made of potential smell from the rubber, or durability, and no indication has been discovered about how long the mattresses were in use on the *St. Louis*. The basic concept was felt to have a great many beneficial applications ashore and afloat in everything from mattresses to seats for the home to life rings. It was mentioned that one staid New England church recently had bought a complete set of air-filled cushions for its pews.[5]

The *St. Louis* attracted a great deal of attention on June 5 when she backed out from her pier and started on her maiden voyage. She had been thrown open for inspection in the morning until the "all ashore" gong, and the ship was overrun with hundreds of curious persons. It was the largest crowd ever to inspect a steamship in New York since the *Great Eastern* 40 years earlier. Griscom spared no expense to make the first sailing of the new American queen as festive as possible. The crew were all outfitted in new white duck suits, and gigantic bouquets of flowers were placed everywhere in the public rooms. The main dining saloon was described as a veritable bower of flowers. Many of the floral displays were composed of red, white, and blue flowers arranged in the shapes of flags or other emblems.

The crowd on the deck was so great that passengers found themselves having difficulty getting on board, and when the supplementary mail arrived at 10:55, five minutes prior to sailing, only a squad of policemen could make enough room for the wagons to reach the ship. At least two steerage-class passengers arrived after the gangplank had been drawn in and missed the ship.

As the *St. Louis* backed out into the North River, she was loudly cheered and the passengers lining the promenade deck responded by waving hundreds of small silk American flags about the size of handkerchiefs. The queen of the American merchant marine was awash with patriotic colors all along the open deck, and the cheering became thunderous. A great silk American flag, also the gift of the city of St. Louis, waved over the taffrail as the *St. Louis* turned downstream and headed for the bay. Unfortunately, the fog was so thick Captain Randle had to anchor off Sandy Hook, since it was

(top left) *First-cabin smoking room of the steamships* St. Paul *and* St. Louis *as outfitted by the William Cramp Shipyard, Philadelphia, Pa.*

(top right) *The Promenade Deck on the new American liners (1895).*

(middle left) *A first-class suite on the* Saints *including sitting room, bedroom, bath, and toilet room sold for $600 per person for one crossing in 1895.*

(middle right) *The ladies' drawing room on the* St. Paul *and* St. Louis.

(bottom left) *The libraries on the new American liners were the gifts of their sponsoring cities, St. Paul, Minnesota, and St. Louis, Missouri.*

Another view of the ladies' drawing room on the St. Paul *and* St. Louis.

considered unsafe to venture out. Later in the day, the fog lifted and the *St. Louis* cleared The Narrows. Griscom firmly stated that no attempt would be made to beat any record, since the machinery was still being brought up to full power.

About six miles east of the lightship, the Hamburg-American express steamer *Augusta Victoria* (1889, 7,661 tons), inward bound to New York, passed the *St. Louis*. Captain Kaempff of the *Augusta Victoria* ordered her flags to be broken out, and the German liner's orchestra quickly assembled on deck to play American national airs in honor of the *St. Louis* as the two ships passed and saluted each other. On a more somber note, the news also was passed that the German liner had spotted three gigantic icebergs drifting in the middle of the transatlantic steamer lanes. The bergs towered 75 to 120 feet high and were more than 500 feet long. The price of safety, particularly in foggy weather, was eternal vigilance! The maiden voyage of the *St. Louis* from New York to Southampton did not establish any record. The big American liner arrived at Southampton at 4:20 A.M. on June 13 after a crossing of seven days, three hours, 53 minutes. She had averaged 18 knots, with daily runs of 314, 443, 431, 441, 433, 432, 416, and 249 miles. The twin quadruple-expansion engines had worked up to about 80 revolutions per minute, which represented about 85 percent of potential power. With regard to her speed, Captain Randle said it should be remembered that the liner had not been dry-docked for cleaning and painting since her launching in November 1894, and that no great results should be expected before this was done, since the hull was foul.

The *St. Louis* brought with her a full complement of cabin passengers (335 first, 175 second) and 265 steerage passengers. All commented most favorably on the stability of the ship and on the almost total absence of engine vibration. One of her most distinguished passengers was Sir Julian Pauncefote, Her Majesty's ambassador to the United States, who was returning home on leave. Sir Julian chaired a meeting on the *St. Louis* at which a resolution was passed by the first-class passengers praising the Line and the builders for the magnificent new American steamship.[6] Later a question was raised in the

The Friesland *(1889) was built in Glasgow, Scotland, by James and George Thomson, builders of the* New York *and the* Paris, *and was designed nearly upon the same lines as those steamers. She was built of Siemens-Martin steel and to the standards of Lloyd's of London and the Bureau Veritas.*

House of Commons about why the British ambassador was using British government funds to travel on an American ship, but the matter was dropped when Sir Edward Grey, foreign minister, said he was not prepared to respond.

At Southampton, a crowd gathered to see the maiden arrival of the *St. Louis* in spite of the early hour. The customs tables were drawn up parallel to the railroad shed, and the special train to London awaited the passengers. Quite a number of the passengers were on deck as the liner was escorted to her berth by two tugs. At the time of her arrival, she dwarfed every other vessel in the harbor. Edmund Taylor, the managing director of the company in England, expressed great satisfaction with the performance of the ship, whose engineers had been instructed to take it easy for several crossings. The liner was open for public viewing at a small charge while in port, and the proceeds were donated to a local charity. Public-relations activities included a shipboard luncheon for civic dignitaries and railroad officials and special arrangements for journalists to accompany the ship as she sailed down Southampton Water on her return trip.

Charles H. Cramp had sailed from New York on the *Augusta Victoria*, and the Hamburg-American liner was approaching Southampton as the *St. Louis* was outward bound. Cramp was on the bridge of the HAPAG ship as his most brilliant creation approached. Passengers crowded the rails of both liners. One cheer broke out from the throng on the *Augusta Victoria* for the new American liner, whose passengers responded with three cheers for the *St. Louis* and her builder. Charles Cramp was deeply touched and doffed his hat as the two big ships sped by each other. This promptly brought another roar from the passengers on the *St. Louis.*

Upon arrival in Hamburg, Cramp explained in an interview with a United Press reporter that the plans of the International Navigation Company originally had been for five ships, but that this had proven prohibitively expensive, even with the inducement of the new mail contract. The Line had cut back its order from five to two first-class ships, and had revised the vessels' specifications in order to allow them to carry much more cargo than originally intended. The *St. Louis* and the *St. Paul* never would be record breakers in the sense of speed, but they were record breakers in the sense of their luxury and in their earnings per voyage. Cramp built his ships to operate 12 months of the year in all kinds of weather, and there was no question that they would be driven hard.

The maiden westbound crossing of the *St. Louis* was destined to be far more eventful. The liner sailed from Southampton on June 15 with high hopes for a fast passage. By Sunday noon, she had made good time under favorable conditions and had logged 431 miles. By Monday noon, another 464 miles had been covered, and the engines worked up to 482 miles by noon Tuesday. Stormy weather was encountered Tuesday morning, and the liner was handling the seas quite well when it was discovered that a large crack or fissure had opened in the massive piece of steel that formed the main section of the rudder. An immediate examination made while the *St. Louis* was under full speed convinced Captain Randle and the chief engineer that it would be dangerous to move the rudder much and that they should dispense with using it for steering. The crack began in the rudderpost and extended downward in a lateral direction. While the rudder might hold all the way to New York under normal use, disaster might result if it broke, so the decision was made to stabilize it. The helm accordingly was steadied amidships and made fast without any play in the rudder.

The remainder of the 1,600-mile crossing to New York was made using the twin screws for steering—a difficult and laborious task involving hundreds of signals from the bridge to the engine room. When the bow sheared to starboard, the port engine was checked and the starboard engine was set ahead at increased speed. Almost without fail, a similar adjustment the other way had to be initiated within minutes. Fair weather favored the *St. Louis* for most of the crossing. The bearings on the engines became hot on several occasions, making it necessary to slow them, and once they were stopped completely for a few minutes to permit an examination of the crosshead on the port engine. A pilot was taken on board from Pilot Boat 6 about 250 miles east of Sandy Hook.

As the *St. Louis* neared The Narrows, a signal was made for a tug but none was at hand. Captain Randle felt confident of being able to bring his ship to quarantine, and the wheel was brought into duty again, using the rudder very gingerly to thread the vessel through The Narrows. Quarantine was reached shortly after 5 P.M., and the anchor was dropped with a huge sigh of relief from everyone on the bridge and in the engine room.

The second-class dining rooms on the St. Louis *and* St. Paul *were not as luxurious as the first class. There was less carpet on the floor and the seats were solid wood without padding.*

The second-class smoking room for gentlemen on the new American liners was done in different woods, with checkers prominent as a source of entertainment. Note the spittoons on the deck.

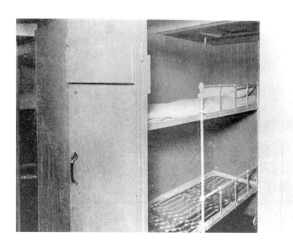

This unusual picture of a steerage cabin with two berths on the Saints *emphasizes the fact that the beds were of a superior quality and had actual springs. One of the mattresses has been removed to show this fact to potential travelers.*

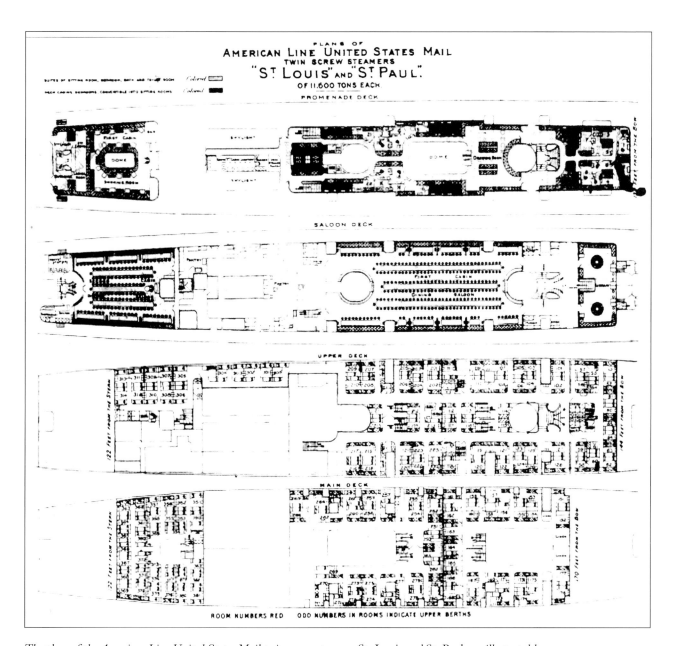

The plans of the American Line United States Mail twin-screw steamers St. Louis *and* St. Paul *are illustrated here. In these ships "the luxuries have been reckoned as being the necessaries."* American Line brochure

SUMMER RATES — PROMENADE DECK

	FOR 1 ADULT.	FOR 1½ ADULTS.	FOR 2 ADULTS.	FOR 2½ ADULTS.	FOR 3 ADULTS.
	Per Room.				
Suites of Sitting Room, Bedroom, Bath and Toilet Room {1-3, 2-4, 5-7, 6-8, 15-17, 16-18, 19-21, 20-22}	£110	£120	£130	£140	£150*
Deck-Cabins ...7, 8	80	85	90	97	105
If with Private Bath and Toilet Room	100	105	110	117	125
Deck-Cabins ...1,2,3,4,9,10,15,16,21,22	75	80	85	92	100
If with Private Bath and Toilet Room	95	100	105	112	120
Deck-Cabins ...5,6,17,18,19,20	65	70	75	82	90
If with Private Bath and Toilet Room	85	90	95	102	110
Deck-Cabins {11, 12, 13, 14}	70	75	80	...	...
Deck-Cabins {23, 24, 25, 26}	65	70	75	...	...
Deck-Cabins ...27, 28, 29, 30	58	62	65	72	80

SUMMER RATES — UPPER DECK

	Per Room.		Each.	Per Room.	Each.
Outside Rooms					
107, 128	65	70	40	85	30
55, 60, 105, 124	55	60	35	77	28
53, 57, 58, 62, 101, 103, 109, 111, 118, 120, 122, 126, 201, 203, 205, 207, 209, 216, 218, 220, 222, 224	50	55	30	67	25
Inside Rooms					
102, 106, 110, 119, 121, 127	42	47	26	60	22
56, 59, 104, 125, 202, 206, 208, 210, 213, 217, 219, 221, 225	40	45	25	55	20
106, 112, 113, 116, 117, 123, 204, 223	38	43	24	53	19
50, 51, 52, 54, 61, 63, 64, 65, 114, 115, 211, 212, 214, 215	34	39	22	50	...

SUMMER RATES — MAIN DECK

	Per Room.		Each.	Per Room.	Each.
Outside Rooms					
153, 157, 161, 168, 174, 256, 277	46	51	28	62	23
151, 159, 170, 172, 176, 253, 255, 257, 259, 261, 263, 264, 265, 271, 272, 274, 276, 278, 280	40	45	25	55	20
Inside Rooms					
152, 154, 155, 156, 160, 162, 163, 164, 165, 166, 167, 171, 173, 175, 177, 250, 262, 283	34	39	22	50	19
158, 169, 251, 252, 254, 258, 260, 266, 269, 270, 273, 275, 279, 281, 282	30	35	20	46	17

WINTER RATES — PROMENADE DECK

	FOR 1 ADULT.	FOR 1½ ADULTS.	FOR 2 ADULTS.	FOR 2½ ADULTS.	FOR 3 ADULTS.
	Per Room.				
Suites of Sitting Room, Bedroom, Bath and Toilet Room {1-3, 2-4, 5-7, 6-8, 15-17, 16-18, 19-21, 20-22}	£80	£90	£100	£110	£115
Deck-Cabins ...7, 8	65	70	75	82	90
If with Private Bath and Toilet Room	80	85	90	97	105
Deck-Cabins ...1, 2, 3, 4, 9, 10, 15, 16, 21, 22	58	62	65	72	80
If with Private Bath and Toilet Room	73	77	80	87	95
Deck-Cabins ...5, 6, 17, 18, 19, 20	50	55	60	67	75
If with Private Bath and Toilet Room	65	70	75	82	90
Deck-Cabins {11, 12, 13, 14}	50	55	60	...	...
Deck-Cabins {23, 24, 25, 26}	45	50	55	...	...
Deck-Cabins ...27, 28, 29, 30	40	45	50	57	65

WINTER RATES — UPPER DECK

	Per Room.		Each.	Per Room.	Each.
Outside Rooms					
107, 128	40	47	27	60	22
55, 60, 105, 111, 118, 124, 203, 222	32	38	25	55	20
53, 57, 58, 62, 101, 103, 109, 120, 122, 126, 201, 205, 207, 209, 216, 218, 220, 224	28	33	22	50	18
Inside Rooms					
102, 108, 110, 119, 121, 127	28	33	22	50	18
56, 59, 106, 112, 113, 116, 117, 123, 204, 212, 213, 214, 223	25	30	20	44	16
50, 51, 52, 54, 65	23	27	18	40	15
114, 115, 211, 215	21	25	17	38	15
	20	23	15	33	15

WINTER RATES — MAIN DECK

	Per Room.		Each.	Per Room.	Each.
Outside Rooms					
153, 157, 161, 168, 174, 256, 277	25	30	20	44	17
151, 159, 170, 172, 176, 253, 255, 257, 259, 261, 263, 264, 265, 271, 272, 274, 276, 278, 280	23	27	18	40	16
Inside Rooms					
152, 154, 155, 156, 160, 162, 163, 164, 165, 166, 167, 171, 173, 175, 177, 250, 262, 283	22	26	17	38	15
158, 169, 251, 252, 254, 258, 260, 266, 269, 270, 273, 275, 279, 281, 282	20	23	15	33	15

Summer rates (1897) for the St. Louis *and* St. Paul *are shown in British pound sterling. Multiply by five to get the fare in dollars for 1897 ($550). A century later the highest fare for an Atlantic crossing by sea would be approximately $16,000, which proportionately has nowhere near the buying power of $550 in 1897.*

The tugs *Evarts* and *Fulver* ran alongside. On board the *Evarts* was Edwin Cramp, ready to inspect the damage immediately and advise the owners about what could be done.

The *St. Louis* cleared quarantine quickly and steamed up the harbor to her pier, where, with the tugs' assistance, she slowly turned into the berth. The operation was prolonged in order to save the rudder as much as possible, and the big ship had to be manhandled into the slip by the tugs. She finally was secured around 7 P.M., and passengers and cargo were gotten off expeditiously. In view of the accident to the rudder, the crossing was quite respectable. Prior to discovery of the damage, the average speed had exceeded 19.5 knots, and even after the problem was realized, the *St. Louis* still averaged 18.5 knots for the crossing.[7]

Cramp had experienced misgivings about the size of the funnels for the *St. Louis* and the *St. Paul*. He had felt that they were too small and did not permit sufficient draft for the fires. Hence, they were impeding the fullest development of the power that the engines could produce. Cramp suggested to Griscom that the *St. Louis* be removed from service in July in order to replace the funnels, drydock the ship for scraping and painting, and undertake maintenance on what had been discovered. Griscom was exceedingly reluctant to remove the vessel from service at the height of the season, and so shortly after her maiden voyage. Moderately fast runs were preferable to no ship so soon after commissioning, and the decision was made to keep the *St. Louis* in service until the normal time for her overhaul.

SUMMER RATES.   TWIN S.S. "NEW YORK" AND "PARIS."   **WINTER RATES.**

Summer Rates

PROMENADE AND SALOON DECKS.		FOR 1 ADULT.	FOR 1½ ADULTS.	FOR 2 ADULTS.	FOR 2½ ADULTS.	FOR 3 ADULTS.
		Per Room.				
Suites of Sitting Room, Bedroom, Bath and Toilet Room	{3, 4, 5, 6, 7, 8, 20, 55, 56, 57, 58}	£110	£120	£130	£140	£150*
Deck Cabins, with Private Bath and Toilet Room	{1, 2	80	85	90	97	105
	{50, 52	50	55	55	...	...
	{19, 21	70	75	80	87	95
Deck Cabins	{9, 10, 11, 15, 17, 22, 23, 24, 25}	65	70	75	82	90
	{12, 13, 14, 16, 18	58	62	65	72	80
	{51, 53, 54	50	55	60	67	75

UPPER DECK.		Per Room.		Each.	Per Room.	Each.
Outside Rooms.	G—307, 312, 313, 316 E—100, 101, 102, 103, 104, 109, 110, 115, 116, 122 F—200, 205, 206, 211, 212, 217, 218, 219 G—300, 306	55	60	35	77	28
		50	55	30	67	25
Inside Rooms.	F—201, 202, 203, 204, 207, 208, 209, 210, 213, 214, 215, 216 G—314, 315, 317, 318	40	45	25	55	20
	E—105, 106, 107, 108, 111, 112, 113, 114, 117, 118, 119, 120, 121 G—301, 302, 303, 304, 305, 308, 309, 310, 311	34	39	22	50	19

MAIN DECK.						
Outside Rooms.	P—250, 256, 257, 262, 263, 268, 269, 274 R—350, 353, 354, 358, 359, 362	40	45	25	55	20
	O—150, 153, 154, 157, 158, 161, 162, 167, 168, 173 R—363, 368	34	39	22	50	19
Inside Rooms.	O—159, 160 P—271, 272, 273 R—355, 357, 360, 361	34	39	22	50	19
	O—169, 170, 171, 172 P—251, 252, 253, 254, 255, 258, 259, 260, 261, 264, 265, 266, 267	30	35	20	46	18
	O—151, 152, 155, 156, 163, 164, 165, 166 P—270 R—351, 352, 356, 364, 365, 366, 367	30	33	19	45	17

Winter Rates

PROMENADE AND SALOON DECKS.		FOR 1 ADULT.	FOR 1½ ADULTS.	FOR 2 ADULTS.	FOR 2½ ADULTS.	FOR 3 ADULTS.
		Per Room.				
Suites of Sitting Room, Bedroom, Bath and Toilet Room	{3, 4, 5, 6, 7, 8, 20, 55, 56, 57, 58}	£80	£90	£100	£110	£115
Deck Cabins, with Private Bath and Toilet Room	{1, 2	60	65	70	77	85
	{50, 52	40	45	50	...	...
Deck Cabins	{9, 10, 11, 15, 17, 19, 21, 22, 23, 24, 25}	50	55	60	67	75
	{12, 13, 14, 16, 18, 51, 53, 54}	40	45	50	57	65

UPPER DECK.		Per Room.		Each.	Per Room.	Each.
Outside Rooms.	G—307, 312, 313, 316	32	38	25	55	20
	F—200, 205, 206, 211, 212, 217, 218, 219 E—100, 101, 102, 103, 104, 109, 110, 115, 116, 122	28	33	22	50	18
	G—300, 306	25	30	20	44	17
Inside Rooms.	F—201, 202, 203, 204, 207, 208, 209, 210, 213, 214, 215, 216 G—308, 309, 310, 311, 314, 315, 317, 318	23	27	18	41	16
	E—105, 106, 107, 108, 111, 112, 113, 114, 118, 119, 120	21	25	17	39	15
	E—117, 121 G—301, 302, 303, 304, 305	20	23	15	38	15

MAIN DECK.						
Outside Rooms.	R—354, 358, 359, 362	25	30	20	44	17
	O—150, 153, 154, 157, 158, 161, 162, 167, 168, 173	21	25	17	39	15
	P—250, 256, 257, 262, 263, 268, 269, 274 R—350, 353, 363, 368	23	27	18	41	16
Inside Rooms.	O—159, 160 P—271, 272, 273 R—355, 357, 360, 361	20	24	16	37	15
	O—151, 152, 155, 156, 163, 164, 165, 166, 169, 170, 171, 172 P—251, 252, 253, 254, 255, 258, 259, 260, 261, 264, 265, 266, 267, 270 R—351, 352, 356, 364, 365, 366, 367	20	23	15	33	15

Summer rates (1897) for the New York *and* Paris *were slightly lower across the whole range of first-class cabins, since they were five years older than their new consorts,* St. Louis *and* St. Paul.

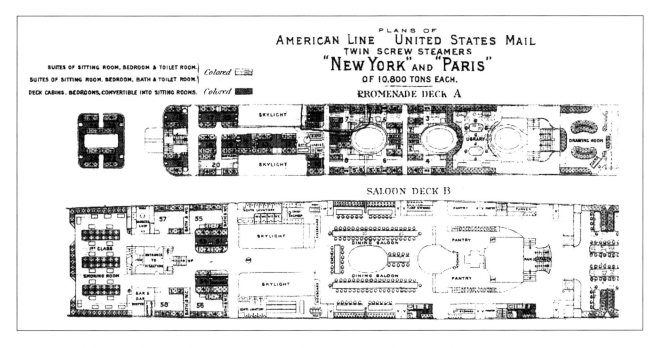

The Promenade Deck and Saloon Deck accommodations of the New York *and* Paris *are shown in these plans. The library and drawing room are noted on the Promenade and the first-class smoking room and dining saloon on the Saloon Deck. The three funnels of the* New York *and* Paris *rise through the first-class accommodations.*

SUMMER RATES. — **S.S. "BERLIN" AND "CHESTER."** — **WINTER RATES.**

	FOR 1 ADULT.	FOR 1½ ADULT.	FOR 2 ADULTS.	FOR 2½ ADULTS.	FOR 3 ADULTS.	FOR 3½ ADULTS.	FOR 4 ADULTS.
	PER ROOM.	EACH.		PER ROOM.	EACH.	PER ROOM.	EACH.
"BERLIN." SALOON DECK. OUTSIDE ROOMS. 3, 4, 6, 9, 12, 15, 16, 18, 20, 22, 23, 24, 25, 26, 27, 28, 29, 30, 31, 32, 33, 34, 35, 37, 39, 41, 42, 44, 46, 48, 67, 68, 69, 70, 71, 72, 78, 74, 75, 76, 77, 78, 80, 82, 84, 87, 90, 93, 95, 97, 99	£30	£33	£18	£40	£15	£48	£13
INSIDE ROOMS. 1, 3, 5, 7, 8, 10, 11, 13, 14, 17, 19, 21, 36, 38, 40, 43, 45, 47, 79, 81, 83, 85, 96, 88, 89, 91, 93, 94, 96, 98	24	27	15	...	...	...	...
MAIN DECK. OUTSIDE ROOMS. 100, 102, 104, 106, 108, 110, 112, 114, 116, 118, 120, 122, 124, 125, 126, 128, 130, 132, 134, 136, 138, 140, 142, 144, 146, 148, 150, 152, 154, 155	26	29	16	37	14	45	12
INSIDE ROOMS. 101, 103, 105, 107, 109, 111, 113, 115, 117, 119, 121, 123, 127, 129, 131, 133, 135, 137, 139, 141, 143, 145, 147, 149, 151, 153	22	25	14	32	12	40	...
"CHESTER." SALOON DECK. OUTSIDE ROOMS. 3, 6, 9, 10, 11, 12, 13, 14, 15, 16, 17, 18, 19, 20, 21, 22, 23, 24, 25, 26, 27, 28, 29, 30, 31, 32, 33, 34, 35, 36, 37, 38, 39, 40, 41, 42, 43, 45, 49, 51	30	33	18	40	15	48	13
INSIDE ROOMS. 1, 2, 4, 5, 7, 8, 44, 45, 47, 48, 50	24	27	15	...	...	...	...

	FOR 1 ADULT.	FOR 1½ ADULT.	FOR 2 ADULTS.	FOR 2½ ADULTS.	FOR 3 ADULTS.	FOR 3½ ADULTS.	FOR 4 ADULTS.
	PER ROOM.	EACH.		PER ROOM.	EACH.	PER ROOM.	EACH.
"BERLIN." SALOON DECK. OUTSIDE ROOMS. 2, 4, 6, 9, 12, 15, 16, 18, 20, 22, 23, 24, 25, 26, 27, 28, 29, 30, 31, 32, 33, 34, 35, 37, 39, 41, 42, 44, 46, 48, 67, 68, 69, 70, 71, 72, 73, 74, 75, 76, 77, 78, 80, 82, 84, 87, 90, 93, 95, 97, 99	£20	£23	£15	£33	£12	£38	£12
INSIDE ROOMS. 1, 3, 5, 7, 8, 10, 11, 13, 14, 17, 19, 21, 36, 38, 40, 43, 45, 47, 79, 81, 83, 85, 86, 88, 89, 91, 92, 94, 96, 98	15	18	12	...	...	...	...
MAIN DECK. OUTSIDE ROOMS. 100, 102, 104, 106, 108, 110, 112, 114, 116, 118, 120, 122, 124, 125, 126, 128, 130, 132, 134, 136, 138, 140, 142, 144, 146, 148, 150, 152, 154, 155	18	21	14	31	12	36	12
INSIDE ROOMS. 101, 103, 105, 107, 109, 111, 113, 115, 117, 119, 121, 123, 127, 129, 131, 133, 135, 137, 139, 141, 143, 145, 147, 149, 151, 153	14	16	12	26	12	34	...
"CHESTER." SALOON DECK. OUTSIDE ROOMS. 10, 11, 12, 13, 14, 15, 16, 17, 18, 19, 20, 21, 22, 31, 32, 33, 34, 35, 36, 37, 38, 39, 40, 41, 42, 43,	22	23	15	33	12	38	12
INSIDE ROOMS. 23, 24, 25, 26, 27, 28, 29, 30	15	18	12	...	...	...	...

SUMMER RATES. — **RATES FOR CHILDREN.** — **WINTER RATES.**

Under 2 years ......Free, provided only one infant in a family | Under 2 years ......Free, provided only one infant in a family.
Three adults and one child occupying entire room, 3½ full fares at the 3 adults in a room rate. | Three adults and one child occupying entire room, 3½ fares at the 3 adults in a room rate.

Servants berthed in First Cabin at £15 on the s.s. "St. Louis," "St. Paul," "New York" and "Paris" and £12 on the s.s. Berlin" and "Chester."

The summer rates for the secondary steamers Berlin *and* Chester *were significantly lower than for the first-class units. The most expensive cabin was priced at 30 pounds ($150), roughly one-fifth the fares on the* St. Louis *and the* St. Paul.

Repairing the broken rudder on time for the next sailing was to prove a challenge. The *St. Louis* arrived from Southampton on Saturday, June 22, and was immediately inspected. By working through the night and morning, early Sunday it was possible to unship the damaged rudder and swing it onto the open end of the American Line pier. This was no small feat, since the rudder, with all its parts, weighed 27 tons. To assist in the operation, the American Line agents, on the advice of Edwin Cramp, hired a powerful derrick as well as the wrecking steamer *Hustler*. Late Saturday, the Cramp Shipyard in Philadelphia loaded a spare rudderstock onto a Pennsylvania Railroad flatcar and shipped it to New York City, where it arrived alongside the pier on Sunday afternoon. Simultaneously, the portions of the old rudder assembly that still were useful were being unbolted in preparation for reassembling on Monday. By Tuesday, the delicate job of shipping the new rudder assembly was undertaken, and by late that afternoon, it was possible to begin testing the steering mechanism.

On top of the repairs to the rudder, the *St. Louis* also had to be fully coaled and provisioned for a transatlantic crossing. The hazards of coal dust and coaling in close proximity to active welding equipment must have been acute as well. Everyone heaved a huge sigh of relief when the early morning hours of Wednesday saw the ship fully provisioned, coaled, and with her new rudder in place. The *St. Louis* backed out into the North River promptly at 11 o'clock with a very full passenger list consisting of 375 saloon, 170 second-cabin, and 250 steerage passengers. On board was a bevy of notables, including Mr. and Mrs. Charles A. Dana of the *New York Sun*, Senator Nelson W. Aldrich,

The sharp lines of the St. Louis *are well defined in this photograph as she approaches Southampton, England, after a fast transatlantic crossing. Her 17 bulkheads and double bottom made her among the safest ships afloat.*

Congressman James J. Belden, and Sir Donald A. Smith. When Captain Randle was asked by a reporter if the *St. Louis* would try for a record passage this time, he replied that it was not his intention to press the ship. "Wait until the stiffness, which is inherent to new machinery, is worn off, and then we will see just what the *St. Louis* can do."[8]

By midsummer, the *St. Louis* still had not completed a crossing at more than 20 knots, and it did not appear that she would do so in the near future. The October deadline for the beginning of the mail contract loomed ominously on the horizon for the International Navigation Company. The decision was made to have extended trials in the English Channel between August 14 and 24, with American naval observers on board. A drydocking at Southampton would make the ship's hull as clean as a whistle and enhance her performance to the ultimate level possible. In Washington, Secretary Hilary Herbert designated Captain Royal Bradford and Lieutenant Richard T. Mulligan as the board to conduct a speed trial on the *St. Louis* in accordance with the provisions of the Postal Aid Act.

Captain Bradford and Lieutenant Mulligan were familiar with running and certifying trials on steamships. It was decided that they first would sail on the *St. Louis* August 7 for Southampton in order to be able to observe the working of the ship and her machinery during a regular transatlantic crossing. For the trials, the two naval officers were ordered to lay off a 100-mile course in the English Channel, which the *St. Louis* would steam over to determine whether she met the requirements of the postal law. The American legislation required that any first-class vessel (at least 8,000 tons) must be able to maintain a speed of 20 knots for four hours to qualify for the subsidy. There was little doubt expressed that the *St. Louis* was capable of making 20 knots over the time and distance specified, but there was great hope expressed that she might put on a phenomenal burst of speed and astonish everyone. Hope springs eternal.

Naval Constructor Frank Fernald, stationed at the New York Navy Yard, was also ordered to inspect the *St. Louis*, the *New York*, and the *Paris* to ensure that they met all the requirements of the legislation prior to the official award of the mail contract. The terms of the Act required that vessels also be readily available to serve as naval auxiliaries in the event of war. This meant that the decks had to be strengthened and reinforced so they were capable of mounting four six-inch, rapid-fire guns. With their carriages and equipment, these guns weighed more than 30,000 pounds and required careful positioning. The legislation also was designed to reinforce and enhance the number of trained sailors available to the American merchant marine and to the United States Navy. In order to accomplish this, the American Line was to provide accommodations and apprenticeship training for at least one American boy under 21 years of age for every 1,000 tons of displacement. The apprentices were to be trained in seamanship and to carry the rank and pay of petty officers.

The attempt to get the Pennsylvania General Assembly to appropriate the funds necessary for deepening and widening the steamship channel in the Delaware River failed. All the wining and dining of the legislators in connection with the launch of the *St. Paul* had been to no avail. The International Navigation Company accordingly reacted by withdrawing its two large new steamers from the Philadelphia–Liverpool trade and reassigning them to the New York–Antwerp service. The explanation given was that the ships were too large to navigate the Delaware River to Philadelphia using the existing channel, and that they met with frequent delays at low water or when heavily laden.

The *Southwark* was the first to go when she sailed from Philadelphia on July 6, bound for Europe with a large passenger list. The passengers included the Rev. Dr. Sidney Strong of Cincinnati, leader of a group planning to tour Europe by bicycle, as well as 27 members of the Century Wheelmen's Club of Philadelphia, who were disembarking at Queenstown for a bicycle tour of Ireland, Scotland, England, France, Switzerland, and Belgium. Bicycle riding was coming into its own as a form of recreation and sport in the mid-1890s. Dr. and Mrs. Gilbert J. Palen of Philadelphia were on their honeymoon, but a bit of a social cloud surrounded their departure. Dr. Palen was socially prominent as a nephew of the famous financier Jay Gould. The day before he

A beautiful broadside of the St. Paul *with her decks crowded by passengers as she approaches port.*

sailed on his honeymoon, he was sued for alleged breach of promise by Margaret May Thompson, a professional nurse, who demanded $25,000 in compensation.

The last departure of the *Southwark* from Philadelphia was followed by that of the *Kensington* on July 20.[9] The *Southwark* and the *Kensington*, at 8,600 tons, were the largest and fastest steamers to carry only second-cabin and steerage passengers. As their replacements, the Red Star liners *Pennland, Belgenland, Rhynland,* and *Waesland* began to sail on the American Line Liverpool service.

The transfer of the *Southwark* and the *Kensington* to the New York–Antwerp service of the International Navigation Company meant that the average size of the steamers in that service was a very substantial 7,800 tons, and it was exceeded only by the premier North Atlantic services of the American, Campagnie Générale Transatlantique, Cunard, HAPAG, and White Star Lines. Furthermore, the *Berlin* of the American Line periodically enhanced the Red Star sailings when she was not required as the substitute vessel on the New York–Southampton route. The Philadelphia–Antwerp supplementary service of the Red Star Line was maintained by the vintage *Pennsylvania, Illinois, Nederland,* and *Switzerland* until 1897.

When the *St. Louis* reached Southampton on the evening of July 3, the American cruiser *Columbia* was anchored in the harbor and saluted the American liner as she came up Southampton Water. This set the crew to thinking about the next day being the

Fourth of July and an American holiday. The men worked overtime on their own initiative and finished everything that was to be done by midnight. The next morning, the *St. Louis* was decked with flags from stem to stern. Her crew prepared to celebrate the Fourth of July by taking the day off. When they were ordered to work on what they considered unnecessary jobs, they elected two men from each watch to form a committee to ask for the day off. The request was refused. When the seamen's committee returned, the refusal was debated, and the entire force of firemen and stokers, numbering 179 men, marched off the ship. They celebrated the Fourth of July in Southampton and returned that evening none the worse for their run ashore. This was admitted by somewhat envious officers. The firemen and stokers worked the *St. Louis* back to New York on a creditable run of six days, 18 hours, 47 minutes, at 19.5 knots. Once docked, they were brought before the United States deputy shipping commissioner, W.J. Bradley, who knew he had been handed a labor-relations pickle. The law prescribed a penalty of up to two days' wages for every day a seaman refused to work in a foreign port. Chief Engineer John Walls testified that it had been necessary to hire additional laborers, at a cost of $93 to the American Line. Commissioner Bradley looked up the law on that point and found that when a company had been put to extra expense, the guilty seamen must be fined. Accordingly, he fined each man one day's pay ($1.00), which they treated as a joke.

Timothy Sheehan, a brawny stoker on the *St. Louis*, sought and was granted leave by Commissioner Bradley to stay over in New York in order to find out what the American public thought about the incident.

> "We were," said Stoker Sheehan yesterday, repeating his former explanation of the patriotic occurrence, "on an American ship, flying the American flag, and hailing from an American port, and we thought we were entitled to a holiday."

Sheehan went on:

> "The ship was safe at dock at Southampton and 'dressed' for the National holiday. Everything was protected and safe, and we celebrated the holiday like gentlemen.
>
> "There were twelve nationalities in those who took the holiday at the cost of $1 fine each, but all were either American citizens or had their first papers. None was drunk, and there was not a single disturbance the whole day. It was claimed that our absence cost the ship $68 [sic] in extra labor. In that case a profit of more than $100 was made out of our patriotism.
>
> "Secretary Herbert has declined to give an official decision on the case, but he will again be invited to decide, and we would like the great American public to pass an opinion. Were we right or wrong?
>
> "The matter will not be allowed to die out. All mechanics and those interested in other industries on American craft are going to have a say about it, and

CONNECTIONS AT SOUTHAMPTON

In connection with sailings and arrivals of American Line steamers, fast twin-screw steamers, with excellent accommodations for cabin passengers, have been placed on the line between Southampton and Havre, thus affording a most desirable route between New York and Paris. The steamers leave Southampton at 12 midnight every week-day and make the passage in about six hours. Passengers usually arrive at Havre in good time to proceed by the first-class express train leaving there at 8 A.M., due in Paris (St. Lazare Station) at 11.30 A.M. Baggage can be checked from the steamer at Southampton to Paris, or *vice versa*, without examination by the British custom officials. There is also direct connection at Southampton with all points in Great Britain, the Continent, Channel Islands, Central America and the Southern Pacific, South Africa and all Australian, Chinese, Japanese and East Indian ports, and it is the port of departure of the ROYAL MAIL LINE. CASTLE LINE and UNION LINE for West Indian, South American and African ports.

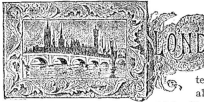

LONDON

Sailing from New York, steamers of the American Line proceed direct to the Empress Dock at Southampton, and suffer no delays from tides. Passengers land on terra firma, and find waiting on the pier, alongside, a special train, the Eagle Express, which will convey them to London in about one hour and forty minutes. This train is provided with smoking rooms, lavatories and toilet rooms.

I propose to leave no stone unturned in behalf of myself and my comrades. We are seeking no notoriety, but we acted without precedent, and we would like to know, if the public sustains us in declaring a National holiday in a foreign port in spite of the prohibition of Engineers Higgins and Boyland."[10]

The American Line was holding its collective breath over the speed trials of the *St. Louis,* for a great many subsidy dollars were at stake. After disembarking passengers, the liner went into drydock for cleaning. The trial course already had been determined—from Portland Bill to Start Point, a distance of 52 knots. The coal was loaded and everyone was well rested in anticipation of the challenge. The big American liner left Southampton at 8:30 A.M. with Captain Bradford, and Lieutenant Mulligan on board to conduct the test. Other dignitaries included Clement A. Griscom, who could not stand to be anywhere else at such a time; Commander W.S. Cowles, naval attaché of the

American Embassy; Frank L. Fernald, United States naval constructor; W.S. Kinhead, U.S. Consul at Southampton; and James Wright, New York agent of the American Line.

The day was misty as the *St. Louis* moved down Southampton Water, drawing 23 feet forward and 24 feet aft. Only 450 tons of coal were loaded, rather than the 2,000 tons she would normally carry for a transatlantic run, when she also would be drawing a foot more water. By the time she reached The Needles, the weather was clear and there was no wind. Outside The Needles, the *St. Louis* turned twice in circles to adjust her compasses. The time consumed was 15 minutes for each turn. Steam was now up to full power, and just as the tide was running full, the *St. Louis* slammed across the starting line at Portland Bill. It was 11:38:06; she ran with the tide for two hours, 12 minutes, and five seconds, at an average speed of 23.6 knots. The giant quadruple-expansion engines were producing 95 revolutions per minute, but the ship was perfectly steady, almost devoid of vibration. The sun shone brightly on the *St. Louis* as she knifed through the smooth seas, going as fast as she ever had since she took to the water.

The liner passed the end of the course at Start Point at 1:50:11 and, still going full speed, made a long, graceful turn, in order to come back on course. She passed the same point on her return at 2:09:38. With two clouds of black smoke streaming behind, she began the race for The Needles. Hundreds of fishing smacks, steamers, and ships of various descriptions saw the performance. The return trip was made in two hours, 26 minutes, 37 seconds at a speed of 21 knots, slicing through a smooth sea but without a favorable tide. Everyone on board was delighted and relieved by the performance of the *St. Louis*, and the naval officers announced that they would certify the liner as a 20-knot ship for the purposes of the mail subsidy. The challenge had been met!

Griscom said he was glad that the first great American ship had made the finest measured mile on record. It was an engine test that did credit to the firemen, all of whom were Americans and had been shipped in New York. Griscom also stated that he was confident that the *St. Louis* would do far better the next year after her new and larger funnels were fitted. During the seven hours of the test, the machinery had been in perfect order and had not overheated at all. The fact that the liner had only previously attained a speed of 19.5 knots became clear when she went into drydock at Southampton. Her hull was covered with foot-long grass, which must have created incredible drag. Subsequently, after recalculating all their figures, the naval observers certified to the United States government that the *St. Louis* achieved 20.14 knots for the 114 nautical miles, which was just enough to secure the contract.

A boost for the profits of the American Line occurred when the Cunard Line raised the average fares to the United States from $20 to $26.50. The explanation by Agent Floyd of the Cunard Line in New York was that the ratios simply were too low, and this represented a necessary adjustment. In addition, discount railroad tickets in Britain to the port of embarkation were abolished. Other European lines said they expected no change, since the Cunard decision reflected uniquely British conditions. Negotiations were underway among the major North Atlantic lines about a general agreement on rates for the whole industry, but they met with little success. Furthermore, even the Cunard decision affected only westbound crossings. There had been such a decline in eastbound steerage traffic between the serious depression year of 1894 and the recovery period of 1895 that far too many berths were chasing far too few potential passengers. In the severe depression year of 1894, more steerage passengers traveled back to Europe than went to America! Jobs, particularly in U.S. coal-mining regions, simply were not available, and people went back to Europe to wait for better times. In 1895, the reverse was true, and the eastbound traffic of the Hamburg-American Line alone had dropped from nearly 4,000 to fewer than 2,000 steerage passengers.[11] The American economy was righting itself after the collapse of 1893, and more jobs existed to draw people to America and keep them there.

The very survival of some of the North Atlantic steamship lines, and the profitability of all of them, depended on greater sanity in determining steerage rates. The difficulty in the final stage of negotiations was that a number of lines wanted differentials based upon the speed and size of a ship. A smaller, slower vessel should not have to charge the same rate for steerage passengers that one of the Atlantic greyhounds received. Officials were reluctant to say too much about the negotiations among the steamship lines, because they were afraid that speculators would buy up tickets at the old rates and hold them until the increase went into effect, thus making larger profits. However, by September 10, 1895, the news from Hamburg was that an agreement appeared imminent. The very next day, a new transatlantic agreement was announced in Liverpool between the British and the foreign transatlantic lines by which the largest and fastest ships would charge $27.50 (£5 10s.), and the slower ships $26.25 (£5 5s.), while the very slowest would be allowed a rate of $25 (£5). If the agreement among the members of the Continental Conference (as it was called) could be maintained, the financial picture for the steamship lines would be greatly improved.[12] The new rates, announced by Lawson S. Sandford, secretary to the Continental Conference, represented as much as a 500 percent increase over the rates some charged during the previous rate war ($5), and a minimum 100 percent increase over the cutthroat ticket selling that had nearly ruined the transatlantic trade. The agreement would not endure forever, but at least during a period of American economic prosperity, it brought peace for five years. Saloon and second-cabin passenger tickets were increased across the board as part of a subsequent agreement negotiated by the lines in additional talks.

The Cunarder *Campania* beat the *St. Louis* in a westbound crossing of late September 1895, coming across from Queenstown in five days, 11 hours, 34 minutes, while the American liner took six days, seven hours, 25 minutes from Southampton. While all the transatlantic lines consistently denied they were racing each other, no effort was spared to humiliate a rival. The *Campania* came up on the *St. Louis* in a stern chase, overtook her, and passed her in mid-Atlantic. Since the *Campania* was something in the nature of 1,320 tons larger, and her engines could produce nearly a third more power, there was no possibility of a contest between the two vessels. That did not make the officers or the passengers on the *St. Louis* feel any better about the situation when the big Cunarder pulled away from them. Intense competition between the officers and crews of the great rivals would lead to near-disaster in the future.

The builder's trials for the *St. Paul* began on Sunday, September 29, 1895, when the second of the big American Line ships sailed from the Cramp Shipyard around 7:30 A.M. In spite of the early hour, virtually every steamer she passed saluted her, and her throaty horns thundered in reply. She made the 40-mile run to Reedy Island in four hours and anchored there to await a high tide in order to pass over the bar. The additional 65-mile run to the Delaware Breakwater took another 4½ hours, and the *St. Paul* anchored at The Brown, a shoal a few miles above the breakwater. There she awaited the arrival of the official party from Philadelphia, which came down to Lewes by train. In the morning, Captain John Jamison passed the Capes and the *St. Paul* took her baptismal plunge in the Atlantic Ocean. A stiff gale was blowing from the stern, helping her along at a rapid gait. Once outside the breakwater, Jamison steamed around in circles in order to check the compasses before taking the official party on board. Conditions for boarding the liner outside the Capes could not have been easy. A tug brought the official party of about 30 men, led by Clement A. Griscom, from Lewes out to the waiting liner.

About 2 o'clock, the tug came alongside the towering sides of the *St. Paul* and successfully transferred all the distinguished passengers. Others besides Griscom were Assistant Secretary of State A.A. Ades; Lieutenant Richard T. Mulligan, one of the trial board to verify the speed of the liner; William E. Marsily, one of the co-founders of the Red Star Line with Griscom 22 years earlier, who was still the Antwerp agent of the International Navigation Company (INC); S.C. Heal, the INC's Washington attorney; E.F. Chamberlin, commissioner of navigation; C.H. Higbee, general manager of the INC; B. Comegys, president of the Philadelphia National Bank, on whose board Griscom served; J.H. Michener, president of the Bank of North America of Philadelphia; J.S. Doran, superintending engineer of the INC.; J.B. Swartz, treasurer of the INC; T. Cangdon, chief inspector in the United States of the British Lloyd's; E.T. Wright, dock superintendent of the INC; and H. Pussy, private secretary to Mr. Griscom.

Edwin S. Cramp, chief engineer of the Cramp Shipyard, was already on board, and after the Griscom party boarded the liner, the ship headed for the open sea. Since the water was shoal as far as the Five-Fathom Bank Lightship, the *St. Paul* went at a snail's pace until the lightship was passed around 4:30 P.M., when Jamison turned her north toward Cape Ann, 413 miles away. A stiff northwest breeze was blowing, and she showed her weather qualities to advantage. Like her sister, she proved uncommonly stable and remarkably free from the engine and propeller vibrations that disturbed trips on many contemporary vessels. "She stood up to the breeze and choppy seas as stiff as a church, and steamed along with little more roll than does a river steamer caught in the wash of a steamship."[13] During the first day, she "jogged" along at 18 knots while the engineers watched the engines. Toward the end of the day, Edwin Cramp gave the order to run her at full speed for an hour, and she worked up to 94 revolutions on 20,000 horsepower, which resulted in a speed of 21 knots into the gale that was blowing. Everyone was delighted.

Cramp wanted another run to limber up the machinery, so the official trials were put off for a day while the *St. Paul* steamed over the measured course, testing everything. This was good thinking, because the liner's boilers were untried and fouled by the grease and dirt that had built up during construction. A couple of hours were spent in getting up steam, and then a run at speed was made from Cape Ann over the 44-mile official course to Cape Porpoise, Maine. The liner began to increase speed with every mile covered, but then the boilers began to "prime" as the grease and dirt boiled off. The ship's speed fell off slightly, because steam could not be manufactured as efficiently or as speedily. By "priming" was meant that the water in the boilers was not made into steam rapidly enough. The result was that bubbles and some water were carried over into the cylinders with the steam, and power was reduced. A further slight delay occurred from a hot crosshead on the port engine, necessitating the stopping of that engine for a few minutes. Another exasperating delay occurred when the big liner was about eight miles from the finish line off Cape Porpoise and a lumber-laden schooner exercised New England independent-mindedness and refused to give way. The schooner was dead ahead of the *St. Paul*, and Captain Jamison blew the ship's horns for him to sheer off, but he had the right of way and held steadily to his course. The big American liner was compelled to make a wide detour to avoid cutting the schooner in half. The average speed for the outward run from Cape Ann to Cape Porpoise was 19.5 knots. The time was two hours and 15 minutes, and the ship had made 21 knots for a brief period. During the afternoon, she jogged back to Cape Ann at 18 knots, with everyone enjoying the ride and complimenting Edwin Cramp on his good judgment. The decision was made to take Thursday for recoaling the vessel, flushing her boilers, refilling them with clean water, and totally cleaning the fires.

Griscom was asked for a statement and obliged the press:

> The *St. Paul* was put over the course today for preliminary trial. The boilers primed so badly that the speed trial will be deferred until the boilers are washed out and refilled. She was run over the course at 19½ knots speed to the eastward, and jogged slowly back.
>
> Like the sister ship, the *St. Louis*, the *St. Paul* was remarkably steady and entirely free from vibration. Her preliminary performance today gives every assurance that she will make the required speed with ease when she is put in proper condition for it. It should be borne in mind that since she started from the shipyard the boilers have not had more than thirty-four hours' steaming before she went over the course today, which was not enough preliminary work to get them free of the dirt and grease which accumulate during construction. The engines worked smoothly throughout. The only heating developed was in

two crossheads, which was of no importance. A thorough investigation was made as to the cause of the priming of the boilers, and it was attributed to the fact the water taken in at the end of the pier just previous to the departure of the vessel from Philadelphia was found on examination to be brackish, owing to the protracted drought.[14]

Griscom's hopes were buoyed by receipt of the news that the *St. Louis* had just completed the fastest eastbound crossing of her career, making the trip from New York to Southampton in six days, 13 hours, 25 minutes. This beat the best performance of the *Paris* (six days, 16 hours, 43 minutes) and came near to the best crossing of the *New York* (six days, 11 hours, 30 minutes). The record for the crossing from New York to Southampton was held by the *Fürst Bismarck* (1891, 8,242 tons) of HAPAG, which had raced across in six days, 10 hours, 35 minutes. Someone made the comment that if the hull of the *St. Paul* had been scraped and painted, she would have performed better. Knowing this, it defies comprehension that Cramp and Griscom would run such important trials with a liner whose hull was trailing a foot-thick coat of weeds from the Delaware River. Certainly it was expensive to drydock a vessel and it took precious time, but the mail subsidy was at stake, and it should not have been jeopardized at any cost. Their confidence in the ship does not appear to be justified by the incredibly small speed margin they were getting out of quadruple-expansion engines.

On Friday, October 4, 1895, the *St. Paul* sailed on her trials, with every possible care taken in the selection of her coal and the purity of the water in her boilers. The engines and boilers were working smoothly as she left Boston, Massachusetts. On board to conduct the trials were Commander Royal Bradford, Lieutenant Commander Beaton Schroeder, Lieutenant M.T. Patch, and Lieutenant Richard Mulligan—the trial board of naval officers appointed by President Cleveland to certify the American Line ships. At 6 A.M., the *St. Paul* got underway and was off Gloucester, Massachusetts, around 7 A.M. Chief Engineer John Patterson warmed up the machinery as far as possible and finally gave the signal for the start of the trials. The colossal 20,000-horsepower quadruple-expansion engines began to turn over at maximum speed, and the *St. Paul* sliced through the seas toward the starting line with Pilot Lewis Chambers at the wheel. At 8:50, the big steamship swept past the tug and buoy that marked the beginning of the measured distance off Cape Ann, and the race for the subsidy was underway. The liner headed for Cape Porpoise, 44 miles away, with two towering plumes of smoke streaming from her funnels. The *St. Paul* passed the second stakeboat, 32 miles from Cape Ann, at 10:22, making the speed to that point a bare 20.09 knots. After passing the second stakeboat, everything was let out and the speed of the ship increased appreciably, so that she crossed the line off Cape Porpoise at 11:01, for an average speed of 20.11 knots. The run from Cape Ann to Cape Porpoise was made against the tide and the prevailing wind in two hours and 11 minutes. If the *St. Paul* could achieve that, then the most difficult part of the trials was over. The liner swept around in a giant circle off Cape Porpoise and came racing back at full power for the second leg. She made the run back to Cape Ann in two hours and seven minutes, for an average speed of 20.8 knots. The increased speed on the way back brought the average up to a more respectable 20.5 knots for the trials as a whole and the subsidy was ensured. The actual engine revolutions going east were 89, and west 90, so the liner still had some power in reserve. Everyone onboard was jubilant. The information was important enough to be sent by Reuters to London, where *The Times* took note of the accomplishment.[15]

Following the successful completion of her trials, the *St. Paul* called at Gloucester, Massachusetts, to drop Commander Bradford of the trial board, and then set course for New York. The *St. Paul* was close to completion by her builders at the time of her trials and was scheduled to take the place of the *Paris* on the Wednesday, October 9, sailing. Carpets still had to be laid and furniture covers removed before she would be ready for passengers, but otherwise she was fully outfitted. She was sighted south of Fire Island at 10 A.M. on October 5 and three hours later passed quarantine, where, for the last time, she did not have to stop. Harbor craft saluted the new liner as she made her way up the bay. Tugs whistled, ferryboats acknowledged her presence with deep-throated blasts, and outward-bound steamers sounded their whistles and dipped their colors as she passed.

The rush to prepare her for her maiden voyage began immediately, and she received the finishing touches in the next three days. At 11 A.M. on October 9, the *St. Paul* backed out into the North River with a full complement of cabin passengers and began her first run to Southampton. The daily runs were 394, 382, 409, 412, 439, 324, 399, and 319 to The Needles—not a record, but it did allow her passengers to arrive at Southampton at 8:15 A.M. in plenty of time to reach London by noon and make any necessary connections. In short, the schedule was maintained, and the American Line, with the *St. Louis*, *St. Paul*, *New York*, and *Paris*, possessed the best-balanced fleet of first-class liners on the North Atlantic. A slight problem with a feed pipe delayed her a little on one day, but everyone expressed delight with how steady she was during a somewhat rough crossing. Captain Jamison and his officers were invited to a civic reception hosted by the mayor of Southampton, and the prospects seemed excellent for a long and fruitful association with Southampton. Furthermore, since the French government had just announced that there would be a huge exposition in Paris during the summer of 1900, and the United States had been invited to participate, the prospects for transatlantic travel seemed to be blossoming.

If the American Line could keep its fleet in good repair and be able to maintain the sailing schedule, then success appeared assured. This would be no mean challenge. With great chagrin, the agents in Southampton had to announce on October 24 that the *St. Louis* had again damaged her rudder on the eastbound crossing, so there was no way she could make the westbound departure on October 26. The *Berlin* would sail instead that Saturday, but she could not accommodate all the first-class passengers booked on the *St. Louis*. The American Line offered first-class passengers the option of taking the *New York* on November 2. All second-cabin and steerage passengers could be accommodated on the *Berlin*, since private facilities were not an issue where they were concerned, and additional persons always could be fitted into extra berths.

By the time the *St. Paul* reached New York on the return leg of her maiden voyage, Griscom must have wondered if he were living under an unlucky star. The *St. Paul* made the crossing in six days, 17 hours, 51 minutes—an acceptable crossing but nothing to brag about. The problem was that the port engine had broken down in mid-Atlantic and had to be shut down. Captain Jamison had felt sure that the *St. Paul* was capable of a record run.

> "It is in her to do it," he remarked, "and she will smash that record yet. Of course the breakdown was unfortunate, but it was not at all a serious one, and such things are to be expected in a new ship. Besides this ship's bottom is very foul. She has never been drydocked, and her bottom has never had a coating of anti-fouling paint. By next summer, I feel sure that this steamer will astonish people by her performances. She is not built to be the speediest thing afloat but she will prove herself no slow coach."[16]

The *St. Paul* gave good service during her next two round trips and appeared to be settling in when disaster struck. She had arrived in New York from Southampton on schedule, Saturday, December 14, and the preparations were begun immediately for a speedy turnaround so she could take the "Christmas sailing" of December 18, which was designed to get her passengers to England in time for the holidays. For several hours prior to the 11 A.M. sailing time, engineers and machinists had been preparing the engines to answer the command of the captain to move out into the North River and begin the run to Southampton. As was usually the case, a very large passenger list had booked for the Christmas crossing, and very heavy mails were expected.

Just as the steam from the boilers was let into the main steam pipe at the low pressure of 130 pounds, the pipe exploded, and live steam and shrapnel sprayed the engine room of the liner, with murderous effect. At the time of the accident, there were about 30 men in the engine room, led by Second Assistant Engineer James Fawns. The noise of the explosion and escaping steam was heard on deck and created considerable excitement. The horror of the accident was brought home when several badly scalded machinists and engineers staggered to the deck and collapsed. Police were notified immediately and ambulances were summoned from the Hudson Street Hospital, which was alerted about the disaster on the ship. Two doctors came with the ambulances to the pier in order to care for the victims. Five members of the engine-room staff, including Fawns, were killed outright, and four others were so severely scalded that they died in the hospital shortly thereafter. Fawns and the four men with him had been near the pipe when it exploded, and they never had a chance. The New York coroner and his staff went to the pier to investigate the accident, make out death certificates, and render what assistance they could. It was made known that the American Line would pay for the burial expenses of the dead, and they would be interred in either a company plot or one of their choosing.

Since few personal tragedies represented a greater financial drain on poor working-class families than death, this news was no small consolation to the bereaved.

Chief Engineer James Carnegie was stunned by the accident and too busy securing the engine room to make a statement to the press. He and Superintending Engineer Clark were sitting in his cabin discussing their plans for the ship when the pipe burst, and they heard the explosion. Both men raced for the engine room, only to meet a couple of the scalded survivors stumbling up the stairs. The explosion shattered a lot of windows and was so enormous that it blew out a part of the bulkhead. The main steam pipe had blown at its elbow and taken off the main stopvalve. The pipe had been tested with steam at the Cramp Shipyard at 400 pounds of pressure, and it normally operated at 200 pounds of pressure. Hence, the 130 pounds of pressure at the time of the explosion was within appropriate range. The only conclusion the inquiry panel could draw was that the elbow of the pipe must have had a casting flaw that had escaped detection and testing. The builders and the owners were exonerated of all negligence in the accident.

The immediate problem for the American Line was that one of their largest ships had been fully loaded and provisioned for an Atlantic crossing and now, as a result of this tragedy, the liner could not sail.[17] The second-cabin and steerage passengers were transferred immediately to the Red Star liner *Kensington*, scheduled to sail the same afternoon. Twenty of the first-class passengers also elected to sail on the *Kensington*, although they would not reach England for Christmas Day. Some first-class passengers transferred to other ships of other lines, and some opted to wait for the next sailing of one of the "big four" of the American Line on the following Saturday. The Christmas mails were transferred to the *Campania* of the Cunard Line, sailing three days later (Saturday, December 21), too late for Christmas delivery in Britain. The postal employees traveling on the *Campania* and charged with sorting the mail could only handle a small fraction of their avalanche of work during the crossing.

The cargo of the *St. Paul* had to be taken out of the ship and placed on the pier to await the next sailing of an American Line vessel. It was expected that repairs would take at least 10 days, and that the *St. Paul* would have to lie at her New York pier until her next scheduled sailing.

Assistant Engineer James Fawns and his men—Andrew Heard, George Williams, Robert Wilson, and Adolphus Folkner—were buried side by side in solemn ceremonies on December 21 at the American Line's plot in the New York Bay Cemetery in Jersey City, New Jersey. Many family members, friends, and a large representation of company employees attended the funerals. The bodies were in black cloth caskets. Handsome wreaths lay on two caskets, and floral anchors on the other three. The services at the cemetery were conducted by the Rev. John Kraus of Trinity Methodist Church, who complimented the International Navigation Company for its generosity in caring for the dead and for their relatives who were so suddenly bereaved. The burial service was read over each body, a hymn was sung, and the crowd dispersed.[18]

One further incident was to round out the year for the American Line in the awful month of December 1895. The *Berlin* sailed from Southampton in the place of the disabled *St. Paul*, passed The Needles, and headed down the English Channel. There was considerable shipping in the waterway as always, and the *Berlin* collided with the ship *Willowbank*. The force of the collision caused enough damage that the *Berlin* had to return to Southampton in distress. Some passengers now had been booked on two American Line ships without being able to complete a successful crossing. At Southampton, a survey revealed that the *Berlin* would be out of service for some time. Her cargo was transferred to the *Nederland*, which called at Southampton on December 29 after having left Antwerp three days earlier. There can be no question that the American Line was delighted to see 1895 depart.

Chapter 11

PERILS OF THE SEA

The United States Mail Steam Ship St. Louis *leaving New York for Southampton with the Statue of Liberty in the background.*

The 1895 calendar year saw a total of 96,558 cabin-class and 258,560 steerage passengers landed in New York by the North Atlantic steamship lines. Of these totals, the American Line carried 16,146 cabin-class and 19,580 steerage passengers from Southampton and the Red Star Line brought 4,890 cabin-class and 12,554 steerage passengers from Antwerp. The International Navigation Company proudly could claim well over 20 percent of the cabin-class trade and nearly 9 percent of the immigrant trade. These were quite commendable figures.[1] The stabilization of the steamer rates through the Continental Conference, and the steady improvement of the American economy as it continued to recover from the depression of 1893, contributed to the revival. In view of the substantial indebtedness the fleet was carrying, this was welcome news indeed.

Another factor in favor of the American and Red Star Lines was that they needed far fewer ship voyages to amass their passenger totals than many of their competitors. North German Lloyd held the record with 130 voyages to New York, Hamburg-American was next with 93, Cunard made 56, the French Line 54, Red Star 53, Holland-America 52, White Star 51, and the American Line 50. In other words, Cunard, French, Red Star, Holland-America, White Star, and American all sent one ship a week across the Atlantic during 1895. The two big German lines had numerous freighters on the North Atlantic, in many cases carrying small numbers of passengers, and they were operating far more extensive cargo-liner operations all around the world, with periodic stops in New York.

The *St. Louis* found the winter conditions on the North Atlantic to her liking and came romping home from Southampton in six days, nine hours, and 32 minutes at 19.8 knots—which subtracted nearly four hours from her previous best. This voyage, over a tract of 3,046 miles, was completed on January 17, 1896, meaning that only the record passage of the *New York* among the American Line quartet was faster. The *New York*'s passage of September 14, 1894, still held the record, with a time of six days, seven hours, 14 minutes. The *St. Louis* was taken off service for 10 weeks and sent to her builder's yard in Philadelphia, where her funnels were lengthened and enlarged. The chief engineer of the *St. Louis*, John Walls, and his counterpart on the *New York*, Taylor, were as great a pair of rivals as their ships. Just before the January 11 sailing from Southampton, Taylor on the *New York*, which had just arrived, sent Walls on the *St. Louis* a note reminding him that the *New York* still held the record and to look out for another smashing of it. Walls was a sturdy Scot. He promptly wrote a reply: "John Walls was chief engineer of the *New York* when she broke the record. I have no doubt of the machine, but what about the mon?" Walls nearly took the record away from the *New York* as the *St. Louis* slammed across at full speed through numerous January snow squalls in the attempt. Walls was convinced that as soon as her new funnels were fitted, the *St. Louis* would have the record.

Some of the most ominous and foreboding headlines that American newspapers ever carried about the American Line screamed across the front page of the *New York Times* on January 26, 1896: "ST. PAUL, SPEEDING IN FOG, GOES AGROUND—IN THE SAND OFF EAST BRANCH, N.J., AFTER A CLOSE RUN WITH HER RIVAL, THE CUNARDER *CAMPANIA*."

The *Campania* and the *St. Paul* frequently found themselves competing against each other during the fall and winter of 1895 and 1896 just by virtue of the luck of scheduling. Both lines sent one first-class steamer a week across the North Atlantic, and these two liners were scheduled to sail from Liverpool and Southampton at about the same time. The *Campania*, larger and more powerful than the *St. Paul*, was the second largest passenger liner in the world, at 12,950 tons (just two tons smaller than her sistership, *Lucania*). The *St. Paul* was the fourth largest, at 11,600 tons. The machinery of the *Campania* was rated at 30,000 horsepower, whereas the quadruple-expansion engines of the *St. Paul* were rated at 20,000 horsepower. The *St. Paul* also was designed to carry substantially more cargo than the *Campania*, while the Cunarder far exceeded the number of passengers (600, 400, 1,000) that the American liner could accommodate (350, 220, 800).[2]

Captain Walker of the *Campania* gave his version of the race for New York on January 25, 1896:

> "It was about 8:30 o'clock Friday morning," he said, "when we sighted the *St. Paul* about fifteen miles ahead of us off our port bow.
>
> "We watched her smoke for some time without being able to determine who she was, and about the time that we recognized her she must have recognized us, for we both went at it as hard as we could.
>
> "We kept following her, but did not have her abeam until 1 o'clock P.M. We steamed on until 8:30 o'clock P.M., when we ran into the fog, and then ran at a fair speed until 1 o'clock this morning.
>
> "From 1 o'clock until 5:30 o'clock our movement was slow, and we then anchored. The lead at 5:30 o'clock indicated but ten fathoms of water, and so I backed the ship until I found fifteen fathoms, and then dropped anchor.
>
> "After the anchor was down I knew we were fast to America, and was determined to stick to her. I was satisfied with my position.
>
> "The fog lifted this morning at 9:30 o'clock, we then got underway. I had no idea of where the *St. Paul* was until the lifting of the fog, and I then saw her on the beach."[3]

The facts of the accident appear quite clear. The *St. Paul* was approximately 400 miles from New York on the long tract from The Needles to Sandy Hook when the *Campania*, westbound from Liverpool/Queenstown to New York, began to overtake her. Captain John Clark Jamison of the *St. Paul*, sighting his arch competitor in pursuit, asked for and received all possible steam from the engine room. A race for New York began with both the big ships producing all the revolutions they could throughout Friday. As a result, the *St. Paul* was able to keep abreast of the *Campania* for the bulk of the day—until a fog bank rolled in and obscured the view. Subsequently, without regard to conditions, the second and third largest liners in the world continued to slam through the fog, ignoring everything except the competition. Foghorns thundered at regular intervals, but they appear to have been the only concession to the elements. As both ships hurtled through the night, passengers reported constantly hearing the other liner's foghorns. So caught up in the race were the officers on both huge liners that they lost all reckoning of where they were, and where their ships should be. As a result, both liners were approximately 15 miles off course. Even though they had slowed appreciably in the early morning hours, they both were still underway at several knots, feeling for the entrance to New York Harbor, when the *St. Paul*, which was slightly in the lead, suddenly rammed her bow on the sands at East Branch, New Jersey. So gently did she touch that many passengers were not aware of her predicament until they awoke in the morning. The *Campania*, immediately behind her, was warned of the danger by the sudden thunderous blasts of the *St. Paul*'s horns. The lifesaving crews along the New Jersey coast had a busy night. Charles Sexton, a member of Life-Saving Station crew no. 5, and Joel Woolley of crew no. 4 were the first to discover the *St. Paul*. They were on duty patrols shortly after 2 A.M. when they saw the approaching lights of the big American liner puncturing the gloom into which they had been staring. They frantically lighted beacons to warn the vessel of her peril, but she had struck, or was just about to strike, the sands before the signal could be seen. The two life-savers hurried to their respective stations, and crew of no. 4, under Captain Mulligan, responded immediately. Captain Wardell of crew no. 5 said that he thought he would have the huge *Campania* on his hands, so he did not come at once. At his direction, a red light was burned; shortly thereafter, it was answered by the *Campania*. For about a half hour, the lights of the Cunarder were seen to pass south of West End, after which she was swallowed by the gloom. Seeing that she was out of danger, Captain Wardell hurried to the aid of the *St. Paul*. Life-Saving Station no. 3 also had been summoned, so there was a team of 24 trained life-savers on the shore near the grounded liner. With great difficulty, the life-savers launched three boats through the surf. At daybreak, a breeches buoy was rigged, and Captain Mulligan boarded the *St. Paul* to confer with Captain Jamison. When he reached the deck of the American liner, the first question hurled at him by an excited crewman was: "Where is the *Campania*?" Mulligan was a little taken aback by this inquiry, because it seemed as if anyone asking such a question was more interested in the Cunarder than the *St. Paul*. Subsequently, the explanation was given that if the *St. Paul* was ashore, then the *Campania* must have hit the beach also. Fortunately for Cunard, this was not the case.

There was no immediate danger to the American Line ship, although the seas were heavy, dashing against the side of the steamer and sending spray high over the deck. Captain Jamison made the decision to keep all passengers on the *St. Paul* and await a tender from New York. The stopping of the engines and the pounding of the waves against the side of the ship soon awoke any passengers who were still asleep. Those who ventured out on the open deck to view the scene were far from reassured about the safety of their position. The long waves rolling in broke on shore with a muffled thunder that was unsettling to the nerves. When the fog thinned, it was evident that the liner had struck the sand bow-on and then swung around broadside to the shore. She was firmly stuck and had gone on the bar during a high tide, so no one thought she would come off immediately. In fact, the comment was made that except for the push of an exceptionally large wave, the *St. Paul* was as stable as in drydock. This must have been cheerful news to Clement Acton Griscom, faced with yet another crisis.

Captain Mulligan of the Life-Saving Station sent word to the American Line agents in New York that they had a big problem. The offices of the International Navigation Company immediately went into high gear. Tugs were dispatched by the Merritt and the

The St. Paul *knifes through the sea in a remarkably detailed photograph.*
The Everett E. Viez Collection, Steamship Historical Society of America, Inc., University of Baltimore Library

Chapman Wrecking Companies, and about 7 A.M. the tugs *I.J. Merritt, Chapman, Jones, Hustler,* and *Right Arm* were at the side of the stranded vessel. A wreck this size called for the big brass. Captain Thomas Kivlin, wreckmaster, Arthur M. Smith, secretary, and William M. Chapman, vice president, all went to the *St. Paul* with the intention of staying with the stranded liner until she was free. Shortly afterward, the tugs *Pulver, Millard,* and *Everett* of the New York Towboat Company fleet also arrived and anchored near the *St. Paul.* Eight tugs were not going to budge the heavily laden 11,600-ton hull until she was vastly lightened.

Immediately, three heavy anchors were set offshore as moorings in order to retard or stop the landward drift of the ship. The hawsers running from the anchors to the steam capstans on the *St. Paul* were taut cables that halted her movement. If it was impossible to pull her free, at least it might be possible to ensure that her situation would get no worse.

American Line Marine Superintendent Captain Shackford hurried down from New York to assume charge of the work of trying to refloat her. He found that the *St. Paul* was about one-quarter of a mile north of the Iron Pier, almost beam-on to the beach, with her bow pointed to the southwest. News of the stranding soon spread up and down the New Jersey coast, and a crowd began to gather. By noon it had swelled to thousands, and

The Boat Deck of the St. Paul *showing the two funnels and companionway (starboard side).*

The Everett E. Viez Collection, Steamship Historical Society of America, Inc., University of Baltimore Library

The Boat Deck of the St. Paul *showing the two funnels and companionway (port side).*

The Everett E. Viez Collection, Steamship Historical Society of America, Inc., University of Baltimore Library

the beach on either side of the stranded liner for several hundred yards was black with people braving the elements to see the big ship. To some it was a grand holiday. One young girl clad in bright bloomers and a jaunty cap daringly rode her bicycle up and down the beach. In sharp contrast, the scene offshore was impressive, as the seas swept ridges of foam along the *St. Paul*'s black sides, the sky had become somber gray, and the loudest sounds were the panting respirations of the eight tugs striving to render aid.

The second-class dining room of the St. Paul, *showing the profusion of electric lights and ceiling fans— unusual for 1895. The tables basically can seat only six and are not the long boarding-house tables seen even in first-class.*

Shortly after noon the paddlewheel steamer *George Starr* appeared, and the transfer of passengers and a small amount of hand luggage began. The *St. Paul* had on board 140 cabin passengers and about 120 steerage. They were embarked in lifeboats from gangway ladders lowered from the starboard (leeward) side. The transfer was very tedious with the seas that were running, and it was impossible for the *George Starr* to leave for New York much before 4 P.M. Hence, the cabin-class passengers did not reach the American Line pier until around 7:30—by which time they were cold, hungry, and irritable. Some first-class passengers were highly incensed that they had to travel on the same paddle steamer as those passengers who had booked second cabin. They were just lucky they had not been traveling in steerage. Those 120 hardy souls had to withstand a three-hour trip in January up the coast in heavy seas on the open foredeck of the tug *L. Purvel*!

The revenue cutter *Hudson* left New York Harbor with Deputy Surveyor D.F. Dowling and his staff on board to go to the *St. Paul*, but the *Hudson* had to return to quarantine around 5 P.M. because heavy seas and all the tugboat lines created such an obstacle that the vessel could not be boarded. In order to expedite disembarkation for cabin-class passengers, quarantine officials had boarded the *George Starr* so that they could do the processing en route to New York. The *St. Paul* also had on board 200 sacks of transatlantic mail, which had to be unloaded with great care to a waiting tug. Only two bags at a time could be handled in safety, so more than 100 trips had to be made before the mails could begin the final leg of their journey to the U.S. Post Office. Besides a substantial general cargo, the American liner also carried more than a million dollars in her strongboxes, which had to be guarded. The money was consigned to W.H. Crossman & Son.

A crowd watches the efforts to free the St. Paul, *which went aground at East Branch, New Jersey, on January 25, 1896, in dense fog. The American liner and the Cunard liner* Campania *had lost their way while racing each other for the entrance to New York Harbor.*

The Everett E. Viez Collection, Steamship Historical Society of America, Inc., University of Baltimore Library

When Captain Jamison of the *St. Paul* finally was interviewed by the press, he was singularly noncommittal about the circumstances of the accident. One reporter asked him if he thought the stranding was due to any negligence on the part of the officers or the pilot of the ship, and he absolutely refused to take a position. He did state that he was on the bridge at the time the *St. Paul* struck the beach, but that the ship was in charge of a pilot. Consequently, the accident could not be laid at his door. He also let it be known that the liner had steamed through the fog at about three knots and that soundings had been made throughout the night. The last sounding just before the liner struck indicated 17 fathoms of water, which was more than adequate. After hitting the shore, Jamison had surveyed the hull of his ship from one end to the other and had seen absolutely no sign of damage or leaking. The hull was as solid as the day she was launched.

With one of his great ships aground, Clement Griscom could not stay away from the scene. Arrangements were made for a special train to carry the president of the

International Navigation Company from Jersey City to East Branch in order to see the *St. Paul*. One can imagine the delight with which he viewed the scene, and the trepidation of the liner's officers when they saw "the old man" on the shore scowling up at them, his handlebar mustache twitching. As night fell, the liner was lighted from stem to stern with electric lights, which cast an ethereal glow on the shore. Old-timers along the Jersey coast said that if the liner was refloated within a week, she would be lucky.

That evening at her berth in New York, the officers and crew of the *Campania* were counting their blessings. Some passengers on the big Cunarder claimed, with substantial reason, that she also had buried her bow in the sand, but not as deeply as the *St. Paul*, and had been able to back off into deeper water. On board the *Campania*, now empty of passengers, there was a feeling of heartfelt relief—from coal passers to captain—that it was not their ship that was fast in the East Branch sands.

> So intent was every one aboard the *Campania* upon the result of the stern chase that she was giving the *St. Paul*, that the fact that both were out of the regular course was not noticed until one had gone aground and the other received warnings that she fortunately heeded and dropped her anchor.[4]

It was noted in the newspapers that the coastline of the United States in the approaches to New York Harbor hardly represented terra incognita, since almost every foot of the distance between the southeasterly point of Long Island and Sandy Hook has its water depth marked on the charts. It should have been possible for the officers of the ships to learn their positions—even with the fog as dense as it was—by judicious use of the lead and close inspection of the log. Few captains in the world had been over this route more often than Jamison of the *St. Paul* and Walker of the *Campania*. They were the acknowledged masters of their craft by virtue of having two of the largest ships in the world entrusted to their care.

In hindsight, one man who was on the *Campania* said he had never been carried through the fog at such a rate of speed in his life as he had been that night. He said he was frightened from the moment the *Campania* entered the fog bank, and he expected some accident until the welcome order to let go the anchor was given. Chief Officer Pierce of the *Campania* refused to speak about the ship's narrow escape until told that she was saved only because of warnings received from shore. That was too much for Pierce, since it flew in the face of the Cunard story, and he then denied that he had seen or heard anything that called his attention to the position of the ship. The decision simply had been made on the bridge of the *Campania* to stop and drop anchor. A number of passengers vehemently denied that story, since even though they were not supposed to be looking and listening for danger, they had seen the lights from shore and had heard the horns of the *St. Paul* thundering their warning. In response, the big Cunarder immediately had begun to reverse her propellers in order to try to stop her forward momentum and back into deeper water, where she might anchor in safety. One witness on shore stated that he saw the *Campania* with her bow in the sand struggling to get off, and that she only did so after substantial power was put into going astern. The life-savers of crew no. 5 were positive that the *Campania* was aground when they were watching her, since she took a while to back away from the shore. They certainly were the resident experts.

During that time, the whistles of the *Campania* were heard sounding regularly from one position in the fog, and she gave no evidence of moving for a prolonged period—until the sound of her whistles finally indicated she was backing off into safe water. The Reuters news report published in *The Times* of London attributed the narrow escape of the *Campania* to hearing the whistles of the *St. Paul* once she had gone ashore.[5] The Cunard Line officially denied any grounding, at the same time that they were denying that their ship was racing the *St. Paul*, and that anyone in authority had heard the *St. Paul*'s distress whistles. The proof to some was that the *Campania* was anchored only about a mile from the stranded *St. Paul* when the fog lifted the next morning. At the conclusion of one contemporary account, it was stated:

> The log of the *Campania* corroborates the statement of some of her passengers
> that her commander did not know the position of his vessel after she entered the
> fog, for on it is a reference to being abeam of the Fire Island Light, but no time is
> given, and a pen has been drawn through the entry. The racing vessels were fully
> fifteen miles out of their course when one ran aground and the other anchored.[6]

The American Line and the Cunard Line could protest all they wanted, but only providence, and no act of their employees, had spared the North Atlantic what might have been one of its greatest single disasters.

The wrecking tugs working on the *St. Paul* wasted no time trying to get the ship free from the sands of East Branch. No one knew when another winter storm might come howling down the coast and irretrievably compromise the vessel. Through Saturday night and Sunday morning, the American Line crew, assisted by numerous other personnel, succeeded in getting her passengers' baggage and some of the cargo out of the holds and loaded onto the lighter *John Haggerty*, which then took it to the company piers in New York. This lightened the hull by several thousand tons. The gold in the strongbox was left on board until the next-to-last trip of the *John Haggerty* on January 28, when it went to New York under the guard of three ship's officers. The removal of the cargo continued through January 29, by which time everything that could be transshipped had been. Meanwhile, continuous efforts were made to move the stranded vessel.

On Sunday, January 26, the liner lay 75 to 80 yards from shore, and thousands of people watched the tugs straining to move her into deep water. The bow and forepart of the liner remained stuck in about 14 feet of sand and mud. The efforts of the tugs succeeded in dragging the ship about 150 feet farther northward, but since the essential movement was parallel to the shore rather than into deeper water, the end result was not gratifying. Calculations indicated that the *St. Paul* had rammed her bow into the sand at about 2:30 A.M., only 90 minutes before high tide on the morning of January 25. High tide on January 26 was only 13 inches higher than the day before—not enough to free the liner from the sand. The highest tide of the month was coming on January 29 at 6:28 A.M., and the plan was to use everything possible to free her at that time. On the morning of January 26, six immense kedge anchors were planted in the sea about 1,000 yards from the stranded vessel. Fastened to the kedges were steel hawsers, which were connected to the powerful steam capstans of the ship. Six of the big wrecker tugs were secured to the ship by powerful hawsers, and another 50 tugs were anchored in the ocean nearby, waiting to help if called upon. Even though it was a Sunday, if 56 tugs were occupied off East Branch, virtually nothing else in New York Harbor could have been moving. Everything was ready, and on a given signal, the 20,000 horsepower engines of the *St. Paul* were put full astern, the steam capstans of the ship strained at the hawsers made fast to the kedge anchors astern, and the tugs whipped taut their lines and strove mightily to drag the big steamer from her bed of sand. Little by little she moved, until she had traveled about a third of her length in distance. Then she came to a final stop and could not be budged. One of the results was that whereas she had been on a relatively even keel before the attempt, she now had a substantial list, and her starboard waterline was about 10 feet in the air. Soundings showed that the stern was touching but just barely, which meant the propellers were still safe. During the afternoon high tide, the tug hawsers and capstan lines to the kedge anchors were kept tight so that the hull would not shift farther ashore. Griscom and Cramp, of the Cramp Shipyard, visited the ship and conversed for hours with Captain Jamison and the other officers. A novelty item was the use of the first ship-to-shore telephone, although not in the familiar sense. In this instance, a telephone line was run from the Ocean Avenue offices of the telephone company to the smoking room on the *St. Paul*. The line was kept slack so that movement of the ship would not snap it, allowing personnel on the liner to telephone New York.

More than 10,000 people visited East Branch, New Jersey, that Sunday. They came from New York, the New Jersey coast, and inland as far as Philadelphia. Farmers drove into town from as far away as 20 miles to see the stranded ocean greyhound. The scene on Ocean Avenue resembled nothing so much as a country fair. Quickly improvised lunchrooms, cigar stands, traveling speakeasys, and restaurants furnished food and drink to the multitude of hungry, thirsty onlookers. On the front portico of one of the big summer hotels, an enterprising individual had put up a sign, SEATS TO RENT, and he reaped a harvest from the weary. Bicyclists were everywhere, as was the omnipresent amateur photographer taking hundreds of shots of ships, tugs, and people. Customs Officer Patterson telephoned from the *St. Paul* that a major attempt would be made to get the ship off the shore at 5 the next morning.

In the meantime, the *St. Louis*, which had been sent to Philadelphia for overhaul and the installation of enlarged smokestacks, was recalled urgently to take the next eastbound sailing of the stranded *St. Paul*. The *St. Louis* had just arrived at the Cramp Shipyard. The rivets had been driven out, preparatory to the removal of both funnels, when the news about the *St. Paul* was received. Work was held up for a few hours until a second telegram detailed the stranding and requested that the *St. Louis* be made ready for sea immediately. The bolts and rivets were replaced and the scaffolding was removed so that the *St. Louis* could sail for New York.

When the paddlewheeler *George Starr* came alongside the *St. Paul* once again on Monday, January 27, it was to transfer crew members. When the *St. Louis* left for 10 weeks at the Cramp Shipyard in Philadelphia, most of her crew members were let go. Since she suddenly was being placed back in service, replacements were needed, and if there was one thing the *St. Paul* did not need at that moment, it was a full crew. The *George Starr* was chartered by the American Line once more to bring 70 stewards, 32 seamen, and 70 stokers from the stranded *St. Paul* to New York for reassignment to her sistership.

As the *St. Louis* came up the New Jersey coast a little after 8 P.M. on January 26, she edged close to the shore to salute and exchange signals with her stranded sister. The whistle of the *St. Louis* was blown and the unfortunate *St. Paul* responded. Then red, white, and blue lights were burned for the American Line, and with a final toot on her whistle, the *St. Louis* altered course toward Sandy Hook and the entrance to New York Harbor. Once there, she had to be fully coaled and provisioned for an Atlantic crossing in half the normal time, as well as taking on all the cargo and baggage of the *St. Paul.* After heroic efforts, the *St. Louis* was able to take her sister's sailing only a few hours late, and the American Line staff could congratulate itself on a difficult job very well done.

Clement Griscom ordered an American Line inquiry into the stranding of the *St. Paul.* At the hearing on board the liner, Captain Jamison and his officers were examined closely about their actions on the evening of the stranding. At the hearing's conclusion, no one said anything, but Clement A. Griscom, Jr., manager of the American Line, later indicated that he felt Captain Jamison had handled himself well.

The efforts to lighten the ship continued. The lifeboats and davits were removed from the liner and sent to New York, along with the two topmasts and every detachable deck fixture. Attempts to move the *St. Paul* on January 29, 31, February 1, 2, 3 often resulted in small gains that eased her toward the open sea, but they did not refloat her. Clement A. Griscom, Sr., and his son both spent the night of January 29 on the ship, hoping against hope that it would be freed at that time, but they went away disappointed. Old hands were beginning to say that only a winter storm with higher than normal seas would free the hull. Since the liner was getting low on coal, 200 tons were brought by barge on January 28, and another 100 tons on January 29.

February 2 was another Sunday, and the notoriety of the stranded liner surpassed every expectation. East Branch, New Jersey, became the center of the world for the American public eager for a midwinter break. It was the greatest day Long Branch and East Branch, New Jersey, had ever seen. The Central Railroad of New Jersey advertised a special train for the accommodation of visitors who wished to see the stranded ship but who did not want to catch the early morning train. Instead of running one excursion, there was such a crowd at the New York station that four trains brought sightseers to the scene. The Pennsylvania Railroad also advertised an excursion to accommodate travelers, and the railroad men were flabbergasted by the response. When the hour came for the special train to depart from Philadelphia, a mob of nearly 20,000 was waiting to board. A second train was announced, and then another. Eventually, the PRR sent nine trains of between eight and 15 cars each to the Jersey shore. This was only one day after a snowstorm, and the weather was both raw and nippy. M.R. Mulford, a conductor on the Jersey Central, contributed to the humor of the occasion when he announced, "Change cars for *St. Paul*" as his train pulled into Branchport. The tourists knew what he meant, and all jumped from their seats to go see the ship. Once again, the thrifty natives of the Jersey shore opened their businesses to handle the hungry and thirsty throng, which may have numbered 100,000. In spite of widespread fines the previous Sunday, liquor was still available for a price. It was reported that every restaurant in East Branch was sold out of all food by 1 P.M. At that point, even the enterprising butchers, grocers, bakers, and delicatessen owners opened and were soon stripped of their inventory. Boys selling pictures of the *St. Paul* minted money, and, it was said, professional pickpockets and crooks of all descriptions fleeced the unwary.

The fact that the bow of the *St. Paul* was embedded below the sand in the sticky clay was making it difficult to break her loose from the beach. The tugs did move the hull a little at various times, but a good storm was needed to complete the job. The beginnings of a good nor'easter on February 3 rocked the vessel a bit and helped the tugs shift her some 28 feet seaward in the morning and 196 feet that night. The wrecker tugs were pulling in tandem, with the *Jones* and the *I.J. Merritt* on one cable and the *Chapman* and the *North American* on the other. They might even have accomplished more if the waves had not been coming in so high that part of the time their propellers were out of water as they rode the crest of a wave. The distances the *St. Paul* moved since going ashore on Saturday, January 25, were: Sunday, 160 feet; Tuesday, 6 feet; Wednesday, 24 feet; Thursday, 6 feet; Friday, 6 feet; Saturday, 15 feet; Sunday, 8 feet; Monday morning, 28 feet; Monday night, 196 feet. Hundreds of people saw the ship move the largest distance yet on Monday, February 3, in spite of driving rain and blustery conditions. Finally, on Tuesday morning, February 4, after having been ashore for 10 days, the hull of the stranded liner loosened from the grip of the sand and clay.

When the wrecker tugs resumed work on Tuesday morning, there was still 200 feet between the stranded liner and deep water, but the high water brought by the nor'easter, and the rocking the hull had taken during the night, made them think this was the time. The supreme effort was set for 9 A.M., and the *St. Paul* had a full head of steam up for the occasion. Her big propellers went full astern to assist the tugs. First came a long pull, then a strong pull and a pull all together, and the big ship moved from her bed, grating her keel in the sand and bumping and jolting over the bar. When she slipped into deep water, the air was filled with the shriek of jubilant tug whistles. None of the tugs, however, wasted any steam in idle exuberance before the *St. Paul* actually was afloat. Long Branchers streamed to the beach to wave farewell to their most famous ship as she bobbed a curtsey in the Atlantic swells.[7]

Enlarged and lengthened funnels were installed after a year's operations and helped the St. Louis *and* St. Paul *to increase their performance. Additional updraft was needed for the fires to burn more effectively.*

Almost immediately, the tugs cast off and the *St. Paul*, under her own steam, turned her prow toward New York. The queen of the American merchant marine had survived an incredible experience, and no one was more relieved than Captain Jamison. The North German Lloyd steamer *Lahn* (1888, 5,099 tons) was rounding Sandy Hook just as the *St. Paul* arrived. The captain of the *Lahn* dipped her colors and blew three blasts on her whistles, while her passengers lined the rail and cheered. The *St. Paul* proudly returned the flag and whistle salutes. She cleared quarantine at 12:25 P.M. and Clement Griscom, Jr., came out to board her on the tug *C.E. Evarts*. Two wrecker tugs, the *W.E. Chapman* and the *J.D. Jones*, maintained an escort through the harbor and up to her berth, just in case anything might go wrong.

If the *St. Paul* attracted little attention an she steamed up the bay, this was not the case as she neared her pier. Her incognito arrival was broken by the salute of an observant tug captain on the North River, and soon river craft of all nature were saluting the liner on her safe arrival. On the bridge at the docking were Captain Jamison, Pilot William Germond, Clement A. Griscom, Jr., and Captain Shackford, shore captain of the American Line. An immediate examination of the liner was undertaken by the insurers, who found very little on which to comment. However, they did insist that the ship be drydocked for a more complete inspection of the hull, necessitating a trip to Newport News, Virginia. The insurers were responsible for paying the salvage claims, the cost of lightering the cargo off the ship and into New York, and the cost of the repairs to the vessel.

When Griscom was asked if Captain Jamison would be fired, he replied, "Absolutely not." The American Line had every confidence in him as master of any of their ships. In the subsequent hearings before the Board of Steamboat Inspectors, Captain Jamison handled the testimony well. He was fully in command of his facts and could prove that he had stopped the *St. Paul* on several occasions to cast the lead to try to determine where he was. At the time the *St. Paul* went on the beach, he was steaming at less than five knots, and a recent heaving of the lead had indicated 17 fathoms of water.[8] In the face of this information, which was substantiated by other officers and the ship's records, the Board of Inspectors of Steam Vessels exonerated Captain Jamison of all negligence in the stranding of his ship.[9] The issue of whether or not the *St. Paul* and the *Campania* were racing does not appear to have been raised by anyone.

The salvage claim of the Merritt Wrecking Company ultimately ended up in court, where the decision of the District Court was affirmed by the United States Circuit Court of Appeals in April 1898. The award of $131,012.48 was the second largest on record against a ship, and an additional $28,987.52 was affirmed against the cargo. In court, the American Line claimed that the evaluation of $2,000,000 for the *St. Paul* was too high, but Merritt produced records that showed the *St. Paul* actually cost $2,650,000 to build just two years earlier. The wreckers got nearly all they wanted, since the cargo was valued at $2,000,000, more than half of which was gold packed in bags and easily handled. Judge Lacombe, deciding there was no reason the gold should not bear a fair share of the cost of the operations, ruled in favor of the Merritt Wrecking Company.[10] The drydocking of the *St. Paul* at Newport News, Virginia, revealed that the hull was virtually undamaged by the grounding of the liner, and that all aspects of the machinery were perfect. The *St. Paul* left Virginia on Sunday, February 23, and returned to New York in preparation for taking on the Wednesday sailing on February 26. Once again the American Line had four liners to handle the weekly mails. This was fortunate, because other units in the fleet also were in for a rough winter.

Early in February, the *New York* crossed westbound in one of the most violent winter storms ever recorded. The waves were said to be more than 1,000 feet in length, and on one occasion, the wind shifted and dangerous cross seas threw the liner about. The seas were so violent that in spite of the buoyant nature of the *New York*, her rails were constantly under water, and no passenger was allowed on deck. In fact, the liner was lurching so wildly that even crew members were having difficulty remaining upright. Briefly, the *New York* went to the aid of a crippled British steamer, the *Oceanic*, from Sunderland bound for Hampton Roads. She had broken her screw and was bobbing about in the storm with a sea anchor. As a mail ship, the *New York* could not undertake a tow unless it was necessary to save lives, and this was not regarded as being the case. The American liner offered to report the *Oceanic's* position and notify Lloyd's, which was acknowledged, and then she continued on her voyage.

Saturday, February 29, 1896, was one of the worst days for accidents in the history of New York Harbor. *La Bourgogne* of the French Line ran down and sank the *Ailsa* of the Atlas Line, which was anchored in The Narrows waiting for the fog to lift. On the same day, the Old Dominion liner *Guyandotte* met the Clyde Line steamer *G.W. Clyde* and smashed a hole in her port side, forcing the *G.W. Clyde* to beach herself off Fort Hamilton to prevent a sinking. The ferryboat *Arizona* and a tug, *E.S. Atwood*, smacked into each other with damage to the latter, and the *New York*, inward bound from Southampton under the charge of a pilot, went aground in the channel near the Quickstep Buoy.[11]

The *New York* carried 225 cabin passengers and 215 steerage passengers at the time of the grounding. She had been boarded by Richard Begley, one of the Sandy Hook pilots, at 3:15 A.M. Captain Charles H. Grant was in command and on the bridge, but he felt no need to tell the pilot anything. The tide was flood and the weather overcast, with patchy rain squalls, when the *New York* crossed the bar. The engines were slowed at one point to avoid a schooner at anchor in the main channel. There were vessels ahead of the liner going through The Narrows on both sides of the ship. The *New York* struck so easily that no one realized it until the forward momentum suddenly stopped. Her bow was dug into about seven feet of mud, and tugs were summoned promptly. There was no point in trying to free her until the next high tide, at 8:30 in the evening. At that time, the tugs managed to get the *New York* out of the mud and underway again. There was no damage to the steamer anywhere, but her passengers were nearly a day late in reaching New York. Subsequently, Captain Grant and Pilot Richard Begley had a falling out over who was at fault. Begley said he had requested that Grant get the anchors ready, and when the captain neglected to do this, it forced the pilot to bring the liner on into the harbor, when in fact he wanted to anchor and wait for the fog to lift.[12] The American Line officers vigorously defended Captain Grant and testified in his defense that the anchors were ready if needed.[13] In turn, Captain Grant testified that Begley had the *New York* nearly 700 feet west of the channel when she went aground, and that this was due to the pilot's miscalculations. The publicity all around was not good, and Captain Grant resigned from the American Line. The resignation evidently came quickly, because Grant was listed as master of the *New York* on the preliminary passenger lists on Tuesday, but his name was replaced with that of Captain Frederick Watkins on Wednesday. Vice President James A. Wright of the International Navigation Company refused to say whether or not the company had asked for Grant's resignation but the line had always been quick enough to deny anything it did not want known.

No sooner was the *New York* towed off the West Bank Shoal in the Lower Bay than the *Paris* took her place. The *Paris* was inward bound from Newport News, Virginia, after drydocking and overhaul. Captian F. M. Passow, formerly of the *Southwark*, had been promoted to the *Paris*, although at the time of the grounding she was in charge of Pilot Arthur Gridley. In an incredible series of events, the big liner touched the shoal for the first time around 1 P.M. on Sunday, March 29, and successfully backed off. Then, as the

Paris felt her way up the channel, another vessel appeared ahead. Trying to avoid that ship, the *Paris* rammed her bow into the muddy shoal for the second time.[14] This time, reversing her engines did not get her off, and tugs had to be called. Contemporary accounts said that the West Bank Shoal was beloved of American Line ships, since they had spent so much time on it. According to the American Line, both incidents happened during clear weather just south of the Quickstep Buoy. Pilot Gridley contended there was some fog. The *Paris* was drawing her full 26 feet of water at the time she went aground, because she had come north from Virginia with full bunkers of more than 2,000 tons of coal, ready for an Atlantic crossing. She had only used about 130 tons of fuel, so all the rest, 1,850 tons, had to be shoveled out of her in order to lighten the vessel so she could be refloated. An attempt at frugal foresight in having her coaled in Virginia, where fuel was cheaper, ended up producing two long, dirty jobs. First all the coal had to come out, and then, once she was refloated, it all had to go back into the bunkers.

At high tide on Monday night, March 30, the *Paris* was helped off by fleet tugs and made it to her pier shortly after midnight. At Pier 14, she had to be provisioned and recoaled in time to take the Wednesday, April 1, sailing of the American Line. In connection with the *Paris*, the American Line registered a formal complaint against Pilot Gridley, for grounding the liner twice. One week later, on April 7, Gridley was reduced in grade by the Board of Pilot Commissioners to the 20-foot license class for one year. This meant that for a year, he could not bring into harbor a vessel drawing more than 20 feet of water.[15]

With the return of the *St. Paul*, the *Paris* replaced the *St. Louis* in the schedule so the *St. Louis* could get to Philadelphia for the overhaul that the stranding of her sister had delayed. Back on line, the *St. Paul* raced home on May 15, 1896, in six days, nine hours, and five minutes, at an average speed of 20.34 knots. She had to reduce speed for 12 hours because of fog, and if that had not been the case, Captain Jamison felt sure she would have broken the record of the *New York*.

In 1896, scientific journals had given full rein to descriptions of a total eclipse of the sun, which was to be visible from the Northern Hemisphere on August 8. Northern Scandinavia was heralded as the best place for seeing this unique astronomical event, and the International Navigation Company proposed to take advantage of this phenomenon to promote a cruise. The 3,392-ton *Ohio* of the American Line was especially fitted for cruises and was advertised as one of the largest and most luxurious steam yachts afloat. Only a limited number of first-class passengers would be carried, with no freight, no cabin class, and no steerage. The voyage was described in glowing terms as "a yachting cruise for health and pleasure in every sense of the word." The *Ohio* sailed from New York on June 27, bound for a Baltic and North Cape cruise that would include calls in England, Norway, Sweden, Russia, Finland, and Denmark. All the arrangements for visiting the various ports were in the hands of the well-known tourist agents Thomas Cook & Son, who produced a special pamphlet for the occasion. On August 8, when the solar eclipse occurred, she was scheduled to be off Bodo, Norway. This opened up a whole new world of money-earning possibilities for the American Line, which in the future would assign a number of vessels to cruising when the trade warranted.

Life along the waterfront never was dull. A case of robbery on the *St. Louis* captured the public's imagination in July 1896. A wealthy brother and sister, Frank A. Watson and Miss Eliza Watson of New York City, were sailing on the American liner on July 15. Miss Watson had packed a quantity of precious jewels in a steamer trunk, which was damaged during loading into the ship's hold. The lock was broken, and the contents of the jewelry box fell into the hands of William Doyle, a 21-year-old sailor working as a longshoreman to load the *St. Louis.* The temptation was too great, and he pocketed a couple of handfuls of jewels. Subsequently, he asked Josoph Flynn, an acquaintance, to pawn one of the diamond earrings for him. Flynn took the 2½-carat earring to the pawnshop of Louis Simon on Varick Street around noon—one hour after the liner sailed. Since Flynn in no way matched the description of a person normally having access to diamond jewelry, Simon refused to have anything to do with the matter. Furthermore, Flynn only asked two dollars for the earring, which was worth more than $150.

No sooner did Flynn start to leave the pawnshop when Simon saw Detectives Frazee and Jackson of the Macdougal Street Precinct passing on the opposite side of the street; he signaled to the two officers to grab Flynn. Before he knew what happened, Flynn, who still had the diamond in his hand, was arrested. "Where did you get this?" one of the officers asked, and Flynn pointed across the street to where William Doyle was standing. "He gave it to me." One of the detectives took off after the sailor, who fled down the street but was caught after a short chase. The detectives searched Doyle and found a substantial quantity of diamond jewelry, including a gold bracelet set with gold balls and diamonds, sapphires, and rubies; one butterfly breastpin studded with a daisy shaped with 34 diamonds; one breastpin, violet-shaped with one large diamond; and the mate to the earring Flynn had tried to pawn. Doyle also was carrying $12.75 in cash, at the time considered a large sum for a sailor.

The men were taken to the Macdougal Street Station, where they were questioned. The diamonds still in Doyle's possession were in pasteboard boxes bearing the names of Black, Starr & Frost, Jewelers, and Tiffany. When they told confusing stories about mysterious well-dressed men asking them to pawn the jewels, Doyle and Flynn were taken to the Jefferson Market Police Court, where they were remanded until the case could be investigated. The jewelers were contacted to identify the pieces in hopes of discovering who had bought them, since there was no idea of the ownership.[16] In due course, Black, Starr & Frost, Jewelers, reported to the New York police that the diamond-studded bracelet had been sold to H.R.C. Watson of Babylon, New York, a relative of the Watsons, and that the diamond earrings were sold to Frank A. Watson in 1894. When a formal arraignment of the prisoners occurred, H.R.C. Watson appeared to press charges against them. American Line personnel also were present to testify that Doyle and Flynn were working in the hold of the *St. Louis* when the liner was taking on baggage, although no one had seen them do the pilfering. The buildup of evidence was so convincing that William Doyle confessed and said he had picked up the jewels when they "fell out of the trunk." This exonerated Joseph Flynn, although he was not immediately released pending additional questioning.[17] Upon receiving this information, James A. Wright, superintendent and vice president of the American Line, cabled a message to be delivered to the Watsons at Southampton when the *St. Louis* arrived. Since the steamer trunk had been consigned to the hold of the vessel, the Watsons remained unsuspecting of the robbery. When the Watsons landed at Southampton on July 22, they were informed by British Customs that the lock on their trunk had been forced by "an expert." At the same time, Wright's cable was delivered to them, explaining the situation and asking them to cable descriptions of the missing jewelry to New York.[18] The stolen gems were valued at more than $5,000. In a footnote to the case, when Doyle was running from the detectives, he threw away a five-pointed diamond star pin worth $900. This item was picked up by 18-year-old Martin Kelly, who gave it to another man, who in turn sold it for $30 and divided the money with him. Such news traveled quickly on the street, and the detectives soon had Kelly in court as well, while they looked for his accomplice. Rarely has a sequence of events brought the solution to a robbery before the victims even knew that they had suffered a loss.

While all westbound transatlantic races began from The Needles, the American Line ships upon occasion may have wasted no time in getting to the starting point. The Solent, a relatively narrow body of water, could be subject to substantial wash from a big, fast-moving ship. This situation brought a complaint to the newspapers from Baron Colville of Culcross, chairman of the Great Northern Railway Company, who insisted that the American Line ships and others were making The Solent dangerous. He complained that a wave from the *St. Louis* nearly swamped a small steamer off Cowes on August 29, and that a wave from the North German Lloyd *Spree* dashed on the shore and knocked over a woman who was using the footpath of the Cowes Road. The American Line denied that its steamers were guilty of speeding in The Solent.

The 1896 fall season went well for the American Line, and it even appeared as though a majority of the transatlantic steamship lines might reach a universal understanding on rates and scheduling that would contribute to the profitability of all of them. So encouraging were the prospects when Thomas H. Ismay of the Oceanic Steam Navigation Company (White Star Line) proposed a London conference of the heads of the great steamship lines that Clement Acton Griscom, Sr., accepted and prepared to cross the North Atlantic for the meeting. So enthusiastic was Griscom about the conference that preparations even were made to hold some of the sessions in the American Line headquarters in London. With his son as manager of the American Line, Griscom, now 55, could play the role of elder statesman. He chose to cross on the *Paris*, which was scheduled to sail from New York on Wednesday, October 7, giving him a little time to settle in before the conference began.

The departure from New York was uneventful, and the *Paris*'s 18,000-horsepower engines were soon running at full power. Sailing time from New York had been pushed

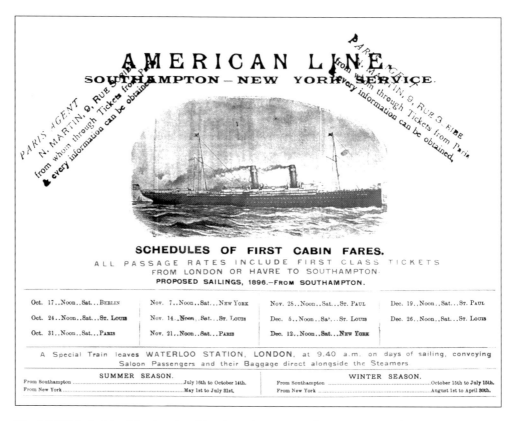

AMERICAN LINE.
SOUTHAMPTON — NEW YORK SERVICE.

SCHEDULES OF FIRST CABIN FARES.

ALL PASSAGE RATES INCLUDE FIRST CLASS TICKETS
FROM LONDON OR HAVRE TO SOUTHAMPTON.
PROPOSED SAILINGS, 1896.—FROM SOUTHAMPTON.

Oct. 17..Noon..Sat...BERLIN	Nov. 7..Noon..Sat...NEW YORK	Nov. 28..Noon..Sat...ST. PAUL	Dec. 19..Noon..Sat...ST. PAUL
Oct. 24..Noon..Sat...ST. LOUIS	Nov. 14..Noon..Sat...ST. LOUIS	Dec. 5..Noon..Sat...ST. LOUIS	Dec. 26..Noon..Sat...ST. LOUIS
Oct. 31..Noon..Sat...PARIS	Nov. 21..Noon..Sat...PARIS	Dec. 12..Noon..Sat...NEW YORK	

A Special Train leaves WATERLOO STATION, LONDON, at 9.40 a.m. on days of sailing, conveying
Saloon Passengers and their Baggage direct alongside the Steamers.

SUMMER SEASON.	WINTER SEASON.
From Southampton ....July 16th to October 14th.	From Southampton ....October 15th to July 15th.
From New York ....May 1st to July 31st.	From New York ....August 1st to April 30th.

The fall 1896 schedule of the American Line shows the return to the express service of the St. Paul, *November 26, 1896, which gave the American Line a first-class transatlantic service second to none. The* Berlin *had filled in for her during her overhaul.*

up to 10 o'clock A.M. in order to give the American Line ships an extra hour to reach Southampton. At 8:40 Thursday morning, as the *Paris* was slicing through the Atlantic swells 320 miles east of Sandy Hook, the liner shuddered. A propeller shaft had fractured and broken in its tunnel, and the starboard engine was stopped. Captain Frederick Watkins conferred with Griscom about the alternatives. He could turn the *Paris* around and limp back to New York or he could keep on going on one screw at 15 knots, which would get the ship to Southampton a few days late. Spare propeller shafts were stored at Southampton, and the drydock was there, so the liner could in fact be repaired more expeditiously in England than in the United States. There was no question in Griscom's mind that he would much rather have Captain Watkins take the *Paris* to Southampton. The havoc to the American Line schedule also would be much less.

The wisdom of this decision was underlined when the HAPAG liner *Fürst Bismarck*, westbound to New York, met them four hours later. As the *Paris* was lying-to and flying a signal that she wanted to communicate, Captain Albers immediately responded to the signal to stop. A boat was put out from the *Paris* as her passengers lined the rails, waving to their counterparts on the other liner, and the American officer boarded the German liner. He informed Captain Albers of their broken shaft and requested that he deliver urgent letters from Watkins and Griscom to the American Line headquarters in New York. The American officer stayed only a few minutes and then returned to the *Paris*. The *Fürst Bismarck* immediately resumed her voyage. As the German liner left with the dispatches, the *Paris* also got underway for Europe. Both Watkins and Griscom could breathe easier, because Southampton would be made aware of the problem by cable and arrangements would be made to drydock the *Paris* as soon as she arrived. In New York the next day, Vice President James A. Wright of the International Navigation Company released a statement to the press that no one had been injured in the accident and that the *Paris* would complete her voyage with one propeller. The previous day's position of the American liner indicated that the ship was doing a comfortable 15 knots under one engine, even though she was dragging the other propeller.

An Atlantic crossing under one propeller was not going to be easy, although the engines on the *Paris* were so powerful that she easily could do 15 knots on one—just five knots slower than usual. The *Paris* was carrying 98 first-class passengers, 60 second-cabin, and 190 steerage passengers. During the crossing, the disabled American liner was sighted by many ships. The *St. Louis*, inward bound to New York, passed the *Paris* at 11:46 P.M., October 8, 458 miles west of the Sandy Hook Lightship. In the darkness, the two ships exchanged signals, but the officers on the *St. Louis* did not even know the *Paris* was having any difficulty, since she was underway and steaming well. The progress of the American liner across the Atlantic was watched with interest, and many reports found their way into the newspapers. The *Teutonic* (eastbound) arrived in Queenstown (October 13) and reported seeing the *Paris* on Thursday, October 8, stopped with a boat lowered. It turned out that this was before the *Fürst Bismarck* came alongside the *Paris*, so it could be discounted. The steamer *Benbridge* (westbound) from Colombo to Philadelphia reported passing the *Paris* making steady speed off Newfoundland on Friday, October 9. The *Kensington* of the American Line (westbound) reported passing the *Paris* at considerable distance nearly a thousand miles east of Sandy Hook. She was flying her code signals: "We are the *Paris*, American Line," which indicated she was all right and did not need assistance. Considering the fact that the *Paris* must have hit the fringe of a major storm in the North Atlantic, she was making fair speed. Reckoning from the time she was sighted by the *Fürst Bismarck* on Thursday afternoon until she was sighted by the *Kensington*, she was making 11 to 14 knots. At that rate, she should have been alongside her Southampton pier by Saturday night. This was only slightly optimistic.

The *Paris* came alongside her Southampton berth at 9:15 Sunday morning (October 18), 11 days out from New York. Captain Watkins had declined all offers of assistance, having every confidence in the ability of his ship to make the crossing on one propeller. The weather had proven to be somewhat rough, but the passengers were well contented with the handling of the situation. During the crossing, the *Paris* had spoken no fewer than 20 other ships in the steamer lanes. She averaged 12.5 knots and would have done better had she not been dragging a screw. On Friday, the first-class passengers had held a meeting in the saloon and presented a testimonial to the captain and the chief engineer as Clement Griscom beamed.

Griscom reached London in time for the conference with the other heads of the transatlantic steamship lines. He was treated with respect as the creator of a great maritime enterprise. The conference opened with a formal dinner hosted by Thomas Ismay of White Star on the evening of October 22. Subsequent sessions were held at the American Line headquarters in London, where an agreement was signed by all the lines relating to the transatlantic passenger business. There was no suggestion of an alteration of freight rates or passenger fares, and the principals refused to discuss with the press anything else about their deliberations. Only the Holland-America Line indicated that the smaller lines also would like a conference with the managers of the bigger and faster lines, with the goal of getting a lower steerage rate for their ships.[19] The participation of Griscom in the steamship conference in London clearly underlined the fact that the International Navigation Company's American Line could command the respect of all its competitors.

The twin-screw steamer Vaderland *(1900) and her sisters were the largest and fastest ships in the Antwerp–New York service. This illustration for a passenger list in 1905 shows the Red Star liner approaching the Statue of Liberty.*

Chapter 12

SHIPWRECKS AND RESCUES

The potential peril to Atlantic shipping from flotsam, jetsam, and abandoned wrecks that had not sunk was well known to mariners. The ocean in the nineteenth century was littered with the remains of sailing vessels and steamers as well as natural perils. It was essential for every captain to mark their last noted position and to keep abreast of any changes. At sea, warning of potential danger might appear by virtue of scattered wreckage, but even the most skilled lookout could miss a half-sunken hull drifting with deadly menace just beneath the waves. This is what happened to the Holland-America liner *Veendam* and her gallant captain, G. Stenger, in February 1898.

Captain Stenger already had earned the reputation of being one of the most competent master mariners on the North Atlantic. He was a highly skilled ship handler and very popular with the knowedgeable traveling public. In mid-career, Stenger had risen to the command of the premier units of the Nederlandsch-Amerikaansche Stoomvaart Maatschappij (Holland-America) fleet. He sailed from Rotterdam in command of the *Veendam* on Thursday, February 3, 1898, with a typical winter passenger list of four saloon, five second-cabin, and 118 steerage passengers. The crew of the liner numbered 85, and the general cargo was valued at between $300,000 and $400,000.

The *Veendam* originally had had a distinguished career as the White Star liner *Baltic* (1871, 3,707 tons). She was purchased by Holland-America in 1888 and given triple-expansion engines in 1890. The *Veendam* had a reputation for being a good, solid, steady sea boat under most North Atlantic conditions.

The voyage down the English Channel was uneventful, and the *Veendam* turned her bow westward for the run to New York. Weather conditions in February rarely were ideal, and the liner encountered strong northwest gales and high west-northwest seas. As darkness settled on Sunday, February 6, the Dutch liner was 500 to 600 miles west of England. Some wreckage was seen bobbing in the waves, and the lookouts were keeping sharp eyes for anything more serious. Suddenly the *Veendam* was lifted by a wave, up and over a large submerged wreck, and then slammed down on top of it. In the engine room, Chief Engineer Lichtenbelt was shaken by the blow and the deafening grating sound that followed. The engines were stopped at once, and Lichtenbelt ran aft to the shaft tunnel entrance, only to be driven back by inrushing water. The after half of the liner had suffered severe damage. The propeller shaft was broken and two bulkheads were shattered by the impact. The *Veendam* had suffered mortal wounds and immediately began to sink. The ship's construction involved seven watertight compartments, and three were open to the sea. Frantic efforts reinforced the bulkhead between the fire

The Veendam *(I) (4,036 tons, 420 feet by 41 feet, 14 knots), was built by Harland and Wolff for the White Star Line as the* Baltic *(1871). She had accommodations for 166 first and 1,000 third. The* St. Louis *rescued all her passengers and crew after she hit a wreck in the mid-Atlantic (1898).*

room and the number-three hold. The steam pumps were started up, but the water flooded in twice as fast as it could be pumped out. Hand pumps were worked and a bucket brigade was begun, but nothing could counteract the steadily rising water. The activities of the crew slowed the rate of sinking and did everything possible to try to keep the liner from making a sudden dive for the ocean floor. As darkness set in and the stern sank deeper, the *Veendam* wallowed without power in the North Atlantic. The inrushing water from the fractured shaft tunnel filled the engine room and fire room, inexorably pulling the liner under the stormy seas stern-first. The watertight bulkheads could not save the ship, but there was a chance they could buy enough time to save the lives of the 212 passengers and crew. All lifeboats were made ready to leave the liner, but no one was willing to go until the last possible moment, because the seas were so rough and the wind was so strong. Rockets were fired off at regular intervals in hopes of attracting the attention of a passing vessel. During the next eight hours, every able-bodied crew member and passenger took turns at the pumps, desperately trying to keep the *Veendam* afloat. Throughout the night, Captain Stenger's solid courage and personal heroism sustained all those under his care.

In what is exceedingly rare in maritime lore, there are some steerage-passenger accounts of this disaster. Mandel Mandoff and David Devinishke, both hailing from Kovno Guberna, in Russian Poland, told what happened to them:

> It was after 5 o'clock on Sunday that there came a terrific crash. We did not know what was the matter. The women sprang from their cots, forgetting their seasickness, and began to rush about shrieking in alarm. We asked to be told what the trouble was, but received no information.
>
> The ship stopped, and there began a terrible rushing about overhead. We knew that there must be some terrible trouble, and we began to pray. Suddenly one of the officers appeared in the steerage and ordered all the men on deck. We obeyed and were put to work on the pumps.
>
> Oh, how we worked those pumps. We knew that our lives depended on keeping the water down, but pump as hard as we could it was impossible to lessen the immense quantity that poured in. We were all exhausted....

Chaia Nyitka, who emigrated to America with her father, Israel, from Sushkovalen, Kalish Guberna, Russia, spoke for the women:

> Nearly all of us were sick, and most of the women and children were in their beds when the crash came. But then our sickness was frightened away. I fainted though, as did some of the other women. But we soon revived and ran around trying to discover what had happened. When we saw the men saying the "Shema" and the children gathered around us crying, we felt as though the last moment had come.
>
> We followed the men on deck because we were afraid to stay where we could not see. We strained our eyes to see a ship, but nothing was in sight. Then there was a report and great lights shot up. They were firing rockets. When finally we saw the lights of another vessel it seemed too good to be true. The rockets were sent up faster, and the lights on the other vessel grew bigger and brighter. Then we knew they saw us.[1]

At 1:30 the next morning, the lights of a large steamer were seen east by south of the *Veendam*, and every possible effort was made to attract her attention. To the infinite relief of those on the Dutch ship, the steamer was observed to turn slowly and make for them. As the liner drew near and her searchlights swept the turbulent sea, those on board the *Veendam* were overjoyed to see that the vessel coming to their rescue was one of the newest, largest, and best-equipped liners on the North Atlantic—the *St. Louis* of the American Line.

The Veendam *(I) (1888), painted by Stephen Card, is shown making a morning departure from New York at the start of an Atlantic crossing to Rotterdam in the summer of 1889. The* Veendam *is wearing the original Holland-America funnel colors, black with white and green bands. The HAL funnels were painted yellow at the start of the Spanish-American War so that the HAL ships could not be mistaken for American Line ships.* Illustration courtesy of Stephen Card

Not a moment was lost, since the *Veendam*'s situation was critical. The *St. Louis* was sighted at 1:30, and by 1:43 Captain Stenger was making arrangements to transfer his passengers and crew to the American liner. Captain William G. Randle of the *St. Louis* took one look at the sinking *Veendam* and wondered if there would be enough time for any rescue. He had sailed from Southampton on February 5 with 221 cabin and 183 steerage passengers, most of whom continued sleeping through the night. Randle took the *St. Louis* to within a quarter of a mile of the *Veendam* but feared to approach any closer because both liners were laboring hard in the high seas. The chief officer of the *St. Louis*, Thomas G. Segrave, made a name for himself that night as the leader of the rescue mission. Segrave called for volunteers from the crew, and eight husky seamen answered his call. Four got into a lifeboat, which was lowered away while they tried to keep it from slamming against the side of the liner. The other four seamen slid down the ropes to the bobbing boat, which nearly swamped even though everyone was as quick as possible. One sea nearly upended the lifeboat and slammed it against the steel side of the ship, but frantic rowing prevented disaster. Segrave said it had been a very close escape, followed by a hard pull to the side of the *Veendam*, but the crack American crew was alongside the sinking liner in seven minutes. Happily, the earlier darkness of the night was broken by a bright moon, which greatly enhanced visibility. Once alongside the Dutch liner, the men faced new challenges, since she had no power and was rolling uncontrollably. Captain Stenger was at the rail, overseeing this critical stage of the operation. After some effort, a line thrown from the *Veendam* was seized by the lifeboat. For the rest of his life, Segrave remained impressed at the total command of the situation that the Dutch captain showed and at how his own exhausted crew obeyed him and followed his leadership without question. Since there was no such thing as wireless communication yet, Segrave brought a message from Randle that if more boats were needed, the *Veendam* was to make more fire, and this was done immediately. Segrave made ready to receive passengers in the lifeboat, and, as he reported: "Captain Stenger sent down the children first, and first of all was a wee babe of six months. Life slings were used, and the Captain personally examined the line to see that it was properly tied before any one was let down. The babe was placed in the stern."[2] Segrave got 20 children and five women in his lifeboat, which was all he thought he could take in safety, given the precious nature of his cargo. The seas were running so heavy that those on the *St. Louis* saw the returning lifeboat only occasionally. Every time it dropped from view in the trough of a wave, gasps arose from the promenade deck of the American liner, when it looked as though the lifeboat had been lost. Furthermore, on occasion it looked as though Segrave lost sight of the *St. Louis* and had to alter course while at the top of a huge swell as his men strained with all their might to row back to their ship. Two additional lifeboats from the *St. Louis* passed Segrave as his lifeboat struggled to get back to the big American liner.

As the first lifeboat neared the *St. Louis*, an amusing incident occurred. Captain Randle, looking down at the approaching boat, could hardly believe his eyes. It looked as though only the American sailors were in it. From the deck of the *St. Louis*, he bellowed at Segrave: "Why don't you bring back the people?" Segrave, somewhat outraged, hollered back: "People! Why I've got twenty-five babies aboard." And so he did! A boatswain's chair was used to get the women and children on deck, while the men in later lifeboats were hoisted aboard by ropes under their arms. In spite of all possible care, every one of the American lifeboats suffered some damage. The process of boarding the *St. Louis* was somewhat slow, but, as one observer commented, haste was out of the question in that sea. As soon as the babies and children reached the deck, American Line stewards grabbed them and whisked them inside to the kitchens and dining rooms, where they could find warmth as quickly as possible. Rescued passengers were taken to the appropriate class, where all could be provided with accommodations, perhaps ones even superior to what they had left on the *Veendam*.

Archer Brown, a *St. Louis* passenger, told reporters in New York about the events following the rescue. "The women, having partially recovered, began to demand their children, and if it had not been so tragic, it would have been ludicrous to see the way they ran about seeking their children. And how they cried with joy when they found

In one of the most famous of Cassiers' sketches, a rag-tag group of fishermen and laborers, accompanied by a dog, admire the magnificent St. Louis *as she steams by. "The lure of the sea is potent and the American Line is there to serve you" (1902).*

their little ones. I tell you there were many snivelers among us, too. The galley was astir, and hot coffee was being brewed in a jiffy. This, and good, fresh rolls were distributed, and lots of warm milk for the children. How they ate! I never saw such a sight."[3]

Launching the additional boats was not easy. George Beckwith, second officer of the *St. Louis*, had one lifeboat stove in against the side of the ship and had to pull it up and try with a second before he made it to the *Veendam* to rescue an additional 18 women from steerage. It may have been the intention to take the first-class and cabin passengers off in the second boat, but the uproar from the terrified women, some of whom had seen their children go ahead of them, altered this. "Beckwith said that the steerage passengers were clamoring to be taken off first, and the cabin passengers, who displayed splendid control of themselves, drew back and said: 'We will wait.'" Nothing adds more to the tale of this rescue than the humanity of this gesture. Rescue may have been at hand, but death was also imminent.

The third American Line boat, under the command of Second Extra Officer Campbell, took off another 18 women. Before the third lifeboat got back to the *St. Louis*, Segrave was alongside the *Veendam* again, rescuing another 20. In all, Segrave's boat would save 90 lives in four trips, and Beckwith's and Campbell's boats each would save 36 lives in two trips. The crew of the *Veendam*, even though exhausted from their struggle to keep their ship afloat, also participated. Two of the Dutch liner's lifeboats were smashed against the side of the ship while launching and were lost. A third finally reached the sea successfully. Manned by Dutch sailors, it succeeded in transferring an additional 50 persons, mostly crew, to the *St. Louis*.

Captain Stenger was the last to leave his ship. "Before he left he went into the main saloon, and piling up everything inflammable, including a lot of furniture, he poured oil over it and touched it off with a match. This was to insure the craft sinking, that she might not float about as a derelict, dangerous to navigation."[4] He did not want anyone else to experience the hell he had just gone through! Since the *Veendam* had 17 feet of water in her hold, Stenger did not feel that she could last more than another six or seven hours. The burning *Veendam* lighted the sea with a huge column of fire. Aemilius Jarvis of Toronto, Canada, a delegate from the North American Yacht Racing Union to the British Yacht Racing Association, was a passenger on the *St. Louis*. He commented, "It was an impressive sight, and I watched it until the hull of the *Veendam* had fallen below the horizon. Even then its reflection shone in the sky."[5]

The rescue effort was concluded at 4:53 A.M., a little more than three hours after starting. Every single passenger and crew member on the *Veendam* was safe. The passengers of the *St. Louis* were so proud of their brave crew that they held a meeting and raised a purse of $700, of which $400 was for the three boat crews and $300 for the destitute steerage passengers, who had lost everything they possessed. A testimonial also was prepared honoring the officers in direct charge of the rescue. When the *St. Louis* reached the bar at 2:38 A.M. on February 12, she was held up by fog and did not reach her berth until midafternoon. The news that she brought the passengers and crew of the *Veendam* was sent up to the city from quarantine. The information was garbled, and some thought that the *St. Louis* had experienced trouble. The cheers that greeted the docking of the big American liner at Fulton Street belied that.

Captain Stenger was generous in his praise of the efforts of the American Line officers and crew. Interesting in itself was the fact that the passengers from the Dutch ship reached New York three days ahead of schedule on the much faster *St. Louis*. August William H. Vandentoorn, the New York agent of Holland-America, held the *Spaarndam*, which was preparing to sail at the company pier, for one day so that she could take the officers and crew of the *Veendam* back to The Netherlands. They sailed for Rotterdam the morning after their arrival in New York. Captain Stenger released a letter to the press:

> Before leaving New York I wish to make public acknowledgment for myself and
> for the passengers, officers and crew of the steamship *Veendam*, of our deep

Henri Cassiers (1858–1944), the Belgian artist, produced some of his most beautiful work for the American Line. Here the liner Haverford *(1901, 11,635 tons, 531 feet by 59 feet, 14 knots) prepares to pass a fisherman, who salutes the new American Line ship. The* Haverford *was engaged in the Philadelphia–Queenstown–Liverpool service of the American Line from April 1902 to December 1908.*

gratitude to Captain Randle, Chief Officer Segrave, Senior Second Officer Beckwith, and Extra Second Officer Campbell, also to the other officers with the crew and passengers of the American Line steamship *St. Louis*.

Their assistance was promptly, cheerfully, and most judiciously given, when my vessel was sinking. The hearty welcome on board the *St. Louis*, and the constant kindness received during the rest of the voyage, from the ship's company and her passengers, are far above our praise and shall never be forgotten. God Bless the good steamer *St. Louis*, her gallant commander, and brave officers and crew.[6]

Stenger was no stranger to rescue operations himself. He and the *Veendam* had stood by the stricken American schooner *Mary Wells* in January 1894, and he had been presented a gold watch for his efforts by President Grover Cleveland. A critical comment found its way into the press that the *Veendam* was not equipped with sufficient lifeboats. This was vehemently denied by Holland-America, which pointed out that the Dutch liner complied with all requirements for lifesaving equipment and that, while she was carrying 212 souls, her lifeboats had accommodations for 328—34 percent more than necessary. Holland-America faced a substantial problem with the *Veendam* immigrants, who were now destitute. By American immigration law, those immigrants having no resources were subject to deportation at the expense of the steamship line that had brought them. Agent Vandentoorn made appropriate financial arrangements with the Immigration Bureau so that almost all of the immigrants could be released. After all, it was cheaper than shipping them back to Europe, and their efforts had been instrumental in manning the pumps to buy time to keep the *Veendam* afloat. One young man from Italy, Michael di Jorio, had to be deported because he had a prison record. He had been found guilty of poaching on a nobleman's estate near his home in Italy. He protested that he had only been guilty of taking some kindling wood lying on the ground, but the Immigration authorities were firm that the law refused admittance to the United States to anyone who had been convicted of any crime. They were sorry, but di Jorio would have to go back to Italy at the expense of the Holland-America Line. The *Tottenham*, a freighter, was chartered to take the cargo of the lost *Veendam*.

Subsequently, Captain William Randle and the officers and crew of the *St. Louis* were recipients of handsome testimonials in recognition of their bravery in rescuing the captain, crew, and passengers of the *Veendam*. The presentations were made on board the *St. Louis* at her dock on March 17, 1898. Holland-America's representative, Vandentoorn, made a brief address and then presented Captain Randle with a large silver cup, suitably engraved. Segrave, Beckwith, and Campbell each received a similar cup, and every member of the crew engaged in the rescue operation received a sum of money in a sealed envelope. The Life-Saving Benevolent Association presented gold medals to Captain Randle and to the three officers, and money to the crew members.

Clement Acton Griscom also was very proud of the officers and crew of the *St. Louis*, and the International Navigation Company awarded $200 to Captain Randle, $100 to each of the three officers, and $25 to $30 to each seaman, depending upon his term of service. The efficiency displayed in the successful rescue of the passengers and crew of the *Veendam* reflected very favorably on the American Line. Captain Randle, in returning thanks for himself and his men, remarked, "Events are transpiring now in this country which may lead us into war, and we may be called upon to sacrifice life in defense of our country. But the satisfaction will not be as great as the saving of life, which is more gratifying than the taking of it."[7] War with Spain over Cuba seemed certain, and there was no question that the American Line fleet would have a large role to play.

The American Line spent another anxious week in March waiting for news of the *Paris*, which was overdue again. She sailed from New York under the command of the experienced Captain Frederick Watkins on March 2 and was due at Southampton on March 9. The *Paris* was carrying a light passenger load of 67 first-class, 44 second-cabin, and 70 steerage passengers. The crossing proved eventful even before the vessel left the harbor. The American liner was following the *Trinidad* down the main channel when the Bermuda boat started to cross in order to go out by the Swash Channel, a shorter route to the open sea. As her pilot was executing this maneuver, he suddenly realized that the much larger and faster *Paris* was overtaking his ship. Changing his mind, he sought to bring the *Trinidad* back onto a straight course in the main channel when the American liner's clipper bow caught her on the quarter and smashed in the counter. Passengers on the *Trinidad* were thrown to the deck by the force of the collision, but neither the Bermuda boat nor the *Paris* was damaged enough to return to port.[8]

News was received of heavy fog along the English coast, which delayed the departure of a number of vessels, and it was assumed that the American liner was creeping toward Southampton. In the end, the news was received that the *Paris* was safe after an 11-day crossing. Once again, she had broken her starboard shaft, rendering the propeller useless. This incident had occurred only 375 miles from Sandy Hook, but Captain Watkins had again felt secure in taking the liner across on one screw. By this time, the American Line had learned to stock spare propeller shafts on the *Paris* and the *New York*. Repairs in some instances could be made at sea, but Watkins reasoned that it was better to make for Southampton, where the work could be undertaken much more conveniently in drydock. Only a month earlier, the *Paris* had been forced to abandon a sailing from England when a flaw was discovered in her port propeller shaft. The cracked section was removed at Southampton and replaced with a new piece. The recurrent episodes with the propeller shafts on the *New York* and the *Paris* were a constant problem, and it was evident that structural alterations would be needed at some future date.

The deterioration of relations between the United States and Spain over Cuba saw the American government taking some preliminary measures to guarantee the availability of oceangoing tonnage should hostilities occur. The creation of an auxiliary fleet in support of the United States Navy became a prime goal of the administration. The Naval Auxiliary Board was established, and the vessels in the American merchant marine were reviewed in order to determine which ones might be appropriate. It was announced on April 5 that the Morgan Line had sold the coastwise steamers *El Rio*, *El Sol*, *El Sud*, and *El Norte* to the U.S. government for cash. Three liners of the Old Dominion Line also were acquired *(Jamestown*, *Princess Anne*, and *Yorktown)*, as well as the *Kansas City* of the Savannah Line. It was rumored that the *Caracas* and the *Venezuela* of the venerable Red D Line would be bought, and the Maine Steamship Company's *John Englis* was being surveyed.[9] The Ward Line service to Cuba was an early casualty of the deterioration in Spanish-American relations, and the vessels in its fleet were placed at the disposal of the U.S. government *(Vigilancia*, *Yucatan*, *Saratoga*, *City of Washington*, and *Orizaba)*. In regard to the fleet of the International Navigation Company, the Auxiliary Board recommended the purchase of the *Illinois* immediately, and rumors were flying that the government would pay as much as $4,000,000 for the *St. Louis* and the *St. Paul*. Particular interest arose in connection with the *St. Louis*, because she was scheduled to sail for Southampton on April 6, and there was discussion about whether she should be allowed to go. C.A. Griscom, Jr., general manager of the American Line, remained constantly in contact with the Auxiliary Board and refuted the high prices mentioned in the press. He made the point that under the terms of the Postal Aid Act of 1891, all the American Line ships were at the command of the government at any time.

Having exhausted the slim resources of the American merchant marine, the Naval Auxiliary Board turned to foreign-flag steamship lines. The big German concerns always seemed to have secondary tonnage available for solid cash. Gustav Schwab, New York agent for North German Lloyd (NGL), was in constant contact with the Naval Auxiliary Board. The three smaller liners in the fleet's Mediterranean service—*Ems* (1884, 4,730 tons), *Fulda* (1883, 4,816 tons), and *Werra* (1882, 4,817 tons)—were mentioned. If the price was right, it even was suggested that the *Aller* (1886, 4,966 tons) might be sold to the desperate American government. None of the seven first-class units of the NGL fleet were available at any price, since the premier German line was not going to jeopardize its competitive advantage on the Southampton–New York run for any reason. This was particularly true if it appeared as though the American Line ships might be removed for any period of time.

NGL created a flurry in the American press when it was suggested that the German line had offered three of its ships to the Compania General Transatlantica of Barcelona, the principal Spanish-flag North Atlantic line. Schwab was highly incensed and cabled Bremen for an explanation, which was sent to him immediately. NGL claimed that the big shipbrokerage Moss & Co. had made inquiries about the ships, and details had been supplied to them. However, when it was discovered that Spanish authorities were the interested party, NGL's general manager, Herman Winter, cabled: "The Company will positively not sell any steamers to Spain at this time, but we will part with such vessels as we have for sale to the United States."[10] NGL seized the opportunity to accuse HAPAG of being willing to sell its ships to anyone—HAPAG agreed. It had just sold the

Normannia and the *Columbia* to Madrid. The Beaver Line of Montreal, in financial difficulties, immediately offered its entire fleet to the United States government. It was stated that since its four ships—*Lake Ontario, Lake Huron, Lake Winnipeg,* and *Lake Superior*—had been chartered by the British government to take troops to Egypt, they were already outfitted for troop-transport duties. Nothing came of this, and the Beaver Line was acquired by Elder Dempster before the year was over.

The suspense ended for the American Line when Clement A. Griscom cabled the New York office on April 15, 1898, that the *St. Paul, St. Louis, New York,* and *Paris* all had been chartered by the United States government. Interestingly, while the "big four" were chartered by the United States, the Naval Auxiliary Board knew nothing of the action, because the liners were chartered by the U.S. Navy itself, for employment as "armed merchant cruisers." The liners were to go to the Cramp Shipyard as soon as possible for conversion to auxiliary cruisers. Captain Randle's words that the American Line ships might soon find themselves involved in a war were most prophetic.

The Red Star service from Belgium to the United States was maintained by a fine fleet of ships. Here the Vaderland *is shown westbound just after leaving her berth in Antwerp.*

Chapter 13

THE SPANISH-AMERICAN WAR

The New York *with bunting on the bowsprit and all flags flying approaches Southampton. Passengers line the decks as the liner lets loose with a thunderous blast to announce her imminent arrival.*

The policy of arming merchant ships in time of war and regarding them as legitimate additions to the regular naval establishment was a controversial subject in the 1880s and became even more so in the 1890s with the publication of Alfred Thayer Mahan's treatises on sea power. One of Mahan's conclusions was that the *guerre de course*—literally, the running war—against an enemy's seaborne commerce did not pay. Yet Mahan, a keen student of the War of 1812, reached this conclusion despite the strong evidence that American commerce raids in that war produced significant results. By the fall of 1814, more than 1,600 British vessels had been taken by American naval vessels and privateers.

Mahan may have concluded that the success of the American privateers and naval vessels was the exception that proved the rule. But there were other exceptions during the Civil War. The Confederate raider *Tallahassee*, formerly the twin-screw, 700-ton *Atlanta*, originally built in England for the opium trade, terrorized the eastern seaboard from New York to Matinicus, Maine, in a month-long voyage during which she captured 35 prizes.

The first great raider in the days of steam, the CSS *Sumter*, was converted from a 500-ton passenger steamer. Her success was not measured as much in the prizes she took, or the federal ships she burned, but in the disruption she caused to Union seagoing commerce. Because of the *Sumter's* activities and panic-producing reputation, scores of commercial vessels were transferred by their owners from American to foreign registry.

When the *Sumter* was finally blockaded at Gibraltar by Union vessels, her commander, Captain Raphael Semmes, sold her and went with most of his officers to England. He then took command of a newly constructed vessel that became the most feared raider of the Civil War, the *Alabama*. With a crew made up mostly of seamen off the streets of Liverpool, Semmes attacked Union commerce wherever he found it. When he could no longer find it in the North and South Atlantic, he ranged the waters of the Far East.

Finding precious few American ships as he prowled the waters of East Asia, Semmes sounded far more like an American than a Southerner as he wondered, "Where is the Yankee? that he is permitting all this rich harvest of colonization and trade in the East to pass away from him. It was at one time thought that he would contest the palm of enterprise with England herself, but this dream has long since been dispelled."[1]

Semmes found most of his missing ships in Singapore. "There were," he recalled, "twenty-two American ships there—large Indiamen—almost all of which were dismantled and laid up! The burning of our first ship in these seas, the *Amanda*, off the Strait of Sunda, had sent a chill of terror through all the Yankee ships, far and near, and they had hastened to port, to get out of harm's way."[2]

Perhaps it is understandable that, in the 1880s and 1890s, it was the British who voiced the harshest criticism of the armed merchant cruiser theory. England was now indulging herself in honoring and revering Mahan as it had few foreigners before or since. Britons argued openly that modern vessels could never be made adequate to the task because of their thin-hull construction; privately, it was stated that any expansion of such a program undoubtedly would deprive the Royal Navy of funds needed for new ships. As is usually the case, the partisans for both sides continued to make their arguments, with everybody talking and nobody listening.

The possibility of war between America and Spain did not settle the case, but it added some interesting new evidence. By early April 1898, diplomatic relations between the United States and Spain had deteriorated to the point where war appeared certain. President William McKinley was being pushed steadily toward a belligerent stand by the war hawks in his own party and by the anti-Spanish press campaign fueled by the Hearst–Pulitzer newspaper war in New York City. Secretary of the Navy John D. Long and his ambitious assistant secretary, Theodore Roosevelt, sought to raise the U.S. Navy to a high degree of readiness for any eventuality.

An important aspect of the preparedness program was the requisitioning of U.S.-flag shipping to serve as armed merchant cruisers, transports, and fleet auxiliaries. The four largest liners flying the American flag were among the first units called up. These were the International Navigation Company's *New York*, *Paris*, *St. Louis*, and *St. Paul*, which maintained the North Atlantic ferry of the American Line between New York and Southampton.

The American Line quartet of express liners was composed of two sets of sisterships. The *New York* and the *Paris* were the older pair, having been constructed in Great Britain for the Inman Line as the *City of New York* (1888) and the *City of Paris* (1889). When commissioned, the *Cities* were 528 feet in length and 63 feet in breadth. They had a gross tonnage of 10,499 tons, and machinery consisting of compound engines driving two screws at 20 knots. Accommodations of the highest quality were provided for 290 first-class, 250 second-class, and 725 third-class passengers. Both of these superb greyhounds won the celebrated Blue Riband of the Atlantic as the fastest ship in service. Moreover, with the simultaneous events of their commissioning and the breaking up of the 30-year-old, 18,915-ton *Great Eastern*, they became for a short while the largest steamships in the world.

Their record crossings of the early 1890s were run at average speeds of more than 20 knots, and while faster ships were constructed in the intervening decade, they remained among the swiftest vessels afloat. The *City of New York* and the *City of Paris* were regarded by many as the most beautiful passenger liners ever built. Their refined greyhound lines swept forward to a graceful clipper bow, while their white superstructures were crowned by three towering funnels and three slender masts. Each bow was adorned with a figurehead—an eagle on the *New York* and a young girl on the *Paris*.

On April 13, 1898—approximately two months after the destruction of the battleship *Maine* in Havana Harbor, and only 12 days before the United States declared war with Spain—the U.S. Navy formally requisitioned the *St. Paul* and the *St. Louis*. The orders for the *New York* and the *Paris* followed the next day.

The *St. Paul*, nearing New York on her normal transatlantic run from Southampton, was the first liner to be converted. She steamed through The Narrows on April 16 and, after feverish activity, was ready to be handed over to the U.S. Navy at 6:00 A.M. on April 17. The command of the *St. Paul* was considered important enough to be given to Captain Charles D. Sigsbee, who had commanded the battleship *Maine* on her ill-fated visit to Havana. Within minutes of entering the navy lists, the sleek American liner was underway for the Cramp Shipyard, Philadelphia, and a quick conversion into an armed merchant cruiser. The *St. Paul* was commissioned a United States auxiliary cruiser on the eve of the declaration of war. She spent only a week at the Cramp Shipyard, during which the newly established Naval Auxiliary Cruiser Board placed several thousand tons of bagged coal in the vessel to provide some protection in lieu of armored plate. An armament of 30 guns was planned for her, but orders came to sail before the installation of much of the weaponry could be completed. The new addition to the U.S. Navy steamed down the Delaware past thousands of cheering people and seven miles of wharves crowded with vessels, which saluted the liner as she headed for the open sea.[3]

On the day the *St. Paul* arrived in New York, both the *St. Louis* and the *New York* quietly slipped down Southampton Water under urgent orders to come home. The *St. Louis* sailed with cargo and passengers, but the Navy Department's instructions had been so imperatively worded that the *New York* sailed completely empty of passengers and

The St. Paul *was the first ship of the American Line express service to be requisitioned on April 17 for government duty. She sailed in battleship gray from the Cramp Shipyard after a one-week conversion into an armed merchant cruiser.*

cargo—all dollar-earning commodities. The hotel staff must have enjoyed the freedom during the crossing, but one suspects they were busy packing anything fragile.

The formal declaration of war was only a day away when, on April 24, the *St. Louis* and the *New York* steamed past The Battery. Both liners were immediately requisitioned, and nearly all of their crews volunteered to stay with the ships. Captain Caspar R. Goodrich, USN, took command of the *St. Louis*, and Captain Charles S. Cotton, USN, assumed command of the *New York*. The civilian commanders of the respective liners, Captain W.G. Randle and Captain F.M. Passow, remained with their vessels as "navigation officers" and were given temporary commissions in the United States Navy. Perhaps to avoid confusion with the armored cruiser of the same name, the *New York* was renamed the USS *Harvard* for the duration of hostilities. Within four days, both vessels were ready to sail as armed merchant cruisers. Their temporary weaponry consisted of four rapid-firing six-pounders mounted forward and aft, with three-quarter-inch steel shields to protect the gunners.

The last of the American Line quartet, the graceful *Paris*, sailed from Southampton on April 22. Alarming reports circulated the next day in New York that she had been captured off the Irish coast by a Spanish cruiser. This was not an impossibility, since a Spanish torpedo boat, the *Audaz*, was known to have been fitting out in Cork Harbor. However, the International Navigation Company firmly denied the rumor and announced that the *Paris* could outrace any vessel, naval or otherwise, flying the Spanish flag.

True to her owners' boasts, the *Paris* made a fast, unmolested Atlantic crossing and six days later received a triumphant welcome to New York Harbor as she steamed up the bay. Captain Frederick Watkins of the American Line had taken a slightly different course than usual and had run without lights in order to outwit any hopeful captors. Within three days, the *Paris* received her eight five-inch guns, her six six-pounders, and some 4,600 tons of coal. Under sealed orders, she put to sea again. Captain William C.

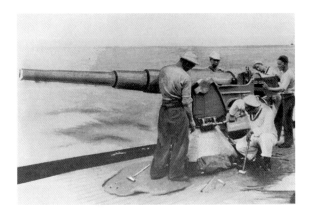

(top left) "Mounting the Guns"—The International Navigation Company in 1898 produced a handsome commemorative book on the Spanish-American War activities of the American Line ships. A team of seven distinguished marine artists were commissioned to illustrate the work— H. Reuterdahl, F. Cresson-Schell, G.A. Traver, F.W. Jopling, George A. Coffin, Howard F. Sprague, and Alfred Lenz.

(top right) One of the five-inch guns aft on the St. Paul *with its crew. The heat in the Caribbean on a ship designed for the North Atlantic apparently forced the relaxation of U.S. Navy regulations on clothing.*

(lower left) The Spanish-American War was the last American war fought without radio communication. In this picture sailors "wig-wagged their observations" from the deck of the Paris, *renamed* Yale *for the war.*

Wise, USN, assumed command of the *Paris*, which, like her sister, was given a collegiate christening upon entering naval service, becoming the USS *Yale*. If coordinated names make similar ships memorable, this was truly the case in the Spanish-American War. When the students of Yale University learned of this, they began a fund with which to purchase guns for their nautical namesake. They soon raised enough to buy and install two six-pounders, which they christened "Eli" and "Handsome Dan" to distinguish them from the other batteries.

Early in May 1898, intelligence reached Washington of the departure from Cartagena of the Spanish fleet—four modern cruisers and three destroyers—under Admiral Pascual Cervera y Topete. It was imperative that news of the whereabouts of the Spanish fleet in the Caribbean be obtained quickly. The best means by which this could be accomplished was through the strategic deployment of the four newly armed merchant cruisers.

View on the forecastle of the St. Paul *with five-inch guns, capstans, and winch following her conversion to armed merchant cruiser in 1898. The photo was taken by C.H. Graves.*
U.S. Naval Historical Center photograph

The situation for the United States Navy was far from reassuring. The Atlantic fleet was adequate to meet the combined Spanish fleet in the Caribbean, but there were far too few American warships to provide individual protection for all U.S. East Coast and Gulf Coast ports. Horrified American planners foresaw the possibility of Cervera dividing his fleet into a number of cruiser squadrons, which could conduct raiding operations and bring the war right onto America's doorstep. A Spanish cruiser squadron off any American port between Texas and Maine, unhindered and unopposed by comparable American strength, was the nightmare the Navy Department faced. Cervera had to be found as soon as he entered the Caribbean.

The *Harvard* and the *St. Louis* proceeded to the man-of-war anchorage off Staten Island following their commissionings, but they did not remain there long. On April 29, Navy Secretary Long sent sealed orders to the captains of the two armed merchant cruisers to get underway immediately. The purpose of their mission was to ascertain whether the Spanish fleet, which had been seen at the Cape Verde islands, intended moving into the Caribbean—and if so, to what locality. The cruisers were to search out the Spanish fleet and immediately notify the Navy Department and the commander on the Cuban station of its whereabouts.

The two vessels were assigned specific areas to patrol east of the Windward Islands. The *Harvard* was closest to the Windwards, with the *St. Louis* in a patrol area just

The Yale (Paris) *in Cuban waters during the Spanish-American War.*
Wartime service has taken its toll on her sides.
U.S. Naval Historical Center photograph

beyond. Both vessels were to maintain station until 1200 hours on May 10, after which the *Harvard* was to proceed to Martinique for further orders. Simultaneously, the *St. Louis* was to explore Guadeloupe for signs of the enemy. Between May 4 and May 9, the *St. Louis* overtook and examined three merchantmen, all of which flew American or neutral flags. While all were permitted to proceed, the activities of the *St. Louis* as an American warship, rarely seen in those waters since the Civil War, underscored the potential value of the armed merchant cruiser as a commerce destroyer.

By noon on May 10, with nothing significant having developed, the *St. Louis* put into her assigned port of call and the *Harvard* steamed to St. Pierre, Martinique. On May 11, Captain Cotton anchored the *Harvard* off St. Pierre, a bustling French commercial center that would be destroyed by the explosion of the volcano Pelée in a few years (1902). Within hours, two Spanish torpedo boats, the *Furor* and the *Terror*, put into Fort de France, Martinique, 15 miles down the beautiful coast. Captain Cotton, learning of the arrival of the torpedo boats, sent two officers in a small boat to evaluate the situation. To their horror, the two officers nearly sailed into the center of the Spanish fleet, which had followed the two torpedo boats into the anchorage. They returned to the merchant cruiser as quickly as possible, and Captain Cotton notified the Navy Department by coded cable. Thus, the honor of first contact with the Spanish fleet by any United States naval vessel went to the armed merchant cruiser *Harvard*.

Cervera had been discovered, and he was in the West Indies! It seemed, however, that the *Harvard*'s situation was about to change from hunter to hunted when the French authorities notified Captain Cotton that, as a belligerent, he had 24 hours to leave Martinique. A similar message was sent to the Spanish fleet, which sailed immediately, stationing some of its fastest vessels just beyond the three-mile limit. The Navy Department sent Captain Cotton a lengthy cable describing in detail his rights under existing international treaties. With the smoke from the Spanish destroyers on the horizon, this must have been comforting. If the situation became absolutely intolerable, it was suggested that he might take the *Harvard* out to a point just within the three-mile limit and steam as fast as possible in hopes of finding an escape route to the open sea.

Meanwhile, the smoke of the Spanish watchdogs was ominously visible to those on the *Harvard*, and time was fast running out. It was clearly a moment for human ingenuity to assert itself. Certainly, in a country full of men who were capable of making machinery go, there ought to be some cunning individuals who could make it stop. Thus, "unfortunately," some of the *Harvard*'s machinery was discovered to be temporarily "inoperable." After an official inspection by the sympathetic French authorities, the liner was given seven days' grace during which repairs could be made. Neutrality laws could have wonderful loopholes when one figured out where to find them.

Admiral Cervera, anxious to reach Cuba, steamed away, leaving one torpedo boat on guard. On May 17, the highly vulnerable but swift *Harvard* steamed out of St. Pierre and easily eluded the enemy warship. Once out in the open sea, she raced for Haiti, where news of her escape was cabled to Admiral William T. Sampson, commander of the U.S. Atlantic Fleet. The *St. Louis* put into St. Thomas on May 13 and, before the afternoon was over, the U.S. Navy tug *Dauntless* brought dispatches from Admiral Sampson requesting the armed merchant cruiser to perform one of the single most important missions of the war. Sampson ordered Goodrich to take his cruiser to Puerto Rico and sever the telegraph cables linking San Juan with the rest of the world. After completing this assignment, the *St. Louis* was to proceed to Cuba and sever the cables running from Santiago and Guantanamo to the outside world. These lines of communication were vital to the Spanish authorities, since they connected into a transatlantic grid independent of American installations. The cutting of these cables would be a crippling blow to the Spanish war effort, since it would stop any fast form of communication with Madrid.

The *St. Louis* possessed a special asset for the cable-severing operations in her chief officer, T.G. Segrave, who formerly had commanded the West Indian cable-laying steamer *Grappler*. Segrave was familiar with the exact locations of the West Indian cables, and under his supervision in America, the *St. Louis* had been equipped with the most modern cable-grappling gear available. Owing to his foresight, the liner was well prepared to execute Admiral Sampson's orders.

The merchant cruiser arrived off San Juan on May 14. After only a two-hour effort, she succeeded in hooking and severing the San Juan–St. Thomas cable, which lay in 40 fathoms of water. St. Thomas was in neutral Danish territory, and the cutting of this

cable isolated Puerto Rico from contact with the rest of the world. After severing the cable, the *St. Louis* steamed away from Puerto Rico at full speed. Early the next morning, she overtook Admiral Sampson's slower-moving battle fleet off Cape Isabella, and Captain Goodrich went on board the flagship to report his news.

In the ensuing naval effort to determine the exact whereabouts of the Spanish fleet, the orders of Admiral Sampson on May 15 illustrate the high priority that he placed on the activities of the American Line greyhounds as the eyes and ears of the American forces. They were critically important to Sampson as high-speed, wide-ranging vessels. The auxiliary cruisers were ordered to patrol as follows: *Yale* to assist *St. Paul* between Jamaica, Môle St.-Nicolas (Haiti), and Cuba; *Harvard* in Mona Passage and on the north side of Puerto Rico: *St. Louis* cutting cables at Santiago and Guantanamo, then via Puerto Rico to St. Thomas about May 19 to await orders. All four of the American Line express steamers were figuring prominently in Admiral Sampson's plans, and all were proving invaluable to a United States Navy that was critically short of fast tonnage.

The *St. Louis*, bound for Santiago, swiftly drew away from the fleet. She was accompanied by the small fighting tug *Wompatuck*, which soon fell so far astern that the *St. Louis* dropped back and took her in tow in order to maintain the critical timetable. The crew of the *Wompatuck* may or may not have enjoyed their "Nantucket sleighride" on a towline in the wake of the 20-knot *St. Louis*. On the night of May 16, the *St. Louis* and the *Wompatuck* arrived off Santiago Harbor to begin their dangerous assignment. The decision was made to begin grappling for the cables immediately, before the presence of

the American ships became known. Captain Goodrich, Chief Officer Segrave, and a selected crew transferred to the *Wompatuck* and slowly steamed toward the harbor entrance, where the cable reportedly lay in some 55 fathoms of water.

After several hours of grappling, the party at last snagged the cable and slowly began to raise it to the surface. Just as it seemed that success was within their grasp, a Spanish patrol boat suddenly appeared across the bay and began to race toward the *Wompatuck*. There was only one possible course of action. The cable was slipped and the *St. Louis* steamed in to take the tug in tow and hold off the attacker. When the patrol boat sighted the *St. Louis*, the smaller Spanish vessel decided not to press the issue, and the two American vessels quickly departed from the area.

The Santiago cable-grappling operations were suspended for a day on May 17 while the *St. Louis* recoaled the *Wompatuck* and the cable crew rested and planned. The decision was made to attempt a daring frontal attack on the cable in broad daylight. Early the next morning, the *St. Louis* and the *Wompatuck* returned to the scene of their previous grappling operations. The armed merchant cruiser steamed directly for the harbor entrance and audaciously opened fire on Morro Castle.

The Spanish batteries were wide awake and immediately returned the fire. While this distraction was underway, the *Wompatuck* crept in toward the cable area and took soundings. It had been agreed that the grappling operations would have a better chance for success closer to shore—particularly if the merchant cruiser undertook them rather than the tug. The *St. Louis* continued to provide a diversion by steaming back and forth across the harbor mouth, while gradually getting closer to the forts. The *Wompatuck* soon completed its survey and signaled Captain Goodrich that the water was deep enough to accommodate the liner. The Spanish batteries had ceased firing when, quickly from her stern, the *St. Louis* lowered the grappling hook on 630 fathoms of line to begin dragging for the cable.

The St. Louis *was ordered to sever the undersea cable off Santiago de Cuba in order to isolate the Spanish fleet. The liner, assisted by the tug* Wompatuck, *succeeded in cutting the cable but was shelled by the batteries. The drawing was by George A. Coffin for the American Line commemorative book.*

The St. Louis *off Morro Castle, Santiago, Cutting the Telegraph Cables, by G.A. Traver for the American Line book.*

It was noon when the grapnel caught the cable and the *St. Louis* came to a dead stop in the water. The Spanish, apparently aware at last of the nature of the cruiser's activities, resumed firing. A six-inch gun to the east of Morro Castle opened fire, and the first shot sent up a geyser 200 yards short of the steamer. Captain Goodrich ordered the fire to be returned from two six-pounders mounted on the starboard side of the *St. Louis.* The marine gunners enjoyed considerable success in silencing the Spanish fire, but they could not reach a mortar battery whose shots began to fall uncomfortably close.

Another Spanish battery west of the entrance to the harbor opened fire suddenly and, after firing a few shots, sustained a hit from the *St. Louis*'s guns, which put it out of the fight. The signaling station near the harbor mouth was also silenced by a volley of well-placed shells, one of which took the roof off the building.

AMERICAN LINE UNITED STATES MAIL TWIN SCREW S. S. PARIS (U. S. AUXILIARY CRUISER YALE)
CAPTURING SPANISH S. S. RITA MAY 8 1898.

The U.S. Auxiliary Cruiser Yale *Capturing the Spanish* Rita, *May 8, 1898, by George A. Coffin. The* Yale *surprised and captured the* Rita *off San Juan, Puerto Rico, and sent her back to the United States as a "prize of war." She brought $150,000, of which half was divided amongst the crew of the* Yale.

When the grapnel finally broke the surface with the cable dangling from two of its prongs, a jubilant cheer rose from the crew of the *St. Louis*. A long section of the severed cable was pulled onto the deck of the merchant cruiser, where it was cut into pieces as souvenirs for the officers and crew.

The engagement had lasted 52 minutes. The *St. Louis* fired 172 shots, while the little *Wompatuck* fired 73 shells from her three-pounders. Chief Officer Segrave and his picked crew had remained at their stations on the exposed stern of the *St. Louis*, hauling in the vital cable, throughout the Spanish fire. Having accomplished this ticklish assignment, the *St. Louis* left the area. Three hours after her departure, Admiral Cervera steamed into Santiago Harbor to find his communications with Spain severed.

Within the next week, the mischievous *St. Louis* performed her duties to perfection by cutting the French cable running from Môle St.-Nicolas (Haiti) to Guantanamo, and the Spanish cable from Cienfuegos (Cuba). Thus, all telegraphic communication between Cuba and the outside world, except for the American-controlled Key West cable, was disrupted. After completing the cable-cutting operations, the *St. Louis* reinforced the naval blockade off Puerto Rico for a few days before steaming to St. Thomas for new orders.

While the *St. Louis* was busy off Santiago, the *Yale* was confounding the Spanish garrison of Morro Castle in San Juan, Puerto Rico. The *Yale*'s orders were to survey the harbor for enemy shipping and, in order to do so, she had to get in close. The *Yale*'s skipper, Captain Wise, was mindful of the fact that there had not been sufficient time to

give her a coat of military grey; she still wore her commercial colors. An ensign on the bridge of the *Yale* recorded the discussion between Captain Wise and Commander Frederick Watkins, who had been her civilian captain: Captain Wise and Commander Watkins were both on the bridge, and as they neared the entrance of the harbor, the former asked, "What ship does the *Yale* most resemble?" "She might pass for the *City of Rome*," replied Commander Watkins. Thereupon, Captain Wise ordered the English colors run up and the *City of Rome* signals displayed, and he steered close under the Morro, where every corner of the harbor could be seen. Then, having made quite sure that Cervera's fleet was not within, Captain Wise ordered the borrowed colors to be dipped in salute to the Spanish colors on the Morro, and as the ship passed under the guns that could have sunk her, the courteous and unsuspecting gentlemen in the fort dipped the standard of Aragon and Castile.[4]

The *Yale* steamed away and, once out of range, raised the Stars and Stripes again. Almost as soon as this was done, the Spanish steamer *Rita*, bound from Liverpool to San Juan, came in sight, was chased, and captured as a prize of war. Under the U.S. Navy's rules governing prizes of war, the *Rita* was taken to Charleston, South Carolina, and auctioned off for $150,000, half of which went to the officers and crew of the *Yale*. During the Spanish-American War the *Rita* became one of the few vessels to be disposed of as a prize of war by the United States government.

The days of the Spanish fleet in the Caribbean were numbered. On May 18, the *St. Paul* took up station off Santiago shortly after the departure of the *St. Louis*. Captain Sigsbee on the *St. Paul* was unaware of the presence of the Spanish battle fleet. He did not know that, in the brief interval between the *St. Louis*'s departure and the *St. Paul*'s arrival, Admiral Cervera had slipped into the harbor of Santiago undetected.

The *St. Paul* rigidly enforced the blockade, and when a small British freighter was seen making a dash for the harbor, she was pursued and captured. The mystery of why the British-flag *Restormel* was so determined to enter the harbor was revealed almost immediately. She was loaded with 3,000 tons of Cardiff coal for the Spanish fleet, and her owners were paid handsomely to have their ship run the blockade. Unaccountably, the Spanish cruiser force within the sheltered harbor made no effort to protect the *Restormel* from the threat of one thin-skinned armed merchant cruiser.

The British consul in Santiago maintained a diary of the events surrounding the capture of the *Restormel*. He recorded that the Spanish battleship *Cristobal Colon* got underway, and onlookers felt that she was planning to leave the harbor to prevent the capture of the blockade-runner. Qualified observers thought the Spanish battleship easily equal to the task, since she reportedly was capable of more than 18 knots, and the American ships were regarded as "simply mail steamers fitted with guns." However, the *Cristobal Colon* only steamed down the bay and dropped anchor near the entrance.

Throughout the day of the dramatic capture of the *Restormel*, the Spanish force remained relatively inactive. The flagship also moved from the Juragua Wharf to Cajuma Bay and anchored there, while the *Viscaya* or *Oquendo* took her place at the wharf in order to take on water. The British consul summarized the day's activities: "It seems incredible that this should have been allowed right in front of the port, and the squadron with steam up." The British captain of the little steamer who had tried his best to deliver his contraband cargo was furious, sputtering at Captain Sigsbee: "I am glad you Yankees have the coal since those duffers inside didn't have the nerve to come out and back me up when their guns were right within range." The presence of the Spanish fleet was great news indeed to Captain Sigsbee, who, a few short months earlier, had known the depths of despair with the loss of his ship and 260 men in Havana Harbor. One ship under his command had triggered a war. Now, another was playing an important role in ending it. Sigsbee now knew that the honor of obtaining the first information about the exact location of Admiral Cervera's force along the Cuban coast would go to his command, the armed merchant cruiser *St. Paul*. Having received the information from the "plucky blockade runner," and with every wish to maintain the valuable propaganda support of Great Britain, the United States freed the *Restormel* after formal confirmation was received of her British registry.[5]

Two of the Spanish battleships made a brief foray on May 28, and Captain Sigsbee was able to identify the *Cristobal Colon* by her peculiar rig of a military mast between two smokestacks. The *St. Paul* relayed this information to the other American blockading vessels. Later on the same day, Commodore Wingfield Scott Schley steamed up with his squadron and relieved the *St. Paul*, the *Yale*, the *Harvard*, and the USS *Minneapolis*, which had maintained the blockade and kept the harbor entrance floodlit with their searchlights throughout the nights.

The *St. Paul* left for Havana and, after a rendezvous with Admiral Sampson, proceeded on to New York. The orders for New York were welcome, since the crew and stokers were nearly exhausted. The *St. Paul* reached New York on June 2, 1898, and was replenished with stores, supplies, and coal. The tensions of the first six weeks of naval

The American Liner Was Already Rounding in Upon Him Under the Very Guns of Old Morro Castle, *by G.A. Traver, captures one of the more dramatic incidents of the war—when the* St. Paul *captured the British-flag collier* Restormel *with 3,000 tons of coal for the Spanish fleet off Santiago. The intelligence gathered from the prize confirmed the presence of the Spanish fleet in the harbor.*

St. Paul *Coaling and Receiving Her Ammunition at Newport News, Virginia, by Howard F. Sprague for the American Line book.*

warfare were noticeably relieved as a result of the discovery of the Spanish fleet and the blockading of those warships in Santiago. Hence, the *St. Paul* did not return to the Caribbean until the middle of June. During the last two weeks in June, the armed merchant cruiser carried ammunition and rations to the American marines and Cuban insurgents fighting at Guantanamo. Ironically, the American beachhead at Guantanamo made imperative the restoration of cable communications—which the *St. Louis* had just ripped up—and this was soon accomplished.

The *St. Paul*, while in company with the old battleship *Texas*, the *Marblehead*, and the *Suwanee*, joined in the second bombardment of Fort Calmanera. Captain Sigsbee's well-trained gun crews had an excellent opportunity for target practice at a range of a thousand yards. To the astonishment of many, "general quarters" was sounded on the *St. Paul* in the midst of the bombardment of the Cayo de Toro fortifications. A troop of

The New York *was renamed the*
Harvard *for the duration of the*
Spanish-American War. This is a
view of target practice on the
Harvard. *After the Battle of*
Santiago de Cuba, she carried
many Spanish sailors to
Portsmouth, New Hampshire, and
Spanish officers to Annapolis,
Maryland, where they were paroled
and quartered at the Naval
Academy. The Harvard *was*
manned by 35 officers, 381
Bluejackets and 50 Marines.

Working the Rapid Fire Guns *on*
the St. Louis, *from the American*
Line commemorative book.

Spanish cavalry was sighted galloping from the hills, and all attention was concentrated on them. A shell from one of the five-inch guns aft scattered the cavalry, and the demoralized horsemen were completely routed by a fusillade from the forward port Hotchkiss. After this bombardment, the American forces were firmly established at Guantanamo, and the *St. Paul* received new orders for San Juan, Puerto Rico.

When the *St. Paul* took up her new station, she relieved the *St. Louis* and the *Yale* and provided the crews of those cruisers with a much-needed break in the routine of the blockade. When the *St. Paul*'s lookouts sighted a large vessel leaving the harbor, Captain Sigsbee ordered full speed ahead, and the two ships began to close the seven miles between them. The Spanish vessel was the cruiser *Isabella II*, and she began firing while still well out of range, dropping several shells within a thousand yards of the approaching American merchant cruiser. Captain Sigsbee swung his vessel around in order to present a broadside to the Spanish cruiser, but he was disappointed when the *Isabella II* simply tried to lure the *St. Paul* into approaching within range of the Morro Castle

A new and much feared addition to the Spanish fleet was the destroyer Terror. *She attacked the* St. Paul *off San Juan, Puerto Rico, and was crippled by a lucky shot from the armed merchant cruiser that went through the destroyer's engine room.*

batteries. At this point in the stalemate, one of the *St. Paul*'s officers noticed a small, dark craft slipping around the Spanish cruiser. This opponent was identified as the new Spanish naval warship, the destroyer *Terror*. A milestone in naval history was about to occur, as the scene was set for the first daytime torpedo attack by a modern-type destroyer on a larger vessel.

Several years after the event, Rear Admiral Sigsbee wrote a personal account of the incident for the widow of Commander Don Francisco de la Rocha, who had commanded the *Terror* during this historic confrontation between two somewhat unorthodox naval units. Sigsbee recalled that the *Terror* steamed toward the *St. Paul* without any hesitation whatsoever. Naturally, the *St. Paul* did what it could to make the position of the *Terror*—a small and fast ship—as unfavorable as possible. This was accomplished by maneuvering in such a manner as to make it impracticable for a torpedo to be fired at the *St. Paul*, and by keeping the *Terror* continually in the trough of the sea. Since the seas were quite substantial on the day of the battle, the odds were decidedly against the destroyer.

The seas, Sigsbee knew, would make the aim of the *Terror*'s guns impossible to maintain, but, as it turned out, the *Terror*'s three-inch guns had never been installed and never could have been brought into play. The *St. Paul*, being as large as she was, had no difficulty keeping her bow to the wind and sea. When the *Terror* began her direct attack, Sigsbee stopped the *St. Paul* dead in the water in order to provide as stable a platform as possible for the gunners, in whom he had very considerable confidence. Sigsbee stated that the battle conditions were those of a large and stable ship that presented to the struggling *Terror* a broadside of three six-inch guns, three six-pounders, and three three-pounders, all of which were rapid-fire guns and considered to be quite effective. What Sigsbee did not tell de la Rocha's widow, however, was the risk he himself had run. He was submitting the *St. Paul*'s 500 men and 25 officers to the attack of a vessel new to the

F. Cresson-Schell captured the drama of the Spanish destroyer's attack on the St. Paul *when he sketched this scene entitled:* The Terror *Reeled in Her Headlong Course, . . . and One of Her Smokestacks Dropped Into the Sea.*

annals of naval warfare, one whose fighting capacity and effectiveness were totally unknown. In view of the fact that the destroyer was regarded as an extremely important development in the evolution of naval warfare, the risk was not inconsiderable, and only a very courageous officer would have considered stopping his ship dead in the water to await such an attack. Few would repeat such tactics.

The *Terror* attacked cleverly and without the least hesitation, fully accepting all the risks on her part. Sigsbee let the destroyer approach until she was in range, and he only permitted the firing of one gun to ascertain this. Then, when the *Terror* was irretrievably committed to the attack, Sigsbee ordered all guns to open fire. The *St. Paul* proved very steady in the water, and her guns were so well served that the accuracy of the fire reminded Sigsbee of target practice. The *St. Paul*'s fire was incessant, and one foreign consul, observing the battle from shore, stated that at one point he had seen six of the *St. Paul*'s guns fire simultaneously. The hail of metal was too much for the destroyer, which was soon put out of action. The deciding blow was a hit from a shell that entered her engine room and severely damaged her ability to maintain the attack.

The Spanish commander, Sigsbee assured de la Rocha's widow, could have pursued the engagement—but only at the cost of his ship and the lives of many of his crew. With considerable wisdom, he returned to the safety of San Juan, having acquitted himself in the handling of the destroyer *Terror* as well as any man could have in similar circumstances. In 1905, when Sigsbee wrote his description of the battle for Señora de la Rocha, his aim was to vindicate the memory of a brave adversary who had experienced considerable unwarranted criticism in the postwar years for not continuing the attack. Sigsbee stated that, in view of what had been learned since 1898, the attack was doomed to failure, but at its conception, it represented a daring move with a relatively untried naval warship. He emphasized that he had never heard any member of the U.S. Navy speak unfavorably of Commander de la Rocha for his decision to withdraw to San Juan.[6]

The explosion of the magazine on the Almirante Oquendo *destroyed the Spanish warship during the Battle of Santiago de Cuba, July 3, 1898. The scene was drawn by George A. Coffin.*

The Harvard *anchored off St. Pierre, Martinique, French West Indies, early in the war and nearly was captured by the Spanish fleet, which had put into Fort de France just down the coast.*

Within two weeks of the San Juan duel, Admiral Cervera elected to make a try for the open sea, and the Spanish fleet in the Caribbean ceased to exist in the Battle of Santiago de Cuba. During the previous two weeks, the *St. Louis*, the *Harvard*, and the *Yale* had been engaged in ferrying troops to the Cuban front. The *St. Louis* and the *Harvard* were present off Santiago on July 3, 1898, when the key battle occurred. The *Harvard*'s log recorded the events of the day: at 10:45 A.M. Transport No. 2 off the harbor showed the signal 4.1.6.4 ("The Spanish fleet has fled"). Captain Cotton immediately recalled all his boats, which were being used in landing operations, but he was unable to regain all of them before the situation became critical.

AMERICAN LINE UNITED STATES MAIL TWIN SCREW S. S. NEW YORK (U. S. AUXILIARY CRUISER HARVARD
RESCUING CREWS OF DESTROYED SPANISH FLEET NEAR SANTIAGO JULY 3 1898.

The *Harvard* Rescuing the Crews of the Destroyed Spanish Fleet, *after the Battle of Santiago de Cuba, drawn by George A. Coffin for the American Line book about the war.*

The *Harvard* was cleared for action, every man at his post, as she steamed at high speed past the entrance to Santiago Harbor and exerted every effort to bring her five-inch guns within range of the escaping Spanish vessels. The Battle of Santiago de Cuba was not to last long, and the *Harvard* was not to fire many shots in anger this day. Her principal role would be to rescue the survivors. Throughout the afternoon and into the evening, Spanish sailors were transferred to the *Harvard*, until she had nearly 900 on board. The passions of the battle were not yet spent, and approximately 20 of the prisoners attempted a sudden assault on the *Harvard*'s crew shortly after midnight. The Spanish prisoners made a rush on the Massachusetts militiamen who were guarding them, and only prompt action averted a catastrophe. The American soldiers opened fire, while all available personnel were called to general quarters to defend the ship's armory against the Spanish. In the melee, a number of Spanish sailors were shot, while others jumped overboard and had to be rescued from the sea once again. Nearly an hour passed before order could be restored.

On July 10, the *Harvard* sailed from Cuba for Portsmouth, New Hampshire, where she arrived on July 15 and disembarked the Spanish sailors. On July 18, she sailed for Annapolis, Maryland, and there discharged the Spanish naval officers, who were paroled and quartered at the Naval Academy. Thereafter, the *Harvard* made one more round trip between Cuba and Camp Wiloff, Long Island, before being decommissioned and returned to the International Navigation Company on September 2, 1898.

The *St. Louis* also transported Spanish prisoners to Portsmouth and Long Island before returning to the Cramp Shipyard for the removal of her guns on August 24. She was decommissioned as an armed merchant cruiser on September 3 and then underwent a major refit before reentering the American Line's express service. The *St. Paul*'s transport duties consisted of two voyages to Cuba carrying much-needed supplies to General William Shafter. Her last voyage was from Newport News, Virginia, to Ponce, Puerto Rico, with 1,300 men of the 8th Ohio Volunteers. The *St. Paul*'s return track was from Guantanamo to Long Island with prisoners and wounded, and from there to Guantanamo for decommissioning.

Meanwhile, the *Yale* had returned home early in June and had arrived off Hampton Roads with just enough coal for another hour's steaming before she would have had to begin burning the woodwork. During the next three weeks, the *Yale* finally was painted a dull gray, and she received a number of additional guns. A relatively minor detail omitted in the heat of war—the commissioning of the *Yale*'s officers and crew—also was accomplished at this time. Note was taken that they had been fighting for six weeks! The armed merchant cruiser also acquired a small black goat, named Eli, as a mascot. On June 24, 1,300 men of the 33rd and 34th Michigan Volunteers came aboard, bound for Cuba. After disembarking all of the troops in one day, the *Yale* steamed up and down the Cuban coast to collect homeward-bound mail from the many ships of the squadron and transport fleet. During this time, she was visited by a number of foreign military and naval attaches, who evinced the liveliest interest in the details of converting a great passenger liner into an auxiliary cruiser. In the beginning of July 1898, the *Yale* was home again to embark the 6th Massachusetts Volunteers at Charleston, along with General Nelson A. Miles, who was to be the commander of the United States Army. Miles was landed at Siboney, Cuba, on July 12. After the Cuban capitulation, General Miles returned to the *Yale*, which became the flagship for the Puerto Rican expedition. This enterprise began on July 22, when the long line of transports left Cuba bound for the unsuspecting Puerto Rican anchorage of Guanica. The *Yale* acted as the command ship for some days and then returned to New York for one more voyage to Cuba before being decommissioned on August 30 to resume her career as the gracious *Paris* of the American Line.

The American Line express service from New York to Southampton was resumed late in October 1898, when the *St. Louis* sailed with the war veteran, Captain William G. Randle, in command. The *St. Louis* received a triumphant welcome at Southampton on the occasion of her maiden postwar arrival. The American Line made the most of the event by decking out the *St. Louis* in her signal flags and encouraging the maximum amount of publicity. All four of the International Navigation Company's express liners were returned to the North Atlantic commercial service during November, and the weekly mail sailings were resumed.

The role of the American Line quartet in the Spanish-American War certainly provides food for thought as to the value of armed merchant cruisers in naval affairs. What

The United States Navy, 1898, *lithographed by C.A. Musselman, Philadelphia. The print depicted all the active ships of the Navy at the time of the Spanish-American War. The* Yale (Paris) *and* Harvard (New York) *are shown on the upper left and the* St. Louis *and* St. Paul *are in the center. The battleship* Maine, *whose loss in Havana Harbor contributed to the conflict, is in the cameo on the upper right.*
U.S. Naval Historical Center photograph

may have been a far less satisfactory arrangement in later world wars seems to have been eminently successful in 1898. The *New York*, *Paris*, *St. Louis*, and *St. Paul* admirably fulfilled the roles assigned them. While none of the ships quite made the transition from a commercial vessel to a destroyer of enemy commercial vessels, their contributions were extremely valuable. They more than lived up to expectations by discovering the whereabouts of the Spanish fleet, successfully severing vital cable communications, and maintaining important blockade stations. Moreover, the four express liners served as the eyes and ears of a fleet critically short of high-speed tonnage. After the Spanish threat ceased to exist, the ships made a more mundane, but no less valuable, contribution to the American war effort by carrying troops and supplies all over the Caribbean. No other vessels did as much. In the annals of American naval history, the role of the armed merchant cruiser in the Spanish-American War has received far less consideration than its importance warrants.

Chapter 14

A TRIUMPHANT RETURN

The *St. Louis* at Southampton (October 1898). "*When, having resumed her service as a transatlantic liner, she again appeared in England, looking fresher and brighter than when she had sailed away, she was accorded a reception such as Southampton had seldom, if ever, before witnessed.*"
— *International Navigation Company*

The American Line quartet was demobilized quickly after the conclusion of the Spanish-American War and each unit received a triumphant welcome at Southampton as she put in an appearance. While most European nations were critical of America's role in the war with Spain, Great Britain remained benevolently neutral toward the United States. On no occasion during the previous century had London and Washington been on better terms, and this was reflected in the public response toward the American Line ships at Southampton.

The good will between the nations was expanded when the *Paris* went to the rescue of 23 seamen from a sinking British tanker during the 1898 Christmas season. The *Vindobala* of 1,865 tons was bound from Rouen, France, to Philadelphia in ballast. Built on the Tyne in 1880, the tanker and was owned by J.A. Salton & Company of London, where she was insured by Lloyd's. She sailed on December 15 from the French port and on December 23, in the midst of a violent North Atlantic storm, sprang a leak. Chief Engineer Wood went to the bridge and informed Chief Officer Alfred Backmann that water was coming into the tanker's bunkers and engine room. Wood felt that the ship must have ruptured some rivets during the storm of the previous day, but he could not find the leak and only knew that water was entering the vessel amidships. Immediately upon being informed, Captain Michael J. Clarke ordered the bilge pumps, and later the water-ballast pumps, to be started. The effort to clear the engine room of water soon

The Paris *is captured here by John Nicholson (1920–) of Leeds, England, one of the foremost maritime artists of the twentieth century. The background was inspired by a photograph taken by the author in mid-Atlantic from the* France *(1962). The* Paris *westbound flies the American flag on both the sternpost and the foremast.*

proved unsuccessful, because so much coal dust was mixed in with the water that the pumps became clogged and useless. The crew struggled to slow the rising waters without success, and the tanker began to settle by the head.

Realizing that the situation was deteriorating rapidly, Captain Clarke ordered the flag flown upside down during the day. When night fell, flares burned, with rockets occasionally sent up. As she lost headway, it was impossible to keep the bow of the *Vindobala* pointed into the seas, and the empty tanker rolled heavily. The logical expedient was to put out a sea anchor. This was made of spars lashed to form a triangle, over which canvas was laced. Grate bars were then lashed to two of the points to make the device float with the third point upward. This was run out with about 700 feet of hawser. As soon as the sea anchor took hold, the steamer swung around and was able to keep bow-on to the sea.

On December 24, all fires on the *Vindobala* were extinguished by the rising seawater, and the tanker wallowed helplessly on the North Atlantic as the weather worsened once more. Around 7:30 A.M. on Christmas Day, everyone's hopes soared when the lookout sighted a large four-masted steamer coming over the horizon, heading northwest. In Captain Clarke's words:

> It was known that the tanker was doomed. A few hours it was believed must
> settle her fate, and probably the fate of her crew. There was therefore great

American Line publications provided a wealth of information, including: "Rates from Southampton to African Ports via Union and Castle Liners"; "Rates from Southampton via Royal Mail Line"; "Approximate Rates from Southampton to Points in Great Britain and Ireland"; and information on the "American Line Express," intended as a convenient means by which passengers could ship packages home.

rejoicing at the present, seemingly, of life itself, that Christmas had brought. The gray of early morning spread over the ocean. The wind blew in terrific squalls, and the waves flung themselves so high that they filled the air with spray and flecks of spume. They thickened the atmosphere with a mist that rose high, like that from the foot of Niagara, and it was only at times that the steamer, growing bigger on the horizon, could be made out. The men on the wreck knew that they, too, could be made out with difficulty, if at all. But flares were burned and rockets sent up. It was just light enough to obscure the fire and it was not seen. Then the stranger grew smaller again and was lost to view."[1]

The seamen on the *Vindobala* became disheartened. Captain Clarke remarked that it was the saddest time of his life. The men kept at work, however, and obeyed orders. Incredibly, the tanker survived another night, although morning brought additional bad news that seawater had got into the freshwater tanks, and all that was left for the 23 men were three beakers carried in the lifeboats. No water could be spared for cooking, and the men only had biscuits. Miraculously, the *Vindobala* made it through yet another night in the mountainous seas.

The storm was still raging fiercely, and many on the British tanker had given up hope, when around 8 A.M. on December 27, the lookout sighted yet another ship on the horizon, bearing north and about eight miles distant. The men all gathered at the rail and strained their eyes. The British merchant flag was flying upside down at the truck of the tanker's mizzenmast. The *Vindobala*'s crew could not believe their eyes when the three tall black funnels marked with white bands of the American Line, familiar to all North Atlantic sailors, were seen slowly blending into one as the liner altered course for the stricken ship.

The *Paris* bore down on the helpless tanker and signaled, "What assistance do you need?" Captain Clarke promptly flew the signal flags N and D of the international code, signifying, "I must abandon the vessel." The *Paris* responded that she would send a boat. The waves were running so high, and the wind was driving so hard, that those on the *Vindobala* regularly saw the liner taking water over her bow. It was thrown up and over the funnels as she righted herself, or cascaded over the deck before rolling back into the sea.

It took a brave person to cross the Atlantic in midwinter even on the *Paris*. You knew that the weather would be wretched, and that the North Atlantic would have a mean bag of tricks. James Davison, a New York businessman who lived in East Orange, New Jersey, wrote an account of this crossing. The *Paris* had left Southampton promptly at noon on Saturday, December 24, and passed The Needles at 1:34 P.M. Davison wrote:

> The weather along the coast was fair and clear until the Lizard was abeam when old Neptune asserted his sway, and many of the passengers retired to their berths to reflect upon the frailty of man and to contemplate his weakness, and the wonderful mechanism of his inner organism. On Christmas Day a heavy beam sea caused many of the passengers to continue their meditations in the seclusion of their berths, away from the spray and the seas that were constantly washing the decks. On entering the main saloon on the morning of Christmas Day a very pleasing decoration of United States and British flags was arranged in festoons at the head of the saloon. Between the flags was suspended a large bunch of mistletoe, and underneath the whole, another flag bearing the name *Paris*. A rough and confused sea prevailed all day Sunday and Monday, constantly increasing in power, deluging the decks with spray, so that the passengers for their own comfort were compelled to remain below. Tuesday morning the gale increased in severity, producing very high and dangerous seas. A little before 8 o'clock a steamer was sighted, showing signals of distress; the course of the *Paris* was altered and in half an hour we got sufficiently near to read distinctly the signals, which, being interpreted, read that she would have to be abandoned. The distressed vessel lay in the trough of the sea, perfectly helpless. The vessel proved to be the English tank steamer *Vindobala* of London, Captain Michael J. Clarke, in ballast from Rouen, France, to Philadelphia for a cargo of oil.
>
> The *Paris* swung around in the lee of the *Vindobala* and immediately began preparations for rescue. A volunteer crew comprising the First Officer, John Bradshaw, Fourth Officer R.H. Webb, and a crew of eight noble seamen manned a lifeboat, each man wearing a life belt and taking off all superfluous clothing, even their shoes, so that in case of being thrown into the sea, they would be better able to swim and cope with the waves. In such a terrific sea it was no easy matter to launch the boat, though somewhat protected by the lee side of the ship, but in about five minutes it was successfully done, amid the

plaudits and cheers of the passengers and crew. The passengers for the time being seeming to forget their sickness in the desire to witness the thrilling scene of a rescue at sea amid conditions so hazardous and adverse.

The boat when it took to the water was struck by several heavy waves drenching its occupants to the skin. The crew pulled away from the ship, and although but a third of a mile from the tanker, it took over an hour against such terrific seas to get near enough to speak to her, the seas and wind being contrary. It soon became evident that the rescuing boat could not run alongside the *Vindobala* without eminent peril to its own crew, and that the distressed seamen themselves would have to develop heroic measures.[2]

On the *Vindobala*, Captain Clarke already had cut away the sea anchor so that the tanker would offer a more sheltered lee for the rescue boat, but this proved inadequate under the circumstances, since the very worst of the storm was blowing. At one point, the *Paris*'s lifeboat got within 12 feet of the side of the rolling tanker before having to pull back for fear of being crushed against the hull. So close had the lifeboat come that Captain Clarke had thrown his log and papers into her. An attempt was made to float a line to the rescue boat, but this proved impossible. Then a new scheme was attempted. The strongest swimmer among the sailors on the *Vindobala*, P. Fitzgerald, an able seaman, was lowered overboard with a line tied around him, and he struck out bravely into the tumultuous waters, trying to reach the lifeboat. Time and again, he was flung back, narrowly escaping being dashed and mangled against the steamer's side. Exhausted, he was hauled back on board.

The *Vindobala* was outfitted with four lifeboats, but it was impossible to launch any vessel from the weather side of the ship in such a storm. Of the two lifeboats on the lee side, one had been damaged. Captain Clarke ordered the launching of the only remaining usable lifeboat. Eight of the tanker's crew made the daring attempt and narrowly succeeded. They moved as quickly as possible to launch and whipped their oars into the sea in order to pull away from the hull. As the tanker's lifeboat neared First Officer Bradshaw shouted for it to make for the liner, which they did.

Back on the *Vindobala*, the 15 remaining sailors had no alternative left except somehow to reach the rescue vessel bobbing just beyond their reach. Captain Clarke tried another strategy. He threw overboard a lifebuoy attached to a line, and this time he succeeded in floating it out to the *Paris*'s lifeboat. It was picked up, and the painter of the boat was tied to it. Then it was hauled back to the tanker, the painter dragging after it. Thus, they had created a trolley that could be pulled back and forth. Just as the line was got out, the carpenter of the *Vindobala*, A. Oesterrvick, grabbed the end and jumped overboard, apparently expecting to be picked up by one of the two lifeboats. He was wearing a cork vest and bobbed in the water. The American sailors watched in horror as a large wave swept the struggling figure aft under the raised counter stern of the tanker, which then crashed down on top of him. The man breached the turbulent seas, and the boat from the *Paris* succeeded in getting to within a couple feet of him when he was

The British marine artist John Nicholson has captured the sleek lines of the New York (1889) *in this painting, which shows the American Line greyhound knifing through a choppy sea against a threatening sky. The scene was inspired by a photograph taken in mid-Atlantic by the author.*

flung around, face toward them. Bradshaw hollered, "Cheer up, old man," but there was no response. His face was white, and it was obvious he was dead, probably of a fractured skull. A cry went up from the remaining crew members on the tanker—"Save the living"—and the boat was rowed back into position for the next attempt. The lifeboat was kept between 40 and 100 feet of the plunging and rolling tanker as one after the other of the remaining 14 crew members donned cork life jackets, took hold of the lifebuoy, dropped overboard, and was hauled to the lifeboat. There was no life jacket left for Captain Clarke, who saw all his crew safely away and then leaped himself into the sea, through which he was quickly pulled to the lifeboat. As fast as possible, the American sailors rowed to the waiting *Paris*, where ropes were hanging down the sides of the ship to aid in bringing the exhausted rescuers and rescued on board. As each man stepped foot on the deck of the *Paris*, cheer after cheer went up. The doctor stood by and ladled out liberal quantities of hot whiskey to the frozen men which was followed by food and hot baths. The sailors also received quantities of clothes from the passengers. In James Davison's words:

> Too great praise cannot be awarded to the gallant crew who made the rescue at
> the peril of their own lives. As they left the ship on their errand of mercy many
> a silent prayer was said. During the rescue the *Vindobala* was frequently lost to
> sight, except the topmasts and a portion of the funnel, the waves being so high.

The small lifeboats disappeared again and again, only to rise on the crest of a huge wave. The rescue took about three and a half hours, and was a time of intense excitement on the *Paris*, as well as to the rescuing crew and the distressed seamen. About noon the *Paris* proceeded on her voyage, leaving the *Vindobala* in Latitude 49 degrees 29 minutes, Longitude 31 degrees 29 minutes, with hatches uncovered, sea anchor cast loose, and sixteen feet of water in her hold. It was believed that she must soon founder.[3]

The officers and crew of the *Vindobala* were well cared for on the *Paris*. Hot baths and solid meals did wonders for their recovery, and they were loud in their praise of the officers and crew of the American liner. The cabin passengers traveling on the *Paris* expressed their pride and appreciation for the officers and crew who had participated in the rescue by raising a purse of $300, from which $25 was awarded to each of the eight seamen and a suitable watch was to be purchased for each of the two officers. In a formal ceremony on the last evening out, as each of the men from the lifeboat crew entered the main saloon on the *Paris*, he saluted Captain Frederick Watkins and received an ovation from the assembled passengers. Subsequently, the officers and crew of the *Vindobala* joined the group and also were cheered. Captain Clarke offered sincere thanks on behalf of himself and his crew to their rescuers and to the many passengers who provided clothing to the destitute seamen. As the celebration was nearing its end, a call came for the very popular fourth officer of the *Paris*, Richard H. Webb, to speak. Webb was one of the volunteers who had manned the American lifeboat. Normally, he would have been in command of no. 6 lifeboat, but when the call came for volunteers, he had been first. When his offer was declined in favor of Bradshaw, who was senior, Webb had offered to go in the place of a seaman, and this was permitted. He may have been a bashful young man of 21, but his courage was unquestioned. His response was: "Ladies and gentlemen, I thank you for your kindness. We only did for these men what I am sure they would have done for us under like conditions."[4]

The *Paris* reached New York on New Year's Day—one day late—after a crossing in which the weather never let up once! The Committee of Lloyd's subsequently bestowed silver medals for heroism upon Captain Watkins, First Officer John Bradshaw, and Fourth Officer R.H. Webb of the *Paris* for saving 22 of the 23 members of the crew of the *Vindobala*.

In the United States, the American Line was engaged in a difficult struggle with the American government in an effort to increase the mail subsidy. The amount awarded the North Atlantic express liners was a vigorous subject for debate again in 1899. Clement Acton Griscom, by now one of the most senior and respected men of commerce on either side of the Atlantic, traveled to Washington to give testimony before Congress about the inadequacy of the government grant. Needless to say, he wanted the subsidy revised upward by a substantial margin, and he argued before the congressional committee that the return on investment for the *St. Louis* and the *St. Paul* was totally inadequate. Griscom stated that the liners had cost $1,100,000 more to build in the United

On the Bridge in a Gale *helps one appreciate the challenges of successfully navigating a ship across the North Atlantic in the days when bridges were totally open to the elements and offered little protection. Sou'westers are the preferred overcoat in an effort to cope with foul weather.*

States than was the case in Britain. Furthermore, the cost of interest, insurance, and manning were higher in the United States than in Europe. Therefore, as far as the International Navigation Company was concerned, the annual postal subsidy of approximately $750,000 received by the American Line from the United States government was $113,000 short of meeting the basic costs of maintaining the ships under the American flag. At this rate, Griscom stated, when these four ships are worn out, they will not be replaced. Griscom also made the point that while the American Line covered its expenses, it was impossible for the steamship line to declare a dividend to its stockholders.

Not everyone accepted the figures or the views that Griscom put forward. John Codman of New York, a knowledgeable critic of Griscom, offered the observation that the reason the American Line had not paid a dividend was that Griscom was pumping all the profits of the line into building two new ships on the River Clyde. These vessels, Codman contended, were designed to fly foreign flags and operate with foreign crews in order to serve the interests of the International Navigation Company in whatever service it desired. There was no question that INC was building new tonnage on the Clyde. Whether or not those vessels were draining income from the American Line can be debated.

Early in 1899, the International Navigation Company Inc., the parent organization of the American Line and the Red Star Line, underwent a major recapitalization. The financial reorganization and fund raising was handled in Philadelphia by associates of J.P. Morgan. The INC issued $20,000,000 of 5 percent mortgage bonds—considered an enormous sum at the time. Griscom pointed out that this was an astute financial move, since $12,000,000 was to be used to retire bonds that had been issued at 6 percent. The balance was to be used for the acquisition of new property as the business of the company might demand. It was stated that the extra $6,000,000 afforded ample provision for the expansion needs of the International Navigation Company for years to come.[5]

The passenger market for the first half of 1899 appeared weak, and the White Star Line reacted by lowering the minimum first-class fares from $75 to $60 until April 15, from $100 to $75 through June 1, and to $100 through July 6. A 20 percent fare reduction was quite substantial, and it produced a renewed era of economic instability on the North Atlantic. Cunard reserved judgment on the situation, but the American Line immediately matched White Star's new rates. North German Lloyd, which ran in direct competition on the Southampton route, waited a few days for instructions from Bremen before following suit. A point of interest made in the newspapers was that the reductions announced represented no sacrifice on the part of the steamship lines. It was contended that all the minimum-grade cabins had been sold out a long time before, and the announcement about new discount fares would apply only if passages were canceled and the cabins went on the market again. The steamship lines responded somewhat heatedly that they had a number of cabins available at the reduced rates and would be pleased to sell them to travelers.

The American Line also sought alternative profitable employment for its vessels. This produced a unique opportunity when the *Paris* was assigned in 1899 to take a West Indies cruise to sites of the Spanish-American War. (The *Paris* had served the United States as the auxiliary cruiser USS *Yale*.) Prospective passengers were told that they would have nearly three weeks of cruising under sunny skies in tropical seas, visiting places where no one had ever been before on a first-class liner. The publicity was very well done, and the *Paris* was soon fully booked to take 400 fortunate passengers on a March cruise to the Caribbean sun. The liner would sail from New York on March 4, 1899, and the cruise was to last 31 days, covering some 6,000 miles. The longest run of the cruise was from New York to Môle St.-Nicolas, Haiti—1,270 nautical miles. After that, the *Paris* was to steam between points of interest, calling at Puerto Rico, St. Thomas, Barbados, Trinidad, Martinique, and Jamaica. Along the Cuban coast, the liner was scheduled to call at Guantanamo, Daiquiri, Siboney, Santiago, Cape Cruz, Cienfuegos, Cabo San Antonio, and Havana before heading north to Nassau, Fort Monroe, and back to New York. Attention was paid to shore excursions to famous settings of the Spanish-American War, such as Daiquiri, Siboney, Las Guasimas, and San Juan Hill in Cuba. At Santiago de Cuba, the *Paris* would steam by the hulls of the Spanish fleet sunk by the United States Navy during the Battle of Santiago.

An observer commented that the rates charged by the American Line for cabins were "exorbitant"—which they probably were by 1899 standards. An inside cabin for two persons went for $200, and suites were available at $1,500 for the cruise—with some wealthy travelers taking more than one. These rates were less than half what the facilities would have cost for a similar time span on the North Atlantic (four crossings), but for the more leisurely business of cruising in the off-season, the prices shocked some. Nevertheless, the *Paris*'s 400 passengers were booked long before sailing, and there was a substantial waiting list. As far as New York society was concerned, the 1899 season was proving dull, and the departure of the *Paris* on her cruise promised to be a new sensation. Every available

After the Spanish-American War, American Line ships periodically cruised during the winter months to the Caribbean. This employment began in 1899. The New York *is shown around 1903 while coaling at the East Asiatic Wharf, St. Thomas, Danish West Indies. For cruising, the* New York *had been painted white in order to make her cooler in the hot sun of the Caribbean.*

automobile was engaged to carry the travelers and their friends to the American Line pier. The event was newsworthy enough to have the full passenger list printed on the day of departure. Among society leaders who booked on the *Paris* were ex-Secretary of State John Sherman, Anson Phelps Stokes, and Augustus S. Peabody.

The record passages between Southampton and New York of the American Line quartet of express liners. The remarkable balance of the fleet is shown by the fact that the fastest passage speeds for the four liners were separated by only 1.18 knots.

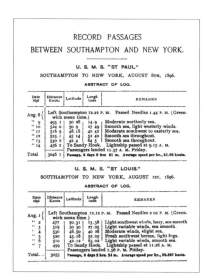

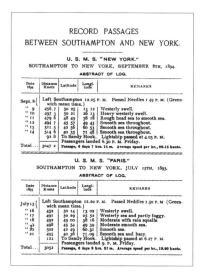

The International Navigation Company's Facts for Travellers *(1897) provided "Mileage Tables," "Table for Converting Knots Into Miles," "Table of Proportional Speed of Ships," and "Distance Objects Are Visible at Sea Level."*

Saturday, March 4, was a miserable day for a gala sailing. Rain, fog, waterproof wraps, dripping umbrellas, and muddy carriages were features of the scene. The crowd that gathered on the pier to see the *Paris* off on her maiden West Indies cruise were determined to make merry. A reporter commented that the sailing parties made the whole occasion into one big picnic. Captain of the *Paris* was Frederick Watkins, who had served on the ship during the war and held the rank of commander in the United States Navy.

No sooner had the *Paris* sailed than a minor tempest erupted over why she had been given clearance papers by the collector of customs of New York to take passengers to Cuba and the various American-held islands of the Caribbean. Maritime gadfly John Codman sent a open letter to the *New York Times* in which he asked why the *Paris*, which had been given the right to fly the American flag on the North Atlantic but not to engage in the coastal trade, suddenly found herself cruising in the Caribbean. As a foreign-built vessel, she and the *New York* specifically were denied the right to carry passengers in the American coastal trade. Codman said that the law was ridiculous as far as he was concerned, but it was the law, and until Congress repealed it, he did not know by what authority the collector of customs had authorized the liner to sail with American passengers.[6] Codman's letter created a bit of a stir. Deputy Customs Collector Frank Raymond was given the job of replying, and neat distinctions were drawn. Raymond said that Codman was perfectly correct about the status of the *Paris* in regard to her exclusion from the coastal trade of the United States. However, Raymond contended that the liner was on an "excursion" in which she was delivering neither passengers nor cargo to any destination, and therefore was exempt from the regulation. A cruise to the Caribbean was acceptable and legal.

Codman refused to let the matter die on that note. In a subsequent letter to the editor, he insisted that the collector for New York would have to ensure that every passenger taken out by the *Paris* came back on the same ship, and that no new passengers were

The City of Chester *(1893, 4,791 tons, 445 feet by 44 feet, 14 knots) was the relief boat for the express quartet, although considerably slower. Renamed* Chester *in 1893 for the American Line, she was sold in 1898 to the United States government for use as a transport and renamed* Sedgwick.

picked up anywhere en route, or the law would be broken. If any violation occurred, either the *Paris* would be subject to seizure or the law was illegal and the American coastwise trade would have to be opened to everyone. The debate rumbled through the New York newspapers for the duration of the *Paris*'s cruise without affecting anything.

On board the *Paris*, her passengers had a wonderful time. The first great American cruise ship received a tumultuous reception wherever she went. Nowhere was this truer than at Santiago de Cuba, where the liner anchored on March 25. The arrival of the *Paris* with 420 passengers—all of whom wanted carriages and hotel accommodations—strained the limited local resources. There were only 30 hacks, each of which could accommodate four passengers at most, and that left 75 percent of the passengers without transportation. Ambulances from the local hospitals and from the United States Army were pressed into use, taking care of another 100 passengers, but no more than 200 could be handled at once. Furthermore, only about 200 individuals could be accommodated in the local hotels for the three-day stay; the remainder had to resort to their cabins on board the liner. Air-conditioning was noteworthy by its absence in 1899, and while the *Paris*'s ventilators would have relieved the tropical heat somewhat when she was underway, the atmosphere in port must have been stifling.

Every one of the American tourists wanted to obtain relics or souvenirs of the recent war. Local initiative rose to the occasion, and some natives reaped a golden harvest from the gullible tourists. Every man and boy around the city who could gather anything that could be termed a relic of the war, by any stretch of the imagination, soon sold it. New machetes recently arrived from the United States were kept in salt water for a few days in order to give them a coat of rust. They were then sold at $5 to $15 each, depending on the ability of the seller as a romancer. The locals became very good at adding historical narrative to their sales spiel, and they excelled in the art of storytelling. An estimated 1,200 machetes were sold to those aboard the *Paris*. To supply the heavy demand, even the knives used in the hotel and restaurant kitchens were requisitioned and sold. When the *Paris* finally sailed, it was difficult to find a machete in Santiago for any purpose. Another outstanding local success story involved the young "guides to the battlefields." Most had never been to the sites before, but they managed to provide dramatic narratives for the tourists.

A special reception was given by General and Mrs. Leonard Wood. General Wood was the American military governor of Cuba, and he and Mrs. Wood received their distinguished guests surrounded by a glittering staff in full dress, with the governor himself wearing the full-dress uniform of a major general. On the following night, the American Line responded with a formal ball aboard the *Paris*, anchored in Santiago Harbor. The liner was brilliantly illuminated from stem to stern with Chinese lanterns, bunting, and flags. Anyone with the slightest claim to social distinction in Santiago was invited. Music was provided by a Cuban band and the Fifth United States Infantry band. All agreed that the entertainment was a great success. When the *Paris* steamed back to New York, her passengers expressed delight in their cruise and their treasures, including the 1,200 rusting steel machetes—relics of war.

On the North Atlantic, the American Line decided that the continental market was worth more consideration than it had received. In March 1899, the *New York* became the first American liner to call at Cherbourg. She sailed from Southampton as per the normal schedule, but then she crossed the English Channel to Cherbourg, where she boarded 25 first- and five second-cabin passengers before proceeding to New York. This made the trip a little longer, but it provided a very substantial convenience to passengers traveling from the Continent. Individuals on the crossing saw a great deal of ice off the Grand Banks as the liner picked her way through an ice field for two days. When a crank pin broke, she stopped 25 minutes, then proceeded on the starboard engine for about three hours before full power would be restored.

The additional funds provided to the International Navigation Company by the successful floating of the 5 percent mortgage bonds allowed the INC to order four large new units for the fleet. The goal of the International Navigation Company was to improve the quality of both the American Line and the Red Star Line fleets. Orders for the vessels were placed with the Clydebank Engineering and Shipbuilding Company of Scotland.

The Red Star steamers were named *Vaderland*, reviving the name of the first unit of the fleet in 1873, and *Zeeland*. The general dimensions of the new steamers provided for large capacity, with a length of 500 feet, a beam of 60 feet, and a measurement of approximately 12,000 gross tons, 20,000 tons displacement. They were outfitted with twin screws and bilge keels to enhance stability. Standard operating speed was intended to be 17 knots, making possible transatlantic crossings of eight days. Passenger accommodations were for 300 first, 250 second, and 750 steerage. A majority of the first and second cabins were deck cabins, and there was a limited number of suites with bedroom, sitting room, and bath—as had proven so popular on the *New York*, *Paris*, *St. Paul*, and *St. Louis*. The public rooms on the large promenade deck featured a well-equipped library and a smoking room. As was normal in any Griscom vessel, particular attention was given to ventilation, and the point was made that a large number of cabins had private bathrooms. Steerage accommodations involved two-, four-, and six-berth cabins, which were well lighted and well ventilated, with lavatories and bathrooms readily available. A large social hall was provided for steerage passengers, and there was plenty of open deck space.

The two vessels for the American Line were intended to upgrade the Line's Philadelphia–Liverpool service, which had been languishing for some years. These ships, named the *Merion* and the *Haverford*, were similar in dimensions to the Red Star Line vessels (530 feet by 59 feet, 10,000 tons), with twin screws and bilge keels. However, at 13 knots, they were appreciably slower. Following the custom of the Philadelphia service, they were outfitted for only a single class of cabin passengers, with a capacity of 130. The cabins, to be situated in the upper deckhouse amidships, were the equal of many first-class accommodations on other vessels. Public rooms on the promenade deck provided a smoking room and a social hall. Accommodations for 800 in steerage were divided among two-, four-, and six-berth cabins with good light and ventilation. This point was emphasized, since many vessels continued to carry steerage passengers in large dormitories, rather than cabins.

With the new tonnage on order, the International Navigation Company seemed to be heading toward a prosperous turn of the century. Then disaster struck. Early on the morning of May 21, the *Paris*, westbound to New York from Southampton and Cherbourg, ran bow-on onto one of the most dreaded hazards to navigation along the southern coast of England—The Manacles. The *Paris* sailed from Southampton under the command of Captain Frederick Watkins, the commodore of the American Line fleet and one of the most highly respected master mariners on the North Atlantic. Watkins was 61 and had never known any other occupation except the sea since the age of 13. He transferred from sail to steam in 1862 at the age of 25 and joined the Inman Line one year later. Since 1877, he had commanded virtually every vessel in the Line. He was the first master of the *City of New York*, and then of the *City of Paris*. As captain of the *Paris*, over the previous 10 years, he had brought the big liner safely through a number of accidents and near-catastrophes, partly because of the unsatisfactory structural supports for the propeller shafts, which had cracked on a number of occasions. The worst of these disasters, in March 1890, had resulted in the dropping of a shaft and the total destruction of one of the ship's engine rooms off Ireland. The *Paris* had survived, with great praise going to Watkins, and various provisions and safeguards had lessened the risk somewhat by 1899. Watkins was known personally to nearly every prominent American who visited Europe for business or pleasure. In 1898, when the *Paris* was converted to an armed merchant cruiser for the U.S. Navy, Watkins remained with his ship as executive officer. Any ship with Watkins in command always was considered in good hands. Knowledgeable individuals booked passage on the *Paris* just to sail with this trusted, popular, and safety-conscious master.

The *Paris* was nudged away from her Southampton berth promptly at noon on Saturday, May 20. The weather was questionable as the American liner slipped down Southampton Water with approximately 330 passengers, the mails, and general cargo on board. In accordance with the new service of the American Line, her first destination was the French port of Cherbourg, where she arrived at 5:21 P.M. and embarked an additional 45 passengers and their baggage. The Cherbourg call was proving very popular, and well worth the extra time and effort. Watkins took the *Paris* safely out of Cherbourg Harbor and entered the departure time in the log as 5:52 P.M. He then set course for the first leg of the run to New York. The usual procedure was to steam from Cherbourg to just south of the Lizard Light, where the final positioning could be made for the transatlantic crossing. Misty weather set in, and the *Paris* steamed along at full speed. Captain Watkins noted that Cap de la Hague was abeam at 6:38 and the Casquets Lighthouse at 7:35 P.M.[7]

During the late evening, the fog dispersed over the English Channel and the *Paris* continued to steam at full speed toward the southwestern tip of Britain, where the course would be altered for New York. When Captain Watkins next consulted the log, his ship was near Eddystone Light, but the lookout could not see it through the fog and mist. Apparently Watkins felt he had plenty of time to make the next course adjustment, and since the weather was uncertain, he went down to his cabin to get his mackintosh. What he failed to realize was that in addition to the tide pressing against the bow of the *Paris*, a variable current was flowing in off the Atlantic at two to three knots. These factors steadily pressed the clipper bow of the *Paris* farther to the north.

An unfortunate series of circumstances conspired against Watkins and the *Paris*. Just as the misjudgment on time placed her in peril, nature lay a thick fog bank over the land and obscured the coastal warning lights, while the sea remained clear. Captain Watkins had barely reached his cabin when the officer of the watch suddenly saw a warning flare from a pilot boat almost in the path of the liner. Quick maneuvering swerved the *Paris* around the pilot boat, and to the horror of the English crew, they saw the liner return to her original course. The flare had been intended to warn the *Paris* of the rocks, not just to inform the liner that a vessel was nearby. Watkins reached the bridge just in time to hear the lookout howl, "Land, dead ahead!" The time was 1:21 A.M. on May 21. Almost immediately, the *Paris* swept by the wreck of another ship previously obscured by the fog and narrowly missed hitting her. The vessel was the Atlantic Transport liner *Mohegan*. She had gone on the rocks in a fierce storm on October 14, 1898, only nine months earlier, with the loss of 106 lives out of the 150 on board. The *Mohegan's* superstructure and masts, suddenly rearing out of the fog, were a grim testament to the unforgiving nature of this coastline.

On the *Paris*, as soon as the lookout screamed the warning, the helm was put hard to starboard and the order was given to put the port engine hard astern in a frantic effort to turn the bow of the liner away from the impending disaster. Before these measures could slow the forward momentum of the *Paris*, she slammed onto a rocky shoal a cable's length from the beach. Attempts to reverse the engines proved fruitless, as the 10,800-ton liner was firmly aground on a high tide. The bow lay about 150 yards from shore and the stern about 200. Shortly after striking the rocks, the fog that had totally obscured the coast lifted, and St. Anthony's Light suddenly appeared bright and clear. The sea was as calm as a millpond, and the fate of the passengers and crew members on the *Paris* looked much more encouraging than that of the poor souls on the *Mohegan* nine months earlier. There still was concern, however, that the liner might suddenly slip off the rocky ledge and sink in water that was more than 100 feet deep on either side.

Rockets were sent up and signal guns fired from the *Paris*. With the clearing conditions, the rockets were seen at Coverack, where the Coast Guard station responded with a rocket and the *Paris* acknowledged with her signal gun. Chief Jeffers at Coverack launched a lifeboat with a crew of four for the stranded ship. The weather was sufficiently clear that the large liner could be seen without difficulty. Upon reaching the stranded ship, the lifeboat crew prepared the rocket apparatus and fired the first line from the shore toward the bow, which missed. A second rocket carried a lifeline to the bow of the *Paris*, where it was secured quickly. The Port Houstock lifeboat also responded. Captain Watkins ordered the launch of the gig, which quickly reached shore. A message was telegraphed to Falmouth for tugs to assist the ship.

When the *Paris* struck the rocks, those on board heard a grating sound as the liner slid over the edge of the rocky shoal, followed by a severe jolt as the hull stranded. Some slept through the entire event. The crew was summoned on deck, and all passengers not on deck were awakened and told to dress warmly. When they appeared in the companionways, they were met by stewards with comforting words and assurances that all would be well. Exceptional calm was shown on all sides, with no signs of panic. Stewards provided coffee and stimulants to all who desired them. Watkins' survey of the ship revealed that she already had 16 feet of water in the forward compartments and was filling fast. One passenger, Thomas Allen of London, reported:

> I was in bed when the accident happened. I heard a grating sound, and then several hard thumps on the rocks shook the ship. The vessel then seemed to stop dead. A few minutes later I heard someone calling "All hands on deck!" I roused my chum, who was still asleep, and we went on deck. We were told to secure our lifebelts, and we returned below and got them.
>
> We were not allowed to return to the deck at that time. All were kept waiting below. At the first summons a few of the passengers appeared in their night clothes, but as soon as they discovered that there was no danger they returned to their rooms and made themselves ready to leave the ship. The passengers all

behaved in the best possible manner. There was no screaming on the part of the women, and the most perfect order was maintained. We were kept waiting below for an hour. Coffee and biscuits were served out, and then we were ordered to the ship's boats. Steam tugs brought us to Falmouth.[8]

One gentleman leaped from his berth and grabbed whatever was handy in the rush. He arrived on deck dressed only in his drawers and his wife's fur cape. This generated some humor on the part of others, but his wife was not amused. She did not care whether or not the *Paris* was sinking. He was going to return to their stateroom immediately and dress properly. Chagrined, he went below, but only to grab some additional clothes and speedily return to the music room, where he finished dressing before an audience of passengers awaiting rescue. His wife's additional comments were not recorded.

The *Paris*'s own lifeboats were launched on the port side and as dawn came tugs arrived, so the area was swarming with vessels that had come to render assistance. Passengers were reassured by seeing the shore on one side and the waiting lifeboats and rescue vessels on the other, but they were also mindful of their danger by being able to see the masts of the wrecked *Mohegan* and to hear the mournful clamor of The Manacles bell buoy nearby. Owing to the calmness of the seas, the boats fortunately could be managed with complete safety.

Captain Watkins was said to have told one first-class passenger: "I am unable to understand how this happened." Nevertheless, he stood on the bridge giving orders, and his calm demeanor had a comforting effect on the passengers. Watkins ordered that all the women and children were to be taken off first, and an observer commented that such perfect order was maintained that the disembarkation simply involved a slow procession of women and children walking in single file to the boats.

The greatest challenge, according to Mrs. Batchelor, sister of U.S. Senator George Graham Vest of Missouri, arose in transferring the young and the aged from the lifeboats to the waiting tugs. "The officers and crew worked like Trojans in getting the old people and children off, and they certainly deserve great praise."[9] The passengers soon were safe on tugs, which carried them to Falmouth, where they landed at 7 A.M. The local agent of the American Line met them as the tug tied up and provided the first- and second-cabin passengers with accommodations at local hotels. The steerage passengers were given facilities at the local Sailors' Home. No passengers had brought with them anything except the clothes on their backs, yet all passengers were lavish in their praise of Captain Watkins and the crew of the *Paris* for their care, concern, and efficiency. At Falmouth, they were informed they would be transferred to the *St. Paul*, which was preparing to take the next Saturday sailing from Southampton. Passengers also had the option of crossing on a ship of any other line at the expense of the American Line, or postponing their departure to any later sailing of the American Line.

One of the passengers taken off the *Paris* was Louis Rhead of New York. Nine years earlier, he had been aboard the same liner when her starboard engine blew up off the Irish coast. On that occasion, he had spent six days awaiting rescue when the cotton steamer *Aldersgate* finally had arrived. After this latest incident, Rhead served as secretary of the passenger meeting at the Falmouth Hotel, where they gave thanks for their safe deliverance. When he was asked why he continued to travel on American Line vessels, he said that he had always met with kindness and courtesy on the American Line ships and that, insofar as he was concerned, the *Paris* always managed to save her passengers! At the meeting, prayers were offered, Captain Watkins and the crew were praised, and a collection of £30 was taken up for the Coast Guard, which had been so prompt in coming to the rescue.

Watkins made one attempt to free the *Paris* shortly after she struck the rocks. Unfortunately it was only an hour before high tide that the liner had gone ashore. As soon as possible, Watkins tried to reverse engines full speed to see if he could free his ship. This met with no success. If anything, it only wedged her more firmly on the shoal. The remaining tugs left the stranded liner at 5 P.M., and by that time, lighters and workmen were busily engaged in removing the passengers' luggage, the mail, and the cargo. It was announced that the mails on the *Paris* were to be transferred to the *Kaiser Wilhelm der Grosse*, which was due to sail from Southampton on Wednesday, May 22. Thus, the mails lost only two days in transit. The sea remained calm, helping the discharging of the ship.

Others besides Captain Watkins failed to comprehend how the accident could have occurred. Captain Scott of the ship *Kinross* was bringing his vessel into Falmouth when the *Paris* accident occurred. From his perspective, St. Anthony's Light was clearly visible for five or six miles, and the bell on The Manacles buoy was loud and clear as the *Kinross* steamed along. A misty rain was falling, but there was no fog, and the coastline was visible nearly all the way from The Lizard. Captain Scott said, "It is impossible for me to understand how the *Paris* got into that position any better than the *Mohegan*. The possibility of mistaking the St. Anthony's Light for the Lizard Light is ridiculous, as the former is a revolving oil light, low down, and the Lizard Light is two fixed electric lamps on a high cliff."[10] The answer appears to lie in the fact that fog is fickle. A coast can be clear one minute and obscure the next.

Henry Wilding, the well-known managing agent of the American Line, arrived in Falmouth by special train from Southampton to supervise transportation of the passengers. He arranged for the North German Lloyd *Bremen* to call at Plymouth on May 22 for any passengers who wanted to resume their journeys immediately. None felt up to facing the North Atlantic within 24 hours of rescue, so no passengers accepted the offer. In the absence of any means of contacting the *Bremen*, she made her call at Plymouth for nothing.

When Wilding was asked about the situation of the *Paris*, he refused all comment prior to the official investigation. At the same time, it was noted that in response to substantial public agitation after the wreck of the *Mohegan*, Trinity House finally had agreed to erect a gas-lighted, automatic sound-producing buoy on The Manacles in place of the bell buoy still there.

The Paris *in dense fog ran onto The Manacles off the Cornish coast, May 21, 1899, and was feared a total loss. Against all expectations the liner was refloated on July 10 and taken into Falmouth for temporary repairs before going to Belfast for a complete reconditioning that would take two years. Before resuming service in 1901 she was renamed* Philadelphia.

The crew of the *Paris* remained on the liner to assist in the unloading of luggage and cargo. Two Admiralty gunboats were sent from Plymouth by Admiral Sir Edmund Robert Fremantle to assist the *Paris*, but the feeling was that she probably would be a total wreck. Torpedo boats also were being held in reserve should additional pulling power be needed. The great concern of all parties was that the wind might shift off the Cornish coast and place the stranded liner in extreme peril. Divers were summoned, but the messages sent to Vice President James Wright in the New York office were not encouraging. The specific location given for the *Paris* was "off Lowland Point," which encouraged American Line officials to believe she might be resting on sand. This wishful thinking was soon dispelled. The *Paris* had considerable water under her stern and on either side of her, but her bow was hard aground on a rocky shoal that had punctured the forward compartments, which were full of water. Taking all information into consideration, if the wind and weather held, the prospects were favorable for saving the vessel. If the wind changed and the seas began to roll in, she was doomed. That part of the Cornish coast was treacherous indeed, with the list of wrecks during one year exceeding 60 vessels. The *Paris* lay about a mile away from Fenwin, the outermost of the rocks generally described as The Manacles.

One major problem for the International Navigation Company, parent company of the American Line, was that it held a substantial portion of the insurance on the vessel. Hence, the idea of abandoning the liner to her insurers was less attractive than it might have been, and clearly a last resort. It was stated in London that the ship was insured for $1,000,000 and her cargo for another $750,000. It was expected that the cargo was heavily damaged by water and would represent a substantial claim. Once the cargo was removed from the *Paris* and sent ashore, the crew turned to the task of heaving her coal overboard. She was loaded with more than 2,000 tons for an Atlantic crossing, and its removal appreciably lightened the vessel.

The divers exploring the forward holds of the *Paris*, under arduous conditions, found four or five large openings to the sea. Some of these could be patched, but others were less certain. One assessment stated that the hull was wedged on top of one of the rocks, and that since she had gone on them nearly at high tide, her chances were dismal. If she had not been warned of impending danger by the Falmouth pilot boat, she would have ended up virtually on top of the wreck of the *Mohegan*, with far more serious consequences. After the removal of the cargo and coal, the *Paris* began to show movement with the swells—indicative that she was not wedged solid on the rocks. After evaluating the damage, the divers reported that four of the forward holds probably could be pumped dry, there was no hope for the fifth one, but the six after compartments were all dry. Heavy-duty pumps were ordered from the Liverpool Salvage Association in hopes of emptying the ship quickly. The heaviest damage to the hull ran from the bow for about 70 feet aft. It was thought that if she could be pumped out, she might come off the rocks fairly easily, since she would be well balanced. A Cornish diver who had inspected the liner was far more pessimistic. He felt that there was little or no chance the liner could get off the rocks, and that if she did, she probably was so badly holed that she would go straight to the bottom.[11]

When a representative of the British Board of Trade boarded the *Paris* and tried to interview the officers, he was politely but firmly rebuffed. The American Line officers refused to answer any questions put to them by a British official because the *Paris* flew the American flag and was subject to the jurisdiction of the United States. Any investigation would have to occur in New York, not London.

During the latter part of May and early June, various attempts to pull the *Paris* off the rocks failed. Then the weather conditions worsened, and heavy seas began to roll in, slamming against the port side of the *Paris*. Most of the remaining crew members were removed from the liner, and only Captain Watkins and about a dozen hardy souls remained on board the stranded vessel. By June 11, the *Paris* had been ashore for nearly three weeks, heavy swells had begun to shift the hull toward the shore, and very little hope remained.

On their return to New York, the crew of the *Paris* complained bitterly to the Office of the Shipping Commissioner about their own poor treatment. To a man, they had stood faithfully by the stranded liner—saving passengers; unloading the mail, luggage, and cargo; and finally doing the dirty job of throwing the coal overboard. In return for their faithful service, as soon as they reached Falmouth they were informed by the American Line agent that they were discharged (fired) on the spot. Their pay stopped immediately, and they could get home any way they wanted, but the Line would not help them. Adding insult to injury, the crew members then had to buy their own steerage tickets on the *St. Louis* from Southampton to New York. The *St. Louis* carried 133 crew members and 17 officers. When they reached New York, they crowded into the office of Shipping Commissioner Dickey to complain about the treatment they had received from the International Navigation Company. They also complained vociferously that the United States consul in Southampton had refused to do anything to help them. Commissioner Dickey was told that the sailors were paid only fourteen dollars for a round-trip voyage. When they were discharged in Southampton, they lost half of their wages and then had to buy their passage home. The net result was that most of them had worked four weeks for a loss of three dollars! What were they or their families to live on? The men claimed that the agents of the American Line had no right to pay them off in a foreign port. They also said that the American consul at Southampton should have ordered the company to send the men home at its expense. Commissioner Dickey expressed his sympathy with the men from the *Paris* but informed them that he was powerless to intervene on their behalf. If they wanted, they could sue the American Line, but the expenses of such a legal action would be high and their chances of winning slight. The courts were not favorably inclined toward the rights of labor.

When the Board of Inquiry into the loss of the *Paris* convened in New York, its deliberations did not last long. According to the statement that Captain Watkins submitted to the board, he accepted full and complete responsibility for the accident to the *Paris*. His explanation was that he had made an unaccountable error in taking his bearings for the run across the Channel from the Casquets Light instead of from Cap de la Hague, 18 miles eastward. The result placed the *Paris* in peril when the fog bank over the land obscured visibility of all navigational lights on shore. At the end of his report, the bluff old veteran paid tribute to the discipline and gallantry of his officers and crew under the trying circumstances following the stranding of the vessel.

The United States Board of Inspectors of Steam Vessels were able to make a report to George H. Starbuck, supervising inspector, on July 10, 1899. Stated simply, their decision was that when the *Paris* grounded on the Cornish coast, Captain Frederick Watkins had not exercised sufficient care in the navigation of his ship. No one could argue with that broad statement. As a result of their deliberations, they suspended Captain Watkins' master's license for two years. The report of the inspectors revealed that they felt Captain Watkins' official statement was somewhat meager:

> . . . inasmuch as he merely states that he made a mistake in making his departure from Cap de la Hague at 7:38, when he was actually abreast of the Casquets at that time, a distance of about sixteen and a half miles. This, of course, would put him sixteen and a half miles ahead of his reckoning, but would not account for his being set in to the northward of his course some seven miles, allowing his intention to pass the Lizard at a distance of three miles. As Captain Watkins does not make any mention of making any allowance for tide, we are of the opinion he did not take that matter into consideration,

whereas when he approached the English Coast he must have encountered the flood tide on his port bow, setting him toward the land. In addition to this he makes no mention of having used the lead and he only discovered that it was thick over the land when the ship was ashore.[12]

After having given due consideration to all these matters, the inspectors felt they had no choice but to suspend Watkins' license for two years.

The American Line was not pleased with the result of the Board of Inquiry. Both Clement Acton Griscom, Jr., vice president and general manager of the Line, and James A. Wright, Jr., publicly expressed their personal views that the punishment was excessively harsh. They were not in a position to state immediately whether Captain Watkins would remain an employee of the American Line, but they had received many letters and testimonials in support of him. Wright forcefully stated, "He is one of the oldest and most respected captains in our service, and he had the confidence of all. We all think that great credit is due him for the frank manner in which he has told of his mistake and the manly way in which he has taken all the blame for the loss of the *Paris*."[13] Young Griscom said that the Line had received the report of the inspectors, and no further action on the part of the company was required. If anything, he was even more outspoken in support of Watkins than Wright had been:

> "The sentence seems a little severe. Other men have lost ships through what was afterward shown to be their own carelessness and only had their licenses suspended for six months or a year at most. Personally, we feel for Captain Watkins. He has been half a century at sea without the slightest accident before, and it seems to be hard upon him. We are liable to err, and it seems too bad that the mistakes should have been made on a night when the atmospheric conditions were such that he received no help from the land lights. Had the same error been made at any other time in ninety-nine cases out of a hundred the land lights would have saved him."[14]

Others made the point that this was only Captain Watkins' second visit to Cherbourg, and that he could be forgiven for taking a quick look at the log and assuming that the starting time was from Cap de la Hague instead of the Casquets. The difference meant disaster for the *Paris* and the ruin of a 50-year career. At the same time, when asked by reporters whether Captain Watkins' statement would affect the insurance on the *Paris*, Griscom snapped that the Line was not responsible for the mistakes of its captain.

It seemed as though the *Paris* would be a total loss. Wright announced that the liner had been abandoned to the underwriters and that Captain Watkins would stay with the ship at their request in the event it could be refloated. When Wright announced on June 12 that two new vessels were being ordered from the William Cramp Shipyard in Philadelphia, it immediately was assumed that one of them was designed to replace the *Paris*. The two new liners were to be in the 12,000-ton class, which made them slightly larger than the *Paris*, although at 17 knots they were not going to be as fast as the *Paris*. It was stated that the new liners would have accommodations for 400 cabin and 800 steerage, with considerable freight capacity. They were to be 600 feet in length, with a beam of 60 feet, which would make them very similar to the four other ships already on order from the Clyde. Six new vessels of this magnitude represented a major financial commitment that would strengthen the position of the International Navigation Company. The expectation that all units would be on line by late 1900 was overly optimistic, however, since a shortage of steel was to delay construction times in American yards.

To the utter amazement of the shipping world, it was trumpeted that on the very day the American Board of Inspectors of Steam Vessels had made its report on the *Paris* stranding (July 11), a group of German salvagers, led by Superintendent Alsbett, had managed to refloat the *Paris*. For some days beforehand, dynamite charges had blown away rocks on either side of the stranded liner, clearing a path to the open sea. The second critical problem was figuring out how to lift the bow off the rocks. The salvagers solved it by loading the stern with a thousand tons of granite, which raised the bow substantially. Then the wind cooperated by picking up just a little and raising the high tide by a foot. When the salvagers began to slew the hull so that the divers could work to patch the holes, suddenly it was seen that the *Paris* was afloat. Immediately, a steam winch was started. It was connected by a strong hawser to an anchor astern, and in a matter of minutes, the winch moved the liner away from the rocks and 150 feet astern to deeper water. Here she was secured with the assistance of only three tugs. The elated salvagers immediately anchored the ship to stabilize her. The pumps were set at full power in order to empty as far as possible the compartments that had been patched. The next day, steam was gotten up in the boiler rooms, and the *Paris* was able to sustain herself with her own pumps even before she reached port. Captain Watkins, a few officers, and 20 members of the salvage crew were on board as the *Paris* drifted free from the rocks. Their elation knew no bounds. Prior to this, Watkins was described as a grief-stricken figure. Whatever else might happen, his joy over having the *Paris* afloat again was indescribable. At least Watkins now could retire to his home in Southampton with some sense of peace.

The pumps were soon coping with the water, and it appeared there was no danger that the *Paris* would sink. However, unfavorable weather was moving into the area and the salvagers did not regard the *Paris* as safe until she reached port. The German salvage company had taken the job on the basis of "no cure, no pay" and would receive a stipulated percentage of the value of the *Paris* when she reached drydock safely.[15]

On July 12, the passengers and crew members on the American Line's *St. Louis*, steaming up the English Channel, suddenly saw a ghost—as the "wrecked" *Paris* came into view, inward bound for safe harbor. The *Paris* was accompanied by an armada of five tugs and three salvage vessels. On board the *St. Louis* were the members of the Yale–Harvard Crew Team bound for England to answer the challenge issued jointly by Oxford and Cambridge. With high spirits, the athletes and passengers on the *St. Louis* cheered and cheered those on the *Paris* who had beaten the odds. At Falmouth, the dry dock could not accommodate a vessel as big as the *Paris*, yet the salvagers wanted to secure the patches on the hull before taking her along the coast. It was decided to run her up on an unexposed sandy beach in the tidal harbor, where temporary repairs could be made prior to taking her to Southampton.

The salvaging of the *Paris* did not immediately settle her fate. Griscom explained to the public that in marine insurance there are "total losses" and "constructive total losses." The latter occurs when the value of a ship, after a disaster, is less than the cost of restoring her to her former condition. This was a question to be determined by a board of survey. In the case of the *Paris*, if the cost of repairing her was more than she was worth in her present condition, she would become the property of the underwriters, and the American Line would receive its insurance money. On the other hand, if she could be repaired for less than her present value, the underwriters would have to restore her to her former condition and return her to the American Line. After all the *Paris* had been through, Griscom was not optimistic. The American Line agent in London flatly stated that he thought the *Paris* might make an excellent ship for another line, since the American Line had no further use for her. Whether or not Griscom and his agent were aware of it, a special train already was scheduled to take shipwrights from Glasgow to Southampton for the purpose of restoring the *Paris*. The insurance underwriters had seen the light at the end of the tunnel, and the liner would sail again if they had anything to say about it.

Ultimately, the *Paris* would be completely rebuilt and refitted. The American Line took the opportunity to order strengthening for the casing and supports for the propeller shafts. New quadruple-expansion engines were installed, and the three funnels were replaced with two. The work was done at Harland and Wolff, Belfast. When the liner returned to service on August 31, 1901, after 17 months out of service, she was renamed *Philadelphia*. At the Cramp Shipyard, the *New York* underwent refitting between May 1901 and April 1903, returning to service on April 15, 1903.[16]

In July 1899, the American Line also announced that Captain William G. Randle of the *St. Louis*, one of its most famous and respected officers, was retiring from the sea at the age of 61 in order to become vice president and general manager of the New York Shipbuilding Company in Camden, New Jersey. The INC held a substantial interest in the shipbuilding firm, and Randle's valuable services would be retained by the corporation. Yet the twentieth century would soon see shipping plans that would dwarf anything anyone had ever dreamed.

Chapter 15

THE BEGINNING
OF A NEW CENTURY

"A Wedding Trip," from a series of vignettes entitled Life at Sea—Incidents on a Voyage on an Ocean Greyhound *by F. Opper for* Frank Leslie's Illustrated Newspaper *(June 30, 1888).*

T he turn of the century saw the International Navigation Company preparing for the future. New steamers building on the Clyde and the Delaware were larger than anything in the American or Red Star fleets. Their moderate speed and large cargo capacity guaranteed that they would be moneymakers. If the White Star Line traditionally has been given credit for switching from greyhounds to big, commodious vessels after 1900, the International Navigation Company already had begun to move in that direction in 1898. Prestigious speed queens frequently did not make money, and Griscom had no desire to build a ship to chase the *Kaiser Wilhelm der Grosse* (1897), the North German Lloyd greyhound.

Among the first-class units, the American Line's *St. Louis* turned in a commendable record during 1899 and was recognized for her achievement. In 34 voyages across the Atlantic between Southampton and New York, she traveled 106,764.5 miles and carried 16,858 passengers, including 5,081 in first class. It was commented: "There may be

Pullman cars on transcontinental trains which in constant service have traversed more than 106,000 miles within a year, but no locomotive nor other vehicle propelled by its own power has approached the record of the *St. Louis*."[1] The *St. Louis* was in service for 50 out of 52 weeks, during which she was in port 133 days and at sea 232. While at sea, she had averaged 460 miles per day. Reading between the lines, these records also testify to how hard the American Line ships were driven year-round, because of the mail contract, whereas many of the first-class units of other lines spent part of the winter either cruising or laid up.

Unfortunately, the new century also carried with it one familiar ring—the *New York* hit some wreckage in mid-Atlantic on May 22, 1900. The debris scraped along the side of the hull until it collided with the propeller, which was turning at full speed. The result was that the propeller, its bracket, and 16 feet of shaft soon lay buried in the Atlantic deeps. By now, such a development was familiar, and after a brief stoppage to check for leaks, the *New York* continued on one propeller. She reached America 36 hours late but maintained a respectable 15 knots after the accident. At her pier, a diver inspected the hull and assured the agent, Samuel Bettle (Clement Griscom's son-in-law), that the liner could take her normal sailing and be drydocked at Southampton for repairs. Those sailing on the *New York* were given a 25 percent fare reduction because she would be crossing at a slower pace. The only alternative was to send the liner to Newport News, Virginia, for drydocking, which would have played havoc with the summer schedule. Much of the equipment and spare parts for the *New York* were stored at Southampton, where a drydock was readily available. After repairs in England, the liner made her fastest crossing to date from Cherbourg to New York—six days, 18 hours, 57 minutes.

In May 1900, when the transatlantic shipping lines evaluated their prospects for the summer season, every indicator looked very good. Some 2,000 additional cabin-class berths (over 1899) would be available as a result of several new vessels, including the *Deutschland* of the Hamburg-American Line. So optimistic were the major lines about the season that all said they were prepared to place extra boats in service should demand warrant. Where the American Line would find any extra boats on short notice was never explained. This all seems to have been whistling in the dark, because within a month, Cunard and White Star announced that they would put their "winter rates" into effect starting August 1—dramatically underlining the fact that there were cabins aplenty to be had. The expectation that the Paris Exposition would sustain a high flow of traffic to Europe was not coming true. Vernon H. Brown of Cunard said, "Our announcement was made independently, and was not due to any agreement with the White Star people. Of course we would have kept summer prices going until later, but our bookings for August and September were not as good as we expected. In most years our winter rates begin on the 1st of August."[2] The difference in fares was substantial. Summer rates on the White Star *Oceanic*, *Majestic*, and *Teutonic* ran around $125 for first cabin, but winter rates dropped to $75. When one or more major lines offered a price break, there was no alternative but for the others to follow suit. Only North German Lloyd felt secure

"In the Cook's Galley" by F. Opper, on a transatlantic express liner of the late 1880s.

In the cooks' galley.

enough to maintain its rates through the August 7 sailing of the *Kaiser Wilhelm der Grosse* because her advance bookings were quite good.

The *St. Paul* brought a distinguished passenger list westbound when she docked in New York on August 31. She steamed from Cherbourg to New York in the exceptional time of six days, seven hours, 52 minutes. A day out from New York, she overtook the Cunarder *Campania* in a stern chase and was already docked when the latter still lay at quarantine. On this crossing, it helped that the *St. Paul* was bringing home Clement Acton Griscom, Sr., founder and president of the Line. Griscom had been on a visit to his son, Lloyd C. Griscom, chargé d'affaires of the United States Legation in Constantinople. The elder Griscom also took the opportunity to shoot grouse in Scotland and to inspect the four steamships that his concern had under construction on the Clyde. The canny old Quaker made the observation that with their large size and moderate speeds, "they are the kind that pays."

The stature of Clement A. Griscom among men of business and commerce was substantial. On one European trip, Griscom, P.A.B. Widener, and J. Pierpont Morgan visited northern Germany, where they were the guests of Kaiser Wilhelm II. The imperial invitation included the promise of a day or so at sea. Griscom, Morgan, and Widener assumed this meant a cruise in the opulent luxury of the imperial yacht *Hohenzollern*, but such was not to be the case. The German emperor took the American captains of industry for a day of racing on the imperial sailing yacht *Meteor*. As Lloyd Griscom later wrote, "It was a rough trip for the old boys, who had done no physical labor since they

The Philadelphia *(ex-*Paris*) is shown after her return to service in August 1901 with quadruple-expansion engines but only two funnels. Harland and Wolff had done a good job of refurbishing her.*

could remember; the Emperor had set them to work immediately hauling ropes. At the end of the day, they were totally exhausted and, having transferred to the palatial *Hohenzollern*, enjoyed a dinner of many courses to the utmost, looking forward to a restful evening over cigars and brandy."[3]

After the huge dinner, the three American millionaires discovered to their horror that their ordeal was not over. To aid his digestion, the Kaiser always stood for a full hour after the evening meal. The three titans of industry, exhausted from the vigorous workout, began to lean up against anything that would take their weight while the Kaiser continued to stand and talk. When Wilhelm II finally sat down, Griscom, Widener, and Morgan collapsed into the nearest chairs. Years later, in the spring of 1908, when Lloyd Griscom was the American ambassador to Rome, he and his wife, Elsa, were invited to a diplomatic banquet given for Kaiser Wilhelm II in Berlin. When the Kaiser strode into the room, his first words to Lloyd Griscom were: "How is your papa? He is an old friend of mine. He helped me sail my boats. Albert Ballin of the North German Lloyd says Mr. Griscom taught him all he knows about steamships."[4] From the Kaiser and, indirectly, from the greatest living German shipping genius, Albert Ballin, those were stunning tributes!

Griscom's national and international standing in 1900 made the industrialist fair game for New York journalists whenever he arrived or departed on a ship. It must be

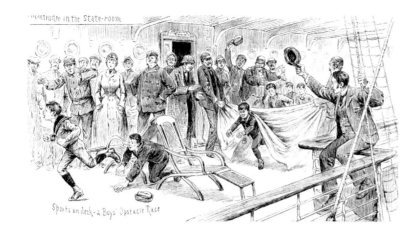

"Sports on Deck—a Boys' Obstacle Race" by F. Opper shows some of the range of homemade entertainment common to transatlantic liners in the days before cruise directors.

added that they rarely got much out of him. On returning from Britain, Griscom was asked whether he had visited Andrew Carnegie (he had not), and whom he was backing for president of the United States (no comment). The passenger list on the *St. Paul* with Griscom included John H. Flagler of Standard Oil, an old business associate; Senator Nelson W. Aldrich of Rhode Island; and Congressmen Payne, Steele, and Dalzell. Griscom and Flagler knew each other because of their mutual interest in oil pipelines and the petroleum industry. Senator Aldrich was an old friend from numerous political battles over the maritime policy of the United States, as also were Congressmen Payne, Steele, and Dalzell. It must have been a convivial group for the crossing.

On September 25, once again the *New York* captured a headline when she fractured her starboard shaft about 370 miles from The Lizard and had to reduce speed in rolling seas until the shaft could be disconnected. She then proceeded to Southampton on one propeller, arriving about 17 hours late. The fracture was a serious one, and as soon as she disembarked passengers, mail, and cargo, she went straight into drydock to have her spare shaft installed. It was imperative that the *New York* maintain her schedule, since the *Paris* was out of service for an indeterminate period while being rebuilt after her disastrous grounding near The Manacles.

In the case of any large liner, such as the *New York*, one of the greatest challenges that the Line faced each week was coaling the ship for another Atlantic dash. The American quartet at full speed consumed between 3,300 and 3,700 tons of coal during each crossing. Their bunkers could carry approximately 4,500 tons, which gave them a margin of about 1,000 tons. Sometimes they reached port with little to spare. As soon as an American Line greyhound docked in *New York*, and even before passengers had begun to disembark, coal lighters swung into position on the opposite side of the ship. They had come down river with 500 to 800 tons of coal on board, and when the steamer was secured, they would begin to pour their cargo into the bunkers of the recently docked ship. Down on the lighters, men shoveled the coal into huge iron buckets. As

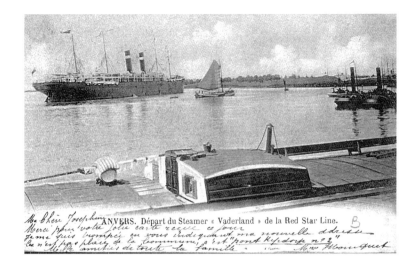

The departure of the International Navigation Company (Red Star Line) steamer Vaderland *(II) from Antwerp, Belgium, shows the liner steaming down the Scheldt River with a sailing barge off her bow.*

each bucket was full, it was swung up and dumped into the chutes leading directly to the ship's bunkers. The monotonous, strenuous work continued around the clock in order to prepare a steamer for her next crossing.

The coaling of the steamer was done by gangs of men employed especially for the work who often worked 12-hour shifts. One reason for starting as soon as a greyhound was tied up at her pier was to give the Line a few hours of grace if anything should go wrong. In 1900, it was realized that any strike by the coalers would prove disastrous to the schedule, since there was no way for the ships to carry any more coal than what was necessary for a normal Atlantic crossing. If any of the ships were delayed more than two days during a crossing, the ability to maintain full speed could be jeopardized. The year-round ordeal of coaling for the American Line was more arduous than for some of its competitors, since the mail contract required the American Line to send one of its principal vessels across the Atlantic every week of the year, regardless of the season. At times in winter, the coal on the lighters at New York might well be frozen into a solid mass by inclement weather. It would have to be thawed with steam pipes before chunks could be pried loose for loading.

Once the coal rumbled into the bunkers, there was plenty of dirty work still to be accomplished before sailing. Coal trimmers had to distribute the fuel so that when the ship sailed, the firemen could get the coal expeditiously. A big ship would need almost an even balance between trimmers and firemen in order to maintain the smooth flow of fuel, with perhaps 50 to 70 of each on duty at any given moment. The work of both groups of men was hot, suffocating, and quite dangerous to all save the strongest. The unventilated bunkers produced a constant swirl of black coal dust, which coated the skin of the half-naked men until they were permanently dyed a dark hue—hence the name, "the black gang." Thermometers in the coal bunkers and the fire rooms on transatlantic greyhounds regularly registered 120 to 130 degrees Fahrenheit or more. The strain was so great that few could stand it for more than four hours, the legal limit of a watch.

When summer heat raised temperatures even more, provision was made for those men who collapsed to be brought on deck for fresh air.

It was considered remarkable that some trimmers and firemen actually survived to retire from such a career. It also was considered remarkable that even men who had fainted usually were able to recover sufficiently to take their next shift. The standard procedure was that if a fireman saw another one about to collapse, a bucket of water was thrown over the fellow's head and he was sent up for a breath of air. This made the work all the more difficult for those who remained, so not too many could have this kind of break in any watch. If those incapacitated exceeded one-third, then the speed of the steamer would be affected and the company would not be pleased. Similarly, if too many neophyte trimmers or firemen were employed for a sailing, then the speed of the ship would be adversely affected. It was stated that several voyages were necessary before a trimmer or fireman could become adjusted to the strenuous, frantic pace and become an efficient part of the "machinery."

On October 27, 1900, the *St. Paul* sailed from Southampton with a full cargo and a substantial passenger list (316 cabin and 245 steerage passengers). Halfway across the Atlantic, on October 31, with a heavy sea running, the liner suddenly lost her starboard propeller and about 10 feet of the shaft, possibly by hitting wreckage. Within seconds, the starboard engine was destroyed. Fortunately, the crisis involved no loss of life, nor did it jeopardize the vessel's safety. The port propeller and engines were intact, and the *St. Paul* continued on to New York at a reduced speed. "So slight were the manifestations of this mishap, and so perfect was the discipline of the crew, that few, if any, of the passengers realized at the time that anything unexpected had occurred."[5]

The destruction of the starboard engine turned out to be substantial. Apparently the starboard propeller came out of the water and started the engines racing. Almost simultaneously, a hidden flaw in the shaft caused it to fracture. Relieved of all load, the engine ran away when the speed governor failed. Within the engine room, the forward end of the crankshaft lifted, stretching the main bearing bolts and cracking the engine seatings. "The stretching of the bolts being greater than the cylinder clearances on top, the result was that the forward H.P. and L.P. pistons went through the heads and a general smash up was started, which but for the presence of mind of the chief engineer, John Hunter, and assistant, Gavin M'Coll [sic], would probably have caused, at least, a repetition of the disaster which befell the SS *Paris* several years ago."[6] Chief Engineer Hunter, on his way to make his 8 o'clock report to Captain Roberts, was walking along the alleyway on the starboard side close to the galley. In the pantry, the builders had installed, as a safety measure, an emergency gear with a stop valve that ran directly to the engine room. Seconds after feeling the shock, the chief engineer flung himself into the galley, yanked the gear, and shut off the flow of steam to the starboard engines. He well knew, however, that the remaining steam in the system would cause the engines to turn over another couple of times, but there was nothing more he could do except pray. Simultaneously, in the engine room, Assistant Engineer Gavin McColl, realizing that a disaster was happening, sought to minimize the damage. McColl was on the starting platform and ran for the reversing lever. He threw the links into neutral and, while the gear was still operative, let steam into both ends of the still-intact intermediate cylinders, thus stopping the engine.

These two men acted with great courage and foresight. McColl's selfless heroism occurred while destruction was going on all about him—cranks bending, gears twisting, and pieces of metal falling. As a result of Hunter's and McColl's actions, the watertight integrity of the *St. Paul* was maintained and she was able to make New York on her port engines.

Once at her berth, the American Line tried to minimize the accident. Acting Manager Samuel Bettle of the International Navigation Company, Griscom's son-in-law, said that the reports of the damage had been greatly exaggerated. This was a lie. He informed the press that he had inspected the starboard engine room and noted only minor damage. Nevertheless, he conceded that it would be several months before the *St. Paul* could return to service. When asked to show the engine room to the press, Bettle declined. " 'No one,' he said, 'would be allowed to see the injured machinery as it was considered one of the American Line's secrets.' "[7] This was a far cry from the openness that had surrounded the accident to the machinery of the *City of Paris* 10 years earlier, but that was before the American Line had secured the valuable mail contract.

The *St. Paul* was given special permission to enter the drydock at the Brooklyn Navy Yard for surveying in order to satisfy the Line and its insurers that the hull was undamaged. Even a quick evaluation underlined the fact that the ship's machinery was seriously damaged and that the starboard engine would have to be replaced. Rebuilding was out of the question. Following the survey, the *St. Paul* left for an extended stay at the Cramp Shipyard in Philadelphia.

Now the American Line had two of its four greyhounds out of service, with no obvious way to resolve the situation quickly. The *St. Paul* would be out of service from November 1900 until May 5, 1901. The *Paris*, undergoing a complete rebuilding at Harland and Wolff, Belfast, was not expected back in commission before midsummer 1901. The International Navigation Company had a big problem. The first-class service of the American Line from New York needed tonnage fast. One solution was to borrow ships from the Red Star Line and from the American Line's Philadelphia service. Almost immediately, the *Kensington* took a November 28 sailing from New York in order to help fill the gap. Meanwhile, John Brown's Shipyard was asked to rush forward the completion of the new Red Star liner *Vaderland*, being outfitted on the Clyde. The Scottish yard put forth a major effort, and the new liner was assigned to take her maiden voyage from Southampton for the American Line. The *Vaderland* sailed from England on December 9, 1900, and would remain in the American Line service for the foreseeable future. At 17 knots, she was slower than the four units of the first-class quartet, but she was slightly larger than any of the other ships. Plus, she was new and available for service!

The *Vaderland* was described as an "intermediate-class" ship, even though her dimensions of 580 feet in length, 60 feet in beam, and 31 feet 4 inches in draft meant she exceeded 12,000 tons and thereby became the largest unit in the fleet. She perpetuated the name of the first ship in the Red Star fleet and was built to conform to the requirement of Lloyd's and the American and British governments. Eleven watertight bulkheads were arranged so that she could remain afloat with any two flooded. The hold and 'tween decks of the vessel were devoted to cargo, with the exception of a space amidships for firemen and aft for stewards. The *Vaderland* could carry 11,000 tons of cargo and 200 tons of water, with additional distillation capacity available. Refrigerated chambers were included for the transportation of meat and perishables. The *Vaderland* had accommodations for 342 first-class, 192 second-class, and 1,000 third-class (or steerage) passengers. Nothing had been spared to make the first-class accommodations attractive. The main dining saloon, which could seat 204, had white woodwork and many oil paintings. The furniture was largely of mahogany, although the sideboards were of satinwood inlaid with various decorative woods. Numerous electric lights and a substantial two-deck-high trunk well, crowned by stained glass, provided the lighting. The kitchens were situated between the first-class dining saloon and the second-class dining saloon, which had seats for 120. Thus, the kitchens and pantries could serve either dining room. On the whole, the *Vaderland* and her three American and British sisters would serve the interests of the International Navigation Company very well indeed and would remain popular for many years.

Two Flemish peasants on a traditional sailing barge watch the modern flagship of the Red Star Line, the Vaderland *(II) (1900) steam up the Scheldt. The beautifully proportioned illustration is by Henri Cassiers (1858–1944).*

Additional ships taking American Line sailings were the *Noordland* on December 30 and the *Southwark* on January 6, 1901, as a piecemeal Southampton–New York service was maintained through the winter months. In January 1901, only one of five sailings from New York was made by a member of the first-class quartet. The *St. Louis* was out for minor repairs, which eliminated three out of four of the first-class ships. The *New York* sailed for Southampton on January 2, followed by the *Kensington* (January 9), *Noordland* (January 16), *Friesland* (January 23), and *Vaderland* (January 30). The best that can be said is that at least there was a weekly sailing to carry the mail. Under these conditions, management must have been pulling its hair, although the replacement units were far less expensive to operate than the first-class ships.

The problems of January 1901 underlined the fact that major decisions had to be made about the future of the International Navigation Company and its principal subsidiaries, the American Line and the Red Star Line. The high cost of building new tonnage in the United States curbed Griscom's enthusiasm for any new replacements for the first-class fleet. This feeling certainly was reinforced by the knowledge that once any new greyhound was commissioned, its earnings stood to be crippled by injurious rate wars. Griscom thought something needed to be done to bring stability to the industry.

Chapter 16

THE INTERNATIONAL
MERCANTILE MARINE (IMM)

T he single most important economic factor at the turn of the century was the creation of trusts. These colossal business organizations set out to control either all the production or all the distribution capacity of an industry, or both. Trusts could be organized along either vertical or horizontal lines of control, but they had to possess a monopoly of a product in order to control pricing and reap substantial profits. All across the economic landscape were examples of huge industrial combinations: Standard Oil; United States Steel; tobacco; sugar; beef. During the period 1899–1902, Clement Griscom and some of his cronies sought to answer the question: Why not shipping? Why not create the largest steamship conglomerate in the world and bring together all the major steamship lines on the North Atlantic so that cutthroat competition no longer could exist?

Griscom discussed this appealing idea with his Philadelphia friend and associate P.A.B. Widener on a number of occasions during 1898, 1899, and the summer of 1900. The concept also was discussed with Bernard Nadal Baker of Baltimore, owner of the Baltimore Storage and Lighterage Company and founder of the Atlantic Transport Company (1881–1934), one of the two most important American-owned steamship enterprises on the North Atlantic.[1] In 1900, the Atlantic Transport fleet was approximately the same size as that of the International Navigation Company. Baker was only 46, but he, like Griscom, had been involved in shipping all his working life. The establishment of ATL in 1881 occurred with the encouragement and assistance of the Pennsylvania Railroad Company. At its conception, the economic judgment was made that American domestic construction and operating costs were too high. Therefore, while the ATL fleet was American financed, its ships were owned through a British subsidiary (Atlantic Transport Company Limited). ATL ordered from British yards; its ships flew the British flag and were manned by British crews. Baker, like Griscom, possessed very broad business interests besides shipping. He was affiliated with one of the largest Pennsylvania coal companies, associated with both the Pennsylvania and Baltimore & Ohio Railroads, and sat on the boards of a number of financial and insurance institutions. Baker enjoyed traveling, and among his international friends were Lord Pirrie of Harland and Wolff, which built most of the Atlantic Transport vessels, and Albert Ballin of HAPAG. Baker's primary shipping interest lay in Baltimore, but in the fall of 1891, he branched out and inaugurated a liner service between London and New York. The ATL agent in Philadelphia was Peter Wright & Sons, Griscom's old firm.

In a dramatic action sketch, Henri Cassiers has one of the big Red Star Liners swinging in the Scheldt River with the assistance of two straining paddle-wheel tugs.

Red Star Line
Antwerp - New York
Antwerp - Boston

In 1896, ATL bought the fleet and goodwill of the National Line of Liverpool, which was down to two ships but had a famous name. When the Spanish-American War broke out, the majority of the ATL fleet was sold to the United States government. Seven ships were transferred by sale and one was donated to the United States to serve as a hospital ship. In 1899, an additional vessel was lent to the British government for use as a hospital ship when the Boer War broke out in South Africa.

Having disposed of his passenger and general cargo fleet on beneficial terms, Baker went shopping and bought the five ships and goodwill of the Wilson & Furness-Leyland Company. This British line, which operated a service between London and New York, had been a competitor of ATL. "Goodwill" alone in this instance cost Baker $1,000,000, but he could afford the price.[2]

After the acquisition of the Wilson & Furness-Leyland Line, Baker considered expansion through purchase or combination with other lines. Merger talks with no less a figure than Albert Ballin were pursued as early as 1891, and again in 1899 and 1900 without coming to fruition. Opportunities in the Caribbean and Latin America were explored, and a freight line was acquired. All this took capital.

The next move to secure additional shipping resources occurred in 1899, when Baker began negotiating a merger with John R. Ellerman of the Leyland Line. Ellerman's Leyland Line dated to 1876 and possessed far-flung maritime interests on the Atlantic, the Caribbean, and the Mediterranean. Ellerman's Leyland Line is not to be confused with the much smaller concern Baker had purchased earlier. The ambitious merger agreement called for the creation of a new British corporation under Ellerman's direction with a capitalization of £5,000,000 ($25,000,000). This endeavor proceeded to the point where it was announced to the stockholders. The new corporation was to commence operations in May 1900 and own Atlantic Transport, Leyland, and two other smaller British lines. Considerable adverse comment was generated in the financial market because the assets of the combined lines barely equaled half of the value of the newly proposed stock. The dilution of equity was substantial. Suddenly, the merger of Atlantic Transport and Leyland stopped dead, even though it had been announced to the public. The possibility of an even bigger plan in the near future may have ended the Atlantic Transport–Leyland merger. Other possible explanations are that Baker no longer wanted day-to-day responsibilities in shipping, and Ellerman was insisting that he join the Leyland board of directors. If Baker was going to have to participate in the management of the fleet, and not be free to do whatever he wanted, then he might as well retain ownership. Ellerman also had been publicly attacked by Furness interests for questionable financial planning, and he may have withdrawn out of anger. Alternatively, Ellerman may just have had second thoughts on the basis of existing freight rates and uncertain future prospects. For whatever reason, the merger of Leyland and Atlantic Transport died in 1900.[3] In Britain, John Ellerman moved ahead on his own, unilaterally increasing Leyland's capital from £1,100,000 to £3,115,000 in order to finance additional expansion plans.

During 1900, J.P. Morgan was creating the billion-dollar merger of corporations that would result in United States Steel. Envisioned was a colossal vertical trust linking cheaply mined Michigan iron ore with scientifically run eastern steel mills and the tremendous moving capacity of the Pennsylvania Railroad. The result would be high-quality American steel so cheap that it could outsell British steel in London and German steel in Berlin.[4] Only one link was missing in this worldwide chain—transportation across the Atlantic Ocean. While Judge Elbert H. Gary sold Morgan on the concept of a steel trust, Clement A. Griscom simultaneously pushed the idea of a shipping trust. To Griscom, such a maritime colossus was an economic idea whose time had come.

The Morgan firm, through its Philadelphia affiliate Drexel & Company, was the International Navigation Company's banker. The Drexel Bank was responsible for floating the new 5 percent first-mortgage bonds of the INC in 1899. Additional assistance had been provided to Griscom since 1898 by the presence on the INC board of directors of P.A.B. Widener and W.L. Elkins, two of Pennsylvania's leading capitalists. A.J. Cassatt, the direct representative of the Pennsylvania Railroad, resigned as part of the restructuring of the INC board to accommodate Widener and Elkins. However, a number of other individuals were directors of both the International Navigation Company and the Pennsylvania Railroad, so close cooperation was assured. Standard Oil Company also was represented on the board of the International Navigation Company. Griscom, because of his great interest in the creation and management of the oil transportation industry, was linked to them. The individuals who served on the INC board must have considered the directorship either a patriotic duty or a personal favor to Griscom, since the American Line paid no dividends for seven years after its creation in 1893. The British and Belgian divisions of INC paid dividends, but the American Line did not until 1900, when it paid 2 percent, and 1901, when it paid 4 percent.

Morgan, Griscom, Baker, and a number of other associates met in the fall of 1900 to discuss the plans for the shipping trust. To Morgan, one of the great benefits of the trust—in addition to ending rate wars—was that the combination of lines would allow a first-class ship to leave New York for Europe every day of the week. "In this way, mails would go forward without delay, and a man who wanted to sail for the other side would not have to wait, unless for his favorite ship. Eventually it would be as simple as going up to the Grand Central Terminal and getting a train to Chicago or San Francisco on any day of the week."[5] The meeting apparently did not go beyond deciding that the new corporation would involve the International Navigation Company and the Atlantic Transport Company.

A legitimate question regarding these proceedings is what did the Morgan firm stand to gain from the creation of these gigantic business trusts? The answer is simple—enormous commissions on a par with the size of each corporation created. The commissions could and did run into the millions of dollars when hundreds of millions of dollars' worth of new stocks and bonds were involved. Furthermore, the Morgan firm could walk away from the infant giants as soon as they were born. The responsibility of the bankers ceased the moment the ink was dry. Some trusts succeeded, others failed, but there was no sense of paternal responsibility here. The Morgan partnership involved only eight members in 1901. Besides the members of the Morgan family—J. Pierpont Morgan, his son, J.P. Morgan, Jr., and son-in-law, Herbert Satterlee (both in their early thirties)—the partners represented a brilliant young cadre of financial minds. Charles Steele was 43; Temple Bowdoin, 37; Robert Bacon, 40; George W. Perkins, 39; and Edward F. Whitney, 48. They stood to share millions of dollars in commissions. Whatever capitalization was felt necessary to achieve the goal of the shipping trust could and would be made available if the Morgan interests were sure they could market the securities.

The climate for international trade could not have been more propitious than at the turn of the century. The year 1900 was enormously successful for international commerce and for the expanding American economy. The total foreign commerce that year exceeded $2 billion for the first time in the history of the nation, and it was $320,252,475 larger than any previous year. Exports far exceeded those of any previous year. More manufactured goods were imported to the United States than ever before. Of even greater significance, American manufactured goods represented a large and growing share of the exports from a nation that heretofore had been most famous as a source of raw materials.

A second meeting of the American shipping magnates led by Griscom and Baker was held later in the fall of 1900. A proposal was discussed for a shipping trust with a capitalization of $115 million consisting of $75 million in preferred stock and $40 million in common. It must be noted that the common stock was largely regarded as a speculative issue without significant value. Dividends might, or might never, be paid. No decision was reached concerning what lines besides Griscom's and Baker's to include in the consortium. Even the agreement of J.P. Morgan to launch such an enterprise was not immediately forthcoming, since he was busy with other proposals.

At another dinner meeting in the fall of 1900, the final decision was made to go ahead with the creation of the United States Steel Corporation. Andrew Carnegie's agreement to sell Morgan his Carnegie Steel Company made possible the new trust, and United States Steel was incorporated in February 1901. The Carnegie price was $400 million, but rumor had it that J.P. Morgan was prepared to go to a billion dollars if necessary to buy out the canny Scot and create the new trust. Griscom and Widener became directors of the giant United States Steel Corporation. Two Morgan partners, Charles Steele and George W. Perkins, also were elected to seats on the board of directors of the steel trust.[6] All four men eventually also would take seats on the IMM board.

Subsequently, when the question was asked about the possibility of creating a shipping trust, Morgan's response was, "It ought to be."[7] The challenge had been accepted and the green light given. Thus, the idea began to grow and develop, eventually giving birth to the most fantastic of all big-business trusts—the International Mercantile Marine. Negotiations rapidly followed in Europe, Great Britain, and America—all swept along by the promise of a tidal wave of American money. The obvious rewards to those who participated swamped most opposition. For various reasons, Morgan and his associates regarded it as important that their plans not become common knowledge too quickly. Therefore, various members of the inner circle of the shipping trust undertook different transactions. Bernard Baker of Atlantic Transport and Samuel Bettle of INC sailed for Britain. Their particular quarry was the Leyland Line, and they were prepared to pay handsomely for it.

Frederick Leyland and Company Limited owned the Leyland Line, which was one of the most successful concerns on the North Atlantic. It had been founded in 1876 and eventually had services from Britain to Canada, the United States, the West Indies, Portugal, and the Mediterranean, and from Belgium to Canada. On the death of Frederick Leyland in 1892, the firm had gone public with stock worth £800,000. Shortly after the Leyland Line became a public corporation, a young accountant, John R. Ellerman, gained control. Under his dynamic leadership, the firm virtually tripled its tonnage in the next decade. The Leyland shares were trading at around £10 and Morgan's representatives offered the shareholders £14 10s—a premium of nearly 50 percent.

John Ellerman was both astute and crafty. He realized that there was no legitimate business alternative but to advise acceptance of the generous offer.[8] The issue was put to the Leyland stockholders: "Is it better that I should sell out my shares to Messrs. Morgan at a very handsome profit or shall I continue in the company as it is and take risks of increased competition in the Atlantic trade?"[9] The owners of Leyland stock acknowledged their good fortune and readily accepted the Morgan offer. At the same time, Ellerman was well aware that some Leyland ships and services did not fit into the Morgan plans. It was also worth something to the trust if Ellerman, personally, would agree to stay out of the United States trade for awhile. The deal to which Ellerman agreed was that after the sale of all the ships and assets of Frederick Leyland and

Company to Morgan, he would be allowed to buy back the vessels in the Portuguese, Mediterranean, and Belgian trades. These services and ships then would run under the label of the "Ellerman Line." In return Ellerman agreed not to compete for a share of the American market for 14 years.[10]

The Leyland deal was consummated on April 26, 1901, putting in place the first piece of the shipping-trust puzzle. This acquisition came hard on the heels of the formation of United States Steel only two months earlier. It was assumed by some observers that since the Leyland fleet contained a number of large freighters capable of carrying steel, the acquisition simply was aimed at guaranteeing inexpensive ocean transportation for the steel trust. The *Daily Express* advised its readership of Morgan's intentions: "He had determined, therefore, to make a sharp aggressive campaign for the steel markets of the world. Prices are to be cut abroad under the cover of heavy profits in America, and every device and trick of the trade is to be used to make the United States Steel Corporation the master in all open markets."[11] Others thought that a large American investment in an oceangoing fleet would stimulate the U.S. Congress to act on a generous subsidy bill, and that the 242,000 tons of shipping in the Leyland fleet soon would be flying the American flag. Some reason had to be found in order to account for the incredibly high price paid for the ships in a falling freight market.

For his part, J.R. Ellerman wrote a biting attack on the British government's free-trade policies, which, when combined with restrictive regulations on steamships, were crippling the British merchant marine. Ellerman thought British shipping companies always would be able to compete if the competition was fair, but the presence of an income tax at the rate of 6 percent of earnings, much more generous immigrant-carrying regulations for foreign-flag tonnage, and antiquated fare regulations made this impossible. When combined with the threat of a major subsidy program on the part of the American government to American-owned shipping, the future for British shipping appeared bleak. This was Ellerman's parting blast, and his justification for accepting the Morgan offer with its generous premium.[12] When the Leyland shareholders met in London, they accepted the Morgan offer by a margin of £1,090,000 out of £1,200,000 outstanding shares.[13] Ellerman took some of his profits and bought the Papayanni Line of Liverpool.[14] The combined fleet's 43,406 tons involved 19 vessels and gave Ellerman by far the largest fleet trading between the United Kingdom and the Mediterranean.

J.P. Morgan traveled to Britain in the spring of 1901 and was in London during the closing stages of the Leyland negotiations. His primary goal was to resume negotiations with Lord Pirrie of Harland and Wolff, the great Northern Ireland shipyard. Pirrie, accompanied by Sir Thomas Lipton, the tea magnate, had visited Morgan in New York, and it was natural for them to exchange visits. In 1899, Pirrie and Lipton had discussed with the American banker the need to curb rampant competition among the steamship lines on the North Atlantic. At that time, the three had tossed around the idea of an interlocking transportation system involving the Pennsylvania Railroad, the International Navigation Company, and others. Harland and Wolff of Belfast, one of the largest shipbuilding yards in the world, had been the principal supplier of tonnage to the White Star Line since 1870. Thus, Pirrie was closely allied to the White Star Line (Oceanic Steam Navigation Company) both as shipbuilder and as one of the principal investors in the line. Morgan decided that no effective trust would be possible without control of White Star. For his part, Lord Pirrie knew that the management and owners of White Star might be susceptible to a generous offer. Thomas H. Ismay, founder of the Oceanic Steam Navigation Company, had died in 1899, and his estate had not been settled yet. His son, J. Bruce Ismay, was the managing director of the White Star Line, but there were others to be considered, and they might want to sell. If the White Star Line were sold to the Morgan trust without Pirrie's benevolent involvement, Harland and Wolff stood to lose one of its most important clients. If Pirrie cooperated with Morgan, he expected assurances that Harland and Wolff would remain the White Star builder and receive other business as well.

Pirrie contacted J. Bruce Ismay of White Star and discussed the ramifications of the proposed shipping corporation. At the very least, Ismay's interest was piqued, and while he protested to the press that White Star was not involved, he traveled to New York on August 28, 1901, for a three-week stay. With him were his principal corporate law attorney, Mr. Dickinson of Hill, Dickinson & Co., and Lord Pirrie. Even in 1901, no one paid the expenses of a top-rank attorney for three weeks for no reason. Negotiations were held at the Waldorf-Astoria Hotel among Ismay, Griscom, and Baker, and the groundwork was laid. The shipping magnates' final session was an elegant, private farewell banquet for Ismay the night before he sailed.[15] When he returned to Liverpool on September 18, he protested: "J. Pierpont Morgan hasn't money enough to buy the White Star Line."[16] This was camouflage. The monetary stakes were enormous, and Ismay, coached by Lord Pirrie, was playing the game for all it was worth. As knowledgeable figures in the international shipping world were aware, Morgan was acting as a promoter of the shipping trust for Clement Acton Griscom. Vernon Brown, the experienced New York agent of Cunard, knowing this, wrote Lord Inverclyde "that it will be found when the facts are made public that the International Navigation Company with all its ramifications is behind all these negotiations."[17]

When Lord Pirrie agreed to participate in the formation of the shipping trust, it was with the understanding that he also would handle the negotiations with yet a third significant British-flag concern, the Dominion Line. Under Pirrie's guidance, the Dominion Line soon became an important unit in the proposed trust.

Many individuals wanted to know what Morgan was up to, and solid information was at a premium. The Cunard Line's premier source was Edward J. Berwind of ATL, who wrote from the Cunard offices in New York to Vernon Brown, who was on a business trip to Liverpool. He said he had talked with Bernard Baker of Atlantic Transport (his boss), who had informed him of the situation. Morgan's plans were to purchase a number of transatlantic steamship lines in order to create a large shipping enterprise. The goal would be to remove the wild fluctuations in ocean passenger rates and to

S.S. "Merion" at Landing Stage, Liverpool.   62398

The Merion *(1902, 11,621 tons, 531 feet by 59 feet, 14 knots) was built by John Brown on the Clyde, with a passenger capacity of 150 second and 1,700 third. Originally ordered by the Dominion Line, she ran for the American Line in the Liverpool–Philadelphia service from 1903 to 1907.*

create stability in freight rates, which would make the great American railroads happy by increasing profitability.[18] No one was to feel threatened by Morgan's acquisitions.

Late in the spring of 1901, when Morgan booked passage for America, he could be well satisfied with the British plans put in motion. Now there were other international avenues that needed to be pursued quickly. Morgan normally crossed on the *Oceanic*, *Teutonic*, or *Majestic*, the first-class units of the White Star Line, his favorite ships, but this time he would cross on a Hamburg-American liner. The reason was simple. The cooperation of the great German lines was essential to the success of the shipping trust. Over the years, Lord Pirrie had carefully cultivated a friendship with Albert Ballin, and Pirrie briefed Morgan on the sensitivities of the great shipping magnate. Ballin was the shipping genius who had brought the Hamburg-American Line to the point where its ships and services embraced the entire world. Pirrie knew Ballin would be delighted that the American financier and friend of the Kaiser was crossing on one of his ships. Another cog in the negotiations was Henry Wilding, head of Richardson, Spence & Company, the American Line's British agency since 1872, who also was an old friend and business associate of Ballin's. The goal of Morgan, working through Pirrie and Wilding, was to swing the enormous economic muscle of Hamburg-American behind the shipping trust. Negotiations with Albert Ballin never were easy. His vigorous leadership of one of the two largest units in the German merchant marine for 30 years made him a legendary figure whose success in competing with rivals was extraordinary.[19]

Ballin returned from a rare vacation and business trip to the Far East in May 1901 to find the Morgan acquisition of Leyland dominating the news. Ballin's round-the-world trip enabled him to survey with a critical eye Hamburg-American operations as well as to evaluate the opposition. In New York, the newspapers had been full of rumors about coming events in ocean transportation. When Ballin sailed from America for Hamburg on the final leg of his trip, he was determined to protect his turf. He was not fooled into thinking that the Morgan moves simply were associated with the steel trust. Ballin immediately drafted a memorandum on the Morgan acquisitions for the imperial German government and for the private eyes of a few friends. This critical analysis, circulated late in the summer, was designed in part to prepare influential German readers for impending changes.

The managing director of Hamburg-American was concerned that if a huge, American-controlled shipping trust were created under Morgan's leadership, then German-flag ships might find themselves at a severe disadvantage in securing cargoes from the American railroads sympathetic to Morgan. In America, Ballin had gone so far as to seek out the president of the Pennsylvania Railroad Company, who had assured him that the giant railroad had no intention of signing a preferential agreement with any shipping trust, even one financed by J.P. Morgan. The fact that the management of the PRR even had a response ready for Ballin's question was enough to increase his sense of apprehension. Ballin knew as well as anyone who sat on which boards of directors and how they interlocked. If the threat of being cut out of the American eastbound trade was not enough, there also was the possibility that the American financier might make a hostile takeover bid for the stock of the Hamburg-American Line. Ballin wanted to avoid this at all costs.[20] Ballin's goals in the subsequent negotiations were to maintain the independence of Hamburg-American while retaining the goodwill of the Morgan shipping trust.

Even before Ballin's ship docked at Hamburg, feelers went out by wireless to his old friend Lord Pirrie, who may or may not have been surprised at hearing from Ballin. During the summer of 1901, open letters and secret messages crackled over the communications systems between Hamburg, Belfast, London, and New York. Ballin traveled to Britain, where negotiations were held in London. Initially, the American interests apparently wanted to buy 18 of the finest HAPAG steamers and leave the matter at that level. Ballin had no desire to see the cream of his fleet transferred to a foreign flag, and he refused. Yet supposedly he still had in the back of his mind the threat of the American railroads ganging up against any steamship lines not connected to the trust.[21] After much maneuvering, the first draft of an agreement between the Morgan trust and Hamburg-American was drafted on September 10. Ballin's biggest challenge proved to be his own board of directors, who were fearful of both the economic and the political ramifications of any agreement with the shipping trust.[22] After many meetings and vigorous discussions, Ballin won the unanimous consent of the Hamburg-American board for his negotiations with Lord Pirrie and Henry Wilding, representing the Morgan trust. But this was not enough—not in the German Empire, where the ruler loved his navy and his

The Haverford *(1901, 11,635 tons, 531 feet by 59 feet, 14 knots). Built by John Brown, she and the* Merion *were sisterships. Switched around by the International Mercantile Marine, she ran for the American Line from 1902 to 1908.*

merchant marine. Ballin knew that he could not begin to execute any agreement with a foreign trust unless he had the support of both Kaiser Wilhelm II and the chancellor, Count Bulow. Fortunately for his plans, Ballin had direct access to the All Highest whenever he needed it.

Ballin's meeting with the Kaiser as usual had to be planned carefully. Those around Wilhelm II were capable of preparing the ground and influencing him. If new ideas were to be comprehended and imperial support solicited, court figures had to be forewarned, and the Kaiser had to be obliquely familiarized with the situation. When the managing director of Hamburg-American finally received the summons from Berlin to attend upon His Imperial Majesty, the climate had to be favorable. The Kaiser's curiosity could not be contained for long, and Ballin traveled to Berlin on October 16, 1901, to explain the negotiations and the proposed agreements. To Wilhelm II, it was crucial that Hamburg-American retain its independence, and Ballin was able to reassure him on this point. Then the Kaiser and Ballin went over the draft of the agreement with the shipping trust, point by point, and Wilhelm II made a number of revisions in the text! The meeting between the All Highest and Ballin went on for several hours, and *thorough* is not adequate to describe the grilling Ballin received. At the end of the audience, Kaiser Wilhelm II "announced his unqualified approval of the plan but also charged Ballin with seeing that the Lloyd as well was brought into affiliation with the trust."[23] When an exhausted Ballin returned to Hamburg, he felt an enormous sense of relief. Yet the fight was not over.

The Kaiser's command that North German Lloyd be included in any agreement with the shipping trust already was in the process of being honored before it was received. On October 17, the day after his long meeting with the Kaiser, Ballin met with representatives of the German Imperial Government and Dr. Heinrich Wiegand, managing director of North German Lloyd. At the meeting were high-ranking representatives of the Foreign Office and the Naval Office. The stated purpose of the session was to discuss "measures to protect German steamship lines from falling into American hands."[24] Wiegand was not convinced of the "shipping-trust peril," and, as Hamburg-American's dedicated rival, he was not prepared to agree to anything. Wiegand cabled Gustav Schwab, his New York agent, to consult his Cunard counterpart, Vernon Brown, to see if there was any truth to the rumor that a controlling interest in Cunard had been sold to the Morgan interests. They were relieved to learn that Cunard was still independent but were troubled to learn that White Star must be involved some way. As Brown told Schwab, "According to the old saying, where there is so much smoke there must be some fire."[25]

Ballin's careful negotiations with the shipping trust appeared to be unraveling amid German dissension, and he was deeply concerned. "Writing in 1900 in support of Tirpitz's early naval expansion, Ballin described how he viewed the world as a jungle: 'In the hard struggle between the nations for air and light, ultimately, only raw power decides. Diplomatic finesse and political chess, alliances and declarations of neutrality. . . ultimately are only effective when backed up by real power.' "[26] So great was Ballin's concern that the good offices of the Kaiser were called upon to calm the waters and settle differences. In pre-1914 Germany, only the All Highest could bring together Hamburg and Bremen. Ballin and Wiegand were commanded to have supper with the Kaiser. With Hamburg on his right and Bremen on his left, Wilhelm II mediated by bullying. He sided with Ballin against Wiegand and berated the managing director of North German Lloyd as an "obstinate Frisian."[27] However, before the evening was over, Ballin realized that Wiegand's principal objection to the plan was a stock-distribution clause that might require the transfer of small amounts of stock in the German lines to the shipping trust on some future dates. Ballin saw the light, and the agreement was modified to eliminate any stock transfer. The clause was replaced by one calling for a dividend payment. Both North German Lloyd and Hamburg-American could accept this, and peace was achieved between the German giants. The Kaiser was pleased, and Ballin probably felt like he needed another long ocean voyage to recover. The Kaiser's and Wiegand's revisions were incorporated into the draft agreement and forwarded to Pirrie on November 6, 1901.

Events moved ahead rapidly in the fall of 1901, and it was clarified in the American press that J.P. Morgan was acting entirely in his professional capacity as a banker for

A Flemish family watches a Red Star liner steam by in this illustration by Henri Cassiers.

The Vaderland *(1900) or one of her three sisters is shown at the Société Anonyme de Navigation Belge-Américaine (Red Star Line) quay at Antwerp, Belgium. Steam is up so she probably is ready to sail.*

Clement Griscom where the shipping trust was concerned. Pennsylvania Railroad interests were credited with having a major financial interest in the proposed purchases of foreign-flag tonnage. With regard to this, it was explained that the interlocking directorates among the Pennsylvania Railroad, the International Navigation Company, and Atlantic Transport were so close that they were the "equivalent to community of ownership management in its broadest sense."[28]

In the dead of winter, the big White Star liner *Celtic* sailed from Liverpool on January 15 with a very distinguished passenger list:

> The *Celtic* had on board J. Bruce Ismay, chairman of the Board of Directors of
> the White Star Line; the Right Hon. William James Pirrie, chairman of the
> Harland and Wolff Shipbuilding Company, of Belfast, a former Lord Mayor of

that city and a director of the Leyland and White Star Lines; Henry Wilding, English Agent of the International Navigation Company, recently elected chairman of the Board of Directors of the Leyland Line; W.S. Graves, director of the White Star Line, and Messrs. Neville and Dickinson, maritime lawyers of Liverpool, who were said to have come at the insistance of Mr. Ismay.[29]

None of the prominent personages would admit to traveling on the *Celtic* for any reason related to a sale of the White Star Line. Ismay and his lawyers were going to New York on a private matter. Pirrie and Graves were surveying the *Celtic* in order to see what she would need for a future cruise. Henry Wilding was traveling to New York to generate new business for Leyland, and his presence aboard the *Celtic* with the others was nothing but coincidence. Yet people of importance across the United States knew who was arriving on the *Celtic*. Waiting on the pier to greet the visiting maritime dignitaries were Clement Acton Griscom, Jr., and James A. Wright, vice president of the International Navigation Company.

Clement Acton Griscom himself traveled from Philadelphia to New York for the purpose of meeting with his British counterparts. The rumor mill mentioned the possibility of a dinner in Philadelphia the following Sunday.[30] In Philadelphia, W.H. Barnes, director of the Pennsylvania Railroad and of the International Navigation Company, "declared that the visit of the representatives of the English steamship companies who are now in this country had no other purpose than a desire to get together and harmonize on the question of ocean steamship rates and other matters pertaining to the business."[31] The "harmonizing" would produce a mighty chorus.

Throughout the negotiations over the next 10 days, Vernon H. Brown, the Cunard Line agent in New York, had an informant, E.J. Berwind of the Atlantic Transport Line, within the meetings who kept him abreast of the deliberations. Brown faithfully cabled or wrote all he learned to Lord Inverclyde, chairman of Cunard, in Liverpool. Griscom and Baker, in their deliberations with Ismay, wanted the whole of the White Star Line, not just the North Atlantic services. This proved a sticking point. The Waldorf-Astoria Hotel was a hotbed of intrigue as bits and pieces of information emerged. Ismay, Graves, Pirrie, and their two British maritime lawyers haggled over the final details with the team of American bankers and lawyers. Ultimately, on the afternoon of February 4, the negotiations moved to the offices of J.P. Morgan and Company, where Charles Steele, one of Morgan's brilliant younger partners, served as the principal facilitator for Griscom. In fact, when the meeting moved to the Morgan offices, it was actually to sign the purchase agreements. Time certainly was short, because Ismay was scheduled to sail with most of his group on the *Oceanic* the next day, and they did so with the agreement in their possession.[32]

Everyone wanted to know what was happening, and the management of the Cunard Line was particularly concerned. Cunard had established an "educational fund" for Vernon Brown, its principal agent in New York, to use as he saw fit to further the interests of the line in America. A war chest in excess of $10,000 was involved; when Brown

informed Lord Inverclyde in April 1902 that he had about $2,700 left, the Cunard chairman added another £1000 ($5,000) to it. This slush fund served as secret lobbying money for use in Washington or New York. It apparently was used to secure information from any and all sources, to wine and dine appropriate individuals, and, if possible, to influence political personages. Corporate espionage was rampant. Brown and Inverclyde so thoroughly mistrusted the security of their own transatlantic cables that they always sent messages in a special Cunard Line code and had special names for such individuals as Griscom (GROOM) and Henry Wilding (WEEP).[33] The "educational fund" also helped to create a favorable working relationship with some of the New York newspapers and journalists. When a highly favorable article on the proposed American steamship subsidy bill appeared in one newspaper, an editorial attacking the subsidy bill immediately appeared in the *New York Post.* Brown's comment to Inverclyde: "You will see that the Editor of the *Post* disposes of it in a very few lines (which lines were sent from 29 Broadway)."[34] "29 Broadway" was the New York address of Vernon Brown's office and of the Cunard Steam Ship Company Limited in New York.

When Ismay sailed from New York on the *Oceanic* on February 5, 1902, the liner also carried a letter from Brown to Inverclyde written in great haste in order to catch the last mails at the White Star dock. Once again, Brown proved his enormous reliability and worth to Inverclyde. Brown wrote about the secret agreements signed the previous afternoon:

> From what I can learn this morning I am satisfied that the White Star outfit
> including all services and also the Dominion Line have been acquired by the
> Morgan Syndicate, and that an American Company will be formed as the par-
> ent company—the different companies will be nominally run separately as at
> present, each Company managing its own business but presumably subject to
> the central company on matters of policy, Mr. Morgan and his friends to have a
> controlling interest in stock and an American Board of Direction.[35]

The business negotiations of the leading figures in the future shipping trust were not as secret as they would have liked. If the days were filled with hard negotiating, the evenings saw one great Victorian banquet after another. When Edward Berwind hosted a dinner (February 1) on behalf of the Atlantic Transport Line, even Vernon Brown of Cunard was invited to join the group. This placed him in a difficult position. The way the newshounds were following the proceedings, if the word ever got out that a Cunard representative was at dinner with such a group, the ramifications could be enormous. Accordingly, Brown declined the invitation and remained content with the information gathered from his reliable informants. Since so much of the information Brown obtained was from highly confidential sources that could not be compromised without harming his and Cunard's position, Inverclyde was faced with a dilemma. The chairman of the Cunard Line wanted to tell the British government some of what he knew in order to begin negotiations with them on Cunard's behalf, but he was concerned about protecting Brown's sources. Inverclyde finally asked Brown's permission to open communication with the British government, provided he was very discreet.[36]

Inverclyde commented to Brown: "I am still somewhat surprised that we should be left out of such a combination. Can you not, through any of your friends, find out the reason for this, and also whether it is likely that we may yet be approached. Of course even if we are not, I am still unable to see that much harm can be done us, and on the other hand I cannot help wondering how the White Star Company can be part and parcel of an American Syndicate, and still continue their agreements with the British Government."[37]

Brown cabled Inverclyde that he did not mind if the information he gathered was shared with trusted members of the Cunard board, but he was very reticent to have it discussed with any member of the British government, since he thought "it would be injudicious and premature" before any formal announcements of the takeovers were made in Britain by those concerned.[38] Brown did not see much reason for questioning the position of the new shipping trust with regard to Cunard. In his view, Cunard had fallen so far behind the competition—with two 17-year-old single-screw steamers (*Umbria* and *Etruria*) and two eight-year-old ships (*Campania* and *Lucania*)—that they could be ignored.

On February 4, the first contracts laying the foundation for the shipping trust also were signed with Griscom of International Navigation and Baker of Atlantic Transport. These established the financial terms under which their steamship lines were acquired by the trust. The International Navigation Company was valued at $14,205,000. The method of payment was an exchange of stock in the new corporation. The old 8 percent noncumulative preferred shares of the International Navigation Company, Inc., were exchanged on an equal basis for the new 6 percent cumulative preferred stock of the International Mercantile Marine Corporation, valued at $9,205,000. The common stockholders in the International Navigation Company were persuaded to accept one share of IMM common for every two shares of INC, which was valued at $2,500,000.

The Haverford *(1901) is shown in the American Line service (1902–8) from Philadelphia to Liverpool with the British and American flags crossed overhead.*

The remaining $2,500,000 of common stock paid by IMM for INC was simply described as an "additional payment." Almost certainly that sum represented the commissions paid to Clement Acton Griscom and his closest associates for their services in bringing about the creation of the International Mercantile Marine Corporation. Similar benefit packages were granted to other expediters of other steamship acquisitions. There were enormous amounts of money to be made by the creators of a trust, but only if you realized your profit quickly.

Baker's Atlantic Transport Company, registered in West Virginia, was valued at $13,716,000. In this case, there were no preferred shareholders. Holders of common stock in ATL received three new shares of IMM preferred, worth $9,000,000, plus a bonus of one share of common stock in the trust, worth an additional $3,000,000. A $15 dividend, declared for ATL shareholders of record, involved a cash payment of $450,000. Almost certainly Bernard Baker was the recipient of the additional $109,000 of IMM preferred stock and $1,157,000 of common stock. Baker remained on the IMM board but took no active role in running the new corporation. On the other hand, P.A.S. Franklin, vice president of ATL and Baker's second in command, became a vice president of the IMM. It is known that Baker made gifts of stock as severance pay to longtime employees who were losing their jobs in the steamship consolidation. These shares would have significant value only if sold immediately. Time would make them virtually worthless.

These acquisitions paved the way for the final round of negotiations to determine the prices to be paid for the White Star and Dominion Lines, and for their managing agencies. Basically, the valuation placed upon the British companies was 10 times 1900 earnings, less depreciation and less earnings from government charters. The payment

Red Star Line.
Antwerpen-NewYork.
Antwerpen-Philadelphia.

On the Banks, July 20th
Bound for Halifax, thence Queenstown.

The Vaderland *(1900) is described as a twin-screw mail steamer. The card was written by a passenger when the ship was off the Grand Banks, Nova Scotia, bound for Halifax and Queenstown en route to Liverpool, July 20, 1902.*

was 25 percent in cash and 75 percent in preferred stock at par, with a bonus of common stock amounting to half of the preferred. Any value for the common shares would depend upon the expansion of future business and earnings.

The price established for the Oceanic Steam Navigation Company Limited was $51,885,188! This was an astonishing figure, even given the eminence of the White Star Line in 1901. Ismay had struck a hard bargain and may never have expected his demands to be accepted. The price paid for OSNC involved $24,502,358 in IMM 6 percent cumulative preferred shares, a 50 percent bonus of $12,251,179 in IMM common shares, interest until distribution, and reimbursement for payments on new ships that now would be delivered to IMM. An additional sum of slightly less than $190,000, deducted from the purchase price, represented severance payments to employees losing their positions because of the merger.

The purchase price for Ismay, Imrie & Company, the managing agency for the Oceanic Steam Navigation Company, was set at $7,371,677. This figure in fact should be added to the total paid for OSNC, since it was an associated expense. Members of the Ismay firm not taken into the management of the IMM agreed to retire from the North Atlantic business for at least 14 years. J. Bruce Ismay remained the president of the OSNC and formed a new firm with Harold A. Sanderson to represent their interests. Here the payment involved 25 percent cash, 75 percent IMM preferred stock, and a bonus of 37.5 percent IMM common stock. The "commission" paid to the White Star facilitators, presumably Bruce Ismay and Lord Pirrie, was $783,963 of IMM preferred and $391,982 of IMM common stock.

The price paid by the International Mercantile Marine Corporation for Frederick Leyland and Company Limited was $11,964,275, which already had been established by Morgan as the figure agreed upon for Leyland the previous year. The Dominion Line, Mississippi & Dominion Line, and British and North American Steam Navigation Company Limited were consolidated in the acquisition because of interlocking ownership and cost the IMM $5,703,348. The managing agency for Dominion and associated lines was Richards, Mills & Company, which was acquired by the shipping trust for an additional $2,520,222. In the case of this acquisition, an enormous "additional payment" included in the total was $808,175 in IMM preferred and $404,087 in IMM common shares paid to Richards, Mills & Company. This probably was required, since the firm was expected to close its doors and cease business activities.

The decision was made by Griscom and the other directors of the International Mercantile Marine Corporation to spend approximately $20,000,000 on new tonnage and the retirement of previous obligations. The exact distribution of funds would take some time to work out. All the lines had ships on order or under construction that had to be completed. General guidelines for distribution of the modernization fund in December 1902 involved White Star $4,000,000, Dominion $3,500,000, Atlantic Transport $6,500,000, and International Navigation $3,000,000.

Organizational expenses for the creation of the shipping trust were a paltry $652,429. However, the second largest figure after the sum paid for White Star was the commission paid to the members of the banking syndicate, led by J.P. Morgan. Altogether, the members of the IMM syndicate were paid $2,000,000 of IMM preferred stock and $22,500,000 of common stock for underwriting the $50,000,000 bond issue. J.P. Morgan's firm itself collected $7,575,051 in cash, $500,000 in IMM preferred stock, and $2,500,000 in common stock for its role in the proceedings.[39] The bankers who stood as godfathers to the shipping trust walked away with their pockets jingling.

No sooner were the British shipping magnates steaming out of New York Harbor on the *Oceanic* (February 5, 1902) than their German counterparts arrived on the *Kaiser Wilhelm der Grosse* (February 12). The crew of the German ship must have had a fit at seeing President George Plate and Dr. Heinrich Wiegand of the North German Lloyd arrive on board at Bremen. Just imagine their additional joy at learning their bosses were to be accompanied by President E. Tietgens and Managing Director Albert Ballin of Hamburg-American. Any one of those powerful men could make a crew nervous, let alone all four in an unprecedented situation. The crossing from Bremen to New York via Southampton appears to have been uneventful, however, and the *Kaiser Wilhelm der Grosse* slowly edged into her Hoboken pier on February 12. Again there was a welcome scene, with American Line dignitaries greeting their German guests.

Since virtually all the leading shipping magnates were known to each other on a personal basis, Tietgens and Ballin specifically took the time to meet with Vernon Brown of Cunard on February 14. A lengthy discussion ensued, during which Ballin indicated to Brown by his questions and observations that he was not totally sure of what had been agreed upon between Griscom and Ismay. Ballin even went so far as to question Brown about whether or not Ismay would remain the managing director of White Star. Ballin may have liked Lord Pirrie, but he was not overly fond of Ismay; he regarded Ismay as a disturbing influence in the transatlantic market. At the same time, Ballin was less than forthcoming with Brown when he told him that the four German maritime leaders simply had crossed "to fully discuss rates with the American

Combination and adopt a protective Policy to their mutual advantage. . . ."[40] Brown may have had difficulty keeping a straight face, since he had known for 10 days that the German lines had concluded arrangements with the Griscom syndicate, even if they had not been bought by the Americans.

Six days later, on February 20, 1902, the agreement was signed between the German lines and the Morgan representatives to cooperate in all areas of passenger and immigrant traffic on the North Atlantic. None of the concerns would acquire any shares of stock in each other. All signatories agreed to support each other against outside competition. IMM would not send ships to German ports without the consent of the German companies and the Germans would restrict their calls at British ports. Additional agreements covered the French and Belgian ports, and a plan was agreed to for pooling passenger traffic. Cooperation among the parties was scheduled to begin on January 1, 1903. The shipping trust guaranteed to Hamburg-American a dividend of 6 percent, but Ballin had to agree to surrender a portion of any earnings over that figure. The agreement between the IMM and the German lines was to last 20 years with the option to withdraw in 10 years. All provisions were void if war broke out.

The deal looked good on paper, and Ballin probably heaved a sigh of relief, since some of the initial discussions had appeared aimed at total acquisition of HAPAG by the shipping trust through an exchange of shares. Peace was bought dearly, however. Between 1903 and 1911, the Hamburg-American Line earned an average dividend of 7.2 percent and ended up paying the American shipping trust more than 1.5 million marks as the price of its independence.[41] This was the most successful business deal the Morgan interests negotiated. Conversely, the agreement to guarantee the dividend of North German Lloyd on the same terms backfired when NGL earned only an average of 4 percent in the same years, and the Bremen concern received payments totaling around 4.5 million marks from the shipping trust.[42]

For the future, the relationship between the IMM and the German lines was to be overseen by a committee sitting alternatively in London and Cologne. The four members were Albert Ballin (for Hamburg-American), Dr. Heinrich Wiegand (for North German Lloyd), and Lord Pirrie and Henry Wilding for the IMM. So far as Albert Ballin was concerned, this arrangement resulted in parity between the Americans and English on one hand and the Germans on the other.

The decision also was made to acquire the Holland-America Line (Nederlandsch-Amerikaansche Stoomvaart Maatschappij), the small but highly respected Dutch concern that in 1902 owned 86,768 tons of shipping. Lord Pirrie approached the owners of Holland-America in February 1902 with an offer from Harland and Wolff to buy 51 percent of the Dutch line on generous terms. The number of NASM shares was increased by approximately 25 percent, and 51 percent of the total shares were sold to the Belfast shipyard. The Dutch agreed to the sale with the understanding that Harland and Wolff was seeking an investment opportunity. Substantial anger was generated in Rotterdam when it was learned that Lord Pirrie had no intention of retaining the shares

Westbound the American Line vessels often crossed from Southampton to Cherbourg for the convenience of continental passengers before setting course for New York. The New York *is shown here in 1903 after she was virtually rebuilt by the Cramp Shipyard.*

and merely had acted as agent for the American shipping trust. In fact, the truth was even worse because the shares Pirrie bought were divided 26 percent to the IMM, 12.5 percent to Hamburg-American, and 12.5 percent to North German Lloyd.[43] Ruffled Dutch feelings were smoothed by guarantees that Holland-America would remain Dutch. Managerial salaries also were doubled! Furthermore, the monopoly of the Rotterdam–New York trade would be preserved, and the dividends of the line would be guaranteed at the same rate paid on IMM shares. In 1910–11, the IMM distributed its Holland-America shares to White Star and Atlantic Transport. During World War I, the Dutch interests were able to buy back control of the line.[44]

The corporate organization of the shipping trust in February 1902 had to deal with the realities of international ownership. At the top was the International Navigation Company Inc. of New Jersey, which owned the International Navigation Company Limited of Britain. INC Ltd., in turn, owned all the shares of White Star, Frederick Leyland, Dominion, and their various agencies and subdivisions. Morgan had until April 30, 1902 (90 days), in which to create a syndicate capable of underwriting and selling a $50 million bond issue. Morgan had been successful in floating a number of huge bond issues, and the IMM syndicate was soon oversubscribed. Once the bonds were sold, the money was available for the final step in the creation of the shipping trust. The International Mercantile Marine Company, on whose behalf the bonds had been sold, was established under the laws of New Jersey on October 1, 1902. Subsequently, IMM formally acquired the International Navigation Company, and Griscom became the first president of the International Mercantile Marine. The shipping trust was born, even if troubled waters lay ahead, since the investment necessary to create it exceeded $185 million.

The financial affairs of the International Mercantile Marine Company were severely influenced by an economic downturn that already was underway in 1902, and by a severe recession in the United States by the middle of that decade. The assumption on the part of the IMM management that earnings would steadily increase was unwarranted.

"Average earnings of the acquired companies for the five years 1898–1902, before depreciation but excluding income from government chartering in the war years, had amounted to about $6,500,000, and with augmented tonnage, income of about $9,000,000 was expected. The annual service charges on the 4.5% bonds and the 6% cumulative preferred amounted to $5,850,000. One provision of the common stock issue was that dividends would be restricted to 10% until the entire new bond issue was retired."[45] In a time of prosperity this might have been possible, but not in a time of economic adversity.

Critics of the shipping trust were quick to voice their well-founded criticism of its finances. It appeared as though the IMM had paid about $185 a ton for the million tons of shipping acquired. In comparison, Albert Ballin valued the huge fleet of Hamburg-American at about $47 a ton! The capitalization of the IMM involved ratios never before dreamed of, ones that appeared totally unrealistic.[46] The respected British maritime publication *Fairplay* caustically commented, "It would be quite interesting to see how the capital of thirty-nine millions sterling could possibly be justified, and it would even be more interesting to see how dividends on such capital, which contains almost as much water as the Atlantic itself, could possibly be earned."[47]

The prices paid for the stock of the early purchases, including the White Star Line, greatly exceeded the earning capacities of those companies. While the example of White Star frequently has been cited by critics, the stock history of the International Navigation Company of New Jersey does not represent an edifying fiscal spectacle. Technically, the INC entered the shipping trust with a capital deficit! Common shareholders in the INC had not received a dividend since the creation of the American Line in 1893 and the incorporation of the company. Preferred stockholders had received a partial dividend only in 1900 and 1901. In view of this situation, the terms afforded the investors in the INC may be viewed as generous. The INC preferred shareholders received a share-for-share exchange of their old 8 percent noncumulative for the new 6 percent cumulative preferred shares of IMM. The holders of INC common stock received one-half share of the new common stock, which technically had only a "bonus value." The common shareholders exchanged worthless stock for expectations. The IMM common stock was to receive dividends only after the interest on the bonds and the preferred stockholders were covered. Later, in some of the intracorporate transactions and deals of 1902 and 1903, the IMM common stock was assigned a value of $18, but no justification for this figure has ever emerged.[48] The comment of the *Wall Street Journal* on the creation of the great trusts of 1900–1902 was: "Caesar, Hannibal and Napoleon were pigmies in their attempted readjustment of national relations compared with the commercial giants of today."[49]

Shipping always was a fickle industry dependent upon too many variables of trade and commerce for the discipline of a trust to be effective. Hard on the heels of the creation of the shipping trust, freight rates from American East Coast ports to Europe dropped from a high in 1899 of $.97 per quarter (480 pounds) to a low of $.33 in 1901, and they were running at $.55 early in 1902, when the trust was born. Furthermore, coal prices had risen, and with them the overall cost of operating steamships. In the future, the years 1899 to 1901 would be regarded as one of the most profitable periods for steamship operation in 50 years, and the prices paid for the component parts of the IMM were based upon that time span. In 1901, the end of the Boer War brought significant tonnage back on the North Atlantic. Freight rates began to dip, with too many ships pursuing even the large amount of cargo crossing the ocean. By the end of 1901, ship resale prices fell 25 percent on the open market. As a result of all these factors, Cunard announced early in 1902 that it was cutting in half the high dividend rate of 1900, and the German corporations prudently reacted in a similar manner. The future was at least questionable, if not bleak.

One of the most beautiful of Henri Cassiers' views of Red Star ships shows a traditional sailing barge passing one of the big 12,000-ton quartet heading down the Scheldt River bound for the open sea. The lithograph was by De Rycker & Mendel, Brussels, around 1905.

Chapter 17

THE PYRRHIC VICTORY

The St. Louis *is shown in an attractive port-side view that shows the vessel very well. She also would serve the United States during World War I as the U.S. Navy transport* Louisville.
U.S. Naval Historical Center photograph

The management of the International Mercantile Marine Company brought together an interesting collection of personalities who among them possessed an awe-inspiring array of American and international directorships. It is impossible to indicate all the affiliations of every member of the management, but a few examples may prove illuminating. President of the IMM was Clement Acton Griscom, founder and president of the International Navigation Company, director of United States Steel, and director of a number of Philadelphia-based financial, insurance, and oil-pipeline companies. The vice president in the United States was P.A.S. Franklin (from Atlantic Transport Line), and the vice president in Britain was Sir Clifton E. Dawkins (partner, J.P. Morgan). Treasurer was James Swartz (INC), secretary was Emerson E. Parvin (INC), assistant to the president and manager of the insurance department was Rodman E. Griscom (INC and son of the president), and general counsel was Francis L. Stetson (U.S. Steel and J.P. Morgan).

The board of directors in the United States, besides Griscom, included P.A.B. Widener (INC, U.S. Steel, and many others), Bernard N. Baker (ATL), E.J. Berwind (ATL), John I. Waterbury (Manhattan Trust Company), James H. Hyde (Equitable Life Insurance), George W. Perkins (partner, J.P. Morgan; U.S. Steel; N.Y. Life), Charles Steele (partner, J.P. Morgan; U.S. Steel).

The board of directors in Britain included, besides Sir Clifton E. Dawkins, William J. Pirrie (Lord Pirrie) (Harland and Wolff), J. Bruce Ismay (White Star Line), Henry Wilding (Richardson, Spence) (American Line, INC), Charles F. Torrey (ATL). The

RED STAR LINE.

TWIN-SCREW S.S. " LAPLAND „
18,694 TONS.

The creation of the International Mercantile Marine in 1902 brought the construction of some large new ships. One such vessel was the Lapland *(1909) built by Harland and Wolff for the Red Star Line, which at 17,540 tons was 5,000 tons larger than any other vessel in the fleet. Statistics were 606 feet by 70 feet, with a cruising speed of 17 knots and an enormous passenger capacity of 450 first, 400 second, and 1,500 third.*

Executive and Finance Committee, the most important subcommittee of the board of directors, consisted of five members—Griscom, Widener, Perkins, Berwind, and Steele.

The managers of the operating subdivisions of the IMM were: American and Red Star Lines (in USA), Clement Acton Griscom, Jr.; White Star Line, J. Bruce Ismay; Atlantic Transport Line (in New York), P.A.S. Franklin; Atlantic Transport Line (in Britain), C.F. Torrey; Leyland, Dominion, and American Lines (in Britain), Henry Wilding. All of the individuals concerned had their work cut out for them.

From its inception, the most important goal of the IMM was to have the U.S. Congress pass a new and meaningful subsidy bill for the American merchant marine. Griscom had sought this for a quarter of a century—since the very inception of American and Red Star. In 1900, the shipping legislation placed before Congress had emphasized the fact that the future profitable employment of American farming, manufacturing, and mining depended upon the creation and operation of a strong merchant marine.

The bill had not passed. During the winter of 1901–2, efforts were renewed for the passage of a shipping subsidy bill. It was universally acknowledged that without a government subsidy program, it was impossible to build and operate a first-class fleet under the American flag. Costs of ship construction and manning exceeded foreign-flag tonnage by approximately 30 percent. One of the reasons why Griscom, Morgan, and their closest associates tried to keep the acquisitions and deliberations as quiet as possible in

1901 was to avoid irritating any wavering member of Congress who might vote for the bill. Trusts were not universally admired, and Theodore Roosevelt was president of the United States. Ideally, the new ships being built for the American Line and the Atlantic Transport Line in the United States would be commissioned in time to reap the benefits of the new legislation. It also was hoped that the equal number of new ships under construction for Red Star and ATL in Britain would receive favorable consideration, even to the extent of being permitted American registry. After all, the *City of New York* and the *City of Paris* had been granted limited American registry in 1892 in response to the Line's promise to build similar or larger vessels in the United States. Projecting this formula ahead, then it should have been possible to pair the new American- and foreign-built construction of the IMM and make many of the ships eligible for the new subsidy. The result would be enough additional income to provide financial stability to the various lines of the shipping trust. One sarcastic observer commented, "A subsidy policy by this government would be just about the right thing to give value to the water in the capitalization of the steamship trust."[1]

The 1901–2 steamship subsidy bill was introduced by no less a figure than Senator Marcus Hannah of Ohio, chairman of the Republican Party. It was supported by Griscom, who testified on its behalf before Congress, and by most of the Philadelphia civic, commercial, and manufacturing groups. Proponents of the legislation emphasized that not only would it strengthen the American merchant marine, but it also would support the United States Navy in the future by providing a supply of indispensable auxiliary and support vessels in time of national crisis. Opponents of the legislation, which constituted a vocal minority of the Senate Committee, lashed out at the bill as "wrong in principle, unjust, vicious, pure class legislation. . . ."[2] The opponents said the bill would tax Americans from all walks of life for the benefit of a few wealthy shipowners. Rich corporations should not be the beneficiaries of public subsidies, they insisted. The point also was made that the International Navigation Company "already was receiving for mail carriage about six times as much as White Star and North German Lloyd were paid for about an equal amount of work."[3] Clement Griscom vociferously denied this, stating that the conditions of service required of the American Line were much stiffer than those of the foreign lines, which were not required to run their best first-class tonnage year-round.

Unfortunately for the IMM, American shipbuilding yards also came out against the bill because of the clauses that would have permitted American registry for foreign-built ships. Bernard Baker, testifying before the Senate committee on the importance of this measure, stated that of the two 13,000-ton ships he had building for the Atlantic Transport Line, the one building in the United States would cost $1,846,000 and the one building in Belfast would cost $1,419,120.[4] The 30 percent surcharge for the American-flag vessel was an enormous burden to carry in a competitive world market.

The United States Senate accepted the majority report of the committee and, under the leadership of Marcus Hannah, passed the Ocean Mail Subsidy Bill on March 17,

Red Star Line, Antwerpen-Dover-New York
Doppelschrauben Postdampfer "KROONLAND"

T. S. S. „Finland"
Length 580 feet. Beam 60 feet.
Tonnage 12,185 gross.

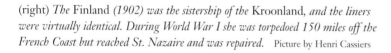

(above) *The* Kroonland *(1902) was the first of two 12,760-ton intermediate steamers built by the Cramp Shipyard for the American Line. They had accommodations for 342 first, 194 second, 626 third (steerage), plus an enormous amount of cargo.* Picture by Henri Cassiers

(right) *The* Finland *(1902) was the sistership of the* Kroonland, *and the liners were virtually identical. During World War I she was torpedoed 150 miles off the French Coast but reached St. Nazaire and was repaired.* Picture by Henri Cassiers

1902. A few days later, J.P. Morgan was in Washington, where congratulations were offered during lunch with Hannah. They were premature. Certainly, if the 1902 subsidy bill of Senator William P. Frye (R–Maine) had been brought to a vote quickly in the House and passed, everything would have fitted together perfectly for Morgan. The basic agreement to create the IMM had been initialed on February 4, 1902, in New York. Morgan had 60 days in which to begin his acquisitions or cancel the whole thing. Timing was of the essence, but complications arose in the House, and Morgan found the situation beyond even his political power. He postponed his normal spring trip to Europe from March to early April in order to be available if his influence were needed in the halls of Congress. Throughout the spring, rumors grew about the fate of the shipping trust in the financial pages of American and British newspapers. Griscom indicated that as far as he was concerned, the negotiations for the mergers were completed, but Morgan waited in vain for news from Hannah that the subsidy bill had passed the House. Finally, in mid-April, he could delay no longer and announced the formation of the syndicate of bankers to finance the trust. Also, with time running out at the end of April, Morgan finally authorized the White Star management to secure the approval of its shareholders.

Everything had looked rosy for the new legislation in the American Congress. However, when the bill reached the House, it was assigned to the Committee on

Merchant Marine and Fisheries and began to gather dust. No action was taken for more than a year. Merchant marine experts such as W.W. Bates, former United States Commissioner of Navigation and editor of the *Nautical Magazine and Naval Journal*, crusaded against the bill. Bates felt that the 1902 bill, if enacted, would involve a multimillion-dollar raid on the federal treasury. His book *American Navigation: The Political History of Its Rise and Ruin and the Proper Means for Its Encouragement*, published in 1902, carried a great deal of weight. When the house committee finally voted in February 1903, it was to kill the bill by never reporting it out of committee for a vote of the full House. By that time, the International Mercantile Marine, personifying a new attempt at commercial monopoly, had already been born and was being subjected to caustic criticism. The *United States Investor* commented, "We suspect that the people of the United States would view a subsidy measure in aid of Mr. Morgan's new steamship combine as too flagrantly indecent to be tolerated."[5]

Somewhat surprisingly, in December 1903 President Theodore Roosevelt again raised the issue of government aid to the American merchant marine in a message to Congress:

> A majority of our people desire that steps be taken in the interest of American shipping, so that we may once more resume our former position in the ocean carrying trade. . . . In 1895, our 20-knot trans-Atlantic mail line was equal to any foreign line. Since then the Germans have put on 23-knot steamers, and the British have contracted for 24-knot steamers. Our service should equal the best. . . . If we are to stay in the business it ought to be with the full advantages to the country on the one hand, and on the other with exact knowledge of the cost and proper methods of carrying it on. Moreover, lines of cargo ships are of even more importance than fast mail lines, save so far as the latter can be depended upon to furnish swift auxiliary cruisers in time of war.[6]

Basically, all that Roosevelt called for was a study of the problem prior to making any decision about enabling legislation. The Progressive Era in American political life was gathering steam, and there was a distinct limit to how far politicians or the general public could be pushed where trusts were concerned. It was bad enough that industrial combinations such as trusts existed without feeding them from the public trough.

Some financial pundits such as John W. Gates of the *Wall Street Journal* continued to follow Morgan blindly. As late as October 1902, Gates said, "I am pleased to say I have a financial interest in the shipping trust. I think it is a good piece of property. I went into it because Mr. Morgan is identified with it. I have no hesitancy in putting my money where Mr. Morgan puts his. He is wise and makes no mistakes."[7]

Others were nowhere near as confident, and some were outwardly critical of Morgan's recent financial creations. The *United States Investor* noted that Morgan's reputation was built on his ability to refinance and reduce the indebtedness of companies. Recent events, however, had seen the creation of overcapitalized promotions without sufficient economic justification. Furthermore, the size of the bankers' fees and the

A spectacular compass was featured on the back of the Philadelphia–Liverpool brochure of the American Line (ca. 1903). The Westernland *is in the center with "International Mercantile Marine Co." spelled out around the compass headings.*

enormous profits realized by the promoters threatened the economic stability of their new creations. Even United States Steel had found it prudent to convert its 7 percent preferred stock into 5 percent bonds in order to bear the financial strain. The tie between United States Steel and the IMM has never been adequately explored. According to no less a figure than Charles M. Schwab, a Morgan partner, "Mr. Morgan's purchases of steamship lines were made with a view of opening England to the steel trust. The shipping facilities we now control will enable us to carry out our policy in England."[8]

In 1902, only the Cunard Line (Cunard Steam Ship Company Limited) rivaled IMM's White Star, and of the two, White Star enjoyed the competitive edge. The takeover of White Star by an American trust was a severe shock to British sensitivities, although the ships were to remain British and virtually no changes occurred in management or operation of the vessels. The news that White Star had been bought by the American trust brought questions in the House of Commons as to the intentions of His Majesty's government. It was as though a piece of the empire had been swiped from beneath the lion's paw. One observer commented, "It is not a great exaggeration to say that the inhabitants of the 'tight little isle' feel somewhat as if Gibraltar had been acquired by the Americans and was to be located henceforth at Sandy Hook."[9]

Opposition in Britain centered upon a number of issues. National pride was bruised by the transfer of ownership in several of the largest British steamship lines to foreign control. Some even regarded the purchases as illegal, given the terms of the British Merchant Shipping Act. Under the terms of the Act of Parliament, foreigners could not own British-flag ships. Griscom always had surmounted this problem by having the International Navigation Company Inc. (of the United States) own the International Navigation Company Ltd. (of Britain). The INC Ltd. owned the British-flag ships, but it was in turn owned by the American parent firm. Some British authorities questioned this as a thinly camouflaged subterfuge of questionable legality. If so, it had been winked at by the British government for the better part of 15 years. The question was raised as

A nice starboard view of one of the Saints *inward bound to Southampton.*

to how the White Star ships could be depended upon to honor the auxiliary-cruiser agreements of the Admiralty if they were owned by foreigners. The criticism was raised that British investors in the affected shipping firms thought more of their bank balances than they did of their loyalty to king and country. Finally, the point was made again and again that the financial terms on which the new trust was founded were so waterlogged that the whole was bound to collapse. So many conflicting factors were at work during 1902 that some wondered whether it was possible for the IMM to continue.

The unwillingness of the American Congress to complete action on the 1902 shipping subsidy bill meant that Morgan had to make peace with the British government as quickly as possible during the summer. It was critical to the future of the IMM that the subsidy paid by the British government to White Star not be canceled. Morgan did not want to find himself in the same position as Griscom in 1886, when he purchased the British-flag Inman Line only to find the Royal Mail contracts canceled two years later. With considerable assistance from Lord Pirrie, an informal understanding among the principals was negotiated in September 1902. This provided the foundation for a formal agreement between the new owners of White Star and the Admiralty and the Board of Trade in August 1903.

The terms of the August 1903 agreement between White Star and the British government were: that the British-flag ships of the company would be treated the same as any other British-flag tonnage; that it was legal for the IMM's British subsidiaries to own British-flag vessels; that a majority of the directors of the British subsidiaries would be British subjects; that the officers of the British-flag vessels in all instances would remain British; and that the same proportion of the crew on the vessels would remain British as was required on any other British-flag vessel. The new White Star management committed itself to enhancing the British-flag portion of the fleet. The agreement between White Star and Arthur Balfour, president of the Board of Trade and future prime minister, was to run for 20 years.[10]

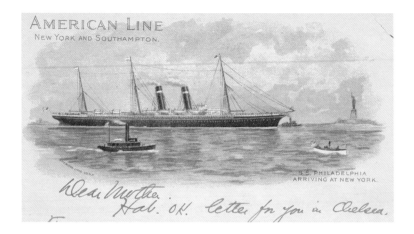

After her rebuilding the Philadelphia (ex-Paris) *was honored with a new set of American Line postcards. Here she is shown arriving at New York with the Statue of Liberty in the background.*

When the announcement was made of the 1903 agreement, more howls of rage were heard in London. Opponents said that the subsidy given to White Star in return for the right of the Admiralty to take ships was unnecessary, because the Admiralty already possessed that right, which needed no augmentation. Why pay for something you already had the right to do? The government remained implacable.

The position of the Cunard Steam Ship Company Limited in 1900 was that of the senior British-flag North Atlantic line. Since its founding in 1840, Cunard had carried the Royal Mail and had been a remarkably successful, if conservative, transportation enterprise. As early as 1900, John Burns, first Lord Inverclyde, managing director of the Cunard Line, had been approached by a number of individuals, including T.A. Bellew of the Liverpool Underwriters Association, Harry MacIver, and various "interests" with an offer from "others" to purchase the line. The "offer" occurred at the same time as the first Leyland deal and never was defined or stated in such a manner as to interest the Cunard board. On March 27, 1900, the Cunard board refused to discuss the sale of the line to anyone who was not a principal.[11]

The simple creation of the IMM placed enormous pressure on the Cunard Line to join the trust as well. A substantial offer from the IMM for Cunard Line shares would have had to receive serious consideration from the directors if they were to exercise appropriate fiduciary responsibility. In simple terms, they could not turn down a good offer from the IMM without running the risk of being sued by their own stockholders. Almost immediately in the fall of 1901, Cunard's management found its stock was in play. No fewer than five separate feelers or offers were made by a variety of parties between September 1901 and May 1902. Besides offers that clearly represented Morgan interests, additional inquiries were received from Messrs. Vickers, Maxim and Co., shipbuilders, and Sir Christopher Furness, chairman of Furness, Withy and Company. Complicating matters, John Burns, first Lord Inverclyde, died unexpectedly in 1901, and a substantial number of Cunard shares suddenly were available from his estate. On March 18, 1902, Messrs. Watson and Smith, a firm of Glasgow stockbrokers, approached the trustees of Lord Inverclyde's estate with an offer to buy an unlimited quantity of Cunard shares at the highest price that they had commanded over the previous 10 years (£20).[12]

George Burns, second Lord Inverclyde, succeeded his father as managing director of the Cunard Line and found that the challenges of his first year might well involve absorption or annihilation. At the same time, the new Lord Inverclyde had the normal challenge of trying to maintain the first-class North Atlantic service with an aging fleet in the face of strong German and now American competition. White Star was commissioning vessels almost twice the size of existing Cunarders, even if they were of moderate speed. With all the new capital available to the IMM, there appeared no limit to what it might decide to order.

Lord Inverclyde's well-planned move was to solicit the advice of His Majesty's government. On March 8, 1902, as soon as he learned of the February agreement signed by Morgan and his rivals in New York, Lord Inverclyde immediately informed Lord Selborne, First Lord of the Admiralty, that they had a major problem on their hands. There was the very real possibility that the Cunard shareholders would accept a Morgan-backed offer if it involved a comfortable premium. Lord Selborne's reaction on March 17 was to suggest that Cunard unilaterally add a clause to its Admiralty contract forbidding the transfer of ships to foreign ownership for the duration of the agreement. Inverclyde told Selborne he could not possibly make such a large concession on the part of his stockholders without suitable adjustments in the agreement. Lord Inverclyde did offer to reserve 13 of Cunard's best ships for Admiralty purposes if the subvention could be increased. Selborne declined, and the next six months were to see protracted negotiations between Cunard and the government.

The Cunard management explained to the British government that it wished to remain totally British in management and ownership but could not guarantee the maintenance of the existing situation because of American economic pressures. If the British government felt it desirable for Cunard and its ships to remain totally British and available at all times for naval service, then a way would have to be found for Cunard to receive assistance not only in operating but also in replenishing its first-class fleet. Lord Inverclyde, armed with a sheaf of pages showing the relative subsidies of various non-British steamship lines, sought to persuade the government to be generous. The terms of the American subsidy to the International Navigation Company were described as superior to that of the British government to Cunard. Furthermore, the generous increases before Congress in Senator Frye's bill were calculated totally to unbalance the situation. Cunard required a much more secure position.

Late April 1902 brought an offer from Clement Acton Griscom through Henry Wilding for Cunard to join the IMM. The offer was at a rate of £18 per share for up to 55 percent of the shares. Lord Inverclyde might have considered £20 per share for the entire company, but not just for a controlling interest. Much later, he wrote to Bruce Ismay, explaining his position: "I stated that neither the basis on which the offer had been made, nor the price indicated commended themselves to me. Further, that unless

U.S. Mail Twin-Screw Steamers " Philadelphia " and " New York."

A beautiful photograph of the U.S. Mail twin-screw steamers Philadelphia *(1901) and* New York *(1903). Both were reconditioned, emerging with new machinery and with their funnels reduced from three to two.*

the offer was for the Cunard Company as a whole, I must be satisfied before placing it before the shareholders, that the proposed combination would have as much interest in keeping up the Cunard Company as in developing any other section of the syndicate."[13]

It seems incredible that in view of what the creators of the IMM already had swallowed, they would draw back from the investment necessary to secure 100 percent control of Cunard. The IMM management blinked and Cunard remained uncommitted.

Between April and August 1902, the British government explored a number of alternative plans to Cunard's request for a substantially increased subsidy. The IMM offer incalculably strengthened Inverclyde's hand in dealing with the British government. The wolf was at the door. Questions were asked in the House of Commons about the future of the White Star ships acquired by the Americans. This further prodded the government to action. In May 1902, the British government asked Cunard to make a new proposal. When they did, it was for a 20-year agreement involving £5.2 million at 5 percent for a new fleet of nine fast liners capable of serving the Admiralty as armed merchant cruisers. In one fell swoop, Cunard's aging fleet would be replaced, but the Cabinet balked at this expense.

Sir Christopher Furness entered the picture again with an offer to buy enough Cunard shares to take over the company, so Lord Inverclyde used this opportunity to turn up the heat a few more degrees on the government. On May 31, he sent a letter to all Cunard stockholders in which he let them know that negotiations on the future of the company were underway. That was vague enough to mean anything, and it served to confuse everyone, as he intended. There was even talk of a rival British shipping

A bow shot of the reconditioned New York *in the Southampton Docks. Even with two funnels she remained a classic ship.*

combine led by Sir Alfred Jones, which might involve Cunard, Elder Dempster, and Allan.[14] Rumors of that upset Lord Pirrie's digestion.

On May 10, Lord Selborne at the Admiralty wrote Lord Inverclyde that the government strongly objected to Cunard's joining the IMM, "and will do all we can to assist you to justify yourself to your shareholders for not doing so."[15] Selborne stopped short of making a firm commitment, and Lord Inverclyde was irritated. "I think the time has come when you should say what you intend to do with regard to the Cunard Company and not continue on the present indefinite course."[16] His Majesty's government encouraged negotiations toward an all-British consortium in June, but the plans came to naught when the participants could not agree. By July 1902, Lord Inverclyde blamed the government for most of Cunard's problems. He had kept Cunard out of the IMM at the request of the First Lord of the Admiralty, and now he had to explain to his stockholders that he had gained nothing by obliging the British government. If the government did nothing, Lord Inverclyde felt Cunard faced catastrophe. Accordingly, he submitted a new plan for immediate action. Joseph Chamberlain agreed to consider the new plan, and the Cabinet met on August 7. The urgency of the problem was acknowledged, and with what constituted minor revisions, Lord Inverclyde's proposals were accepted. The one point on which the Cabinet had refused to be budged was Inverclyde's request for an immediate increase in the subsidy.[17] An exchange of letters then occurred between Gerald W. Balfour and Lord Inverclyde refining a point permitting the Cunard Line to dispose of aging tonnage, and the agreement was certified.[18] Inverclyde, extremely relieved, wrote a friend: "At last my labour has had some result, but, in the end everything has been carried through with such rapidity that I hardly realise that it is all done with."[19]

Absolute secrecy was required until the government decided how and when to announce the agreement, but Inverclyde could hardly restrain his enthusiasm. "Personally I am satisfied and the more I think of it the more do I consider that it is one of the biggest and the most important arrangements which has ever been made between

The United States Mail steamer New York *passing the Netley Hospital near Southampton, England.*

a private Company and the government of this Country."[20] As usual, Inverclyde wasted not a moment in cabling the news to the highly respected Cunard agent in New York, Vernon H. Brown: "Have concluded satisfactory agreement with Grape."[21] Grape was the Cunard Line's secret code-word for "British government," since secrecy was desired. Brown immediately wrote Inverclyde that he was greatly pleased that Cunard would not be absorbed by the "Morgan-Griscom Syndicate."[22] In a following letter, Inverclyde wrote Brown, "I think it will cause a great sensation when it comes out. I am sure that, in this country, at any rate, there will be great satisfaction that the Cunard Company will still be the great British Line on the Atlantic, and once again, I hope, lead the procession."[23] Brown responded to Inverclyde in a private letter dispatched "per *Umbria*": "I shall be very greatly disappointed if the rank and file do not heartily endorse the Government's action in putting its oldest and most prominent line in a position to enable it to stand firm against any and all efforts of the powerful new ship combine to drive it out of business or force its Directors to sell out and transfer its allegiance to a foreign flag."[24] The Cunard stockholders officially were informed of the agreement in a circular on September 30, 1902, when the details were made public.[25]

Cunard's management received appropriate assurances that made it possible for them to rebuff the shipping trust. Specifically, Cunard was loaned the money to build two new ships (*Lusitania* and *Mauretania*), £2.4 million at 2½ percent, and provided with a subsidy of £150,000 once the two new ships were commissioned.[26] Under the terms of the agreement between the Cunard Steam Ship Company Ltd. and the British government, the management of the Cunard Line, its stockholders, and the ownership of its ships were to remain British forever.[27] As Lord Inverclyde told the Cunard stockholders, "The cardinal principle upon which the Government is treating with us, and to which we desire to adhere, namely—that the Company is to be, and is to remain British."[28] By this stroke, the central goal of the creators of the IMM was denied them. They never

The American Line United States Mail steamer St. Paul *approaching Southampton, England. The American Line ships were among the largest neutral vessels afloat at the beginning of World War I and tried to avoid submarines through a new service from New York to Liverpool (1914–18).*

would be able to control all the major steamship lines between Great Britain and the United States, let alone on the North Atlantic, and competitive rate wars would continue to rage throughout the first 15 years of the twentieth century.

Among those concerns that the IMM never could hope to purchase or control was the French Line (Compagnie Générale Transatlantique), which was partially owned by the government of France and always steamed an independent course. Most of the remainder of the significant North Atlantic lines in some way became associated with the IMM.

The IMM and Cunard would have a bitter rivalry over the next decade. Passenger traffic remained highly competitive, with the IMM accused of putting additional ships on already over-tonnaged routes in violation of the conference agreements. Cunard responded by opening new lines from the Continent to America when opportunity presented. IMM changed the New York sailing days to compete more directly with Cunard. In 1904, the rate for a steerage ticket from London to New York dropped to £2, and no one made much money at that figure.

Clement Acton Griscom always had run his steamship enterprises very much as a benevolent authoritarian figure. Decisions traditionally were referred to him on matters big and little, and his word was final. The strain of running the shipping trust was enormous. Within 18 months (October 1903), his health was undermined—although he would live until 1912—and he was feeling the pressure of running so many additional enterprises. Complaints began to be voiced in the White Star organization about the management of the IMM. Dissatisfaction with Griscom's rule even reached the press, where it was rumored that Bernard Baker would be his successor. Those rumors were ended when Baker himself left the IMM board late in 1903.

If J.P. Morgan possessed a shipping prejudice, it was that he loved the White Star ships and the way the White Star Line was run by the Ismays. To him this

An official American Line view from 1910 of the St. Paul *arriving at her pier. Later, as World War I transports in 1918, the* St. Louis *was renamed the* Louisville *and the* St. Paul *became the* Knoxville. *Both survived the war to resume service for a brief time in the early 1920s although they were terribly dated by then.*

meant the "English method"—a quiet, elegant professionalism—which brought him back to the White Star ships year after year when he wanted to book his annual pilgrimages to Europe.[29]

In January 1904, Bruce Ismay, accompanied by Henry Wilding and Lord Pirrie, crossed to New York for a series of meetings with Morgan and Griscom. It was said that Ismay brought demands for total control over White Star. Frank and vigorous discussions occurred among all parties, and Griscom denied the rumor that he was going to resign. Morgan apparently was disturbed enough both by the downward drift in IMM stocks and bonds and by the transatlantic management disagreements to force Griscom to give up power. On February 23, 1904, Clement Acton Griscom surrendered the office of president of the International Mercantile Marine to Bruce Ismay of White Star and agreed to accept the ceremonial office of chairman of the board, which he would hold until his death in November 1912. Griscom's sons and son-in-law resigned at approximately the same time, and direct family control of the day-to-day operations of the American Line and the Red Star Line ceased after 30 years.

Symbolic of the shift of power from Griscom to Ismay was the transfer of the head offices of the IMM from Philadelphia to New York. It also was reported that Ismay was planning to move his home from Liverpool to New York, but this never occurred. For the duration of his leadership (1904–13), he continued to live in Britain, with occasional visits to New York. Later Ismay was to explain his position to the British press as having managerial power while actual control lay with the voting trust. Managerial power was more than adequate for White Star purposes. The White Star Line gave evidence of its

The United States Mail steamer St. Louis *leaving New York for Southampton. After the merger of the American Line into the International Mercantile Marine fleet, American Line artists modified the ships to make them look larger, while the new tonnage for White Star soon was four times larger.*

independence by being the only IMM concern that did not include the name of the parent organization in its advertising or on its bills of lading.

The election of Ismay was not unanimous by any means. Apparently various factions supported Griscom or Baker over Ismay for the top position. After Ismay's selection, Baker caustically remarked, "The English shipping men have their own property again, plus the cash contributed by the syndicate, plus the property of the American lines."[30] At the time of Ismay's accession to power, White Star was the only IMM concern making a profit, and some of the former stockholders reportedly were interested in trying to buy back the steamship line. It was not for sale. Ismay's new annual salary as president of the IMM was rumored to be £20,000 (around $100,000), which in 1904 was a very generous remuneration.

Ismay's appointment as president of the IMM also was designed to reassure senior employees in the British firms that their positions were secure. Substantial instability in employment had occurred as a result of the creation of the International Mercantile Marine. It was said that no one knew what was going to happen next, and that senior personnel afloat and ashore frequently found themselves out of work. In Britain, grumbling occurred about "American methods," which were said to regard length of employment as a deficit because of advanced years and a higher salary. Conversely, the "British method" depended on the building of long-term associations and ties between service personnel on the ships and their frequent passengers. In an effort to reduce costs, salaries were cut, and many captains found themselves earning far less. This undermined morale and hurt service.[31]

Ismay's first great challenge was money. The cash flow of the IMM was far below expectations, and the trust used the expedient of issuing the rest of the 5 percent mortgage bonds still held by the corporation ($6,330,000) to meet expenses and make payments on three new ships from Harland and Wolff. The stocks and bonds of the IMM fell substantially in New York during 1902 and 1903, but they stabilized and advanced a

A Red Star liner slows off Flushing at the mouth of the Scheldt River to drop her pilot. The pilot's job was to bring the ship downstream from Antwerp, Belgium. Now he is being rowed in to Flushing, The Nether-lands, for a rest and to wait for another ship. Henri Cassiers has caught the atmosphere of the twi-light scene magnificently.

little in 1904 under Ismay's leadership. Still, many who had exchanged shares in various steamship enterprises for IMM securities wished they had not done so, and a number of Baltimore banks in 1903 were said to be in difficulty over the large sums they had advanced to the shipping trust. Those banks participating in the underwriting of the IMM by mid-1903 had been asked to put up 100 percent of their subscriptions, when many had expected to be called on for far less than that. The "rising prices" of IMM stocks and bonds, which were supposed to take care of any cash-flow problems, never occurred; even some bankers were caught. It was felt that if anyone could restore faith in the trust, it would be the handsome, charismatic Bruce Ismay.

When Bruce Ismay assumed control of the International Mercantile Marine there was no question about which part of the great shipping combine in the future would be most important—the White Star Line. Under Ismay the American Line always would remain a stepsister and of secondary importance to White Star. This was vividly under-lined when the issue of new tonnage was raised after the commissioning in 1907 of the *Lusitania* and *Mauretania* by the Cunard Line. There was no question of building a series of first-class ships for anything but the White Star Line. Equally, there was no question about building the new ships anywhere but at the Harland and Wolff Shipyard, Belfast. Lord Pirrie had earned the right to continue as the principal builder for the Oceanic Steam Navigation Company by virtue of his invaluable service as one of the godfathers to the International Mercantile Marine.

In the mid-1900's, White Star was the only major unit of the IMM producing sub-stantial profits—in some instances over £1,000,000 a year. Bruce Ismay sought to capi-talize on that by winning the support of Clement Acton Griscom, chairman of the board, and his fellow board members for a trio of superliners designed to be larger and more luxurious than any other ships in the world. Whatever Griscom may have desired personally, he had retired to the position of chairman of the IMM and with this move went the day-to-day control of fleet operations.

Insofar as Ismay was concerned there was no need to chase the Cunard speed queens, because the machinery necessary to propel such a vessel would utterly consume the profits earned by the ship. Instead, Ismay elected to build upon the formula for success that had served White Star so well since 1899 and White Star's commissioning of the second *Oceanic*. Ismay asked Lord Pirrie to create the plans for three ships that would be 25 percent larger than anything in service and still capable of maintaining a service speed that would deliver their passengers across the Atlantic in six days. This would make it possible to maintain a first class service with three ships instead of four. By virtue of their size—over 45,000 tons—they would be able to carry sufficient passengers, and, by virtue of a 21–23 knot speed, to maintain a six-day service. Some of the money saved by building only slightly slower ships than the Cunarders would be lavished on making them the most luxurious vessels of their time. Ships on which even millionaires would feel as comfortable as in their own great mansions, or their private clubs. The names assigned to the White Star trio were calculated to evoke a new sense of grandeur—*Olympic, Titanic, Gigantic*.[32]

The *Olympic* was the name-ship of the class and garnered unto herself and White Star all the journalistic glory when she was commissioned in 1911. She was a sumptuously outfitted, quality product of Harland and Wolff, justifying every possible expectation of her owners and builders. Her sisters were to follow at yearly intervals. Shortly after her commissioning it was realized that her only shortcoming as a palatial floating hotel was that she did not have enough luxurious suites to meet the demands of her fabulously wealthy clientele. This was rectified in her sister, *Titanic*, by enclosing a portion of the promenade deck in order to meet the demand for the utmost luxury and privacy in accommodations. So delighted was Bruce Ismay with the second of his three ships that he elected to sail on her maiden voyage—April 10, 1912. For Ismay, sailing on the *Titanic* must have been a heady ego trip. The plaudits of those people who mattered most to him were his in abundance. The *Titanic*'s maiden voyage almost was cut short at Southampton when the suction of her mammoth hull caused the hawsers holding the American Line's *New York* to snap and brought her swinging out toward the White Star liner in a deadly arc. Only the quick action of tugs prevented the *New York* from taking revenge on the White Star liner, which had usurped the position of the next generation of American Line vessels. The *Titanic* escaped the near miss and proceeded on her voyage to eternity. Bruce Ismay, who expected to establish a reputation second to no one with the White Star trio, lost everything except his life when he survived the sinking of the *Titanic*. He remained in control of his beloved White Star for an additional year and then retired in 1913—dying in relative obscurity in 1937.

What Griscom thought of the *Titanic* disaster is unknown, but he always had felt very deeply anything that happened to his ships. Seven months later Clement Acton Griscom, Sr., suffered a fatal stroke on November 10, 1912, and died at his country estate, Dolobran, in Haverford, Pennsylvania. He was 71. The memorials to him acknowledged that he was the founder of the International Navigation Company and of

The last American Line crossing of the St. Louis *was April 21, 1918. This stern shot symbolizes in many ways the end of an era in the history of the American merchant marine.*

the International Mercantile Marine as well as one of the most important American-born financiers and industrialists of his age.

The American Line formally ceased operations in 1925, although its lineal descendant would be the United States Lines, which ceased passenger operations with the withdrawal from service of the liner *United States* in 1969. The *United States* presently (2000) lies in hollow splendor at a pier in the Port of Philadelphia, where the American Line began 125 years ago.

NOTES

Chapter 1

1. Pennsylvania Railroad Company, "Minutes of the Board of Directors of the Pennsylvania Railroad Company," November 29, 1865. Minute Book #5 (November 1865–November 1871). Pennsylvania Railroad Collection, Hagley Museum and Library (Soda House), Wilmington, Delaware.

2. George H. Burgess and Miles C. Kennedy, *Centennial History of the Pennsylvania Railroad Company, 1846–1946* (Philadelphia, 1949), 304.

3. N.R.P. Bonsor, *North Atlantic Seaway* (Jersey, Channel Islands, 1975–80), 2nd. ed., 5 vols., I, 422ff. The Bonsor masterpiece originally was published in one volume in 1955 by T. Stephenson & Sons (Prescot, Lancashire, UK), and subsequently reissued with a supplement in 1960. In 1975 the first volume of the second edition was published by David & Charles (Newton Abbot, UK). A disagreement between author and publisher caused Bonsor to publish the remaining four volumes of the second edition himself, as Brookside Publications (Jersey, C.I., 1975–80). Hereafter, referred to as: N.R.P. Bonsor, *North Atlantic Seaway*, vol., page.

4. R.S. McLellan, *Anchor Line (1856–1956)* (Glasgow, 1956), 40–41. Bonsor, *NAS*, I, 422; The chronology of the Anchor Line: Handyside Brothers (1838–1852); Handysides & Company (1852–1856); Handysides & Henderson (1856–1873) (Anchor Line); Henderson Brothers (1873–1899); Anchor Line (Henderson Brothers) Limited (1899–1935); Anchor Line (1935–1959).

5. Pennsylvania Railroad Company, "Report of the Committee on Steamships," November 23, 1870, "Minutes of the Board of Directors of the Pennsylvania Railroad Company." Minute Book #5 (November 1865–November 1871). Pennsylvania Railroad Collection, Hagley Museum and Library (Soda House), Wilmington, Delaware. The Committee on Steamships was chaired by E.C. Knight and included John Rice, S.T. Bodine, Josiah Bacon, Washington Butcher, Lewis Elkin, Wistar Morris, J. Edgar Thomson, and Thomas A. Scott. Many of these men subsequently would be active in steamship affairs.

6. *Philadelphia Commercial List and Price Current*, February 4, 1871, Van Pelt Library, The University of Pennsylvania, Philadelphia, Pa.

7. *Philadelphia Commercial List and Price Current*, February 18, 1871.

8. *Philadelphia Commercial List and Price Current*, January 7, 1871.

9. American Steamship Company (ASC), "An Act to Incorporate the American Steamship Company of Philadelphia," February 7, 1871, *Minute Book I, 1871–1876*, 1–3.

[Pennsylvania Railroad Collection, Box 89, Urban Archives, Temple University, Philadelphia, Pennsylvania.] This act created a commission to open the books and solicit funds for the new company.

10. Pennsylvania Railroad Company, John O. James, Chairman, Office of the Board of Trade, (to) E.C. Knight, Chairman, Steamship Committee, March 16, 1871, "Minute Books of the Board of Directors of the Pennsylvania Railroad Company," March 27, 1871. Minute Book #5 (November 1865–November 1871). Pennsylvania Railroad Collection, Hagley Museum and Library (Soda House), Wilmington, Delaware.

11. American Steamship Company (ASC), "Report of the Judges of Election," April 4, *Minute Book I, 1871–1876*, 8–9. *Philadelphia Commercial List and Price Current*, April 8, 1871. Lombaert, Knight, Bacon, Rice, and Butcher simultaneously sat on the board of directors of the Pennsylvania Railroad and it is impossible to think of a more interlocking corporate situation.

12. Inman Line, Red Star Line, and American Line, *Inman and International Steamship Company Limited* (New York, nd [1888?], 49; New York Public Library, N.Y., N.Y. An early publication of the Inman and International Line giving a detailed history of the background to the three steamship lines.

13. American Steamship Company (ASC), "By-Laws of The American Steamship Company of Philadelphia," April 22, 1871, *Minute Book I, 1871–1876*, 12–19. B. H. Bartol's prospectus on the fleet occupies the next page (20).

14. American Steamship Company (ASC), "Minutes," August 9, 1871, *Minute Book I, 1871–1876*, 29–31. The formal contract was dated August 30, 1871.

15. American Steamship Company (ASC), "Minutes," August 9, 1871, *Minute Book I, 1871–1876*, 32.

16. *Philadelphia Commercial List and Price Current*, February 3, 1872.

17. Philip Chadwick Foster Smith, *Philadelphia on the River* (Philadelphia, 1986), 156ff.

18. Thomas R. Heinrich, *Ships for the Seven Seas* (Baltimore, 1997), 61. A very fine work of excellent research.

19. *Philadelphia Commercial List and Price Current*, April 6, 1872. American Steamship Company (ASC), "First Annual Report," April 1, 1872, *Minute Book I, 1871–1876*, 78–80. The engines were guaranteed by Cramp to provide an average speed of 11.5 knots with a coal consumption of 40 tons per 24-hour period.

20. Fairfield Shipbuilding and Engineering Company, *Fairfield 1860–1960* (Glasgow, 1960), un.

21. Augustus C. Buell, *Memoirs of Charles H. Cramp* (Philadelphia 1906), 112.

22. Buell, *Memoirs of Charles H. Cramp*, 112.

23. Buell, *Memoirs of Charles H. Cramp*, 112–113. Chief Engineer W.R. Wilson of the *Italy* later became Inspector of the American Line ships between November 1871 and October 1873.

24. Buell, *Memoirs of Charles H. Cramp*, 113.

25. Buell, *Memoirs of Charles H. Cramp*, 115.

26. Buell, *Memoirs of Charles H. Cramp*, 115.

27. *Philadelphia Commercial List and Price Current*, February 24, 1872.

28. American Steamship Company (ASC), "First Annual Report," April 1, 1872, *Minute Book I, 1871–1876*, 80. [Pennsylvania Railroad Collection, Box 89, Urban Archives, Temple University, Philadelphia, Pennsylvania.]

29. *Philadelphia Commercial List and Price Current*, April 6, 1872.

30. *Philadelphia Commercial List and Price Current*, April 6, 1872. The article on the *Annual Report* is detailed and authoritative. It states that Herman J. Lombaert was elected president with E.C. Knight leading the list of directors. The toll on presidents was to be phenomenal. Lombaert submitted his resignation, because of ill health, via J. Edgar Thomson (December 13, 1872). Josiah Bacon had been serving as "president pro tem" but was succeeded by Washington Butcher, who was ill at the time of his election and could not serve, so Bacon took up the post again. Subsequently Butcher died (January 1873) and was succeeded by Edward C. Knight, who was unanimously elected president on January 15, 1873, and again at the annual meeting in April. The American Steamship Company experienced unique management instability with five changes in the office of president between April 1872 and April 1873. Fortunately, Mr. Knight did have substantial expertise since he also was the chair of the Steamship Committee of the Pennsylvania Railroad.

31. American Steamship Company (ASC), "First Annual Report," April 1, 1872, *Minute Book I, 1871–1876*, 80.

32. American Steamship Company (ASC), "First Annual Report," April 1, 1872, *Minute Book I, 1871–1876*, 79.

33. American Steamship Company (ASC), "First Annual Report," April 1, 1872, *Minute Book I, 1871–1876*, 79. The secretary of the Navy also expressed the view that the encouragement of steamship lines was the best means of keeping healthy the shipbuilding yards of the nation.

34. J. Edgar Thomson to Board of Directors, American Steamship Company, July 29, 1872, *Minute Book I, 1871–1876*, 100.

35. J Edgar Thomson to Edmund Smith, Secretary and Treasurer, American Steamship Company, August 24, 1872, *Minute Book I, 1871–1876*, 104.

36. J. Edgar Thomson to Board of Directors, American Steamship Company, August 29, 1872, *Minute Book I, 1871–1876*, 100. The "terms" with Richardson, Spence & Company were: 1 percent on the collection of all freight charges from the United States; 2.5 percent on all freight charges on all freight shipped to the United States; 5 percent on all passenger receipts.

37. *Philadelphia Commercial List and Price Current*, August 17, 1872.

38. *Philadelphia Commercial List and Price Current*, August 17, 1872. Later commentators remarked that the *Pennsylvania* stuck on the ways during her launch, creating a short-lived crisis, before she finally reached the Delaware River. There is a very slight reference to this situation in contemporary accounts.

39. *Philadelphia Commercial List and Price Current*, August 17, 1872.

40. *Philadelphia Commercial List and Price Current*, April 12, 1873.

41. *Philadelphia Commercial List and Price Current*, May 10, 1873.

42. Buell, *Memoirs of Charles H. Cramp*, 112.

43. Buell, *Memoirs of Charles H. Cramp*, 116–117.

Chapter 2

1. American Steamship Company (ASC), "Third Annual Report," April 1, 1874, *Minute Book I, 1871–1876*, 320–321. [Pennsylvania Railroad Collection, Box 89, Urban Archives, Temple University, Philadelphia, Pennsylvania.]

2. American Steamship Company (ASC), "Report on the Committee on Finance on Officers & Crew and their Compensation," January 3, 1873, *Minute Book I, 1871–1876*. 135–137.

3. American Steamship Company (ASC), "Third Annual Report," April 1, 1874, *Minute Book I, 1871–1876*. 320–321. *Philadelphia Commericial List and Price Current*, April 11, 1874.

4. American Steamship Company (ASC), "Report of the Committee on Reorganization," December 31, 1873, *Minute Book I, 1871–1876*. 282–285.

5. Thomas R. Heinrich, *Ships of the Seven Seas* (Baltimore, 1997), 57.

6. *Philadelphia Commercial List and Price Current*, April 11, 1874.

7. *Report of the Postmaster General* (43rd Cong., 2d sess.), vol. 1638, 13–14.

8. *New York Times*, March 11, 1874, 4.

9. *New York Times*, March 12, 1874, 6: "Captain Lewis T. Bradburn, commander of the *Pennsylvania*, was about forty-two years of age, and had been engaged in the trade between New York and Liverpool for the past twenty-five years. For six years previous to his engagement with the American Line he acted as mate to Captain Sumner on several packet steamers, and when Sumner took command of the *Pennsylvania*, Capt. Bradburn was selected First Officer. Upon retirement of the first-named gentleman, he took command of the vessel on August 21, 1873, and has proved himself a man well-fitted for the position. Capt. Bradburn was a native of Maryland. The deceased leaves a wife, who is at present residing at Glasgow, Scotland. This was his last voyage, as he had been appointed Port Captain at Liverpool. Mr. Sweetman, First Officer, had but recently been promoted to that position, and was pronounced a thoroughly competent man; and Mr. Ross, Second Officer, also bears a high reputation for efficiency. These with two seamen, one James Daltron [sic], American, and the other unknown, comprise the lost."

10. *New York Times*, March 12, 1874, 6. Description of saloon passenger C.H. Walton in New York about the near-disaster to the ship.

11. "Deposition of Cornelius L. Brady (July 11, 1874)," *Brady v. American Steamship Company*, "Amendment to Libel," Papers of John Cadwalader, Judge of the District Court of the United States in and for the Eastern District of Pennsylvania. The Historical Society of Pennsylvania, Philadelphia, mss. p. 2.

12. *Brady v. American Steamship Company*, "Amendment to Libel," 4.

13. "Michael Murphy, Q.M., (Excerpt from Deposition)," *Brady v. American Steamship Company*, Cadwalader Papers, The Historical Society of Pennsylvania.

14. *Brady v. American Steamship Company*, "Deposition," mss., 8.

15. *New York Times*, March 11, 1874.

16. *Brady v. American Steamship Company*, "Deposition," mss., 9.

17. "Joseph Pullius, Q.M., afterward 2nd Offr., (Excerpt from Deposition)," *Brady v. American Steamship Company*, Cadwalader Papers, The Historical Society of Pennsylvania.

18. "Edwin Coleman, Seafaring Man Since 1862, (Excerpt from Deposition)," *Brady v. American Steamship Company*, Cadwalader Papers, The Historical Society of Pennsylvania.

19. "Peter McCarroll, Q.M. (Excerpt from Deposition)," *Brady v. American Steamship Company*, Cadwalader Papers, The Historical Society of Pennsylvania.

20. "Frank Reedstone, Seaman (Excerpt from Deposition)," *Brady v. American Steamship Company*, Cadwalader Papers, The Historical Society of Pennsylvania.

21. "George Keabea, Sailor for 20 Years (Excerpt from Deposition)," *Brady v. American Steamship Company*, Cadwalader Papers, The Historical Society of Pennsylvania.

22. *Philadelphia Commercial List and Price Current*, April 11, 1874.

23. American Steamship Company (ASC), "Fourth Annual Report" (March 25, 1875), *Minute Book, 1871–1876*, 412. *Philadelphia Commercial List and Price Current*, April 10, 1875, printed a slightly different version.

24. *Mitchell's Maritime Register*, April 4, 1873.

25. *Philadelphia Commercial List and Price Current*, November 28, 1874, stated that the *Abbotsford* had been transferred to the Red Star Line. However, the ship appears to have moved back and forth as needed in the services of both concerns.

26. *Philadelphia Commercial List and Price Current*, October 9, 1875.

27. *Philadelphia Commercial List and Price Current*, August 21, 1875.

28. *Philadelphia Commercial List and Price Current*, September 11, 1875.

29. *Philadelphia Commercial List and Price Current*, December 25, 1875.

30. *Philadelphia Commercial List and Price Current*, April 8, 1876.

31. American Steamship Company (ASC), "Fifth Annual Report" (April 3, 1876), *Minute Book I, 1871–1876*, 475–477.

Chapter 3

1. Russell F. Weigley, ed., *Philadelphia: A 300-Year History* (New York, 1982): Dorothy Gondos Beers, "The Centennial City," 460–67.

2. *Philadelphia Commercial List and Price Current*, April 8, 1876.

3. Henry D. Welsh, President, American Steamship Company, To the President and Board of Directors of the Pennsylvania Railroad Company, January 25, 1876. Minutes of

the PRR Board, M85, Board No. 95, Hagley Museum and Library (Soda House), Wilmington, Delaware.

4. Henry D. Welsh, President, American Steamship Company, To the President and Board of Directors of the Pennsylvania Railroad Company, March 3, 1876. Minutes of the PRR Board, M85, Board. No. 95, Hagley Museum and Library (Soda House), Wilmington, Delaware.

5. Minute, Subcommittee of the Finance Committee, Board of Directors, Pennsylvania Railroad Company, Philadelphia, January 24, 1877. M85, Board No. 95. Hagley Museum and Library (Soda House), Wilmington, Delaware; American Steamship Company, "Sixth Annual Report," *Minute Book II, 1876–1911.* [Box 89, Pennsylvania Railroad Collection, Urban Archives, Temple University, Philadelphia, Pennsylvania.]

6. *Philadelphia Commercial List and Price Current,* March 17, 1877.

7. Irvin Anthony, *Down to the Sea in Ships* (Philadelphia, 1924), 247.

8. *Philadelphia Commercial List and Price Current,* March 31, 1877.

9. *Philadelphia Commercial List and Price Current,* May 19, 1877.

10. W.E. Woodward, *Meet General Grant* (New York, 1928, 1946), 458–59.

11. J.T. Headley, *The Travels of General Grant* (Philadelphia, 1881), 17.

12. Headley, *Travels of General Grant,* 17–18.

13. Buell, *Memoirs,* 210.

14. Buell, *Memoirs,* 210.

15. Buell, *Memoirs,* 212.

16. *Philadelphia Commercial List and Price Current,* March 4, 1882.

17. *Philadelphia Commercial List and Price Current,* March 18, 1882. Some of the tonnage figures are slightly variable.

18. American Steamship Company, "Eleventh Annual Report" (March 30,1982), *Minute Book II, 1876–1884,* 336. [Pennsylvania Railroad Collection, Box 89, Urban Archives, Temple University, Philadelphia, Pennsylvania.]

19. *Philadelphia Commercial List and Price Current,* April 8, 1882. In April 1882, most of the same figures stood for reelection and were confirmed in office: Henry D. Welsh, President; John Price Wetherill; D.B. Cummins; N. Parker Shortridge; Strickland Kneass; William D. Winsor; G.B. Roberts; Henry C. Butcher; J.N. Dubarry; Joseph W. Lewis; and Edmund Smith.

20. *Philadelphia Commercial List and Price Current,* April 29, 1882.

21. *Philadelphia Commercial List and Price Current,* July 1, 1882.

22. Robert W. Smith, Secretary, PRR, to Samuel Rea, Assistant to President, PRR, January 13, 1897, M-87, BF-156, Pennsylvania Railroad Collection, Hagley Museum and Library (Soda House), Wilmington, Delaware. The letter explains how the PRR resolved the financial problem of the American Steamship Company, with regard to deciding how to dispose of the cancelled bonds in the 6 percent $1,500,000 bond issue

of the American Steamship Company that the railroad had guaranteed and, therefore, now owned upon their maturity (25 years).

Chapter 4

1. Edward N. Wright, "The Story of Peter Wright & Sons, Philadelphia Quaker Shipping Firm, 1818–1911," *Quaker History*, 56 (1967), 72. The article is most interesting and informative but it provides primary credit to James A. Wright without paying much attention to Clement Acton Griscom. Wright would serve as president of the International Navigation Company, but Griscom remains the driving force, and the two men were very close associates.

2. Hugo P. Frear, "History of Tankers," 135; in Society of Naval Architects and Marine Engineers, *Historical Transactions, 1893–1943* (New York, 1945). Frear was the consulting naval architect for the Bethlehem Steel Company, Shipbuilding Division, Fore River Yard, Quincy, Massachusetts.

3. *Philadelphia Commercial List and Price Current*, January 6, 1872.

4. Lloyd C. Griscom, *Diplomatically Speaking* (New York, 1940), 10.

5. Griscom, *Diplomatically Speaking*, 11.

6. Griscom, *Diplomatically Speaking*, 11.

7. *Mitchell's Maritime Register*, August 30, 1872.

8. *Philadelphia Commercial List and Price Current*, August 24, 1872.

9. George H. Burgess and Miles C. Kennedy, *Centennial History of the Pennsylvania Railroad Company, 1846–1946* (Philadelphia, 1949), 271. The *Centennial History* was published by the Pennsylvania Railroad Company.

10. *Philadelphia Commercial List and Price Current*, November 16, 1872.

11. *Philadelphia North American United States Gazette*, January 13, 1873.

Chapter 5

1. Loyd C. Griscom, *Diplomatically Speaking* (New York, 1940), 9.

2. N.R.P. Bonsor, *North Atlantic Seaway*, II, 830–31. Bonsor regarded the exact nature of this cargo as being questionable. It may not have involved petroleum products, even though James A. Wright of Peter Wright & Sons had discussed the tanks and the arrangements for carrying "liquid freight" just two days before the sailing. In the end the pipes were not ready and no oil was loaded.

3. Griscom, *Diplomatically Speaking*, 9–10.

4. *Philadelphia Commercial List and Price Current*, April 18, 1874.

5. *Philadelphia Commercial List and Price Current*, February 13, 1875.

6. Griscom, *Diplomatically Speaking*, 3–4.

7. Messrs. Peter Wright & Sons, *The Red Star Line, Belgian Royal and U.S. Mail Steamships: Facts for Travellers* (New York, nd (1883?), 3. This item is in the collection of the Independence Maritime Museum, Philadelphia, Pennsylvania, and involves 200 pages of information (pocket size).

8. Messrs. Peter Wright & Sons, *Facts for Travellers*, 3–4.

9. Peter Wright & Sons, *Facts for Travellers*, 5.

10. Peter Wright & Sons, *Facts for Travellers*, 8.

11. Peter Wright & Sons, *Facts for Travellers*, 8.

12. Lamar Cecil, *Albert Ballin: Business and Politics in Imperial Germany, 1888–1918* (Princeton, 1967). An excellent monograph on the most distinguished of the German shipping magnates.

13. Griscom, *Diplomatically Speaking*, 13.

14. Griscom, *Diplomatically Speaking*, 14.

15. Griscom, *Diplomatically Speaking*, 11–12.

Chapter 6

1. Arthur J. Maginnis, *The Atlantic Ferry: Its Ships, Men, and Working* (London, 1900), 205.

2. Inman and International, *History of the Inman Line* (New York, 1887), 1. A company history published shortly after the acquisition of Inman by Inman and International (1886), containing descriptions of the Inman, Red Star, and American Lines and their vessels and sailing schedules for 1888. New York Public Library.

3. *D.N.B.*, "Inman, William (1825–81)," X, 457, contends that the *City of Glasgow* sailed with 400 steerage on board on December 17, 1850. Inman and International, *History of the Inman Line* (1887), 4, concurs in the date but leaves the number indefinite. N.R.P. Bonsor, *North Atlantic Seaway* I, 220, states that no steerage passengers were carried until 1852. Bonsor often is correct in these matters.

4. Arthur Maginnis, *The Atlantic Ferry* (London, 1900), 209–10.

5. Inman and International, *History of the Inman Line*, 1.

6. Queenstown would remain a port of call for some transatlantic liners as late as 1970, when the Holland-America Line had the *Nieuw Amsterdam* call there on several North Atlantic crossings that began in Rotterdam and included stops at Southampton, Cobh, Halifax, and New York. The author fondly remembers one such crossing.

7. Postmaster-General to William Inman (Post 51/46), Contract of 9 March 1869. United States Mails. Liverpool via Queenstown to New York. Historical Records Office, St. Martin's le Grand, London.

8. N.R.P. Bonsor, *North Atlantic Seaway*, I, 231.

9. N.R.P. Bonsor, *North Atlantic Seaway*, I, 231.

10. N.R.P. Bonsor, *North Atlantic Seaway*, I, 233.

11. N.R.P. Bonsor, *North Atlantic Seaway*, I, 234.

12. R.S. McLellan, *Anchor Line 1856-1956* (Glasgow, 1956), 41–42.

13. Maginnis, *The Atlantic Ferry* (London, 1900), 68.

14. N.R.P. Bonsor, *North Atlantic Seaway*, I, 235.

15. Inman Line, Red Star Line, and American Line, *Inman and International Steamship Company Limited* (New York, nd (1888?), 7. A very fine company history and publicity release about the combined firm.

16. Inman and International Steamship Company, *The Inman Line* (1888), 8.

17. International Navigation Company, *American Line* (New York, 1898). Another fine publication of the firm.

18. N.R.P. Bonsor, *North Atlantic Seaway*, I, 235.

19. *Inman and International Steamship Company Limited* (1888), 12.

20. N.R.P. Bonsor, *North Atlantic Seaway*, I, 236.

21. *New York Times*, March 30, 1890.

22. Testimony of Clement A. Griscom (misindexed "Grisco") before the Senate Subcommittee on the "Revival of the Merchant Marine," Senate Miscellaneous Documents No. 149, 56th Cong., 1st Sess., 100–109.

23. Winthrop L. Marvin, *The American Merchant Marine* (New York, 1902), 166–67.

24. Marvin, *The American Merchant Marine*, 419.

Chapter 7

1. Postmaster General, "Report of the Postmaster General," in *The Abridgment, Message from the President of the United States to the Two Houses of Congress at the Beginning of the First Session of the Fifty-Second Congress, with the Reports of the Heads of Departments and selections from Accompanying Documents*, ed. W.H. Michael (Washington, GPO, 1892), 838.

2. Francis E. Hyde, *Cunard and the North Atlantic 1840–1973* (London, 1975), 102.

3. *The Times*, September 1, 1892.

4. *New York Times*, May 21, 1892; quoted from *Fairplay*, May 20, 1892.

5. *New York Times*, December 3, 1892.

6. *New York Times*, March 27, 1893.

7. N.R.P. Bonsor, *North Atlantic Seaway*, V, 1872–1882, (Appendix F. "The Blue Riband of the North Atlantic").

Chapter 8

1. *New York Times*, February 23, 1893.

2. *New York Times*, February 23, 1893.

3. International Navigation Company, *American Line* (New York, 1898). See also *New York Times*, February 23, 1893, which contains a slightly different version of the President's remarks. The text above is a composite.

4. *New York Times*, February 23, 1893.

5. *New York Times*, March 9, 1893.

6. *New York Times*, March 8, 1893.

7. *New York Times*, March 9, 1893.

8. *New York Times*, February 23, 1893.

9. *New York Times*, September 22, 1892.

10. *New York Times*, May 6, 1894.

11. *New York Times*, July 15, 1894.

12. Francis E. Hyde, *Cunard and the North Atlantic 1840–1973: A History of Shipping and Financial Management* (London, 1975), 106–7. Hyde's chapter 4 (90–118) on "Cunard and the North Atlantic Conferences 1860–1914" is a gifted analysis of the problems encountered and created by the steamship lines.

13. *New York Times*, May 9, 1894

Chapter 9

1. Charles H. Cramp, *Commercial Supremacy—and Other Papers* (Philadelphia, 1894), 43. This was a privately published collection of some of Cramp's many essays and papers.

2. *New York Times*, September 16, 1894.

3. *New York Times*, September 19, 1894.

4. Winthrop I. Marvin, *The American Merchant Marine* (New York, 1902), 420–21.

5. *New York Times*, November 16, 1894.

6. *Philadelphia Evening Bulletin*, April 10, 1895. Those citizens of St. Paul who eventually saw the launch of the liner bearing their city's name were: J.J. Parker, president of the councils of St. Paul, Colonel Clough, chairman of the Chamber of Commerce, E.W. Peet, Judge and Mrs. Charles Otis, John A. Stees, Miss Mary E. Stees, Judge W.D. Cornish, Mr. and Mrs. Arnold Kohlman, Alfred Holland Stees, George R. Finch, A.H. Paget, C.H. Holdridge, Mr. and Mrs. E.A. Hendrickson and Master Ward Hendrickson, Mr. and Mrs. E.L. Bonner, Miss Mary Fling, Mr. and Mrs. George A. Armstrong, H.H. Campbell, Miss Luella Hughson, Harry W. Davis, Mr. and Mrs. John Shephard, John B. West, O.N. Hokhanson, Edward Williams, Miss Nellie Williams, J.A. Allen, Mr. and Mrs. F.A. Johnson, Miss Nellie O. Finch.

7. *Philadelphia Evening Bulletin*, March 26, 1895.

8. *Philadelphia Evening Bulletin*, April 10, 1895. Paul Fatout, ed., *Mark Twain Speaking* (Iowa City, 1976), 274–76 contains a copy. I am indebted to Robert H. Hirst, General Editor, Mark Twain Project, UCLA, for this citation.

9. *Philadelphia Evening Bulletin*, April 10, 1895.

10. *Philadelphia Evening Bulletin*, April 10, 1895.

11. *Philadelphia Evening Bulletin*, April 10, 1895.

12. Marvin, *American Merchant Marine*, 421.

13. *Philadelphia Evening Bulletin*, May 25, 1895. Captain William G. Randle was born in Dartmouth, England, April 24, 1838. He followed the sea from boyhood and in 1873 entered the American Line service as the chief officer of the *Ohio*. In 1892, he was placed in command of the *City of Paris;* he was her captain when she became an American vessel in March 1893.

Chapter 10

1. *New York Times*, May 30, 1895.
2. *Scientific American*, June 8, 1895.
3. *New York Times*, June 2, 1895.
4. *Scientific American*, June 15, 1895.
5. *Scientific American*, February 8, 1896, 84–85.
6. *New York Times*, June 14, 1895.
7. *New York Times*, June 23, 1895.
8. *New York Times*, June 27, 1895.
9. *New York Times*, July 7, 1895.
10. *New York Times*, July 18, 1895.
11. *New York Times*, September 3, 1895.
12. *New York Times*, December 5, 1895.
13. *New York Times*, October 2, 1895.
14. *New York Times*, October 3, 1895.
15. *New York Times*, October 5, 1895.
16. *New York Times*, October 27, 1895.
17. *New York Times*, December 19, 1895
18. *New York Times*, December 22, 1895.

Chapter 11

1. *New York Times*, January 7, 1896. The American Line was surpassed in cabin-class passengers only by Cunard, although a number of competitors carried more steerage passengers. The figures for the principal lines were:

Steamship Line	Port	Cabin	Steerage
Cunard	Liverpool	18,844	21,724
American	Southampton	16,146	19,580
White Star	Liverpool	11,805	30,725
North German Lloyd	Bremen	10,805	44,326
North German Lloyd	Mediterranean	2,065	11,691
Hamburg-American	Hamburg	10,543	30,141
French Line (CGT)	Le Havre	7,587	16,469
Anchor	Glasgow	6,604	10,011
Anchor	Mediterranean	41	9,837
Red Star Line	Antwerp	4,890	12,554
Holland-America	Rotterdam	2,855	11,416
Allan-State	Glasgow	2,509	3,512

2. N.R.P. Bonsor, *North Atlantic Seaway*, I, 154 (statistics for *Campania*); III, 944 (statistics for *St. Paul*). The American Line always listed the *St. Louis* at 11,629 tons and the *St. Paul* at 11,600 tons.

3. *New York Times*, January 26, 1896.

4. *New York Times*, January 26, 1896.

5. *The Times*, January 27, 1896. Article based on Reuters telegrams from New York. *The Times* also reported the contents of a "Dalziel telegram" from Long Branch that quoted Captain Jamison, commander of the *St. Paul*, as saying: "We lost our reckoning in the dense fog and were only going about five miles an hour and feeling our way. The man who was heaving the lead reported 17 fathoms two minutes before she struck, but this was evidently a mistake. I was on the bridge when she grounded. The Cunard liner *Campania* was in sight for two days, but there is no truth in the report that we were racing." Owing to Captain Jamison's taciturn nature, it is questionable that he gave this interview to anyone. No one got to the ship to interview him for days. The story has the air of fabrication about it.

6. *New York Times*, January 26, 1896.

7. *New York Times*, February 5, 1896.

8. *New York Times*, February 7, 1896.

9. *New York Times*, February 20, 1896.

10. *New York Times*, April 17, 1898.

11. *New York Times*, March 1, 1896.

12. *New York Times*, March 6, 1896.

13. *New York Times*, March 25, 1896.

14. *New York Times*, April 1, 1896.

15. *New York Times*, April 8, 1896.

16. *New York Times*, July 16, 1896.

17. *New York Times*, July 17, 1896.

18. *New York Times*, July 23, 1896.

19. *New York Times*, October 24, 1896

Chapter 12

1. *New York Times*, February 13, 1898.

2. *New York Times*, February 13, 1898.

3. *New York Times*, February 13, 1898.

4. *New York Times*, February 13, 1898.

5. *New York Times*, February 13, 1898.

6. *New York Times*, February 15, 1898.

7. *New York Times*, March 18, 1898.

8. *New York Times*, March 13, 1898.

9. *New York Times*, April 6, 1898.

10. *New York Times*, April 16, 1898.

Chapter 13

1. Clayton R. Barrow, Jr., ed., *America Spreads Her Sails: U.S. Seapower in the 19th Century* (Annapolis, 1973): William H. Flayhart III, "Four Fighting Ladies," 195.

2. Barrow, ed., *America Spreads Her Sails*, 196

3. International Navigation Company, *American Line* (New York, 1898), un. (7–8). The beautifully done history, produced by the Line, of the activities of the four big ships in the Spanish-American War.

4. International Navigation Company, *American Line*, un.

5. Barrow, ed., *America Spreads Her Sails*, 207–8.

6. Barrow, ed., *America Spreads Her Sails*, 211–12.

Chapter 14

1. *New York Times*, January 1, 1899.

2. *New York Times*, January 2, 1899.

3. *New York Times*, January 2, 1899.

4. *New York Times*, January 2, 1899.

5. *New York Times*, April 8, 1899.

6. *New York Times*, March 23, 1899.

7. "Report of Capt. Watkins," *New York Times*, July 11, 1899.

8. *New York Times*, May 22, 1899.

9. *New York Times*, May 22, 1899.

10. *New York Times*, May 22, 1899.

11. *New York Times*, May 24, 1899.

12. *New York Times*, July 11, 1899.

13. *New York Times*, July 11, 1899.

14. *New York Times*, July 11, 1899.

15. *New York Times*, July 13, 1899.

16. N.R.P Bonsor, *North Atlantic Seaway*, I, 244–45.

Chapter 15

1. *New York Commercial and Shipping List*, January 15, 1900, 12.

2. *New York Times*, June 27, 1900.

3. Lloyd C. Griscom, *Diplomatically Speaking* (New York, 1940), 298.

4. Griscom, *Diplomatically Speaking*, 298.

5. *Marine Engineering*, December 1900, 527; *New York Times*, November 5, 1900.

6. *Marine Engineering*, December 1900, 527.

7. *New York Times*, November 5, 1900

Chapter 16

1. N.R.P. Bonsor, *North Atlantic Seaway*, III, 1075.

2. Marian V. Sears, "International Mercantile Marine Company," Harvard Business School Case Study (Cambridge, MA, 1953), 15.

3. Vivian Vale, *The American Peril: Challenge to Britain on the North Atlantic, 1901-04* (Manchester, 1984), 35–36. An excellent work on the maneuvering surrounding the

creation of the IMM, but not for the historical background of the fleets. Bonsor remains the single authority on the line histories.

4. Herbert L. Satterlee, *J. Pierpont Morgan: An Intimate Portrait* (New York, 1939), 329–30.

5. Satterlee, *J. Pierpont Morgan*, 373.

6. Sears, "International Mercantile Marine Company," 16.

7. Carl Hovey, *The Life Story of J. Pierpont Morgan* (New York, 1911), 253.

8. *The Liverpool Daily Post*, May 1, 1901.

9. *Annual Report of the Commissioner of Navigation*, 1901, 319.

10. *The Liverpool Daily Post*, May 1, 1901. Ellerman also announced his future plans to the Leyland shareholders at the extraordinary general meeting held in London on May 7, 1901 (*The Liverpool Courier*, May 8, 1901).

11. *The Liverpool Daily Post*, May 1, 1901. "Starting a Steel War, Mr. Pierpont Morgan's Plans."

12. J.R. Ellerman, "How We Are Killing Our Shipping Trade, The Moral of the Pierpont Morgan Deal," *Daily Mail*, May 8, 1901.

13. *The Liverpool Courier*, May 8, 1901.

14. *Liverpool Mercury*, June 14, 1901.

15. Vernon H. Brown to David Jardine, Esq., October 21, 1901, Cunard Papers (D42/Ca37), *The University Archives*, The University of Liverpool. A *confidential* dispatch sent "Per *Kaiser Wilhelm der Grosse*."

16. *New York Journal of Commerce*, October 15, 1901.

17. Vernon H. Brown to Mr. David Jardine (Managing Director, Cunard Line), October 21, 1901, Cunard Papers (D42/Ca37), The University Archives, The University of Liverpool.

18. Edward J. Berwind to Vernon H. Brown, May 29, 1901. Cunard Papers (D42/Ca34), The University Archives, The University of Liverpool.

19. Frank Broeze, "Albert Ballin, The Hamburg-Bremen Rivalry and the Dynamics of the Conference System," *International Journal of Maritime History*, III, N.1 (June 1991), 1–32.

20. Lamar Cecil, *Albert Ballin: Business and Politics in Imperial Germany, 1888-1918* (Princeton, 1967), 49.

21. Vernon H. Brown to David Jardine, November 15, 1901. Cunard Papers (D42/Ca37), The University Archives, The University of Liverpool.

22. Cecil, *Albert Ballin*, 51.

23. Cecil, *Albert Ballin*, 51.

24. Cecil, *Albert Ballin*, 52.

25. Vernon Brown to David Jardine, October 21, 1901, Cunard Papers (D42/Ca37), The University Archives, The University of Liverpool.

26. Frank Broeze, "Shipping Policy and Social-Darwinism: Albert Ballin and the *Weltpolitik* of the Hamburg-American Line 1886–1914," *The Mariner's Mirror*, Vol. 79, No. 4 (November 1993), 431.

27. Cecil, *Albert Ballin*, 52.

28. *The Journal of Commerce and Commercial Bulletin* (New York), December 9, 1901.

29. *New York Herald*, January 25, 1902, 4.

30. *New York Times*, January 25, 1902.

31. *New York Herald*, January 25, 1902, 4.

32. Vernon H. Brown to Lord Inverclyde, February 4, 1902, Cunard Papers (D42/Ca37), The University Archives, The University of Liverpool.

33. Vernon H. Brown to Lord Inverclyde, April 12, 1902, Cunard Papers (Ca6/20), The University Archives, The University of Liverpool. There is reason for thinking that Cunard's "Educational Fund" was employed discreetly but forcefully to defeat the passage of the shipping subsidy bill during 1902.

34. Vernon H. Brown to Lord Inverclyde, February 8, 1902, Cunard Papers (D42/Ca37), The University Archives, The University of Liverpool.

35. Vernon H. Brown to Lord Inverclyde, February 5, 1902, Cunard Papers (D42/Ca37), The University Archives, The University of Liverpool. Brown also stated: "I have only just gotten the information referred to and have but half an hour to save [*sic*] the supplementary mail at the dock. Shall frame and send you a cable despatch later. Of course I may not be quite correct in my diagnosis of the situation but I think I am pretty nearly right in my conclusions."

36. Lord Inverclyde to Vernon Brown, February 19, 1902, Cunard Papers (D42/Ca37), The University Archives, The University of Liverpool.

37. Lord Inverclyde to Vernon Brown, February 19, 1902, Cunard Papers (D42/Ca37), The University Archives, The University of Liverpool.

38. Vernon H. Brown to Lord Inverclyde, February 19, 1902 (cable), Cunard Papers (D42/Ca37), The University Archives, The University of Liverpool. The cable is quoted in a letter of Lord Inverclyde to A.D. Mearns, February 28, 1902, in which he requests a copy of the Cunard Code Book so that he can decode Brown's cables wherever he might be. There had been some confusion over the meaning of some of the secret messages.

39. Sears, "International Mercantile Marine Company," Appendix A, 49–55.

40. Vernon H. Brown to Lord Inverclyde, February 14, 1902, Cunard Papers (D42/Ca37), The University Archives, The University of Liverpool.

41. N.R.P. Bonsor, *North Atlantic Seaway*, I, 369.

42. N.R.P. Bonsor, *North Atlantic Seaway*, II, 530.

43. Sears, "International Mercantile Marine Company," 24.

44. Broeze, "Shipping Policy and Social Darwinism," 426.

45. Sears, "International Mercantile Marine Company," 24.

46. *Wall Street Journal*, May 12, 1902.

47. Sears, "International Mercantile Marine Company," 25.

48. Sears, "International Mercantile Marine Company," 25.

49. *Wall Street Journal*, April 25, 1902.

Chapter 17

1. *United States Investor*, April 26, 1902, 770.

2. 57th Cong., 1st Sess., *Report 201*, part 2, March 15, 1902.

3. Marian V. Sears, "International Mercantile Marine Company" Harvard Business School Case Study (Cambridge, MA., 1953), 97.

4. *Annual Report of the Commissioner of Navigation*, 1901, 23–24.

5. *United States Investor*, April 26, 1902, 770.

6. 58th Cong., 3d Sess., Senate Report no. 2755, *Report of the Merchant Marine Commission*, 1905, I, 1.

7. *Wall Street Journal*, October 16, 1902.

8. *Wall Street Journal*, April 21, 1902.

9. *Wall Street Journal*, May 14, 1902. Quotation from a British observer.

10. Francis E. Hyde, *Cunard and the North Atlantic 1840–1973* (London, 1975), 147.

11. Lord Inverclyde to Mr. Jardine, May 3, 1902, Cunard Papers (D42/Ca40), The University Archives, The University of Liverpool. George Burns, second Lord Inverclyde, succeeded his father on the latter's premature death in 1901, and in this letter reviewed the actions of the Cunard board of March 27, 1900.

12. Hyde, *Cunard and the North Atlantic 1840–1973*, 139.

13. Hyde, *Cunard and the North Atlantic 1840–1973*, 141.

14. Hyde, *Cunard and the North Atlantic 1840–1973*, 143.

15. Hyde, *Cunard and the North Atlantic 1840–1973*, 144. Lord Selborne to Lord Inverclyde, May 10, 1902.

16. Hyde, *Cunard and the North Atlantic 1840–1973*, 144.

17. Lord Inverclyde to Mr. Watson (member of Cunard board), August 8, 1902, Cunard Papers (D42/Ca39), The University Archives, The University of Liverpool. "Of course the least satisfactory part of it is that the Cunard Company gain [*sic*] on immediate benefit. That is comparatively small matter to the great future I consider is before it, closely bound as it will be to the Government of this Country. And, of course, the sooner we get the new ships built the better it will be for us."

18. Lord Inverclyde to Gerald Balfour, August 8, 1902, Cunard Papers (D42/Ca39), The University Archives, The University of Liverpool. This is accompanied by the "Memorandum of interview between Mr. Gerald Balfour and Lord Inverclyde," relative to the agreement between Cunard and His Majesty's government and signed by both men.

19. Lord Inverclyde to Mr. Watson (member of Cunard board), August 8, 1902, Cunard Papers (D42/Ca39), The University Archives, The University of Liverpool.

20. Lord Inverclyde to Mr. Watson (member of Cunard board), August 8, 1902, Cunard Papers (D42/Ca39), The University Archives, The University of Liverpool.

21. Lord Inverclyde to Vernon H. Brown, August 8, 1902 (cable), Cunard Papers (D42/Ca39), The University Archives, The University of Liverpool.

22. Vernon H. Brown to Lord Inverclyde, August 8, 1902, "Per *Etruria*," Cunard Papers (D42/Ca39), The University Archives, The University of Liverpool.

23. Lord Inverclyde to Vernon Brown, August 8, 1902, Cunard Papers (D42/Ca39), The University Archives, The University of Liverpool.

24. Vernon H. Brown to Lord Inverclyde, August 22, 1902, Cunard Papers (D42/Ca39), The University Archives, The University of Liverpool. Brown also recommended that no position on the Cunard board should be reserved for any government representative, since that would only create future problems.

25. Cunard Steam Ship Co. Ltd., "The Statement Made by the Chairman at the Shareholders' Meeting, 29th July, 1903," The University Archives, The University of Liverpool, Cunard Papers (D42/Ca42), 9.

26. Cunard Steam Ship Co. Ltd., "The Statement Made by the Chairman at the Shareholders' Meeting, 29th July 1903," The University Archives, The University of Liverpool, Cunard Papers (D42/Ca42), 10.

27. Cunard Steam Ship Co. Ltd., "The Statement Made by the Chairman at the Shareholders' Meeting, 29th July 1903," The University Archives, The University of Liverpool, Cunard Papers (D42/Ca42), 12.

28. Cunard Steam Ship Co. Ltd., "The Statement Made by the Chairman at the Shareholders' Meeting, 29th July 1903," The University Archives, The University of Liverpool, Cunard Papers (D42/Ca42). 12.

29. *Fairplay*, January 21, 1904, 78.

30. *The Philadelphia Press*, March 20, 1904.

31. *Fairplay*, March 26, 1903, 491

32. Roy Anderson, *White Star* (Prescot, Lancashire, 1965), 106. The debate over the name of third White Star liner in this trio will go on forever. Anderson felt that *Gigantic* represented a logical progression and I concur. That she ultimately was named *Britannic* following the *Titanic* disaster represents an equally logical adjustment to circumstances.

BIBLIOGRAPHY

General Bibliographies

Two recent bibliographies represent the best places for any one interested in oceanic history, both maritime and naval, to start their research:

Broeze, Frank, ed., *Maritime History at the Crossroads: a Critical Review of Recent Historiography*, Research in Maritime History No.9, International Maritime Economic History Association, St. John's, Newfoundland, 1995.

Hattendorf, John B., ed., *Ubi Sumus? The State of Naval and Maritime History*, Naval War College Historical Monography Series, No. 11, Newport, Rhode Island, 1994.

Manuscripts

American Steamship Company (ASC), "An Act to Incorporate the American Steamship Company of Philadelphia," February 7, 1871, *Minute Book I, 1871–1876*, 1–3. Pennsylvania Railroad Collection, Box 89, Urban Archives, Temple University, Philadelphia, Pennsylvania.

American Steamship Company (ASC), *First Annual Report, Minute Book I, 1871–1876*, 80. Pennsylvania Railroad Collection, Box 89, Urban Archives, Temple University, Philadelphia, Pennsylvania. The *First Annual Report* covers developments from 1871–1872. The successive "Annual Reports" are pasted into the *Minute Books*.

American Steamship Company (ASC), *By-Laws*, Pennsylvania Railroad Collection, Box 89, Urban Archives, Temple University, Philadelphia, Pennsylvania.

American Steamship Company (ASC), *Minute Books* (2 vols): *1871–1876, 1876–1911*, Pennsylvania Railroad Collection, Box 89, Urban Archives, Temple University, Philadelphia, Pennsylvania.

American Steamship Company (ASC), "Report of the Committee on Finance on Officers and Crew and their Compensation," January 3, 1873, *Minute Book I, 1871–1876*, 135–137. Pennsylvania Railroad Collection, Box 89, Urban Archives, Temple University, Philadelphia, Pennsylvania.

American Steamship Company (ASC), "Report of the Committee on Reorganization," December 31, 1873, *Minute Book I, 1871–1876*, 282–285. Pennsylvania Railroad Collection, Box 89, Urban Archives, Temple University, Philadelphia, Pennsylvania.

Bonsor, N.R.P., Nearly complete sailing schedules of the American Steamship Company, 1873–1884, ms. in the author's collection.

Bonsor, N.R.P., Nearly complete sailing schedule of the Société Anonyme de Navigation Belge-Américaine (International Navigation Company-Red Star Line), 1879–1893, ms. in the author's collection.

Bonsor, N.R.P., Nearly complete sailing schedule of the American Line (1893), 1893–1895, ms. in the author's collection.

Brady, Cornelius L., "Deposition (July 11, 1874)," *Brady v. American Steamship Company*, "Amendment to Libel," Papers of John Cadwalader, Judge of the District Court of the United States in and for the Eastern District of Pennsylvania. The Historical Society of Pennsylvania, Philadelphia. Additional deposition material from other crew members also are included in Judge Cadwalader's Papers.

Cunard Steamship Company Limited Papers, University Archives, The University of Liverpool, England.

Hermans, Francois, lt., January 16, 1966, forwarded by Mr. Paul E.R. Scarceriaux, Chairman of the Belgian Nautical Research Association, dealing with the early history of the Société Anonyme de Navigation Belge-Américaine (Red Star Line).

Herrick, Walter, R., Jr., *The American Naval Revolution 1890–1898*, Winter Park, Florida, 1965. An unpublished doctoral dissertation in the archives of the University of Virginia, Charlottesville.

Pennsylvania Railroad Company, "Minutes of the Board of Directors of the Pennsylvania Railroad Company," Minute Book no. 5 (November 1865–November 1871), Pennsylvania Railroad Collection, Hagley Museum and Library (Soda House), Wilmington, Delaware.

Pennsylvania Railroad Company, "Statement of the Financial Committee of the American Steamship Company," December 8, 1874, Pennsylvania Railroad Company, Secretary's Papers, M-85, Board File No. 95, Pennsylvania Railroad Collection, Hagley Museum and Library (Soda House), Wilmington, Delaware.

Pennsylvania Railroad Company, "Subcommittee of the Finance Committee, Board of Directors, PRR," January 24, 1877, Pennsylvania Railroad Company, Secretary's Papers, M-85, Board File No.95, Pennsylvania Railroad Collection, Hagley Museum and Library (Soda House), Wilmington, Delaware. Discusses resolution of ASC debt to PRR.

Smith, Robert W., Secretary, PRR, ALS to Samuel Rea, Assistant to the President, PRR, January 13, 1897, M-87, BF-156, Pennsylvania Railroad Collection, Hagley Museum and Library (Soda House), Wilmington, Delaware. Discusses the history of the PRR involvement in the bonds of the American Steamship Company.

Welsh, Henry D., President, American Steamship Company, ALS. to the President and Board of Directors of the Pennsylvania Railroad Company, January 25, 1876, Minutes of the PRR Board, M85, Board No,95, Pennsylvania Railroad Collection, Hagley Museum and Library (Soda House), Wilmington, Delaware. Detailed ALS discussing the need for additional ships.

Williams, Osgood, lt., July 23, 1965, from the Past-Director of Peabody Museum, Salem, Massachusetts, Mr. Osgood Williams, relating information on the American Line available at the Museum, but also his personal reminiscences of a crossing on the *New York* in June 1914, among other things. In the author's collection.

Newspapers

Daily Mail, 1900–1905.

Fairplay, 1900–1905.

Glasgow Herald, 1873–1874.

International Journal of Maritime History, 1989–1998.

The Journal of Commerce and Commercial Bulletin (New York), 1900–1905.

Liverpool Courier, 1900–1905.

Liverpool Mercury, 1900–1905.

Liverpool Daily Post, 1900–1905.

Liverpool Journal of Commerce, June 23, 1873.

Marine Engineering, 1880–1905.

Mariner's Mirror, 1914–1998.

Mitchell's Maritime Register, August 30, 1872.

New York Commercial and Shipping List, 1900.

New York Herald, 1865–1905.

New York Times, 1865–1905.

New York Tribune, 1890–1905.

Philadelphia Commercial List and Price Current, December 1870–July 1882.

Philadelphia Evening Bulletin, 1873–1905.

Philadelphia North American United States Gazette, January 13, 1873.

Scientific American, 1886–1905.

The Times, 1865–1905.

United States Investor, 1902.

Wall Street Journal, 1890–1905.

Published Documents

Annual Report of the Commissioner of Navigation, London, 1901.

Buell, Augustus C., *The Memoirs of Charles H. Cramp*, Philadelphia: J. B. Lippincott Company, 1906. Highly edited documents and accounts written by Charles H. Cramp and compiled by Augustus C. Buell.

Cramp, Charles H., *Commercial Supremacy and Other Papers*, Philadelphia, nd., (1894).

(Cramp) *The William Cramp & Son Ship and Engine Building Company*, Philadelphia, nd. (ca. 1894). Philadelphia Public Library.

Griscom, Clement Acton (misindexed "Grisco"), Testimony before the Senate Subcommittee on "Revival of the Merchant Marine," Senate Miscellaneous Documents, No.149, 56th Cong. 1st. Sess, 100–9.

Inman Line, Red Star Line, and American Line, *The Inman and International Steamship Company*, New York, nd (ca. 1888). A privately published description of the ships and services of the three lines preceded by a brief history of the lines. New York Public Library.

International Navigation Company, *American Line*, New York, 1898. A collection of documents and accounts concerning the transfer of the Inman Line to the United States and the formation of the American Line (1893), which introduces a documentary account of the employment of the American Line liners during the Spanish-American War (1898), and which is followed by a detailed description of the liners. Mariners Museum, Newport News, Virginia.

Messrs. Peter Wright & Sons, *The Red Star Line, Belgian Royal and U.S. Mail Steamships, Facts for Travellers*, New York, n.d. (1883?). Philadelphia Maritime Museum Collection.

Postmaster-General (UK) to William Inman (Post 51/46), "Contract of 9th March 1869. United States Mails. Liverpool via Queenstown to New York," GPO Historical Records Office, St. Martin's-le-Grand, London.

Postmaster General (US), *Report of the Postmaster General* (43 Cong., 2d. Sess.), vol. 1638, 13–14.

Postmaster General (US), "Report of the Postmaster General," in *The Abridgment. Message from the President of the United States to the Two Houses of Congress as the Beginning of the First Session of the Fifty-Second Congress, with the Reports of the Heads of Departments and Selections from Accompanying Documents*, edited by W. H. Michael, Washington, GPO, 1892.

Report of the Merchant Marine Commission, 58th Cong., 3d. Sess., Senate Report No.2755, 1905.

U.S. Congress, *Report 201*, 57th Cong., 1st. Sess., part 2, 1902.

Books and Published Sources

Abbot, Willis J., *The Story of Our Merchant Marine*, New York, 1919.

Albion, Robert Greenhalgh, *The Rise of the Port of New York*, New York, 1939.

Anderson, Roy, *White Star*, Prescot, Lancashire, England, 1964.

Anthony, Irvin, *Down to the Sea in Ships*, Philadelphia, 1924.

Appleton, Thomas E., *Ravenscrag—The Allan Royal Mail Line*, Toronto, 1974.

Armstrong, Warren, *Atlantic Highway*, New York, 1962.

Baker, W.A. and Try Trychare, *The Engine Powered Vessel*, New York, 1965.

Barbance, Marthe, *Histoire de la Compagnie Generale Transatlantique*, Paris, 1955.

Barrow, Clayton, ed., *America Spreads Her Sails, A Century of Sea Power, 1873–1973*, Annapolis, Maryland, 1973.

Bauer, K. Jack, *A Maritime History of the United States: The Role of America's Seas and Waterways*, Columbia, South Carolina, 1988.

Bessell, George, *Norddeutscher Lloyd 1857–1957*, Bremen, 1957.

Blake, G., *BI Centenary 1856–1956*, London, 1956.

Bonsor, N.R.P., *North Atlantic Seaway*, Prescot, Lancashire, England, 1955 (supplement added 1960).

———, *North Atlantic Seaway*, Jersey, Channel Islands, 1975–1980, Second Edition in five volumes.

———, *South Atlantic Seaway*, Jersey, Channel Islands, 1983.

Bowen, Frank C., *A Century of Atlantic Travel*, New York, 1930.

Boyce, Gordon H., *Information, Mediation and Institutional Development, The Rise of Large-scale Enterprise in British Shipping, 1870–1919*, Manchester, 1995.

Braynard, Frank O., *Famous American Ships*, New York, 1956.

———, *SS Savannah—The Elegant Steam Ship*, Athens, Georgia, 1963.

Broeze, Frank, "Albert Ballin, The Hamburg-Bremen Rivalry and the Dynamics of the Conference System," *International Journal of Maritime History*, III (June 1991), 1–32.

———, "Shipping Policy and Social-Darwinism: Albert Ballin and the *Weltpolitik* of the Hamburg-American Line 1886–1914," *The Mariner's Mirror*, Vol. 79, No. 4 (November 1993).

Bundy, C. Lynn, *The Maritime Association of the Port of New York, Historical review of the Past Fifty Years*, New York, 1923.

Burgess, George H., and Miles C. Kennedy, *Centennial History of the Pennsylvania Railroad Company 1846–1946*, Philadelphia, 1949.

Bushell, T.A., *Royal Mail: A Centenary History 1839–1939*, London, 1939.

Cable, Boyd, *A Hundred Year History of the P. & O.*, London, 1937.

Carosso, Vincent P., *The Morgans*, Cambridge, Massachusetts, 1987.

Carter, Craig J.M., *Ships of the Mersey*, London, 1966.

Cecil, Lamar, *Albert Ballin, Business and Politics in Imperial Germany 1888–1918*, Princeton, New Jersey, 1967.

Chadwick, F.E., et al., *Ocean Steamships*, London, 1892.

Chandler, Alfred D., Jr., *Scale and Scope: The Dynamics of Industrial Capitalism*, Cambridge, Massachusetts, 1990.

———, *Strategy and Structure, Chapters in the History of American Industrial Enterprise*, Cambridge, Massachusetts, 1962.

———, *The Visible Hand: The Management Revolution in American Business*, Cambridge, Massachusetts, 1977.

Chandler, George, *Liverpool Shipping, A Short History*, London, 1960.

Clark, Alexander, *Summer Rambles in Europe*, New York, 1879.

Corson, F. Reid, *The Atlantic Ferry in the Twentieth Century*, London, 1929.

Dictionary of National Biography, "Inman, William (1825–1881)," X, 457.

Dudden, Arthur Power, *The American Pacific*, New York, 1992.

Duff, Peter, *British Ships and Shipping*, London, 1949.

Dugan, James, *The Great Iron Ship*, London, 1953.

Dunmore, Walter J., *Ship Subsidies, an Economic Study of the Policy of Subsidizing Merchant Marines*, Boston, 1907.

Dunn, Laurence, *Passenger Liners*, Southampton, 1961.

———, *Famous Liners of the Past—Belfast Built*, London, 1964.

Dunnet, Alistair, *The Donaldson Line, A Century of Shipping, 1854–1954*, Glasgow, 1960.

Emmons, Frederick, *The Atlantic Liners 1925–1970*, Newton Abbot, 1972.

Fairfield Shipbuilding and Engineering Company Limited, *Fairfield 1860–1960*, Glasgow, 1960.

Farr, Grahame, *The Steamship Great Britain*, Bristol, 1965.

———, *The Steamship Great Western*, Bristol, 1963.

Fatout, Paul, ed., *Mark Twain Speaking*, Iowa City, Iowa, 1976.

Flayhart, William Henry, III, "Four Fighting Ladies," 195–214, in Barrow, Clayton, ed., *America Spreads Her Sails, A Century of Sea Power, 1873–1973*, Annapolis, Maryland, 1973.

Fry, Henry, *The History of North Atlantic Steam Navigation*, London, 1896.

Gibbs, Commander C. R. Vernon, *Passenger Liners of the Western Ocean*, London, 1952 (rev. ed 1957).

Griffiths, Denis, *Power of the Great Liners*, Sparkford, Somerset, 1990.

Griscom, Lloyd C., *Diplomatically Speaking*, New York, 1940.

Haws, Duncan, *Merchant Fleets in Profile 2*, Cambridge, 1979.

Headley, J.T., *The Travels of General Grant*, Philadelphia, 1881.

Heinrich, Thomas R., *Ships for the Seven Seas, Philadelphia Shipbuilding in the Age of Industrial Capitalism*, Baltimore, 1997.

Heyl, Erik, *Early American Steamers* (3 vols), Buffalo, New York, 1953–1956.

Holbrook, Stewart H., *The Age of the Moguls*, Garden City, New Jersey, 1955.

Holman, H., *A Handy Book for Shipowners & Masters* (7th ed), London, 1911.

Holmes, Sir George C.V., *Ancient and Modern Ships, Part II, The Era of Steam, Iron & Steel*, London, 1906.

Hovey, Carl, *The Life Story of J. Pierpont Morgan*, New York, 1911.

Howarth, David, and Stephen Howarth, *the Story of P & O*, London, 1986.

Hyde, Francis E., *Cunard and the North Atlantic 1840–1972*, London, 1975.

Hyslop, Donald, Alastair Forsyth, and Sheila Jemima, *Titanic Voices, Memories from the Fateful Voyage*, New York, 1997.

Isherwood, J.H., *Steamers of the Past*, Liverpool, 1966.

Johnson, Emory R., *Principles of Ocean Transportation*, New York, 1919.

Johnson, Emory R., T.W. Van Metre, G.G. Huebner, and D.S. Hanchett, *History of Domestic and Foreign Commerce of the United States* (2 vols), New York, 1915.

Keiler, Hans, *American Shipping: Its History and Economic Conditions*, Problems der Waltwirtschaft, Schriften des Instituts fur Desverkehr und Waltwirtschaft an der Universitat Kiel, June, 1913.

Kirkaldy, Adam W., *British Shipping, Its History, Organization and Importance*, London, 1919.

Kludas, Arnold, *Great Passenger Ships of the World* (5 vols), Cambridge, 1975.

Kludas, Arnold, and Herbert Bischoff, *Die Schiffe der Hamburg-Amerika Linie* (3 vols), Herford, Germany, 1979.

Knap, Ger H., *A Century of Shipping*, Amsterdam, 1956.

Labaree, Benjamin W., ed., *The Atlantic World of Robert G. Albion*, Middletown, Connecticut, 1975.

Lee, Charles E., *The Blue Riband*, London, 1930.

LeFleming, H.M., *Ships of the Holland America Line*, London, 1965.

Lindsay, W.S., *History of Merchant Shipping and Commerce* (4 vols), London, 1883.

Lott, Arnold S., *A Long Line of Ships*, Annapolis, Maryland, 1954.

Maber, John, *North Star to Southern Cross*, Prescott, Lancashire, 1967.

McCabe, James D., *A Tour Around the World by General Grant*, Philadelphia, 1879.

McLellan, R.S., *Anchor Lines (1856–1956)*, Glasgow, 1956.

Maginnis, Arthur J., *The Atlantic Ferry*, London, 1900.

Marvin, Winthrop I., *The American Merchant Marine*, New York, 1902.

Maxtone-Graham, John, *The Only Way to Cross*, New York, 1972.

Meeker, Royal, *History of Shipping Subsidies*, New York, 1905.

Morris, James M., *Our Maritime Heritage*, Washington, 1979.

Musk, George, *The Canadian Pacific Afloat 1883–1968*, London, 1968.

Nicholson, John, *Liners of the Clyde*, Glasgow, 1994.

Noble, Dennis L., *That Others Might Live, The U.S. Life-Saving Service, 1878–1915*, Annapolis, Maryland, 1994.

Oldham, Wilton J., *The Ismay Line*, Liverpool, 1961.

Oost, Tony, et al., *Henri Cassiers 1858–1944*, Antwerpen, 1994.

Parker, Captain Walter H., *Leaves from an Unwritten Log-Book*, London, nd (ca.1930).

Phelps, Edith M., ed., *Selected Articles on the American Merchant Marine* (2nd. ed), Debaters' Handbook Series, New York, 1920.

Rentell, Philip, *Historic Cunard Liners*, Truro, Cornwall, 1986.

———, *Historic White Star Liners*, Truro, Cornwall, 1987.

Ridgely-Nevitt, Cedric, *American Steamships on the Atlantic*, Newark, Delaware, 1981.

Robinson, Howard, *Carrying British Mails Overseas*, London, 1964.

Rowe, William Hutchinson, *The Maritime History of Maine*, New York, 1948.

Russell, W.H., *The Atlantic Telegraph*, London, 1865 (rev. ed 1972).

Satterlee, Herbert L., *J. Pierpont Morgan, An Intimate Portrait 1837–1913*, New York, 1939.

Schotter, H. W., *The Growth and Development of the Pennsylvania Railroad Company, A Review of the Charter and Annual Reports of the Pennsylvania Railroad Company 1846–1926, Inclusive*, Philadelphia, 1927.

Sears, Marian V., *International Mercantile Marine Company*, Harvard Business School Case Study, Cambridge, Massachusetts, 1953.

Smith, Eugene W., *Passenger Ships of the World, Past and Present*, Boston, 1963.

Smith, Philip Chadwick Foster, *Philadelphia on the River*, Philadelphia, 1986.

Society of Naval Architects and Marine Engineers, *Historical Transactions 1893–1943*, New York, 1945.

Spears, John R., *The Story of the American Merchant Marine*, New York, 1910.

Staff, Frank, *The Trans-Atlantic Mail*, London, 1956.

Swann, Leonard Alexander, *John Roach, Maritime Entrepreneur*, Annapolis, Maryland, 1965.

Taylor, James, *Ellermans—A Wealth of Shipping*, London, 1976.

Tute, Warren, *Atlantic Conquest*, Boston, 1962.

Tyler, David Budlong, *Steam Conquers the Atlantic*, New York, 1939.

Vale, Vivian, *The American Peril*, Manchester, 1984.

Weigley, Russell F., ed., *Philadelphia, A 300-Year History*, New York, 1982.

Whitehurst, Clinton H., Jr., *The U.S. Shipbuilding Industry*, Annapolis, Maryland, 1986.

Winther, Oscar Osborn, *The Transportation Frontier*, New York, 1964.

Wright, Edward N., "The Story of Peter Wright & Sons, Philadelphia Quaker Shipping Firm, 1818–1911," *Quaker History*, 56 (1967), 67–89.

INDEX

famine relief, *45*

Fawns, James, 222, 223

Fernald, Frank, 212, 216

Fidelity Trust and Safe Deposit Company, 169

figureheads, *105*, 127, 261

Finland, *49, 66, 340*

Firth, Major and Mrs. Thomas T., 37

Fish, Hamilton, 70

Fitzgerald, P., 285

Flagler, John H., 309

Flower, Roswell Pettibone, 151

Floyd, Agent, 216

Flynn, Joseph, 242–43

Folkner, Adolphus, 223

Fort Calmanera, 273

Foster, Charles, 142–45, 158–59

Foster, John W., 152

Fox, Sampson, 38

Frames of the City of New York, *looking forward—July 19, 1887, 122*

France, 156, 221, 349
  in Crimean War, 114, 116
  Russia's relations with, 72

Frank Leslie's Illustrated Newspaper, 132, 305

Franklin, P. A. S., 330, 337, 338

Frazee, Detective, 242

Frederick Leyland and Company Limited, 319–20, 331, 334

freight, 178
  in *Annual Report*, 60
  fresh meat, 59–60, 67
  grain, *45, 91, 93, 96*
  Navel loss of, 53, 57
  in *Paris* stranding, 299–300
  Pennsylvania Railroad income from, 66
  petroleum products, *see* petroleum, petroleum products
  rates for, 40, 56–57, 322, 336

Fremantle, Sir Edmund Robert, 299

French Line, 226, 240

Friesland, 84, 106, 128, 133, 162, 170, 314
  figurehead on, *105*

repainting of, 163

Frye, William P., 134, 340, 345

Fulda, 257

Fulver, 208

funnels:
  of Holland-America Line, *250*
  repainting of, 163
  replacement of, 208, 226, *238*
  of *St. Paul*, *230, 238*

Furness, Sir Christopher, 344, 346

Furness and Evans, 200–201

Furness Line, *118*

furniture, 105, *199*, 313

Furor, 265

Fürst Bismarck, 161, 220, 244–45

Gamble, Fourth Officer, 46

Gary, Elbert H., 317

Gates, John W., 341

General Assembly, Pennsylvania, 18, 19

George Birkbeck, 53

George Starr, 231, 236

Geo. Warren & Co., 32

Germond, William, 238

Ghequier, T. Buckler, 104

Gigantic, 353

Giles, J. H., 194

Gilroy, Thomas F., 151

Girard Point, 88, 96

Glasgow and Lisbon Steam Packet Company, 16

Glasgow Herald, 41

G. M. Papayanni, 67, 163, 320

gold, *54*

Goodrich, Caspar R., 262, 266–69

Gould, Jay, 212

Gourlay & Co., 57

Graham, District Attorney, 187

grain, as freight, *45, 91, 93, 96*

grain elevators, 96

Grant, Charles H., 240

Grant, Jessie S., *63*, 70, 71

Grant, Ulysses S., 31, 54

G.W. Clyde, 240

Hall, George, 151
Hamburg-American Line (HAPAG), 107, 109,
    138, 203, 204–5, 213, 220, 226, 244–45,
    257, 306, 315
  board of directors of, 323
  in competition for steerage passengers,
    165–67, 217
  shipping trust and, 322–25, 332–35
Hamilton, 70
Hancock, R. B., 37, 42
Handyside, Nicol, 16
Handyside, Robert, 16
Handyside & Company, 16
Handyside and Henderson, 17
Hannah, Marcus, 339–40
Hanscom, Naval Constructor, 173–74
HAPAG, *see* Hamburg-American Line
Harbor Board, Southampton, 155
Harland and Wolff, Belfast, 67, *68*, *248*, 304,
    308, 312, 315, 320–21, 333, 338, 353
Harmonides, 100, *108*
Harper's Weekly, *134*
Harris, Thomas R., 53
Harrison, Benjamin, 147–54, *148*, *150*, *151*, 178
Hartranft, John F., 70
Harvard, USS, 262–67, 272, *274*, 277–78, *277*,
    278, *280*
Hastings, Daniel Hartman, 183, 187, 192
Hatton, Frank, 149
Haverford, *254*, *294*, *324*, *330*
H. B. Hume, 77
Heal, S. C., 218
Heard, Andrew, 223
Henderson, Thomas, 16, 17
Herbert, Hilary A., 178, 211
Hercules, 97
Hicks, Elias, 81
"Hicksite" Quakers, 81–82
Hoffman, Christian J., 60
Hohenzollern, 307, 308

Holland-America Line (HAL), 167, 226, 246,
    255
  shipping trust and, 333–34
  see also Veendam
House of Commons, British, 204, 342, 346
House of Representatives, U.S., 36, 134, 152,
    340–41
Houston, H. H., 86, 151–52
Howard Carroll, 147–48, 151
Howden, James, *46*
Hudson, 231
Hunter, John, 311, 312
hurricanes, 42
Hurst, F. W. J., 151
Hustler, 210, 229
Hyde, James H., 337

icebergs, 203
I. J. Merritt, 229–31, 237
Illinois, 23–24, 38, 39, 52, 53, 74, 75, 163, 170,
    213, 257
  fresh meat as freight of, 59–60
  launching of, 35
  repairs needed by, 77
  sailing schedule of, *87*
  sale of, *56*; *see also Supply*
immigration, immigrants, 62, 89, 102, 105,
    169, 225
  Griscom's praise for, 190
  Inman Line and, 113, 114, 116
  landings of, *194*
  in return to Europe, 168, 217, 255
Imperial Russian Navy, *45*, 72–74
Indiana, 23–24, 38, 39, 52, 75, 163, 170
  in famine relief, *45*
  Grant party on, *63*, 70–71, *70*, *73*, 97
  grounded at Bulkhead Bar, 60
  launching of, 35
  and precautions against disease, 165
  repairs needed by, 77
  sailing schedule of, *87*
Indiana, USS, 171

McCarroll, Peter, 51

McColl, Gavin, 311–12

MacIver, Harry, 344

McKinley, William, 260

Madeira, Louis C., 37, 42

Mahan, Alfred Thayer, 259, 260

mail subsidy:

    American, 133–39, 194, 205, 211–12, 216,
       223, *225*, 287–88, 339–40

    of American Line, 42

    American Line's pursuit of, 31–32, 36, 88

    Belgian, *49*, 89, 93, 94, 96

    British, *114*, *115*, 116, 123, 127–28, 133,
       135, 136, 343, 344

    Inman and International loss of, 127–28,
       133, 135, 136

    of Inman Line, *114*, *115*, 116, 123

    Postal Aid Act of 1891 and, 133–36

Maine, USS, 261, 280

Maine Steamship Company, 257

Majestic, 133, 146, 306, 322

Manacles, The, 294, 297, 298, 299, *299*, 309

Mandoff, Mandel, 249

Manhattan, lower, map of, *143*

Mantell, Robert, 69

Marblehead, USS, 273

maritime charities, 196

Marsily, William Edouard, 85, 86, *93*, 218

Martinique, 265–66, *277*

Mary Wells, 255

Massachusetts, USS, 171, 173

mattresses, *206*

    inflatable, *199*, 201

Mauretania, 348, 352

meat, fresh, as freight, 59–60, 67

Mechanical Engineers' Brotherhood
    Association (MEBA), 144

Mechanical Manufacturing Company, 201

Merchants' Exchange, American Line
    meetings in, 19

Merion, 294, *322*, *324*

Merritt Wrecking Company, 228–29, 239

Messrs. Martin, Fuller, & Company, 60

Messrs. Vickers, Maxim and Co., 344

Messrs. Watson and Smith, 344

Meteor, 307–8

Michener, J. H., 218

Miles, Nelson A., 279

Millard, 229–31

Minneapolis, USS, 172, 272

Minzer, Mr. and Mrs. Edward L., 149

Mississippi & Dominion Line, 331–32

Missouri, planning of, 66–67

Mitchell's Maritime Register, 86–88

Mohegan, 296–98, 300

Moniteur Belge, 86

Montreal, 74

Morgan, J. P., Jr., 318

Morgan, J. P., Sr., 82, 288, 307–8, 317–23,
    327, 331, 332, 334, 338, 340–45, 349–50

Morgan Line, 257

Morrison, Captain, *41*

Morro Castle (Cuba), 268–69, *269*

Morro Castle (Puerto Rico), 270–71, 274–75

Morton commuter train, 149–50

Moss & Co., 257

Mulford, M. R., 237

Mulligan, Captain, 228

Mulligan, Richard T., 211–12, 215, 218, 220

Murphy, Michael, 47–48

music, *55*

    organ, 136, 199

Musselman, C. A., *280*

Myers, Leonard, 36

Napier, Robert, 24

National Line, 26, 116, 316

Naval Auxiliary Board, 256–58

Naval Auxiliary Cruiser Board, 261

Navy, Confederate, 72

Navy, Imperial Russian, *45*, 72–74

Navy, U.S. (Navy Department), *59*, 135, 161,
    171–74, 212, 256, 261, 264–66, *337*, 339